THE GLORY OF THE LORD

Hans Urs von Balthasar

THE GLORY OF THE LORD:
A THEOLOGICAL AESTHETICS

By Hans Urs von Balthasar

VOLUMES OF THE COMPLETE WORK
Edited by Joseph Fessio, S.J., and John Riches

1. *SEEING THE FORM*

2. *STUDIES IN THEOLOGICAL STYLE:*
   CLERICAL STYLES

3. *STUDIES IN THEOLOGICAL STYLE:*
   LAY STYLES

4. *THE REALM OF METAPHYSICS*
   IN ANTIQUITY

5. *THE REALM OF METAPHYSICS IN THE*
   MODERN AGE

6. *THEOLOGY: THE OLD COVENANT*

7. *THEOLOGY: THE NEW COVENANT*

THE GLORY
OF THE LORD

A THEOLOGICAL AESTHETICS

BY

HANS URS VON BALTHASAR

VOLUME II: STUDIES IN THEOLOGICAL STYLE: CLERICAL STYLES

*Translated by Andrew Louth, Francis McDonagh
and Brian McNeil C.R.V.
Edited by John Riches*

IGNATIUS PRESS ● SAN FRANCISCO
CROSSROAD ● NEW YORK

First published in Great Britain by T. & T. Clark Limited, 1984,
in association with Ignatius Press, San Francisco, U.S.A.

Authorised English translation © T. & T. Clark Ltd, 1984

Originally published under the title *Herrlichkeit: Eine theologische
Ästhetik*, II: *Fächer der Stile*, 1: *Klerikale Stile* by Johannes Verlag,
Einsiedeln, 1962, second edition 1969.

Library of Congress Cataloging in Publication Data

Balthasar, Hans Urs von, 1905–
    Studies in theological style.

    (Glory of the Lord/Hans Urs Balthasar; v. 2–   )
    Translation of: Fächer der Stile.
    Contents: 1. Clerical styles.
        1. Theology—Methodology.   2. Theology, Doctrinal.
I. Title   II. Series: Balthasar, Hans Urs von,
1905–   Herrlichkeit. English; v. 2, etc.
BT78.B2613 1984 vol. 2 etc. 230s 84–1766
[BR118]   [230]
ISBN 0–89870–048–5 (Ignatius)
ISBN 0–8245–0642–1 (Crossroad)

Typeset in Bembo by C. R. Barber & Partners (Highlands) Ltd,
Fort William, Scotland
Printed in Great Britain by Billing & Sons Ltd,
Worcester, England

CONTENTS

VOLUME II
STUDIES IN THEOLOGICAL STYLE:
CLERICAL STYLES

INTRODUCTION

IRENAEUS

AUGUSTINE

DENYS

ANSELM

BONAVENTURE

Qui tantis rerum creaturarum splendoribus non illustratur caecus est; qui tantis clamoribus non evigilat surdus est; qui ex omnibus his effecibus Deum non laudat mutus est; qui ex tantis indiciis primum principium non advertit stultus est.

BONAVENTURA

The Church, which was once the mother of poets no less than of saints, during the last two centuries has relinquished to aliens the chief glories of poetry . . ., she has retained the palm, but forgone the laurel . . .
Fathers of the Church (we would say), pastors of the Church, pious laics of the Church: you are taking from its walls the panoply of Aquinas; take also from its walls the psaltery of Alighieri. Unrol the precedents of the Church's past; recall in your minds that Francis of Assisi was among the precursors of Dante, that sworn to poverty he forswore non Beauty, but discerned through the lamp Beauty the Light God . . .
What you theoretically know vividly realize: that with many the religion of beauty must always be a passion and a power, that it is only evil when divorced from the worship of the Primal Beauty.

FRANCIS THOMPSON

INTRODUCTION

1. THE CONCERN

The first volume attempted to show that one both can and must consider the revelation of the living God, as the Christian understands it, not only from the point of view of its truth and goodness, but also from that of its ineffable beauty. If everything in the world that is fine and beautiful is *epiphaneia*, the radiance and splendour which breaks forth in expressive form from a veiled and yet mighty depth of being, then the event of the self-revelation of the hidden, the utterly free and sovereign God in the forms of this world, in word and history, and finally in the human form itself, will itself form an analogy to that worldly beauty however far it outstrips it. In Jesus Christ, to whom the revelation in creation and history leads, the 'yet greater unlikeness' of God over against all that is not divine is not simply inferred as it were from certain 'signs', nor simply known (in a *docta ignorantia*), but—no matter how strange the manner of its appearing—read off from the form of the revelation and from nowhere else. Where God freely manifests himself (be he still never so deeply veiled), this is finally intended as a gift, as love and therewith as self-surrender; each *via negativa*—which philosophically considered may be set over the *via positiva*—stands in the service of a positive way, indeed the negating ineffability of the gift speaks only of the still greater overwhelming of man (*via eminentiae*) through this 'ineffable' fact that God wills to be with me, for me and in me. This now, in theological terms, is the 'dazzling darkness' of the divine beauty: it is not that which remains inaccessible when God has manifested himself in Christ, rather it is on the contrary the splendour which breaks forth from this love of God which gives itself without remainder and is poured forth in the form of worldly powerlessness: the superabundant power of the light and meaning of love, as it shines forth in the form, causes it to become necessarily a form of veiling—just because it reveals that which is utmost, the ineffable.

If it is true that the divine revelation of grace perfects created natures—both conferring on the complementary disclosures of beings their final meaning, and also revealing the transparence of all being in the world to the absolute ground of being—then everything of beauty found in the world (and with it too the true and the good) is drawn up into a relationship to this inexhaustible standard, where the living God of love is glorified as he pours out his limitless love for the creature kenotically into the void which is empty of himself, indeed into what is strictly totally other than himself: into the abyss of guilty, godless darkness and godforsakenness. Thus, going to the utmost point of what is not God, he can finally establish his lordship and his glory in what is other than himself, in man, and by the glorified *Kyrios* fashion glory out of humanity and the cosmos, which Christ in his final prayer (Jn 17) declares to have been accomplished, at the same time as he still requires it to be accomplished.

This form stands at the centre of the first volume. Everything else is arranged around it: the subjective possibilities of its being discerned; the demonstration of the objective structure of its form (whose cipher could be broken only in terms of the divine, namely as representation of the trinitarian God) and of the glory of God which breaks forth from it objectively, and which is represented in the form of Jesus; finally the whole historical economy, in which this final form is led up to (Old Testament), and which subsequently shows itself in humanity as the Lord of Glory (the time of the Church).

In all this we may gain a preliminary sighting of the relations between the present theological aesthetic and the projected theological dramatic which will follow this work: if God represents himself in the world, then there lies in that an act of the most sublime freedom, an act moreover which is greatly rich in its consequences for human action. God's advent as Lord of the world and its history can release only the most prodigious drama, which indeed it already contains within itself; there can be here no question of simply perceiving, contemplating, of simply registering what is shown; whoever is moved in faith must go out on the stage (*theatrizesthai*: Heb 10.33, *cf.* 1 Cor 4.9), in the sight of a world which at first imagines it can afford to be nothing more than a spectator itself. The Christian *epiphaneia* of God has nothing about it of the simple radiance of the Platonic sun of the good; it is an act in which God utterly freely makes himself present as he commits to the fray the last divine and human depths and ventures of love: the 'ethical' is realised precisely in the figure of the 'aesthetic': behind the perfection of each word, each gesture, each encounter of the Son of Man there stands, making it possible and bearing it, the harmony of divine and human 'existence', life together with death, heaven together with hell. And again within all this—and not as it were merely as a detached witness—there lies as the object of a theological logic the structure of the truth, which can indeed be nothing other than the discernment of being in the freedom of its self-revelation.

The next task of a theological aesthetic is, then, to lend to these abstract propositions historical colour and fulness. Is it true that mankind (in so far as it has learnt to see in faith) comes to behold in the Christian revelation the glory of the Lord, and in what way does it experience this? The very richness of God in Christ would lead us to expect this to occur in the most diverse ways; to indicate the extent of the fulness of this experience is the task of this volume. It will try to do this by presenting a series of Christian theologies and world-pictures of the highest rank, each of which, having been marked at its centre by the glory of God's revelation, has sought to give the impact of this glory a central place in its vision.

The choice of these theologies and world-pictures has been made—apart from the fact of their intrinsic excellence—by taking into account their historical significance. They are reflected rays of the glory and have in this capacity also illuminated and shaped Christian culture through the centuries. There are more inward reflections, which have in secret perhaps cast no less light and have no less theological power—reflections found in mystical, hidden men of prayer and self-sacrifice, to whom has been allotted no publicly ascertainable historical influence. This is possible in the realm of death and of hiddenness and constitutes no objection to that which has become visible. On the other hand, there is in the time of the Church no historically influential theology which is not itself a reflection of the glory of God; only beautiful theology, that is, only theology which, grasped by the glory of God, is able itself to transmit its rays, has the chance of making any impact in human history by conviction and transformation. This may be regarded as a corollary of the argument of the present volume.

The subject of enquiry is then exactly this: the glory of the divine revelation, as it is presented and unfolded in the length and breadth of the theology of the Church. Therefore not immediately (and more narrowly) the form and beauty of theology, but the ultimate, objective ground which lies in the biblical revelation, as it gives shape and form to theology. In this way this historical *enquête* forms the transition from the delineation of the form of the historical revelation in itself (first volume) to its inward, theological and dogmatic, working-out (third volume). Now it is a matter of the different ways of seeing, which are so manifold not so much because of the limitation of human perception as because of the yet greater fulness of revelation, as it shines forth and overwhelms its beholders. The display of this plenitude of perspectives will prepare us too not to overlook anything essential in the dogmatics of glory and to formulate out of the wide-ranging induction of the Church's theological tradition the leading themes of this theological discipline which today is so neglected as scarcely to exist.

In order to feel where a great theology has been moved centrally by the glory of God it is in no sense enough merely to gather together those passages (often paltry or conventional or dependent on alien philosophies) where the subject of the beautiful is expressly considered. Rather, what is decisive for a theological aesthetic occurs most centrally in the heart, in the original vision and in the middle point where the basic forms crystallize. How the theological form is fashioned around the centre of this original vision determines what and how much of the *kâbôd* descends onto this form and thereby acquires body and visage. Thus in each case an effort has to be made to get the sought-after moments to express themselves as one traces as concisely but as exactly as possible the outlines of the work. As we proceed certain constants will also necessarily appear, which accompany us from form to form and perhaps become more plain in the process—for example, the Augustinian-Anselmian theme of the *cor rectum*, of *rectitudo*, which returns in Pascal and finally in Péguy as the two-in-oneness of *justice-justesse*, or the theme of figure (Old Testament) and fulfilment (New Testament) or that of *eros* and *agape*. But it is perhaps even more instructive to see the themes in complete opposition, pushed even to the very limit of contradiction (let Irenaeus or Dante simply be set alongside John of the Cross!): such tensions must be reckoned with right at the heart of this discipline, and they only can convey an adequate representation of its object.

In the main we have chosen official theologians, so long as such were available, who were able to treat the radiant power of the revelation of Christ both influentially and originally, without any trace of decadence; but after Thomas of Aquinas theologians of such stature are rare. Now it is primarily laity who, out of an adequate theological culture and with a more powerful vision and deeper creative insight than the theologians of the schools, carry forward the concern and guarantee its effectiveness with a breadth and depth which escapes the professional theologians. The dividing-line between this and the next volume which occurs about 1300 is not meant in any polemical way; it simply corresponds to an unfortunate but incontestable fact. That the great upholders of Christian spirituality (amongst whom, in an ecumenical spirit, but also with inward justice, there is included a Protestant: Hamann) not seldom feel themselves to be, and behave like, representatives of the ecclesiastical 'opposition' and have to take on themselves the corresponding fate of the exiled, the misunderstood, the outlawed is not astonishing; rather, it manifests, in the main, a burning concern for the most genuine concern of the Church and of theology—Dante! Pascal! Péguy!—which they see is being inadequately defended by the run-of-the-mill clergy. It would be worth tracing the history of this movement of 'opposition', and then it would appear that, for the most part, it is protesting against a narrowing-down of Christian theology merely to the training of pastors or to academic specialization and the timeless pursuits of the schools and that it is demanding an understanding of revelation in the context of the history of the world and the actual present. And here we must name alongside Dante, Lull, Nicholas of Cusa, Erasmus, Luther, Las Casas; alongside Pascal, Leibniz; alongside Hamann, Boehme, Fénelon, Kierkegaard; alongside Péguy, Bloy, Bernanos,

Mauriac; alongside Soloviev, Baader and Schelling; and alongside Hopkins, Newman.

After Thomas the theology of the schools became essentially a process of commentary on St Thomas which lasted till the eighteenth century and was resumed in the second half of the nineteenth century; the collapse of this, prepared for in our own times by the advance of biblical studies, has yet to produce a new and convincing theological figure who could be ranked with those selected here in their grand array. On the other hand, the great, historically influential saints often stand, like the hidden lovers and men of prayer, apart from the levels dealt with here. Benedict, Francis, Ignatius, even Charles de Foucauld, stamp the impress of glory less through their own words than in the working out of their mission, which often, where they themselves are concerned, appears fairly abrupt. And no more than of the saints have we been able to treat of the artists as such, no matter how alluring and rewarding a theological exploration of their work would have been: what would Giotto, Fra Angelico, Michelangelo, Tintoretto, or El Greco, what would Champaigne, Vivaldi, Bach, Haydn, or Mozart, Mahler or Schoenberg, have had to contribute to our theme! Or the builders of the Romanesque minsters, of the Gothic cathedrals, of the churches of the Renaissance and the Baroque, or even Rudolf Schwarz! Or the Christian poets of antiquity, Synesius and Romanos, the poet of the *Heliand*, Wolfram von Eschenbach, Arnoul Greban, Corneille, Milton, Spee, Eichendorff, Claudel and Eliot! A few representatives of the world of letters had to be selected, but only in so far as their literary work stands in an immediate relationship to the vision and exposition of the biblical revelation and there is a fluent transition from it to theology. Something else is missing too: the Church's own exposition of itself and its understanding of revelation in the liturgy. But apart from the fact that the liturgical witnesses develop on their side a world too extensive to be quickly assimilated, the liturgical utterance depends less on the individual word than on the whole procedure in which forms are evolved. There will be some response to the question which emerges here—of the relation between the form of revelation and the liturgical form—in our third volume. Finally we have omitted anything which relates to theological dramatics, theologians as well as poets (the mystery plays, Shakespeare, Calderon and the *autos sacramentales*): they will find their place in the volumes on dramatics. What remains, as is now manifest, is a quite small selection, which can however stand as representative of the whole of the tradition and offers such a fulness of the experience and form of glory that it will overflow in every respect what can be said in a book.

2. THOSE SELECTED AND THOSE MISSING

A few words in justification of the selection found here; a few sentences to render comprehensible the omission of important names.

Irenaeus stands as the founder of the theology of the Church with his stance which is at once markedly anti-Gnostic and pre-Alexandrian, that is to say, not as yet Platonizing. The emphasis lies on the glorious creation of God—*gloria Dei vivens homo* (the glory of God is a living man)—and on the miracle of the temporal order of salvation. Christian thought is imbued with a good spirit; one can only regret that succeeding ages did not give more careful attention to this beginning.

Augustine brings the period of Western Patristics to a close by accomplishing the move from Plotinus to Christ, by both going along with and going beyond Plotinus; he takes up the aesthetics of the Idea and in particular of number (from Pythagoras to Varro); but beyond that, in the existential theology of the *Confessions*, he praises the beauty ever ancient and ever new of the love of God, and in the *City of God* the glory of the temporal order of the dispensations, and lays down for a thousand years the fundamental rules of theological aesthetics.

Denys the Areopagite, the ancient, Syrian monk, translates for the East Proclus' philosophical world-view into the realm of Christian theology; his hierarchical liturgy is timeless, a crystalline worship offered to the heart of the ineffable Godhead; his world-view, determined throughout in aesthetic categories, becomes after that of Augustine the second pillar of Western

theology from the classical representatives of High Scholasticism down to the great figures of the Renaissance and the
Baroque.

Anselm's Benedictine, contemplative reason is aesthetic in a
new and original way: it is the spiritual intuition of measure and
right relationship, together with the clear knowledge of how
the glorious form of order, which God has placed in the world,
depends solely on his inconceivable freedom and love and bears
witness to it.

Bonaventure's cathedral-like theology unites Augustine and
the Areopagite in the spirit of Saint Francis; his giddy syntheses
are transparent to the mysteries of the glory of the poor heart: of
Jesus, of the *Poverello*, even of God himself whose *expressio* is
nature and grace such that even the mystery of time presses for
the unravelling of his being.

Dante represents the painful experience of the collapse of
monastic and clerical theology into a lay theology: into the
centre of the Platonic and Scholastic world-view there is now
brought—for the first time in Christian intellectual history—
the mystery of an eternal love between man and woman, *eros*
refined by *agape* and drawn up through all the circles of hell and
spheres of the world to the throne of God.

John of the Cross, the Reformer of Carmel as a response to
Luther's Reform, treads the same path from the night of hell
into the glory of heaven, but in mystical solitude with God,
without the Dantean world-view. Everything is made to depend on pure faith, which in the darkness of his final deprivation
veilingly unveils the mystery of the dazzling love of God and of
the eternal marriage.

Pascal, a second Catholic answer to the Reformation, conced-
ing to it the loss of the ancient philosophy of being, fashions a
bridge between pure, theological faith and modern metaphysics
and natural science, but in such a way that he (in contrast to
Descartes) attains in the crucified Christ an intuition of man
(who is in himself the fallen-incomprehensible) and fashions a
proportion out of disproportions, just as 'by joining the
demonstrations of knowledge to the uncertainty of the die'
(*matheseos demonstrationes cum aleae incertitudine jungendo*) he
attained a 'geometry of the die' (*aleae geometriae*), which

brought form and rule to the unruliness of the accidental: the high-point of a baroque theological aesthetics.

Hamann, at the end of the Enlightenment and on the eve of German idealism, of which he is *de jure* (rather than *de facto*) the Christian father, stands as the representative of a Protestant theological aesthetics, as the third therefore who attempts to give an answer to Luther. He celebrates in prophetic intuitions the *kenosis* of Christ and the humiliation of the Holy Spirit in the form of the slave manifest in human nature and the letter of the Scriptures, and in the same breath the glorification of the flesh and the letter as final, unsurpassable bearers of Logos and *pneuma*.

Soloviev stands at the other end of idealistic philosophy, bringing its enormous harvest into Christian theology, while at the same time he draws in the whole theological tradition of the East, from the Greek Fathers, through Byzantium and ancient Russia, to Dostoyevsky, Tolstoy and Leontiev: a thinker of universal genius, who anticipates the vision of Teilhard de Chardin and to some extent corrects it.

Hopkins, the English Jesuit and a poet of the highest calibre, represents the English theological tradition, for which, in contrast to continental thought, there has never been any opposition between image and concept, myth and revelation, the apprehension of God in nature and in the history of salvation: he is able to build a bridge between poetic aesthetics and the Ignatian exercises.

Péguy can therefore close this series because he works out his Christian existence between communism and the Church and maintains that he has found the point at which both concerns run into one another without a break. At the heart of his problem he wrestles to free himself from a certain medieval Augustinianism, of the Reformation and of Jansenism: he thinks in a confrontation with Pascal and the Dante of the *Inferno* and wants in his *Mystères* to draw Christian theology in such a breadth of vision as to make it understandable anew to mankind-to-come.

A Western symposium thus develops: representatives of regions of the original sources—Syria (Denys), Greek Asia Minor (Irenaeus), Africa (Augustine)—are joined by the

Lombards (Anselm), the Italians (Bonaventure, Dante), the French (Pascal, Péguy), the Spaniards (John of the Cross), the Germans (Hamann), the Russians (Soloviev) and the English (Hopkins).

Anyone who perceives the fundamental discontinuity between these twelve creative figures will have to concede that a continuous history of theological aesthetics can therefore not be written, because it simply does not exist. In the new constellations of intellectual history there break out from time to time from the midpoint which is beyond history new and original perceptions which certainly, in the succession of the ages, are related to one another, indeed often expressly measure themselves one against another, and enrich the great tradition or stand aside from it; but all this never consists in a mere further weaving of threads that are already to hand, but rather in the power of a total vision. Only so can Denys' relationship to the Cappadocian Fathers be rightly assessed, or Anselm's relationship to Augustine, or Dante's to Thomas, or Soloviev's to Schelling and Baader, or Péguy's to Pascal. In this realm there is no more scope for development as such, as there is or could be in mysticism, or in philosophy: *les philosophes n'ont pas d'élèves* (Péguy—'philosophers do not have pupils'). This observation could place a gentle mute on any enthusiasm for the development of theological doctrine.

This is naturally not to deny that, between these twelve figures picked out as typical, there is not a host of others who could have clarified the intellectual and historical relations and transitions between them and would in themselves also have been worthy of presentation. So, to give a few examples, between Irenaeus and Augustine, Origen, Gregory of Nyssa and Synesius could have been discussed, alongside Denys Boethius, in the period before Anselm Maximus and Eriugena, in the period after him Bernard, William of St Thierry, Hildegard, Albert, Mechthild and Wolfram, after Bonaventure Thomas and Eckhart, after Dante Ramon Lull, Nicholas of Cusa, Petrarch, Ficino, Luis de León, after John of the Cross Francis de Sales, Boehme and Spee, after Pascal Fénelon and Angelus Silesius, after Hamann the Catholics of Tübingen, Baader, Deutinger and Lacordaire, together with Péguy, Bloy,

Claudel, Blondel and Bernanos, together with Hopkins, Newman and Chesterton.

Meanwhile the discussion of all these great ones (not to mention other lesser beings) would already have led, many times over, to wearying repetitions. Very often important intuitions in theological aesthetics by a Christian thinker can find the same place in the firmament of another, even a greater, thinker. So it is not imperative to deal with Eriugena if one has already dealt with Augustine and particularly Denys. Likewise Baader's concerns are covered by a discussion of Soloviev, and the same goes for Boehme. In John of the Cross the best of Eckhart's mysticism finds its home and in some respects is redeemed and finds a calmer expression. Anyone who sees the primordial power with which Dante grasps the problem of Christian *eros* and resolves it in the form of Beatrice will, as far as theology is concerned, scarcely experience anything deeper or purer beyond that in Claudel; indeed Claudel's ode to Dante can be seen to bear this witness.

A further consideration in the omission of the great names was that while often in Christian world-views great aesthetic values are certainly incorporated, they do not always crystallize into an original, theological aesthetics. It may be that the aesthetic moments are simply borrowed from an alien world-view or that they have not fused with the proper theological vision into a complete unity—this is, it seems, the case with Origen and in some respects with Gregory of Nyssa, and similarly with the Florentines and the Cambridge Platonists. It may be that a deep and lucid philosophical aesthetics has been developed, but that it has failed to achieve a theological translation, that is, to be seen as the unfolding of a theology based on the biblical revelation: that is the reason why Thomas Aquinas has been omitted from our sequence. It would perhaps have been possible, in his case too, to have developed (beyond the philosophical aesthetics elucidated by Kovach) out of the structures of order of the theological parts an implicit theological aesthetics, but with uncertain success. Again, other Christian thinkers may possess a strong sense of the harmony of the truth of revelation (for example, Erasmus or Francis de Sales) but without being able to give it expression in a structured aesthetics, or may have an experience of the fulness and many-sidedness of the truth, in which the Christian can romp without a care (like Chesterton), without feeling any necessity to give to this fulness any other than a paradoxical expression. Finally there are Christians to whose original vision and imagery there has been denied any effectiveness either in the Church or in history—such as Hildegard and Mechthild of Magdeburg.

Because no continuous development can or should be shown, each picture that is to be offered is relatively closed and self-sufficient. That fascinating dialogues open up between one and another, one greeting another across the centuries, grasping something and perhaps making expressible what was once intended in quite a new form, completing what was fragmentary, and bringing to the one-sided a compensating counter-balance: this and similar things the reader will see for himself. Yet such dialogues form together no overall system; for how should man be able to attain an overall perspective on the revelation of the living God? All that develops is a full orchestra, whose various instruments blend well with one another: their mutual harmony proves that they all play from the same score (which both transcends and embraces them). And this concordance in opposition paves the way to the third and final volume, which will treat of dogmatics.

3. FORMS, STYLES

Again it must be emphasized that the formal object of this investigation is the glory of the divine revelation itself, in the multiplicity of its manifestations and understandings, and then, certainly, within that glory theological beauty as such, in its transcendence over all models of secular beauty. Thus the object as such does not embrace directly the choice of secular means of aesthetic expression by individual theologians, as they need them for the presentation of their vision.

The visions themselves in their various articulations can be ordered to some extent in accordance with their grasp of the formal object of theology and the different accents manifest within each individual understanding. If 'God in himself' is contemplated as the formal object, then all the rest has value and meaning only in so far as God is expressed and presented therein, in so far as it is transparent to God and returns to God. That is the prevailing world-view of the East, as it emerges in almost pure form in Evagrius, in Gregory the Great, in Eckhart and John of the Cross, but which also predominates in Fénelon. Glory is here God as God, all else is a veil which bears and mediates him. If one sets 'God's revelation' at the centre, then the shimmering radiance of glory falls on the mediation itself: either purely dynamically as in Origen (where the decisive moment is always when the body is transfigured and the letter yields to the spirit, time to eternity) or in a more static way, so that God is rather discerned as he is displayed in the orders of the world and of salvation, as one more deeply veiled in his manifestation, the Unmanifest (Denys), or as the one who has found the culmination of his self-being in the other, in man, in Jesus Christ: here we find Maximus, Nicholas of Cusa, Soloviev, and in all essentials Thomas Aquinas. If the formal object shifts yet again, and, as with Bonaventure, Christ, as the epitome of reality, as the synthesis of God and the world, now assumes the centre, then the human drama wins a more prominent place: sin, suffering and death are now also represented in the formal object itself. In Christ we can now contemplate the interpretation both of God and of man: the heart of God interpreted in the heart of Christ (Péguy), the heart of man in its fall into inauthenticity and lostness caught up and restored to authenticity in this same heart on the cross (Pascal, Hamann). That the experience of the divine glory has here changed is clear: it has taken on increasingly a kenotic colouring, the true depth of the divine glory is only manifest in suffering love. In the end there is a danger of a slipping into, or a change into, anthropology, when faith in Christ threatens to become simply the 'authenticity' of man (Schleiermacher, Kierkegaard, Bultmann). Finally the formal object can allow the human form of the mediator to become completely transparent to the Holy Spirit, promised by the mediator himself as the conclusion of all divine revelation: then the engagement of the Spirit of God with the spirit of man in the Spirit of Christ is what ultimately bestows form. This we find in Joachim and in Hegel, in such theologies of the Church as those of Schleiermacher, of the young Möhler, of Pilgram, and of a number of Russians. Again the picture of *doxa* has changed: to the all-consuming, dazzling intensity of the Spirit, a picture and experience which leads us back to the first-mentioned view of the East.

Over against these possible shifts in the centre of the formal object of theology stand the secular resources of style, as they are utilised for human utterance in poetry and prose, in rhetoric and didactic, and are available for use by the theologian. The latter can, like Augustine in his *Confessions*, unleash a great, symphonic, lyrical and rhapsodic music in order to give expression to his aesthetic experience of God. He can tune the same orchestra to the impersonal style of liturgical music, as does the Areopagite. He can devote himself to the cutting of tiny jewels of verbal skill to thread on the necklace of his sermons (as—not without some vanity—in the case of Gregory Nazianzen). He can attempt to achieve the same clear-polished, laconic style in the Roman spirit of legislation, as often with Tertullian, as with Leo the Great and occasionally with Ambrose: an example of the utmost concentration, which is conceived as a human and ecclesial answer to the most exact sharpness of the biblical word of God. He can go further in a thorough axiomatization of theology, as with Evagrius in his *Centuries*, or in casting it in mystical and magical proverbs, as with Ramon Lull in the *Book of the Lover and the Beloved*, or with Silesius in the *Wandersmann*. He can also, in his search for overladen formulae, fall into kitsch and gongorism, as in many early Byzantine Marian sermons. He can further, counting the outer form as of little worth, concentrate wholly on the vision of the mystery and, like Origen in his endless dictation, strew his treasures without care and without number, in a simple trust in the fulness and the value of the content. He can also—something very similar— seek to master such superabundance by building dizzying towers, some in this way, some in that, masterpieces of classification such as Bonaventure achieved, gothic sacrament houses, all beautiful and possessed of an inner correctness, and yet lacking any final necessity. He can, on the contrary, concentrate entirely on the inner structure and ordering of the mystery and seek to mediate in his style as faithful an impression and reflection of them as possible, as do Irenaeus or Cyril of Jerusalem, and in particular Anselm and Thomas Aquinas, who strive in their style for the utmost self-stripping and a pure transparency and service to the matter in hand. He can strive after the encyclopaedic, as in the later *Summas* and the modern handbooks, whose apparent completeness, however, often conceals the sieve with the greatest holes, or out of necessity or deliberation prefer the form of the fragmentary, which at best mirrors the not-to-be-grasped fulness of transcendent totality: Nicholas of Cusa, perhaps, when he deserted the form of the *summa* and *quaestio* to wander on the lonely and lofty paths of speculation, or Pascal, who was perhaps conscious that he had more to offer through the openness of his uncompleted fragments than in a closed and finished work, or Newman who pointed only to aspects of the whole truth and completely renounced any systematic account. He can also attempt the perspective of the double form, one side of which interprets the other, without any attempt to exhaust it: Boethius writes profound poems, which he then expounds in prose, as does John of the Cross; but the exposition cannot, and is not intended to, exhaust the content of the poetry. He can clothe the mystery in the drapery of an accomplished 'fine' style, either as an act of homage, or (as often with Bernard) in an attempt to preserve it by veiling it; he can—fully conscious of his powerlessness to mirror the real beauty in any real way—deck out its style with all kinds of blossoms—images, similes, and other delights— which only imperfectly serve the concern in hand, and not seldom detract still further from the seriousness of the vision (as with Francis de Sales). He can, through a labyrinthine form, through a breathless, endlessly whirling dance, seek to set free a sense of the superabundance of God, as with Augustine, whose whole work has become an infinitely extending, rolling sea, or with Ruysbroek, who despises any systematization. He can, like Clement of Alexandria in his somewhat dusty 'carpets', open up, with the touching ardour of a connoisseur, a kind of treasury of antiques, present a bouquet of the best and the finest that he has found in the religions of all people and philosophers, to lay at the feet of the Word made flesh.

At first this bewildering variety of styles alarms one, and there arises the suspicion that between the glory of the divine revelation and its imitative expression there can be achieved no kind of convincing correspondence. Is not perhaps then the paradoxical pointer, consciously intending shock and offence, the only possibility? A human word, which, in witnessing to God's word, witnesses itself to its own inappropriateness, even contradictoriness? Were that all, then the Word of God would not have become flesh. So there is a twofold mediation to be considered: the general phenomenon of the freedom of human expression in spiritual utterance and the humanity of the historical revelation of salvation.

With a certain contrast to the forms of expression of the beauty of nature, the element of freedom holds sway in human expression, and therefore in all beauty of art. Certainly the forms of nature in their inscrutable emergence from the ground of life are never simply released by a mechanical necessity; they too are 'freedom manifesting itself' (*erscheinende Freiheit*— Schiller). In human self-expression, in its highest form in the work of art, the will to express itself not only freely creates suitable form; it incarnates in this very form its freedom. It is only that which gives to the form the radiance from the depths. The more given and established the form, the weaker the creative breaking-forth of freedom accomplished in it; the power of expression can therefore be greater where technique does not yet rule completely, but is rather achieved piecemeal in the process of creation, than where it can be learnt from the masters: greater then with Masaccio and Uccello than in the refinement of the Baroque. The true artist is not so subject to the necessity of creating that he does not preserve sovereign freedom in the choice of form. Goethe could write his *Iphigenie* both in prose and in verse, and no-one can know whether he could not have made of his *Werther* just as good a play, or whether the fashioning of *Hyperion* in verse would not have produced a wholly effective work. What a sovereign freedom in the use of individual themes, individual harmonies, even of complete pieces there is in Bach and Mozart! Wagner's *Leitmotive* are expressive and appropriate, but no-one can prove that they could not have sounded differently. In the case of the beautiful it is not primarily the immanent harmony of number and proportion that is enjoyed, but the considered freedom which is manifested in it and is 'necessitated'.

By analogy, the self-expression of divine freedom in the history of salvation and its written witness, the Bible, has a bodily manifestation, which, considered as such, is a miracle of appropriateness and power of expression, but which, precisely as it allows full scope to the sovereignty of divine freedom, does not bind it to the form, but on the contrary brings it to view and to freely lived exposition. Here too we find a deliberate play with forms of expression that lie already to hand: prose and poetry (alternating in the case of the prophets), historical report, legislation, hymn and prayer, wisdom sayings, etc., all forms both preserved in their purity and, when necessary, amalgamated to the point of total interpenetration. And yet this game with forms in no way expresses contempt on the part of the divine spirit for the limitations of secular forms of expression; its high-point, the Incarnation of the Word, proves the opposite: an absolute acknowledgement and sanctioning of the created vessels of expression, a total harmonisation of content and form, and this precisely in the making manifest of the divine freedom. The freedom of the Holy Spirit, for instance, in selecting the sayings of Christ to be included in the Gospels— thus and not otherwise—bearing witness in the midst of the most evident contingency to the deliberateness and appropriateness of his choice, and not without a measure of divine humour, and a certain challenge to the deadly seriousness of the philologists. The phenomenon of revelation is only truly encountered by those who, like Anselm, see the greatest freedom of the manifestation in the greatest necessity of the form of manifestation: whereby necessity means unquestionably more than what theologians on the whole understand by 'convenience'—which perhaps they are not able to understand any better precisely because of their neglect of the aesthetic analogy.

If these two mediations—the human and the divine/divine-human relation of free expression—are established, then a link seems possible between the content of all theology (grasped in the breadth of the adumbrations of its formal object) and the form of expression of any individual theology. The content is itself already the divine expression: the divine glory proclaimed in mundane terms; and the forms of expression are subject, on their side, to the laws of free, human power of fashioning. They are seen to be essentially not finished 'styles' ready to hand, but a style which develops in the creative process of giving form to this unique content. In so far as the content itself is already the expression of God, theology is the expression of an expression, on the one hand an obedient repetition of the expression of revelation imprinted on the believer, and on the other a creative, childlike, free sharing in the bringing-to-expression in the Holy Spirit—who is the Spirit of Christ, of the Church and of the believer—of the mystery which expresses itself.

In this free but obedient relation, where nothing therefore is left to wilfulness or to chance, there are at least these fixed points: (1) the form of revelation, which as form is the unique content of Christian theology—this form should be made visible, and pondered over, and, as far as is permissible, be rendered intelligible; (2) the teaching of the Church, which has the duty of proposing the binding ground rules of such hermeneutics and to which each orthodox theologian has to conform, for the Church as such possesses the Holy Spirit of interpretation and the theologian only in so far as he undertakes to express himself in the spirit and in the name of the Church; (3) the commissions or theological charisms in which individual theologians can share, in order to see and interpret the form of revelation as a whole or an essential part of it under a particular, perhaps up to now little noticed, aspect. These commissions of charisms can be important as a kind of 'inner form' of a great theology, which is given and poured out from the living revelation, the 'form' here emphasizing the aesthetic side of a personal calling, as it breaks in from the self-revealing God through the Church to the heart and mind of the individual.

This is once more to make the particular standpoint of the following studies clear: they deal primarily not with the external form of the individual theologies, but with their inner form, in so far as this is an active-passive radiance of the divine glory from the form of revelation. Naturally this primary form is only attainable through the secondary form—through words, concepts, images, patterns—but through the secondary form we want to make the primary form present. So once again the questionableness of any historical development in theology becomes clear: each original form breaks out anew from the centre. It has, besides, its own *kairos* in its historical context, is, as an instruction for the Church, indeed of the Church, set into the ways of thought and forms of speech of the epoch and it is in this way that it attains its uniqueness.

One can see certain historical lines being drawn here: for example, that the family of 'platonizing' theologies (from Origen and Augustine, through Denys, Eriugena, the scholastics, Dante, Nicholas of Cusa, to John of the Cross) retreats in the modern period (but where then does Soloviev belong?) and gives place to a more directly Biblical theology, corresponding to a change from a preference for *theoria* (monastic and scholastic) to one for an active involvement in the world. But first, this is not a true opposition: who has spoken more of an active, indeed political, realisation than Soloviev? Secondly, the strongest accents of the modern period—from John of the Cross to Charles de Foucauld—are outspokenly contemplative, and finally the general term 'Platonism' covers so much that it is scarcely more than a slogan. It covers practically the whole of so-called 'natural theology', the world of the religious thought of mankind: a sphere which no Christian theology in any age can dispense with, because faith does not replace reason (even religious reason), but exalts it in perfecting it, and because additionally even the form of expression of the Biblical revelation itself does not renounce it. Even a Biblically based theology, which sees itself as a function of the preaching of the Church, can do no other than engage seriously with the thought of the time, to which it turns as proclamation (Bultmann's use of Heidegger's categories is an illustration of this); and there can be no fruitful engagement unless somewhere there has been some mutual involvement. Christian theology will always be, in whatever form or adumbration it appears, a crystallization of the divine-human content of revelation in human, if also faithful, thinking and understanding, so that precisely through this ever-new incarnation it may witness to and demonstrate the

uniqueness and thus wholly-otherness of the manifestation of
God in Jesus Christ.

Even at the end of this volume it will not be possible to
suppress a feeling of disappointment: for we shall have only
circled round the Biblical and dogmatic meaning of the glory of
the Lord and have not elucidated it from the very centre, and
how many important individual aspects shall we have left
untouched! But that will be the concern of the third volume.

Irenaeus' work marks the birth of Christian theology. With it, theology emerges as a reflection on the world of revealed facts, a reflection which is not just a tentative, partial approximation but achieves the miracle of a complete and organised image in the mind of faith. The first and second post-apostolic generations had indeed made a vigorous start on this task, producing works of inimitable brilliance, but these remained occasional works like Clement's glowing letter to the Corinthians; steep, high, narrow confessions like the blazing letters of Ignatius; attempts at synthesis which remained trapped in the contemplation of a detail or the putting together of elements only just learnt and mastered, like the Didache and so much in the Apologists. But no sooner does Theophilus of Antioch see, however indistinctly, that his task is to present salvation history within the framework of world history, than he runs aground on the sandbank of a dry-as-dust chronology, while the believer's spiritual indignation at the world of lies of the pagan pantheon is expressed in him, in Hermias and in Tatian, in jibes which leave one looking for a more sovereign refutation and treatment. Typical of the form of this theology in search of itself is its most valuable example, the Letter to Diognetus, in which one finds sections without internal structure or coherence side by side with precious intuitions and formulations of an intensity possibly never reached again (especially § § 5–6). The most important preparatory work is done by Justin, whose calm, magnificent intelligence gathers and arranges the scattered pieces and assembles them around a centre which is not just conceived, but really seen, the Logos everywhere present in the world who in the Judaeo-Christian history of salvation nevertheless entered the world and finally became flesh. Without Justin, to whose material he constantly goes back, Irenaeus would never have reached his heights, but his relation to him is that of the genius to the man of ability, like that of Mozart to Christian Bach and his many contemporaries: they gave him the forms out of which they could make only a clever game. Justin, for all his cleverness, has a certain dullness; his industry cannot overcome a feeling of boredom. Irenaeus radiates from every pore; his utterance derives not from academic and pious knowledge, but from a creative sight of the glowing central core. The height of the spring betrays the force of the pressure which drives it up, and here the stimulus is not the general enemy, paganism, but a personal one, fully recognised and fully mastered for the first time by Irenaeus, who not only sees through him to the heart but is also enabled by him to employ his intellectual and existential indignation at such a radical falsifying of the truth in an attempt to capture and represent the centre of reality. Justin and the Apologists had no such enemy. The ordinary pagan religion was too amorphous, and their petitions to the emperor required them to spare it and discover what was good and usable in it; and in the same way the dialogue with the Jews had to be conducted in such a way that it constantly shifted between intimate agreement and an assault on their blindness. But Gnosis, which, largely with the tools and materials of the Bible, had erected a totally un-Christian structure of the highest intellectual and religious quality and won over many Christians, Gnosis was the opponent Christian thought needed in order fully to find itself. Every Christian theology is conditioned by its situation, or it would not be the theology of a historical revelation. Every book of the Bible, every statement of Jesus, is conditioned by its situation, because fully historical. Great Christian theology shares in the mystery of Scripture, in as much as it too possesses, in and through its conditioning by its situation, that special vitality which secures and preserves its supra-temporal validity. Though talking to an opponent long-since vanished, Irenaeus is as fresh and relevant today as ever; his work shares the power of perpetual renewal which he says the Holy Spirit gives to the Christian faith and the Church which contains it. The power may come from the faith, but the opponent was the occasion for the crystallisation. So, at the beginning of the history of theology, we have an illustration of the same historical law which governs the history of thought from Plato onwards: it is only the turning away from the 'aesthetic' and its conquest which provides the power and opens eyes to see real beauty.

1. THE AESTHETIC MYTH

We must therefore glance at Valentinian Gnosis, this late, mature and most ambitious of the systems, the one with which Irenaeus wrestled first and in most detail, treating the others as no more than variants or illustrative sources: 'Once the Valentinians are bested, the whole crowd of heretics will be refuted.'[1] Gnosis was a regression from Platonic philosophy (which had separated itself from myth in order to know being) in the direction of myth: Socratic sobriety and the Platonic ethos of knowledge had been transformed into a new intellectual concupiscence in religious colouring which, lacking the naivety of ancient myth, turned being and existence into a novel. Never have man, his structure, his sufferings and his tragedy, been more plainly projected on to the screen of heaven in order to fascinate him and, professedly, to redeem him by the contemplation of this magnified image of himself. To fascinate, because in the heavenly and cosmic giant portrait he really recognises himself; he sees his own fate in the drama of the wisdom which falls out of the divine fulness and is brought back in a series of romantic reversals. And to redeem, because this phantasmagoria is presented to him on an eternal divine scale in the contemplation of which he can hide and lose himself. Valentinus is 'prophet, poet, preacher and philosopher' in one,[2] but he is also something more: he is a magician and producer of the first rank.

[1] *Adversus Haereses* 2, 48.1 (Harvey 1, 369). Books 1, 2, 4 and 5 are cited from Harvey's edition (Cambridge, 1857), Book 3 from the critical edition of P. Francois Sagnard, OP, since regrettably deceased (Irénée de Lyon, *Contre les Hérésies*, livre III, Sources Chrétiennes 34, 1952 = S), in both cases by page. Quotations from the *Demonstratio* (cited by paragraphs) are based on the translation from the Armenian by L. M. Froidevaux (*Démonstration de la Prédication Apostolique*, nouvelle traduction, avec introduction et notes, Sources Chrétiennes 62, 1959). There is a bibliography on Irenaeus in Altaner, better arranged in Quasten (I, pp. 329f., Paris, Cerf, 1955). Indispensable aids are the two Irenaeus dictionaries by D. Bruno Reynders (Louvain, 1954 and, for the *Demonstratio* and the fragments, Chevetogne, 1958).

[2] Leisegang, *Die Gnosis* (4th ed., 1955), p. 289. We can naturally only outline the system as Irenaeus presents it. For Gnosis itself *cf.* in addition to Sagnard esp. the essays by G. Quispel and his book *Gnosis als Weltreligion* (1948), H. C. Puech and Festugière.

At the origin of all things is the unbegotten 'primal father', the 'groundless one' (*Ungrund*) 'in complete silence and calm': to the religious sensibilities of the time the unknowability of the ultimate is a guarantee of genuine and lofty thought. In the bosom of the 'groundless one', resting eternally with him, is the true image, also called 'silence' or 'grace'. From this first pair, which is in truth only a single being, there proceed in sequence 'for the glorification of the Father' three united pairs (syzygies): Nous (reason or the only-begotten son) and Truth, Logos and Life, Ideal Man and Church (ideal election). These eight form the original ogdoad, which is in its turn fertile and expands into the pleroma (fulness) of thirty aeons, by application of the old Pythagorean laws of divine even and uneven numbers, which do not need to be described separately here. The last aeon is that Sophia (love of wisdom) which, in her drive towards the infinite, will become the heavenly initiator of the drama of the world. She is at first a pure drive (Enthumesis) to understand the infinite greatness of the Father, the 'passion' (pathos as a psychological as well as an ethical passion) which, in its expansion into the infinite, 'threatened to disintegrate in the universal being', but then encountered one of the aeons, Horos, Limit or Measure, and was saved by him. She is 'brought to rest' and thereby to herself by him, the pure drive is refined into 'astonished admiration', and so wisdom is kept within the pleromatic divine fulness. But what had to be pruned away and separated from her to this end, the pure, blind 'striving', does not now simply disappear; it is a spiritual but 'formless' substance, a 'rejected fruit' separated from the pleromatic fulness and so 'crucified', for Horos' other name is Cross, since Limit does not only bring being to maturity by strengthening it, but also purifies it by pruning.

To deal with this situation a new pair proceeds from the primal ground, Christ and Holy Spirit. Their mission is to bring to the pleroma the knowledge (gnosis) of the Father's unknowability, to form and comfort the formless substance of wisdom which fell from the fulness,[3] and—this is to be the Holy Spirit's

---

[3] If Irenaeus' account in 1.2, 5 is combined with that of Hippolytus (*Philos.* 6.31, 2).

role—to balance and harmonise the pleroma in itself, where-
upon 'in stability and perfect peace and with great joy it glorifies
the primal Father with hymns'. Each aeon now gives of its truest
and best and all, 'weaving the whole in harmony into a
complete unity, send out, in honour of the groundless one, the
most perfect of all beauties, as it were the very star and heart of
the fulness', its final fruit and quintessence, Jesus, also called the
saviour, and with him his pages and attendants, the angels. The
same process which heavenly wisdom had experienced within
the fulness is now repeated for fallen wisdom on the edge of the
pleroma. Though she is outside, excluded from the light,
wandering and 'boiling' 'in shadow and the void', Christ
stretches himself out for her on the 'cross' of the pleroma-limit
to bring her to herself in her being (*kat' ousian*) and to give her an
awareness of her state, her exclusion from the fulness. Only then
will she be enabled to set her eyes on the things of heaven and,
after Christ has withdrawn into heaven from the cross, to
emulate him in striving after a 'certain fragrance of incorruptibility which he and the Holy Spirit left behind'. She is
now for the first time really (worldly) self-conscious Sophia (in
Hebrew Achamoth), and able to 'deposit' the elements of blind
passion which were in her, as a chemical substance forms a
'precipitate'. What she throws off in this way are the elements of
the material world. She herself, wisdom, is in essence pneumatic, she is the mother of the pneumatic human souls; but what
she throws off is psychic ('animal', the world soul and the
Demiurge) and 'hylic' (the material elements). 'After she had
gone through all the passions, just as she was emerging, she
turned in entreaty to the light she had abandoned, to Christ.
Christ, now returned to the fulness, sent her the Paraclete, that
is, the saviour, whom the Father had endowed with all power
by making all things subject to him, visible and invisible (Col
1.16). On catching sight of him, she wrapped herself reverently
in her veil, then, when she had looked at him, him and all his
offspring (the angels), she hurried to him and received a
"power" from his manifestation.' This encounter now leaves
her formed in her knowledge (*kata gnōsin*). In this the saviour
strips away her passions and makes them into the basic
substances out of which the psychic demiurge will later form

the material world, so that the saviour is the 'potential creator of the world'. There are thus now three worlds or 'places': the heavenly world of the pleroma, the 'centre' between heaven and earth, the seat of Mother Wisdom, who encounters the redeemer (an encounter which gives rise to the pneumatics), and the lower world, formed by the demiurge out of the elements precipitated by Achamoth, psychic and hylic souls and substances. The constructor of the world is formed out of the mother. He is psychic and so has no (pneumatic) knowledge of the spiritual powers which lie above him, work through him and can leave pneumatic seed within his lower world without his knowledge. However, since the psychic, as the power of the centre, can direct its attention upwards as well as down, the world of the demiurge is nonetheless in some way redeemable: the constructor of the world rises eschatologically into the mother's place in the centre. But the elements, the precipitate of the passions (terror becomes earth, fleeing fear water, grief air, the ignorance concealed in the other three the fire concealed in everything), are fundamentally insubstantial and in the universal conflagration disintegrate into nothing, together with the souls of the 'hylics', which are set wholly on the material. The saviour sent from the Father's fulness thus works on the mother and through her, and the mother works on the constructor of the world, who works on the world; but whereas Mother Wisdom knows the saviour, the demiurge does not know the wisdom which works through him, and among men the pneumatics know her but the psychics and hylics do not. Wisdom formed the lower world in the image of the upper, aeonic world of ideas and its numerical relations, whereas the demiurge (the world soul) 'was convinced that he was forming it out of himself when he was in fact only carrying out the ideas of Achamoth'.

This system of dynamic foundations then becomes the basis for the interpretation and integration of Christian theology. The Christ (saviour) of the gospel is the synthesis of four powers. From wisdom he received the pneumatic element, from the demiurge the psychic, and the 'order of salvation' (*oikonomia*) saw to it that he received a similarly psychic (illusory) body so that he should be visible and tangible to material men, though he himself has his origins in the divine pleroma. Thus, in addition to matter, which is doomed to destruction, the saviour took into himself 'the first-fruits of all that he was to save'. It is this psychic saviour that the prophets of the Old Covenant foretold (for of themselves they could see no higher than the demiurge), and the same psychic saviour is the object of the belief and worship of the human beings of the Catholic Church, while only the pneumatics understand his higher powers, the pneumatic and the aeonic. These, of course, are incapable of suffering and therefore deserted the psychic Christ before the Passion. But even the psychic Christ, who, of course, could not really be material, only suffered 'in mystery', so that through his sufferings the mother might be enabled to see the form of the upper Christ, who had stretched himself on the limit-cross, since all earthly things are an image of those in heaven. To find numbers of scriptural references to apply to this sophiology and christology was both exciting and amusing. The woman with the issue of blood was Sophia, whose substance flowed into nothingness until she touched the hem (limit, Horos) of the saviour. The woman who lost the drachma and swept the house until she found it is also Sophia, and so are the lost sheep and the widow Anna. It is because wisdom veiled herself before the angels of the saviour that Paul orders women to veil themselves in church. Jesus sweats blood on the mount of Olives to represent the passions precipitated by wisdom, and so on.[4]

Once one allows oneself to feel the effect of this system which has here been described only summarily, it is impossible to deny it a grandeur and a philosophical and religious completeness: it includes everything that can move a human being, above all everything that could excite the cultivated mind of late antiquity. Plato, the Stoa and the beginnings of Neo-Platonism have their place, no less than Orphism and the Mysteries; it contains both an all-embracing monism and a tragic dualism, a

[4] For Irenaeus' description of the Valentinian system see *Adv. Haer* 1.1–7. There is a study and criticism of this description in W. Foerster, *Von Valentin zu Herakleon* (Beihefte zur *ZNW* 7, 1928), and esp. F. Sagnard, *La Gnose valentinienne et le témoignage de S. Irénée*, (dissertation, Vrin, Paris, 1947).

fatalistic system of world order alongside a dramatic mobility of levels, falls and rises. Ancient heathenism is present, but dressed in the robes of Judaism and paganism, their essences saved, in such abstruse interpretations that no cultivated Christian needed to feel troubled by such illumination. The whole glitters with a strangely immaterial beauty, at once both passionate and passionless. Valentinus—to mention only him, though the same could be said of the other great Gnostic mythmakers—is beyond doubt a powerful poet, and it is easy to see why great poets have constantly felt and succumbed to the Gnostic fascination, poets like Shelley and Mombert and, above all, Blake. There is the same passion for the beautiful, the same spiritualism, the same tragic, Manichean fragmentation, and above all the same aesthetic indifference and ambivalence which simply plays musically with all positions without letting itself be bound by any, and so produces the aesthetic illusion par excellence. It is no accident that the rescuing of the fallen Sophia (with all the ambiguities about earthly and heavenly love) is a favourite theme of Richard Wagner's operas!

Valentinus fails to distinguish adequately between God and creature, in that while the two are distinguished to the point of a rift between the heavenly and the earthly world, God's world is then populated with innumerable emanations and aeons which together make up the divine world and, conversely, the quintessence of the earthly world is deified as the pneumatic Christ and the pneumatic Church. The result is a lack of any real distinction between heaven and earth, such that it is impossible to decide whether the earth is really an image and shadow of the heavenly ideal world (as a genuine fragment of Valentinus says),[5] or whether, as Irenaeus rightly objects, this whole heavenly world is not in fact a clear and essentially simple projection of earthly conditions into eternity.[6] Is it profundity to have an earthly cross matched by a heavenly cross, earthly painful suffering by a divine 'painless pain', and in which direction is the relation of original and image ultimately to be construed? Again there is no real distinction drawn between person and idea (or point of view). The logical and metaphysical

[5] In Clement of Alexandria, *Strom.* 4.13, 89f.
[6] I. 303–305.

dialectic of being and becoming, which is often very reminiscent of Hegel, is turned into a personal drama. Every concept
becomes an aeon, every conceptual tension becomes
a male-female relationship, every example of intellectual
'alienation' becomes an episode of tragedy. However, the
personalisation cannot be maintained; the personalised principles must instead be constantly reabsorbed, and constantly
arc, into the progressive unity of becoming. This is shown very
clearly by the christology, which deliberately talks not about
four Christs, but about one under four aspects. Nor is there an
adequate distinction between the physical and the moral, the
substantial and the accidental, as states solidify into substances,
but arc not really substances and may either evaporate into
nothing or be expelled as waste. So in all this it is the final
category which leaves no choice and is interesting for having
been bought at this price. The divine becomes interesting
because it so much resembles the human, because in God too
there is an abyss, a suffering, a darkness and a drama, infinitely
deeper than in man and yet (as Schelling will say later) always
already overtaken and past and conquered by the light. And the
human is interesting because of the extent to which the divine
displays itself and its life in man, because man himself is a part of
the eternal drama and his small passing passions here receive an
absolute character. This means that nothing is finally fixed;
before it is fixed seriously or irrevocably it is already cancelled,
withdrawn, eclipsed by the arrival of the next vision. But what a
sense of intoxication to look into the inner mechanism of being
itself! This aesthetic spiritual frenzy is the constant element that
holds the rest of the system together and, as Irenaeus will show,
leaves its mark on people even in their general disposition; it
is this that marks them out as sectaries. Irenaeus judges them
as Kierkegaard judged the Hegelians and Nietzsche the
Wagnerians. There is no need, as he puts it, to drink the sea dry
to know that it is salt.[7]

There is no need to evoke again the atmosphere of his
polemic, which has been sharply portrayed by Reynders;[8] a few

[7] I. 320.
[8] Dom D. Reynders, 'Optimisme et théocentrisme chez S. Irénée', Rech. de
Théol. anc. et méd. VIII (1936), 225f.

brushstrokes will suffice. Irenaeus does not judge by hearsay; he
knows his men and has all their mysteries in his head. He
recommends a precise knowledge of one's opponent, lack of
which had hampered his predecessors.[9] And when he tears the
structure of lies apart piece by piece, he does not indulge in
polemics piece-meal (like so many Church Fathers), but attacks
from the vantage of a superior overall view. This view gives
him two things, his great calm which enables him to develop a
whole theology of divine and human patience, and his great
impatience which finds this web of lies intolerable. The fault
here is not, as in the case of other heretics, a mistake on one point
of doctrine, nor even, as in the case of the pagans and Jews, the
absence of the crucial piece, which could however be supplied,
but the falsification of the truth, of the elementary articulations
of being itself. This radical poisoning of thought, which has
been carried to the limit, can expect no mercy. The Gnostics
have blinded themselves like Oedipus in the tragedy,[10] they
chase a shadow and drop the bread, like Aesop's dog,[11] they,
who are constantly talking about God, are more godless than
the pagans.[12] No wonder, for they simply do not know God,
and so are unable to make a single correct statement about him.[13]
They are the fools, the *insipientes*,[14] of the Bible because they
think against nature itself.[15] They lack common sense; they
burrow about in their speculations like blind moles.[16] They
think that as pneumatics they are wiser than the architect of the
world and invent another God above God, despising the
discovery of God and preferring an eternal search to finding.[17]
They have exceeded the measure of thought,[18] which also means
that they have gone beyond God's limits.[19] They themselves
could not produce a flea, yet they look down in contempt on the
creator.[20] They pride themselves on doing theosophical research
and learning something new every day,[21] but the old truth and
simple goodness are too trivial for them. They talk about God as
though he were not the living one, the ever-present;[22] they are

---

[9] 2. 144.   [10] 2. 356.   [11] 1. 275.
[12] 1. 272.   [13] 1. 255.   [14] 1. 344; *para physin*, 1. 85–86.
[15] 1. 347.   [16] 2. 404.
[17] 1. 253, 348; 2. 132, 171, 379; S 400–402.   [18] 2. 380.
[19] 1. 344; 2. 411.   [20] 1. 367.   [21] 1. 188.   [22] 2. 387.

unhappy lovers whose love is in fact not returned, a spectacle more comic than tragic.[23] They open up and dissect the deity;[24] they behave as though they were God's midwives, whose task was to bring him to his own pleromatic fulness.[25] All of which shows that they have no idea who God is or how to think and talk about him. They think they can interpret God 'with a + b and cold figures',[26] and so all their efforts are nothing but posturing and mystery-making with things that are the reverse of divine,[27] an illusion made of sheer false, imaginary infinities, perspectives of worlds which reflect each other back and forth into infinity.[28] At every point, to get their drama going, they have to project an ignorance which is not divine into the divine world, a world in clear contradiction to the divine light which they also proclaim.[29] Their thought bristles with contradictions. If the primal father is the unknowable, how can there be a revelation of him and how can this revelation consist in the knowledge of his unknowability? An eternal seeking without finding is inherently contradictory. And since they already— indeed by virtue of their nature as pneumatics!—know all the mysteries of God, what use is revelation? If they know the truth, they have made obsolete the saying of Jesus that no-one knows the Father except the Son.[30]

The falsehood spills out uncontrollably where they come into contact with Scripture: they break in pieces on its unity, their false mystery is dispelled by its clarity. They have to come to terms with it and cannot. They are left with no other course than to tear apart the indivisible unity of Scripture;[31] not just Marcion, but the others too must rely on eclecticism and hairesis or on a permanent double-talk, speaking a Catholic language to the people and a Gnostic one to the initiates. So they split

---

[23] I. 315.   [24] I. 357.   [25] I. 301, 355.
[26] I. 162.   [27] I. 348.
[29] I. 264 (bottom), 267, 311–12.
[30] I. 299–300.
[31] The whole of the third book is devoted to a demonstration of the indivisibility of Scripture, the Gospels among themselves, the Gospels and Acts, Paul's preaching and Luke's, and, constantly, the inseparability of the Old and New Testaments.

asunder not only Scripture, but the Church as well.[32] They are
not just occasional but comprehensive falsifiers of meaning;[33]
they recast the bronze image of the king in the image of a dog,
claiming that of course the substance remains the same.[34] They
give themselves airs as textual critics: 'The texts are corrupt, are
apocryphal, do not agree.' No wonder, for they do not recognise the tradition of the Church.[35] They take care, however, not
to look for the real causes of the discrepancies in Scripture.[36] The
dark places in Scripture hermeneutically, which ought to be
interpreted and illumined with the aid of the clear ones,[37] are
welcome to them as a pretext for finding hints of their mysteries
and so no longer seeing the plain things.[38] The parables are not
taken in their clear and obvious sense, but turned into obscure
riddles and tied into knots which cannot be unravelled: this is
the result of a refusal to accept any canon of truth.[39] In this way
everyone forges his own revelation and his own God, and they
all, unwilling to be Catholics, have only one common
characteristic, which marks them to the core: they are not the
one Church which,[40] by virtue of its unity that is its
demonstrable tradition, preserves the unity of Scripture, the
source of the unity of the revelation of the one, true, living God.
The indissolubility of these unities is what prompts Irenaeus to
risk the statement which Augustine repeated after him: all
heresy can be reduced to the common denominator of a denial
that the Word became flesh.[41]

So, after describing the heresies in his first book and their
internal contradictions in his second, Irenaeus comes to the unity
of reality. This has already been proved negatively by the
inherent tendency of the Gnostic systems to disintegrate, but he
wishes to prove it positively as well. Since Gnosis presented
itself, not as un-Christian, but as the perfection of Christianity,

---

[32] S 273.   [33] 1. 31.   [34] 1. 67.
[36] S 241.   [35] S 99.
[37] 1. 273. Scripture must be interpreted on the assumption of its unity, 2.
356.
[38] Ibid.; 1. 348 (bottom).
[39] 1. 348 (top).
[40] S 99. Heresy accepts no institution, S 119.
[41] S 185–87.

the fact that the heresy refutes itself in this way is not just an apologetic to those outside, but also a part of dogmatics, just as the one true God of revelation reveals himself as who he is by demolishing the proud and the 'gods' and exalting the humble. This is why Irenaeus attaches so much importance to tracing Gnosis back to Simon Magus, that is, to a situation of revelation within the New Testament.[42]

In Irenaeus apologetics and dogmatics are totally one, because the indissolubility of the inner necessity and harmony between the triune God, the decree of salvation in Christ, Scripture and the Church together with its tradition is both the real content of the *intellectus fidei* and the only convincing proof of Christian truth *ad extra*. Whereas in the Gnostic system everything remains arbitrary, fictional invention—'Let someone tell us the reason for the procession of the aeons, why each is as it is, why the original ogdoad was sent out first and not a pentad or triad or hebdomad,' nor is it based in creation, 'because, according to them, it all lies farther back and therefore needs a separate justification'[43]—in Catholic unity everything is internally plain and bright and can be made clear to anyone who wishes to see within the enduring mystery of God. Although Irenaeus was stimulated in many particular features of his own view by Gnosis, he is, in contrast to the Alexandrians who come after him, the first 'anti-modern' (Maritain), for whom the power of Christianity derives not from its perennial modernity and conformity to the currents of the age, but from the irrefutability and irresistability of its internal obviousness. His account sets out accordingly to be always simple and true;[44] plainness is to be the basis of his explanation. The form of his thought, like that of John's, is a circling within the broad unbroken sphere to which every mystery of the inner divine life and of salvation history belongs; and like John's it is a circling that leads to no loss of clarity, to no dizziness. In this circular motion a line of thought is equally true whether it is followed from below to above or from above to below, from front to back or from back to front.

[42] 1. 190f.; Paul and Gnosis: 1. 345. The root of the whole evil is contained in Simon; here it can be seen in the light of revelation: 1. 189.

[43] 1. 303.   [44] 1. 6.

We can say that the eucharist would not be true if Christ's Incarnation were not true, and it would not be true unless man were truly composed of spirit and flesh, and we can consider the same fact in the reverse order. Again, if God is not the one God of the Old and New Testaments, the basic statements of Scripture are misleading, and it is also impossible to rely on the statements of the Gnostic Jesus, but if Jesus speaks the truth so did the prophets, and the Father is both the God of Jesus and the God of the prophets.[45] Or, if Jesus is the Son of God and the apostles his officially appointed witnesses, and if the Church through her tradition and institution is in possession of the apostolic truth, the Church's kerygma is true, but since the Church's kerygma is true (as absolutely one and homogeneous), it proves the institution of the apostolic office and, as its precondition, the existence of divine authority.[46] So Irenaeus is brought, by the very form of his thought (which is plainly only the crystallisation of its content), to note the continuity above all between reality and ideal, between nature and grace, the work of the Father (creation) and the work of the Son and Spirit (the order of salvation), between Adam and Christ, Old and New Covenant, world and Church. It is this point that is the source of his sober truth, his warming goodness and glowing beauty. For goodness must stand between truth and beauty, the perfection of both and their crown. Irenaeus too, faced with a Gnosis which knows so much, wants to know only one thing, Jesus Christ and him crucified,[47] because he is love. For him, therefore, holiness is greater than gnosis. Holiness is the ideal in the Catholic religion, as opposed to the ideal of gnosis in all Eastern and Greek religions. 'It is better and more profitable that we should be uneducated and know little but draw near to the love of God, than that we should think ourselves deeply learned and experienced and so blaspheme against our Lord. That is why Paul proclaimed, "Gnosis puffs up, but love builds up".'[48]

[45] I. 273.
[46] Cf. S 121–23.
[47] I. 345.
[48] I. 345.

2. THE BIRTH OF THEOLOGICAL FORM

Gnosis was an attack on being itself which led to its dissolution
into visionary apparitions. Theology begins by seeing what is.
Far more than philosophy, which can be and usually becomes
idealist, it is recognition of an accompaniment to and dedication
to reality. It is either realistic or it is not theology at all. 'Truth
helps us to faith, for faith's object is the things which really are,
and so we belive in things as they are and by believing in things
as they are, we retain ever after our firm conviction of them.
And since our faith is the basis of our salvation, we must take
trouble over it to see that it gives us a true understanding of the
things which exist.'[49] This means that the insistence already
mentioned on thinking *kata physin* instead of *para physin* would
lead us to translate these terms, with great profundity and
rigour, as 'in accordance with being' and 'contrary to being', 'in
a manner inadequate to being'.[50] The primary aim is not to
think, to impose Platonic intellectual or even mythical categories on things, but simply to *see* what *is*.

To see. The two words *videre* and *ostendere* fall constantly
from Irenaeus' pen. *Videre*, again, is less Plato's contemplation
than simply standing before the clear message of the facts. The
thing itself is single, whereas the intellectual hypotheses are
countless. In Irenaeus this form takes up the old theo-
logoumenon of the 'two ways': 'For all who see there is only
one way which goes up and is lit by the light of heaven. For
those who do not see there is a multitude of shadowed ways
which lead in the opposite direction.'[51] But whoever wants to
can see the truth. God's light does not refuse itself.[52] To see God
is the distinction of Adam, the distinction too of the prophets
and of Christian believers, though to see God remains equally
the great eschatological promise, *quoniam videbitur Deus ab homi-*

---

[49] D 3; *cf.* Heb 11.1 and Is 7.9 (LXX): 'If you do not believe you will not
understand.'

[50] 1. 85–86.

[51] D 1.

[52] S 100–02. The Gnostics refuse to see, 1. 348. So too the Gentiles: 'They did
not lift their eyes to heaven . . . and would not see the light of truth' (2. 404).

nibus.[53] In the beginning it is the Son, together with the Holy
Spirit, who sees God. 'And no-one in heaven, on earth or under
the earth could unseal the Father's book and see the Father but
the Lamb that was slain, who redeemed us by his blood and,
when the word became flesh, received from the Father, who
created everything by his Word and adorned it by his wisdom,
authority over everything . . . , so that all might see their king,
that the Father's light might be gathered in the flesh of our Lord
and from his flesh strike into us like lightning, so that man might
attain to eternal life, wrapped in the Father's light.'[54] For us,
therefore, seeing means simply the revelation of the Father in
the Son through the Spirit ('for without the Spirit it is impossible to see the Son of God, just as without the Son no-one can
approach the Father,'),[55] that is, the triune God's being for us.[56]
Thus, on the one hand, all revelation is God's becoming visible,
and faith hangs on those encounters in which God has been seen;
similarly the Church's tradition (working backwards) hangs on
the 'autoptics', the eyewitnesses.[57] On the other hand, historical
revelation (moving forwards) has an inherent direction towards
the eschatologically perfected vision of God. The Old Covenant
sees the coming salvation as indeed something which is to come:
'the prophets did not see God's face directly, but saw saving
decrees and mysteries, through which man was to begin to see
God.'[58] Moses saw God and at the same time did not see him, a
dialectic intended to indicate both the impossibility of a man's
seeing God and the fact that, at the end of the ages, through
God's wise decree, man will see God.'[59] The same dialectic is
later upheld by the Son at a higher level 'when he shows God to
men and men to God by, on the one hand, protecting the
Father's invisibility so that man should never become a despiser
of the Father but always have room to progress and, on the
other, by making God visible to men by many saving decrees so
that man should not completely fall away from God and cease

[53] 2. 215 [that God will be seen by men].
[54] 2. 214.   [55] D 7; *cf.* S 94.
[56] D 43: Before the Son revealed himself to us, 'he did not exist for us, for we
did not know him.' D 31: 'Eternal life made itself visible so that we might win
a share in it in every connection.'
[57] 2. 145, 160.   [58] 2. 220.   [59] *Ibid.*

to exist'.[60] The prophets thus looked to the future,[61] the apostles saw in Jesus the presence of God, but a presence obscured and so also granted as a fulfilment, as a promise. The promise of the Old Covenant says 'that God will be seen by men and have contact and conversation with them on earth and be present to his creature and perceiver . . . , for what is impossible for men is possible for God. Man cannot of himself see God, but God is seen by men by his own choice, by those he chooses and when he chooses and in the way he chooses. God has power to do anything: through the Spirit in the past he was seen prophetically, then through the Son adoptively, and one day in the kingdom of heaven he will be seen in his fatherhood.'[62] Seeing the incarnate Son thus remains a seeing in faith:[63] a fulfilment, because God is already coming on earth, and a promise because the final descent of God's glory has not yet taken place. In all this we must never forget that 'the vision of God is the life of man',[64] that what is referred to as seeing is not anything theoretical, but is identical with life-giving, nourishing, purifying and bliss-giving communication,[65] in which the role of the Holy Spirit is of crucial importance.[66] What is seen is 'the living God, who is a God of the living'.[67] This is not a seeing in ecstasy which leaves the earthly senses behind. The important thing is that it is the same eyes which before did not see and which now through the healing miracle of grace have attained vision,[68] that it is 'the Father's ancient creation' which through the Son and Spirit gains access to the glory of the Father,

[60] 2. 219. If the incarnate Son's vision had still been prophetic, the Son would not have been what he appeared and we should have to wait for a further coming (2. 316).

[61] *Nam prophetia est praedicatio futurorum* [For prophecy is the proclamation of things to come], 2. 216; cf. 2. 171 (top).

[62] 2. 216.

[63] *per fidem speculantibus* [for those who see by faith], 2. 225.

[64] 2. 219 (top).

[65] 2. 215: *commixtio et communio Dei et hominis . . . quoniam videbitur Deus* [a mingling and union of God and man . . . since God will be seen by men]; 2. 217: *participatio Dei est videre Deum, . . . et homines igitur videbunt Deum, ut vivant* [To share in God means to see God, . . . and so men will see God that they may live].

[66] D 7.   [67] 2. 155; D 8.   [68] 2. 354.

through the 'economy' of the triune God: 'There was no other
way in which we could have been trained than by seeing our
teacher, hearing his voice with our hearing, so that, having
become imitators of his works and doers of his words, we might
achieve fellowship with him.'[69]

If seeing is the path and goal of the man who advances
towards God, the work of thought can consist in nothing other
than preparation for this seeing. Irenaeus used, to the point of
overworking them, the terms *ostensio*, *manifestatio*, 'display',
'exhibit', 'draw into the light', 'announce', 'make plain'. It is
significant that the process marked out by these words has a vast
range. At one extreme is the polemical 'conviction' and 'ex-
posure' of the opponent—Irenaeus even thinks that with this
bringing to light he has done almost enough, since his opponents' teaching cannot bear the bright spiritual light of day
and refutes itself.[71] Then comes the apologetic *ostensio* of truth
from the Scriptures,[72] and the climax is the theological *ostensio* of
the triune God by God himself. This occurs as the *ostensio Dei per
conditionem*, to which is closely related the *manifestatio Patris per
Verbum*,[73] as the *ostensio* of the inner reality of the incarnate one
by his life and his cross;[74] the self-*ostensio* of the risen one, who
'shows himself',[74a] and thereby at the same time 'shows from the
Scriptures that Christ had to suffer',[75] because faith is related
both to the vision of the risen one and to the pointing of

[69] 2. 314.
[70] 'For you and for all who are concerned about their salvation, one thing is
necessary, to set out with a firm, confident step by virtue of faith, without
deviating' (D 1).
[71] *Cf.* Reynders' dictionaries, which list more than 400 passages in the
Adversus Haereses alone, and the multiplication of terms in the prologues to
Books 1 and 3, *e.g.* 2. 146–47, 178 (bottom), 218 (top), S 396.
[72] *ex scripturis ostensiones* [demonstrations from the Scriptures], S 92; *cf.* S
236: *ostensiones quae sunt in scripturis non possunt ostendi nisi ex scripturis* [The
demonstrations contained in the Scriptures cannot be carried out except from
the Scriptures].
[73] 2. 219 (top) [the conditioned revelation of God, the manifestation of the
Father through the Word].
[74] S 322.
[74a] S 126: *seipsum manifestabat*; 2. 231 (top): *semetipsum ostendens*; D 38.
[75] 2. 236.

Scripture (*fides manifestam ostensionem habens . . . ex scripturis*).[76] Through all this there takes place the *ostensio* by God (which had remained hidden in the Old Covenant) of our likeness to God,[77] which is also the 'opening of God's previously sealed testament in favour of men'.[78] It is therefore natural that the Pauline *parrhēsia*, free access, the confident approach to God which is without fear because nothing obscures it, also constantly recurs in Irenaeus.[79] The Catholic tradition, unlike the secret Gnostic tradition, is marked by its openness and simplicity, its availability to general inspection.[80] It reflects the *ostensio Christi*, in which all appearance and all action is identical with being: *quod parebat, hoc erat*.[81]

This principle of clarity drawn from the clarity of the object itself gives Irenaeus two victories. One is over the Gnostic theory of the secret tradition: Christian teaching is a secret, but 'a holy, public secret'. The second is over the Gnostic theory of the adaptation of the Scriptures of both Old and New Covenants to the mentality, milieu and prejudices of the men of every age, as though the prophets, the Lord and the apostles, out of regard for human weakness (and so out of love for humanity), had not told the whole truth, but 'talked to the sick in accordance with their sickness'.[82] This still popular theory is easily refuted by Irenaeus, who points out that both the prophets and the Lord and his apostles do not shrink from provoking the deepest offence and anger by the directness of their message, or from paying for the welcomeness of their teaching with every sort of torture and even death.[83] If the

---

[76] S 356 [faith having clear proof from the Scriptures].

[77] D 22.

[78] D 8: 'He opened the testament of our adoption as sons'. S 176: 'He opened the testament to men'; S 304: 'to open the New Testament'.

[79] D 15. The most common Latin word is *fiducialiter* (S 94 [top]), but *constanter, audenter, cum fide etc.* also occur (S 219, note).

[80] *Testificatio . . . vera et . . . manifesta et firma, et nihil subtrahens* [A true and . . . clear and firm testimony keeping nothing back], S 270; *sine fuco est veritas et propter hoc pueris credita est* [truth is without deceit and therefore has been entrusted to children], S 272.

[81] S 328 [what he seemed he was].

[82] S 122.   [83] S 125, 223, 245.

principle of adaptation and soft speaking were left unchallenged, any fixed standard of truth would be lost and everyone would be left believing in his own God; any objective revelation would be redundant and everything would remain as it was.[84]

The basic methodological structure reflects not only the central feature of theological truth—it is revelation—but also the most characteristic feature of this particular theologian, his ability to see, above all to see things in their relation to one another, in a compact concentrated whole, in a summary (*epitome, compendium*)[85] which is prevented from being a falsification because it keeps the whole in view of its intensity and is able at any time to reproduce it again. This pulling together of his material produces a formula which outlasts and marks everything; but this is neither a piece of rhetoric, because it lacks the casualness and practical precision, nor a mere product of artistic intuition (although it is that too), because it follows the articulations of saving revelation in total obedience. It is not a trick of polemic, though it would never have been produced but for the pressure of indignation; it is the power of speculation in the original sense of the word. Above all, however, it is not an abstraction, like for example the christological formulas of the councils, but possesses the vibrancy, fragrance and downright poetic quality of direct, spontaneous creation. It is totally traditional; the terms used come from the Bible, are sometimes words of great simplicity, and yet in this use create a fresh, unique effect and have the inexhaustible violence of spontaneous creation. They have the impetuous quality of inspiration—just as for Irenaeus the Holy Spirit in the Church generally is a tempestuous roaring[86]—but at the same time possess a detached calm which matches this thinker's deepest sense of being, his earthy patience with existence. The formulas are therefore engineered to perfection—nothing in them may be altered—and yet open-ended, an invitation to eternal advance in believing, loving and hoping, to an eternally new conversation with God.[87] The concentration shares in the move-

---

[84] S 222.   [85] 2. 88; 2. 95.   [86] S 143, 199f.

[87] 2. 427: *coelum novum et terra nova, in quibus (novis) novus perseverabit homo, semper nova confabulans Deo* [a new heaven and a new earth, in which man will continue as new, always in new conversation with God].

ment from the Old Covenant to the New, from the 'detailed statement of the law' to the 'conciseness of faith and love', since 'love is the pleroma of the law' (Rom 13.10),[88] but this concentration is at one and the same time expansion, a scattering over the globe,[89] so that there is no longer any going back from this unity of fulness to the previous narrowness.[90] This is also to say that the balanced formulas which Irenaeus loves—between the first and the second Adam, between Eve and Mary, disobedience and obedience, etc.—with their *aequa lance*,[91] do not refer to a merely aesthetic harmony and symmetry, but to the unique theological relation of promise and fulfilment, which is at the same time that of fall and restoration.

We have now reached the central concept of Irenaeus' theology, *recapitulation*;[92] on the one hand the material expression of the method's formal aspect, it is at the same time the formative element in the world and history in general. Not just in the world, since for that the philosophical concept of transcendental unity would suffice, the *hen* and *nous* which were later to be used by the Alexandrians and Augustine, but specifically in temporal and historical extension, which cannot receive its meaning from any merely supra-temporal unity, but only from a power immanent in the temporal flow itself which gives the fleeting elements meaning and direction, a goal and substance. Christ, who became man at the 'end of the ages', binds together the disparate strands into that unity of essence and meaning which is their justification before eternity. Here there is no extraction of a permanent content from lost time as in the Platonists; recapitulation gives time itself validity before eternity. The concept retains a characteristic plurality of internally analogous levels which give it its unprecedentedly fertile richness, though it is a richness it must have if it is to express the centre of the mystery and not reduce it to a philosophical proposition.

[88] D 87.   [89] D 89.   [90] D 95.
[91] 2. 376; *cf.* D 31; S 370.
[92] E. Scharl, *Recapitulatio Mundi*, (Freiburg, 1941 with bibliography). More recently J. Lawson, *The Biblical Theology of St. Irenaeus*, (London, 1948); R. Potter, 'Irenaeus and Recapitulation', *Dom. St. N* (1951), pp. 192–200.

(a) There is, first, the dimension of beginning which embraces both the initiation of a work and the final process which brings perfection of inchoative and perfective. However, since we are dealing with a process, these do not simply coexist like comparable entities, nor in precisely the same way as the entities usually described by the two Biblical concepts type and anti-type, but in a way which allows the one which brings the perfection to give the one at the beginning of the process scope in itself for perfection. In Christ's reality Adam's reality comes to its full truth, in Mary Eve, in the Church the synagogue, with the first in each case the outline, the sketch;[93] the vague and complex finds itself under the impress of unity. This is also true of smaller unities within the large, which is why for instance Irenaeus loves to linger over Deuteronomy; he sees it as a unification of the whole Mosaic law which deepens it, clarifies it, and brings it to its culmination,[94] and, in this integrating function, as a 'second giving of the law'.[95] But the concept reaches its complete fulness only in Christ, who, as the God-man, brings perfection because at the same time he 're-capitulated in himself the long unfolding (*expositionem*) of men and gave us salvation in the mass (*in compendio*)'.[96]

(b) The second element is already present here: the active power of the fulfiller to give every emergent thing scope within itself in order, by assimilating it to himself, to bring it to its own fulness: without this active attraction into his own primacy recapitulation would be impossible.[97] So, 'in himself he raises man from the ground to which he has fallen',[98] since by giving the whole of man scope in himself he also assumes man's death

---

[93] S 378 (*praeformare*).

[94] 2. 147: *Moyses recapitulationem universae legis . . . in Deuteronomio faciens* [Moses . . . making a recapitulation of the whole law . . . in Deuteronomy]. *Cf.* 2. 191.

[95] D 28.

[96] S 310–12.

[97] . . . *In seipsum primatum assumens, et apponens seipsum caput Ecclesiae, universa attrahat ad seipsum apto in tempore* [that by taking to himself the primacy and making himself the head of the Church he might draw all things to himself at the appropriate time], S 292. Scharl, I, c. 28f.

[98] D 38.

into himself.[99] With the same vigour he assumes all the prophecies in order to fulfil them too in themselves,[100] a process in which they are fulfilled and redeemed, not outside themselves but in their own essence, with an effect which works back in time.[101] The ground of the advance of the inchoate is thus found in the fulfilling return (*recirculatio*) of the definitive,[102] by whose integrating power everything is decided. Adam is not redeemed just by a moral 'feat' of Christ's, by a 'representative' suffering, by a forensic justification, but is taken up into the redeemer as he is, with all his genuine bodiliness: *antiquam plasmationem in se recapitulatus est.*[103] All Christ's acts must possess this absorptive power, just as he symbolically washed only Peter's feet but thereby made his whole body clean: he redeemed the 'whole body' of the human race by the isolated cross.[104]

(c) This integrating power of Christ's would, however, be only divine and not also human if it did not have some sort of analogy in created mankind, if it did not recapitulate in itself an existing integrating power. Here again, Irenaeus does no more than extend Biblical thinking: Christ is raised and appointed to the position of head by replacing and at the same time redeeming another head, the first one, Adam. This makes it clear why for Irenaeus it is not just a pious wish, but a theological necessity, that the first Adam should be redeemed and saved.[105] So, despite the universality of the redemption of mankind, the full personal relationship of the two heads of humanity is of crucial importance: it is important that what distinguishes the first, namely, his birth directly from the virgin earth and the shaping hands of God, should be repeated in the second at the level of fulfilment, but now the *terra virgo* can no longer be lifeless matter since it is at the same time the 'old Adam' who

[99] 2. 387: *recapitulans enim universum hominem in se ab initio usque ad finem, recapitulatus est et mortem ejus* [For by recapitulating in himself the whole man from beginning to end, he also recapitulated his death]. *Cf.* S 292. In the same way he takes all hostility into himself (2. 304) and recapitulates all the blood of the prophets that was shed (2. 361), which puts an end to death (S 392).
[100] D 86.   [102] S 380.   [104] 2. 228.
[101] D 56.   [103] S 370.   [105] S 384.

must be the 'clay' out of which the new Adam is formed.[106]
From this it necessarily follows that the new *terra virgo*, the
Virgin Mary, as the one who definitively submits to God and is
formed by God, should in her personal answer recapitulate the
first woman, Eve, matching disobedience with obedience. This
quiet, easy conclusion, which is the result of close *attention* to the
biblical complex, is the moment at which mariology is really
born, though here it remains wholly a function of Christology:
the virgin birth is only a sign, the sign by which the uniqueness
of Christ the recapitulator can be recognised.[107] That Christ was
born of the Virgin (and not just of virgin clay like Adam) shows
at the same time, however, his divine status because it is the
distinctive sign of his eternal birth from the Father: *praeclaram
praeter omnes habuit in se eam quae est ab Altissimo Patre genituram,
praeclara autem functus est et ea quae est ex Virgine generatione.*[108]
What for later Church Fathers easily becomes a mere sign of his
divine purity (that he was not stained by any human
conception, which transmits original sin) is for Irenaeus a
double sign of his true divinity and of his true humanity, in that
as man he possesses fully not only Adam's flesh and blood
through Mary, but in addition Adam's archetypal mode of
origin.[109] It is only in this (and not in a mere Platonic lack of
imperfection) that the whole art of the Father is displayed: 'this
was the way it had to happen, so that God might not be
conquered and his art might not succumb to any weakness'.[110]
And even if the transformation of the original uncultivated
virgin earth into the intactness of a virgin is felt to be a sort of
spiritualism, according to Irenaeus God's art goes still further.
This happens in image, when Jesus spits on the ground and

---

[106] S 372–74.

[107] S 328, 348, 362; 2. 266; D 36–37.

[108] S 334 [Not only did he have in himself a glorious begetting surpassing all
others from the Most High Father, but he also enjoyed that glorious birth
from the Virgin].

[109] *servaret archetypum, Adae plasmationem* [that he might preserve the
archetype, the fashioning of Adam], 2. 279. *opportebat ejusdem generationis
habere similitudinem* [It was necessary for him to have a birth of the same
pattern], S 372.

[110] S 382.

makes a paste of clay which he uses to restore sight to Adam who has become blind, *ostendens antiquam plasmationem quemadmodum facta est, . . . quod enim in ventro plasmare praetermisit artifex Verbum, hoc in manifesto adimplevit.*[111] It happens in reality too, when the living second Adam finally also enters into bread and wine, into products of the earth, in order to recapitulate in himself not just man but also nature and the cosmos, the most deeply realistic earth. The eucharist is therefore the culmination of the case against Gnosticism.[112] It now becomes plain to faith that Christ in the end judges everything because he sums everything up redemptively in himself,[113] that he unites heaven and earth in man[114] because he has previously recapitulated them in himself,[115] because he sums up the whole order of salvation and so absolutely everything in himself.[116]

We have looked at recapitulation here first predominantly from the formal point of view, but the fact that the form also proved to be the content has given us a decisive proof of its rightness. Nevertheless we must now also illustrate the method of attention to reality by its most important results, as a preliminary to isolating the specific characteristics of Irenaeus's aesthetic.

3. STILLED CENTRE

Irenaeus wants to see reality as it is. He does not dream; he does not build with bold hypotheses; he places his trust in the logos of being. He does not rake through the background of his subject, but describes its beautiful surface which as such is the true revelation of the hidden depths. *Vere et firme*: the words often recur. His efforts are directed to the *firma et vera de Deo scientia*,[117] but while human knowledge produces a variety of conclusions,

---

[111] [showing how the ancient fashioning was done, . . . for what the Word as maker neglected to fashion in the womb he now made good openly] 2. 365.
[112] 2. 297f., 204, 316, 318; S 189.
[113] 1. 91.   [114] 2. 380.   [115] D 30.
[116] S 292.
[117] 1. 349 [the reliable and true knowledge of God].

convincing and less convincing, the principle nevertheless
holds: *quod verum est et certum et firmum, adjacet Deo.*[118] And only
what is revealed by God in Scripture, *sola illa vera et firma*,[119] this
testimony alone is *vera . . . , manifesta et firma*,[120] and so our faith,
which rests on it, is *firma et non ficta et sola vera*,[121] because it has
chosen as its guide *solum verum et firmum magistrum, Verbum
Dei*,[122] and listens to him in the *vera et firma praedicatio Ecclesiae*.[123]
In contrast to the Alexandrians, who are shortly to follow,
Irenaeus endeavours to hold thought back on the ground of
solid reality and to restrain its tendency to take off into allegory:
*et nihil allegorizari potest, sed omnia firma et vera et substantiam
habentia* (*i.e.*, on the new earth).[124] A further aspect of this firm
and established character of the truth is the *ordo traditionis*
implanted by Irenaeus in the centre of theological truth,[125]
which is no less reliable than the Word of Scripture, since the
Holy Spirit 'has written it in our hearts, without paper and ink',
and the same Holy Spirit guarantees it through the ministerial
succession and the unity of the Church in his truth.

But certainty and truth are only guaranteed if what supports
God's revelation can really take the weight. *Portare* ranges
between the dignity and suitability for receiving the weight of a
burden, the burden of God, the responsibility of carrying it with
oneself, of carrying it to the end, of enduring it,[126] the power to
protect and care for it in oneself as a mother does her child, and
every kind of caring and supportive help. The centre of the
concept for Irenaeus is the notion of the man who bears God: he

[118] 1. 350 [what is true and sure and reliable is close to God].
[119] 2. 52 [only that is true and reliable].
[120] 2. 79 [true, . . . plain and reliable].
[121] 2. 115 [firm and not pretended, but alone true].
[122] 2. 314 [the only true and reliable teacher, the Word of God].
[123] 2. 378 [the true and reliable preaching of the Church].
[124] 2. 426 [and nothing may be turned into allegory, but everything must be
firm and true and have substance].
[125] S 116.
[126] 1. 200: *portare crucem* [to bear the cross]; 1. 227: *portare magnitudinem
luminum* [to bear the strength of the lights]; 2. 293: *magnitudinem gloriae ipsius
portare non poteramus* [we were unable to bear the strength of his glory]; 2. 297:
nobis potestatem divinitatis bajulare non sustinentibus [when we were unable to
bear the weight of the power of divinity].

has the suitability for it, the strength, the power to grasp him: *portante homine et capiente et complectente Filium Dei.*[127] And God accustoms man 'to bear God's spirit',[128] even *capere et portare Deum.*[129] This is more than the underlying Biblical idea, *portare imaginem ejus;*[130] it is the fundamental capacity of the created being to withstand the creator, which certainly presupposes the 'image and likeness': 'Creation would not have borne him if it had been [Achamoth's] cast-off ignorance and taint. . . . How could a creation which was hidden away from the Father and far removed from him have had the power to bear his Word, to bear him who contains all gnosis in himself and is true and perfect? If it had been created by some intermediate being, how could it have borne the Father and the Son together—for the Lord says, "I am in the Father and the Father is in me"? And so the Church's preaching alone is true, namely, that it was creation itself, which derives its existence from the power and the art and the wisdom of God, which bore him; while invisibly it is itself borne by the Father, in the visible world, reversing the roles, it bears his word which is true. But the Father bears creation and his Word together, and the Word borne by the Father gives the Spirit to all.'[131] But the true God-bearer is Mary, by her complete 'obedience to his Word'.[132] Because the creature is not thrust out of the fulness by God but constantly borne by his goodness and patience, it can bear even God. This idea from the heart of supernatural theology receives its justification from an accompanying natural theology: the Old Testament law was able to 'bear' the New Covenant, to serve as a basis for it and to be transfigured into it,[133] and again the general law of 'nature' provided the basis for the commandment to Abraham and the law of Sinai.[134] These foundations do not threaten the radical necessity of supernatural grace, however, since we require the Holy Spirit, 'God's dew, necessarily if we

---

[127] S 282 [man bearing and receiving and containing the Son of God].

[128] 2. 185; *videbitur Deus ab hominibus qui portant Spiritum ejus* [God will be seen by men who bear his Spirit], 2. 217; *portare vitam* [to bear life], 2. 327, 328.

[129] 2. 339 [to receive and bear God].

[130] [bear his image] (1 Cor 15.49f); 2. 348–49.

[131] 2. 372.   [132] 2. 376.   [133] 2. 381, 383.

[134] See the next chapter.

are not to burn up',[135] but they make possible a different sort of positive relation both to the law and especially to nature, and even to the state,[136] from that which normally exists in the Platonising Patristic writings. The ever greater light into which God guides mankind is always at the same time an illumination of the object of the guidance, created nature.

The purpose of the following pages is first of all to indicate the three main points of articulation of Irenaeus' theology. None of these should be considered in isolation, and all three together are only like three static cross-sections through the system, still lacking the dynamic temporal bond which will be described in the next section. Nonetheless these three sections show the theological form: reduction to the simplest basic formulas which, when held up to the light of the Biblical revelation, reveal the organising power and the blazing heat of the recapitulative movement. The first collecting point is God, hidden and revealed in his unity and trinity. The second is the relation between God and creature, being and becoming, especially God and man. The third concerns the relation of time and eternity patterned according to the order of salvation (*dispositio*): Old Covenant, Gospel, Church.

(a) God is the One Totality, outside which nothing can exist, no autonomous separate void (*kenōma*). This is recognised in any sound religious thought. And this is also the original (Gnostic) concept of the pleroma,[138] which does not mean the self-contained fulness of a world of ideas, but that fulness which, as Paul says, fills all in all. However, the pantheistic streak in the Stoic and Gnostic pleroma makes it possible, from the point of view of the particular, to include what is still unfulfilled, still empty, in the all-embracing unity, and this is where Irenaeus' distinction begins. God's fulness (Irenaeus avoids the use of the

---

[135] S 306.   [136] 2. 389.   [137] 1. 349.

[138] As R. A. Markus has demonstrated in an important article ('Pleroma and Fulfilment', *Vig. Christi*, 1954, pp. 193–224), by comparing the *Corpus Hermeticum* and the *Excerpta Theodoti*, where the character of the Valentinian pleroma seems to be better expressed than in Irenaeus' description.

term pleroma of God) does not permit any kind of un-
fulfilledness, limitation or void,[139] whereas the fundamental
Irenaean concept of ful-fulment (*plērein*) is shorthand for the
nature of the temporal order of salvation, though this cannot be
fulfilled in any other way than by being filled out with the
divine fulness. God is not the One merely in a way which would
require him to be at the same time the totality of the world; he is
the *idem ipse*, that is, the free 'creator of heaven and earth and of
this whole universe . . . and the Lord over all things',[140] and as
this eternally free Lord in himself unknowable. It is an apparent
paradox that in reaction to the fashionable Gnostic transcendence, which stamps the highest God as absolutely unknowable,
Irenaeus is himself forced to stress this unknowability. Gnostic
transcendence, however, was nothing other than the inseparable
logical and dialectical obverse of his immanence and filling of
the world as aeon and fulness of the aeons (pleroma), whereas
Irenaeus' God of all is the free majesty which 'encompasses all,
but is alone encompassed by no-one, he the former, he the
founder, he the deviser, he the creator, he the Lord of all things.
And neither outside him nor above him does anything else exist,
not even that mother whom they attach to him, no other God
such as Marcion invented, no pleroma of thirty aeons, . . . no
bottomless depth, no first origin, no heaven, no virgin light, no
indescribable aeon, . . . but the one and only God.'[141] 'Therefore
do not transcend God himself, for he cannot be transcended. Do
not look above the creator, for you will find nothing. He who
formed you cannot be defined, . . . your thought cannot
encompass him, but if you think against nature you will become
a fool, and if you persist you will fall into madness.'[142] 'God
cannot be measured by the heart or grasped by the spirit, he who
encloses the earth in his fist.'[143] Naturally God's three-in-oneness
is also part of his incomprehensibility: the generation of the
Word from the Father is 'indescribable and inexpressible'.[144]
The processions of God cannot be predicted and are not subject
to any human logic. Nor can God's attributes be reduced to a
system which would make them proceed logically (as aeons)

[139] 1. 251–53, 257; 2. 212.   [140] D 8.   [141] 1. 368.
[142] 1. 344.   [143] 2. 211.   [144] D 70; 1. 355.

from the divine ground of being.[145] 'Nor, further, is the All-Father like a composite creature to which the rational spirit was subsequently added; the Father is rational spirit and the rational spirit is the Father.' Father, Son and Spirit are in eternal conversation,[146] but beyond all the imagined drama of ignorance, seeking or finding.[147] For in God there is no trace of darkness,[148] no trace of *anankē*,[149] only eternal light and freedom.

But God has communicated himself and made himself knowable, and this knowledge (gnosis) of God is real, indeed the most real of all forms of knowledge, though it does not prejudice the unknowability of God. Irenaeus here speaks in formal tones: 'In respect of his greatness it is impossible to know God, because the Father is immeasurable, but in respect of his love—for it is his love which leads us to God through his Word—we learn, if we are responsive, more and more how great God is and that it is he who through himself establishes and chooses everything and makes it beautiful and contains it.'[150] This formula is repeated constantly,[151] and is taken from the beginning as a trinitarian formula. For the unknown God is indeed the Father, but he reveals himself through his 'two hands', the Son and the Spirit, with which he makes the world.[152] This enables Irenaeus to repeat the saying that no-one knows the Son except the Father and that no-one knows the Father except the Son and whoever the Son wills to reveal him to (through his Spirit; Mt 11.27), without giving rise to any agnosticism or supranaturalism, because the creation itself is the product of love revealing itself, a love which then, as salvation history, leads us through Son and Spirit ever deeper into the knowledge of the Father. In the last resort Irenaeus knows no other doctrine of the Trinity (and here he keeps to Scripture) than that of the act of revelation and the historical content of revelation.[153] The triune God is accessible to us only where he

---

[145] I. 286.   [146] D 51.   [147] I. 310.
[148] I. 260.   [149] I. 294f.   [150] 2. 212–13.
[151] 2. 215, 216; D 47; S 402.
[152] 2. 145, 213, 317, 333, 365, 403; D 11.
[153] As in the interpretation of Is 61.1 (Lk 4.18): 'The one who anoints is the Father, the anointed is the Son and the anointing oil is the Spirit.'

makes himself accessible to us, so that it is the greatest possible slight to God to disparage the historical self-revelation of his immeasurable love and to look behind it for a non-existent access to the unknown God.[154] The image of the trinitarian God, the highest image which can be sighted from within creation, is the translation of the ark of the covenant into the domain of eternal life, the invisible flanked by the two worshipping cherubim. 'This God is glorified by his Word, which is the eternal Son, and by the Spirit, who is the wisdom of the Father of all. And the powers of these (two), known as cherubim and seraphim, glorify God with incessant cries, and the entire creation . . . glorifies him.'[155] Origen later will again present this image of the Trinity,[156] perhaps following Philo,[157] and make Son and Spirit, at the pinnacle of the entire creation, offer the divine worship. Worship in God carries over into the *dynameis* of Son and Spirit, the highest angels, before communicating itself to the whole cosmos. The emphasis with which the *Demonstration*, Irenaeus' unpolemical dogmatic treatise, dwells on the theme of universal worship is amazing: God's worship of God which carries over into heavenly worship and human worship,[158] the worship we owe to God day and night,[159] the worship of the seven heavens, particularised by the seven gifts of the Spirit and symbolised by the seven-branched candlestick[160] (Denys will later build up his cosmic liturgy on the number nine), the temple worship of the priest Aaron as the core of the

---

[154] S 402.   [155] D 10.

[156] *Hom. on Isaiah* 1, 2 (Baehrens 8, 244–45); cf. von Balthasar, *Geist und Feuer*, 2nd ed. pp. 447f., and commentary on Romans 3.8; PG 14, 948.

[157] *De cherubim* 27–30 (Colson-Whitaker II, pp. 25f.): 'While God is truly One, his supreme and first powers (*dynameis*) are two, goodness and royal power, for it is through goodness that he produced the universe and through royal power that he rules over what he has produced. . . . the cherubim are the symbols of these two powers.' Cf. *De Abrahamo* 24. Dom Emmanuel Lanne ('Cherubim et Seraphim. Essai d'interprétation du Chap. X de la Démonstration de S. Irénée', *RSR*, 1955, 524f.) concludes, rightly in my view, that Irenaeus' idea comes directly or indirectly from the same source, while Daniélou (*Théologie du Judéo-Christianisme*, p. 191), followed by Froidevaux (*Démonstration*, p. 47), prefers to think in terms of Jewish Christian apocrypha as sources. Cf. S 195–97, 201.

[158] D 10.   [159] D 8.   [160] D 9.

Old Covenant, which nevertheless remains binding as worship on the attitude of every worshipper of God,[161] and finally worship in the New Covenant, where God's temple has become the human body.[162] This universe of adoration is inherently trinitarian. What is made known through the love of God is the manifestation of his unknown (because immeasurable) greatness: his love itself is the inconceivable, the indescribable; *benignitas ejus inenarrabilis*.[163] This inconceivability is an attribute of the fact of his concrete presence, which cannot go unnoticed or unperceived by any created thing.[164]

Certainly the model of the God who is at the same time inconceivable and conceivable is prefigured in Gnosticism, as Irenaeus freely admits: 'The ground of the eternal duration of the aeons', he says, 'is the inconceivability of the Father, but the ground of their origin and development is that which is conceivable in him, that is, the Son.'[165] But the difference predominates. Between Father and Son, in the Christian understanding, lies the area of their knowledge of each other, into which they invite whom they will: not only does the Son lead to the Father in the economy, but 'the Father in turn through the Son gives the knowledge of his Son to those who love him',[166] in a free decision of his will which man matches in freedom. No natural salvation, no 'divine core' in man, no overlap between God and the world: Son and Spirit belong unequivocally on the side of the Father.

(b) Here we have the basic articulation of Irenaeus' picture of the world, and it is here that his formulas acquire their greatest force. All 'communion' between God and creature is based on a fundamental opposition of nature, creating and being created, which at the same time implies the opposition of being and becoming and of eternity and time: *Deus quidem facit, homo autem fit; et quidem qui facit semper idem est, quod autem fit, et initium*

---

[161] D 26.
[162] D 96.
[163] 2. 217.
[164] S 402.
[165] 1. 21–22; cf. Sagnard, *La Gnose valentinienne*, pp. 155, 313.
[166] S 190.

et medietatem et adjectionem et augmentum accipere debet.[167] And so
'in the same measure that God needs nothing, man needs
communion with God'.[168] God is *perfectus* because *infectus*,[169] but
man needs *profectus*.[170] The man who transgresses the law of
becoming (*supergrediens legem humani generis*) 'and before he has
become human wants to be like the creator God, who will allow
no distinction between the God who always was and man who
has only just come to be, is more irrational than a brute beast'.[171]
For the creature there is no appeal from the creator 'because he
takes from himself the substance of creatures and the pattern of
his artefacts and the beauty of the individual life-form'.[172] God is
being which is,[173] and therefore eternal;[174] the creature which
comes into being, on the other hand, which necessarily has a
beginning, middle and end, *i.e.*, time,[175] is fundamentally dependent on God, in need of him,[176] and so, if it chooses rightly,
determined by faith, love and hope.[177] Because God is eternally
always greater, it must always entrust itself to God, 'always
hope for new kindnesses from him in order evermore to love
him; always, in obedience to him, learn from him that God is so
great',[178] always serve him in holiness[179] in order 'to get right to
him',[180] and, across the infinite gulf which is bridged by his
gracious power, 'to win communion with him'.[181] And even in
the fulfilment the original opposition persists, but stilled: for the
'flesh . . . does not in the strict sense inherit the divine Spirit, but
is appointed heir by him (*ou klēronomei, alla klēronomeitai*). . . .
Therefore just as the bride cannot take the bridegroom to wife,
but can certainly be taken to wife by him, so "flesh" of itself
cannot inherit the kingdom of God, but can be brought into the
kingdom of God as an heir by the Spirit.'[182] The creature's every

---

[167] 2. 175 [God makes, but man is made, and the one who makes is always
the same but the thing that is made has to accept a beginning, a middle state,
addition and increase]; *cf.* S 148–50.
[168] 2. 184.
[169] 2. 296 [perfect because not made].
[170] 2. 175.   [171] 2. 297.   [172] 2. 213.
[173] D 2.   [174] D 3.   [175] S 398.
[176] 2. 209.   [177] 2. 178.   [178] 2. 212.
[179] 2. 216.   [180] 2. 217.   [181] 2. 314.
[182] 2. 343–44, as an answer to a Gnostic objection to 1 Cor 15.50.

action rests on a still deeper passivity: in order to come into being it must place itself like clay in the shaping 'hands' of God and entrust itself to them.[183]

This difference cuts so deep that the other, Greek distinction between spirit and matter totally pales in comparison. The centre of the created universe is in no sense the angelic spirit (which in Irenaeus plays only an accompanying and subordinate role), but the man who—in a gesture against the Gnostics—is first the clay shaped by God's hands and into whom the breath, *spiritus*, is then infused. This breath, the human soul, is not man, any more than the Holy Spirit of grace is man: *hominis esse possunt, homo autem nequaquam.*[184] The true man is soul in body and grace in both (the Holy Spirit who lives in soul and body as in a temple),[185] and therefore the eschatologically whole man is also not the disembodied soul after death, but emphatically the risen flesh, whose participation in eternal life is no more miraculous in principle than its present participation—like that of a sponge in water and of a torch in fire—in life and the Holy Spirit.[186] The natural 'breath' (*pnoē*) is temporal, but the spirit (*pneuma*) is eternal, and so the natural man dies when he turns away from the spirit (in Adam), but when he is rejoined to the spirit by God he obtains eternal life.[187] Therefore, although it is the man who dies when he loses breath and not just the body, the breath-*soul* can still be called 'immortal',[188] but the man is immortal at the resurrection of the dead. Irenaeus is totally amazed at the miracle of the human body made alive by the soul. It is for him the most fundamental example of what distinguishes the creature: its *being* formed by God's hand: 'The flesh is not without a share in the artistic wisdom and power of God, because God's power, which bestows life, is made perfect in weakness (2 Cor 12.9), that is, in the flesh.'[189] Strange and

---

[183] 2. 299.

[184] 2. 333 [they may belong to man, but can in no way be man]. *Neque . . . anima ipsa secundum se est homo* [Nor is the soul itself, of itself, man], 2. 335.

[185] 2. 335.   [186] 2. 327.   [187] 2. 351.

[188] 2. 337.

[189] 2. 327. Significantly, the tripartite structure of man is divided temporally: man is first body, then soul, and then he can acquire the (Holy) Spirit (2. 351).

impressive exegesis! 'The flesh is devised to be receptive and to be able to contain the power of God, since in the beginning it received the art of God, and one part became an eye for seeing, another an ear for hearing, another a hand for feeling and making, another nerves, tensed in all direction and holding the limbs together, another arteries and veins for the circulation of the blood and the soul-breath, another in turn different internal organs, and another blood, the link between body and soul. It is indeed impossible to describe the whole masterly structure of elements which makes up man; it did not come into being without greatness and wisdom. But what shares in the art and wisdom of God also shares in his power.'[190] Accordingly, for Irenaeus the body does not bear just a trace of God and the soul the image of God, as the Platonising Fathers will later say, but the whole man, made up of body and soul, is created as the image and likeness of God. The language may vary, with the starting-point for this creature of becoming called at one time 'image'[191] and at another 'likeness'.[192] Or the two may be distinguished dynamically, as when it is said that as a result of sin the image lost the likeness or resemblance (*similitudo*) to God, and as a result of God's making himself resemble the fallen creature by becoming man[193] and 'recapitulating in himself the image of the beginning',[194] the resemblance has been re-covered.[195] This dynamic understanding of the image is that of salvation history and authentic Biblical theology: 'The image of God is the Son, in whose image man was created, and that is why the Son appeared visibly in the last ages of the world, to reveal that the image resembled himself.'[196] The revelation and making visible of the resemblance is the distinctive feature of the New Covenant, whereas in the Old Covenant, though man's image-character had been declared, it had not yet been shown

---

[190] 2. 326.

[191] 2. 367; *imaginem habens in plasmate, similitudinem vero ... assumens per Spiritum* [having the image in his matter but taking on ... the likeness through the Spirit], 2. 334.

[192] 2. 145.   [193] 2. 368.   [194] 2. 353.

[195] 2. 297, 317, 334, 339, which also means that the 'image and likeness' should only be expected to emerge with time.

[196] D 22.

---

and demonstrated.[197] Since in Irenaeus human nature is seen as all along embedded in time and becoming, it is not advisable to make a sharp division between the static image and the dynamic process of acquiring the likeness. The doctrine of the image and likeness shows at the same time the trinitarian character of the creature. Because it is a thing which acquires its being gradually, 'God's hands' do not cease to impress their form upon it, the Son objectively, the Spirit subjectively, both in the realm of nature and also in the realm of grace, so that 'over all is the Father as the head of Christ, through all the Word, the head of the Church, and in us all the Spirit, the living water which the Lord offers' (Eph 4.6).[198] And so nature everywhere shows sketches and foreshadowings, the two-dimensional diagram of what is to be developed through becoming and time into the full model. But because God is guiding the direction of the process towards a goal which is unattainable by man, nature can of itself lay no claim to perfective grace.

If man is to be able to follow God's lead, he must be free,[199] and one of the principal places where this freedom can be seen is in that guidance itself, which always takes the form of gentle suggestion (*suasoria*) and never of compulsion.[200] For the same reason he must have an original knowledge of his createdness and of his creator, a *sensibilitas* for God,[201] a natural knowledge of God.[202] In this way it is possible for the wild shoot of nature which grew wild and fell after paradise to be grafted back onto the true shoot of Christ's healing grace. For the process requires that the same substance of wood, and analogously of ensouled flesh, should be found in both states, in other words that the cultivating of the man of flesh into a man of spirit should not involve any change of substance.[203] The important conclusion from this is that the Greek categories of matter and spirit must be assimilated to the Biblical paired concepts of flesh and spirit without suppressing or falsifying them.[204] In other words, the body is not an obstacle to man's true spiritualisation.[205] More

[197] 2. 367–68. [198] 2. 374.
[199] 2. 289. This is where some of man's image character resides (*ibid.*).
[200] 2. 286–89. [201] S 402–403. [202] 1. 264; 2. 160, 163.
[203] 2. 346. [204] *Cf. e.g.* 2. 186. [205] 1. 378.

generally, not only a flight from the world (which, taken in the most literal sense, is impossible) but also a proper use of the world and its goods are both permitted and proper for a Christian according the teaching of Scripture.[206]

(c) Man is perfected according to the threefold order of salvation in the incarnate Word of God. Since the dynamics of the order of salvation will be described later, here for the present we shall discuss only the static perfection, in so far as this can be treated separately. It is after all true that the process of becoming contains the meaning (as the German *Sinn*—from *sinθa* 'journey' as in *Uhrzeigersinn*, 'clockwise'—or the French *sens*, which includes the direction of a process), and every element acquires its meaning in the totality of the developing process. While for the Gnostics and again later for Augustine the distinction between 'wheat' and 'chaff' in the Church and the world has a predominantly static character, in the sense of two classes of people, its meaning for Irenaeus is determined by the position in the organic process of growth: the husk is necessary until the fruit inside it has ripened, and then it becomes dispensable and useless.[207] But to a mode of being which develops there belongs the joy of fulfilment, in other words the believing trust and hope which make existence delightful. As a result, every point in time, even those preceding the fulfilment, receives a fulness appropriate to its particular *kairos*: as each individual in his particular place does the will of God as expressed in salvation history, he has a share (anticipatory or subsequent) in the total fulfilment. Irenaeus applies this temporal interpretation to the simile of the body and its members.[208] Thus Platonic or Gnostic views of being, which break it up into a useless part which runs away into time and a timeless part which is the only valuable one, completely destroy and distort the mystery of the meaning of existence and at the same time the mystery of the economy of salvation and of the mystical body of Christ.[209] The Son who comes last justifies all hours worked in the Lord's vineyard[210] because 'the king has prepared the

---

[206] 2. 248–49. [207] 2. 151–54. [208] 2. 265.
[209] 1. 349. [210] 2. 277, 283.

marriage feast for his son from the beginning'.[211] So Christ is both the fruit of the long organic development of the ages of the world and the one who descends freely from above;[212] as both the fruit of the world and the fruit of the Father he has brought heaven and earth together and united the Spirit with man.[213] That God can do all things was always clear, but that man together with God can also do all things had to be proved. The mediator came to exercise this power together with man,[214] in order 'by his own affinity with both to lead both back to mutual love and harmony, to introduce God to man and man to God'.[215] No question, had he been only man, we would still be 'in the old slavery of disobedience and would die' as 'debtors of death and would not have received the antidote of life'.[216] Everything thus turns on the disposition of the God-man,[217] on the intimate union of the divine Spirit with his flesh.[218] And in this the flesh is crucial: 'If the flesh had not had to be saved, the Word of God would on no account have become flesh',[219] and flesh is really saved only by flesh.[220] If merely a divine spirit were to descend on a pre-existing man, it could and inevitably would leave him again in a crisis, and nothing would have been achieved: no, the Word himself must become flesh.[221] Man must achieve it: 'Had not man conquered the enemy of man, the enemy would not have been properly conquered. On the other hand, if God had not given us salvation, we would not have it for certain.'[222] The same person must be glorified and abased,[223] must penetrate heights and depths,[224] in order to make up by his humiliation for Adam's arrogance,[225] must live through all the ages of man in order to heal all.[226] Salvation lies in the human life and fate of Jesus,[227] and this includes his real death;[228] really

---

[211] 2. 281.   [212] 2. 152–54.   [213] 2. 380.

[214] S 312.   [215] S 326.   [216] S 330.

[217] As the *Demonstratio* heavily emphasises (D 39).

[218] D 41 (and note, p. 95).   [219] 2. 360.   [220] 2. 362–63.

[221] S 158. Everything depends on the 'identity of bodiliness in relation to Adam' (D 32).

[222] S 324.   [223] S 318.   [224] S 336–37.

[225] 2. 383, 385.   [226] S 326.

[227] D 97: 'salvation, to wit, the visible coming of our Lord, that is, his human life'.

[228] S 316.

dying, however, means going down to the realm of the dead, into Hades, and not just leaving the cross to return to the Father.[229] And if everything in the fate of Jesus is the revelation of his Father, so too is his Passion.[230] It is the real suffering and dying man who, by what he completely and utterly is, glorifies the Father, and this man who suffers and is humiliated even to death is much more magnificent than all the bloodless patterns of the Gnostics: 'If one were to pass judgment on the two Christs, far better and more powerful and truly gracious would be the one who, in the very wounds and stripes and all the other injuries and insults, showed himself our benefactor and did not remember the malice shown to him—better far than the one who would have fled from it and would not have suffered any injustice or slight. ... We ourselves, indeed, would be "above the master" (Mt 10.24) if we had to accept and endure things which the master neither accepted nor endured.'[231] But when, as a result, a man treats his suffering and death as discipleship of Christ, when he 'believes' Christ, that is, entrusts himself to him in discipleship,[232] all pain becomes a demonstration of the truth of God in us, even the highest 'attempt to tread in the footsteps of Christ',[233] even martyrdom, whose solemn glory the Gnostics mock with their heavenly limit-cross. In an emotional passage Irenaeus lists the human features of the redeemer. For him they are not, as they are for the later Platonising theologians, sources of embarrassment which have to be artificially reconciled with the perfections of the Son of God; they are, like martyrdom, the halo adorning real existence.[234] And only because all this has been can there also be the *ordo resurrectionis*,[235] the raising of the dead Son through the Spirit in the name of the Father.[236] Only because from its very creation the universe as a whole has received the impress of the sign of the cross, because, that is, the

---

[229] 2. 411.   [230] 2. 368.   [231] S 322-24.

[232] *Credere autem ei est facere ejus voluntatem* [But to believe in him is to do his will], 2. 160, and *infra* the passage on Abraham's faith.

[233] *conantur vestigia adsequi passionis Domini* [they try to follow in the footsteps of the Lord in his Passion], S 322, 320.

[234] S 376.   [235] 2. 411.

[236] D 48 and parallels in the note.

cross has universal dimensions,[237] can the resurrection then set the seal on the whole bodily dispensation of salvation which makes the communion in life between God and man final.[238] Through the suffering flesh of Christ the Father's light reaches us;[239] that is the essence of the *mystērion*.[240] The Church as the unfolding of this mystery is better discussed in the context of the temporal economy of salvation.

4. GOD'S TEMPORAL ART

At this point we can uncover the intellectual bond in Irenaeus' picture of the world which knits together his apologetic method, the essential content of his dogmatics and that new Christian aesthetic with which he conquers the aesthetic myth of Gnosis. The Christian reality is inseparable from history. And, consequently, it is free from time: the Greek demand for proportion, order and beauty must be found again in Biblical time or nowhere. But the fact that human nature which unfolds in time has been taken into the divinely ordained Christian order also gives it proportion and beauty, and through it the whole world. Except that for Irenaeus this cosmic beauty, which tells of the art of the creator, can never be contemplated in isolation from its true artistic intention, from the mystery of *anakephalaiōsis*.[241]

In this section, in accordance with our overall purpose, we

---

[237] D 34, following Justin (1 *Apol.* 55, 60) in a Christianisation of a passage in the *Timaeus* (36 BC) where the demiurge draws a X (chi) over the created world. *Cf.* the Easter homily modelled on Hippolytus which describes the cosmic dimensions of the cross by which the world is held together (Text in *Homélies Pascales*, ed. Nautin, I, pp. 176–78, Sources Chrétiennes 27, 1950).

[238] 1. 360.   [239] 2. 214.

[240] S 232; D 25 (with parallels).

[241] 'Down to the theologians of the "redemptive history" school in the nineteenth century . . . , there has scarcely been another theologian who recognised so clearly as did Irenaeus that the Christian proclamation stands or falls with the redemptive history . . . . Irenaeus is the theologian of antiquity who understood the Greek world in its innermost nature, and yet undertook no . . . violent reductions and reinterpretations of the New Testament message' (O. Cullmann, *Christ and Time* [1946], London, 1951, pp. 56–57).

shall consider the material structure of the apologetics and dogmatics in their aesthetic and formal aspects; first the essence of the divine art, then its temporal dimension, and last the essential content of time.

(a) The demand that the created 'image' should resemble the original which created it is for Irenaeus an elementary demand on the creative artist who is God, 'for if the creator of the worlds did not create things in his own image but, like a poor craftsman or an apprentice, copied other models, where is their "groundless one" supposed to have got its original from?' There is an infinite regress. 'If it is admitted that even men have invented things which are useful for living, is God, who made the whole world, not to be allowed to draw out of himself the beautiful form of created things and the devising of the beautiful ordering of the world?'[242] No, 'God's art does not slacken; has he not the power to raise children of Abraham out of the very stones? . . . The light does not grow weak because of those who have blinded themselves . . . and do not wish to keep his art (*technē*).'[243] Sin would disprove his art only if God were not powerful enough to raise up fallen creation once more and to fill up (*adimplere*) the ages of its banishment.[244]

God creates by his 'artistic Logos',[245] since 'everything was created by a word of God'.[246] But the trinitarian relation is the original measure or proportion in God, 'for it is rightly said that the immeasurable Father himself is measured by the Son, that the Father's measure, indeed, is the Son, because he has his measure. . . . And therefore God creates everything in proportion and rhythm (*metrō kai taxei*), and nothing lacks proportion with him because nothing is without number (*anarithmēton*).'[247]

---

[242] I. 269. Cf. I, 267: *Quod si (emissio) non est similis, Salvatoris erit incusatio qui dissimilem emisit imaginem, quasis reprobabilis artifex.* [But if the (work) does not show a resemblance, the blame will be put on the Saviour who put out an unfaithful image and he will be called a bad artist.] Irenaeus interprets the whole theological image character of the creature in aesthetic categories: I, 266–67.

[243] 4. 299–300.   [244] S 382.   [245] D 38.

[246] D 60.   [247] 2. 153.

From him come not only the substance but also the original and
the form of the ornate things of the world,[248] and the worker is
known by the rhythm of his works.[249] For his creative work
God needs no emanations,[250] no 'radiations' or 'fecundities',[251]
nor does he need any world of ideas.[252] He derives the original
design for the creation of the world from his own power and
from himself,[253] so that the whole Platonic and Gnostic
numerical system becomes redundant, to the extent that it is
conceived as superior to the contingent world and independent
of it. 'We ourselves declare the harmony of created nature,
because, in relation to us, things are suitable for their places
(*aptabilia*) because their own rhythm is appropriate (*apta*) to the
general rhythm for which they were created.'[254] Quite apart
from the fact that the numbers of the earthly and contingent
realm in no way agree with those of the (imaginary) numbers of
heaven![255] The Pythagorean origin of this correspondence of
heavenly and earthly numbers does not impress Irenaeus.[256] The
numbers of the real world are so unbelievably complicated:
who would use them to ferret out the heavenly ones? Irenaeus
leaves them to divine providence, which 'has numbered all the
hairs of our head' and given 'each thing its own pattern of
action, its order, number and particular quantity . . . and done so
with supreme skill in matching them to each other and with
sublime intelligence'.[257] God's work also reveals creative power,
wisdom and goodness: creative power and goodness in the fact
that he has freely established and created what is not yet, and
wisdom in that he created the things that exist to form a
harmony (*eurhythma, apta et consonantia*).[258] The Pythagoreans
are certainly right to talk about a music of being, except that it is
the harmony of the created world which gives glory to God by

---

[248] 2. 213.   [249] 1. 364.   [250] 1. 283–85.
[251] 1. 307.

[252] 1. 269. *Cf.* 1, 304: 'When they say that the pleroma was released by the
Father for the sake of the world which was to be created, to enable him to
organise its being properly, then the pleroma is no longer made for its own
sake, but for the sake of the image which is only to come into being in its
likeness. . . . And then creation is higher in status (*honoratior*) than the pleroma.'
[253] 1. 305.   [254] 1. 304.   [255] 1. 270.
[256] 1. 296ff.   [257] 1. 346.   [258] 2. 295; *cf.* 1. 304.

its existence. 'While creatures are varied and numerous, but skilfully placed in the whole creation and in tune with it, nevertheless, considered separately, they are opposed to each other and not in harmony, just as the sounds of the lyre produce a harmonious melody made up of many contrasting notes as a result of the intervals between them. The lover of truth must therefore not let himself be led astray by the particular interval of each one and postulate one creator for one and another for another, . . . but a single one, to demonstrate the wisdom and justice and grace of the whole work. But those who can hear the harmony must praise and glorify the artist, notice the tautness of one [string] and the slackness of another and listen for the compensating mean between the two, never departing from the canon or straying from the artist.'[259] What is true of the universe is also true of Holy Scripture. If we keep to the canon of faith, 'all Scripture given to us by God will be found to be harmonious (symphōnos). The parables will harmonise with plain speech, plain speech will unlock the parables and through the polyphony of the utterance a single symphonic melody will be audible within us.'[260] Irenaeus is not here describing a literary work made up of different writings and chapters, but the symphony of being and history which is expressed in Scripture and has as its supreme law the recapitulation of mankind through the God-man: 'For if Adam from the earth had received his shaping and essence from the hand and art of God, but Christ had not been formed by the hand and art of God, . . . the work would lack internal consistency (inconstans artificium).'[261] The last chapter does not take its lead from the first, but the other way round, as the true art of storytelling demands. So the physical world is the promise of the supernature which is to follow,[262] because the flesh is itself 'not without the artistic wisdom and power of God', 'but God's hands are accustomed, as they have been from the time of Adam, to give their work a rhythm and hold it strongly, to support it and place it where they choose.'[264]

[259] I. 343. [260] I. 352.
[261] S 374 (and Sagnard's note, 377).
[262] Cf. 2. 326. [264] 2. 330–31.

But the centre of the divine art is man, and the rest of the world has been created for the sake of man rather than man for the world.[265] Already by his very nature as a compound of body and soul, man is a work of art, one in which the soul acts as the artist and the body as the instrument. Moreover the speed of the artist's ideas contrasted with the slowness with which he executes them on the instrument is in no sense an argument against the virtues of the latter.[266] Body and soul, however, each demand their own purity: 'purity of the body as abstinence from all unjust and shameful things, purity of the soul as faith in God without addition or subtraction, . . . for piety preserves its beauty and proportion if truth forever rules in the soul and purity in the body. What value is there in knowing the truth in words while staining the body by bad deeds? And what can possibly foster the purity of the body if truth does not rule in the soul? Both are glad to be together and form a harmony and brotherly unity, in order to present man before God.'[267] It is in this creature alone, a compound of two elements, for which God 'took the purest and finest elements of the earth in order to mix his power with the earth in correct proportion . . . so that man should be like God not only in his breath but also in his shaped flesh',[268] it is in this creature that God has chosen to reveal himself. The whole of salvation history will be written in man himself: 'Man is the receptacle for the action of God and for all his wisdom and power. Just as the doctor shows his skill in his patients, so God is revealed in man.'[269] Especially as the one who pardons: 'in forgiving sins he on the one hand healed man and on the other showed clearly (ostendit) who he himself was.'[270]

This is the source of the central concept of 'glory' as the mutual glorification of God and man. Man, who preserves God's art in himself and obediently opens himself to its disposing, glorifies the artist and the artist glorifies himself in his work. 'You do not create God; God creates you. Therefore if you are

---

[265] 2. 404. Man (as a microcosm) contains within himself the whole macrocosm. This also includes the angels, who are thus at the service of man: D 11–12.

[266] 1. 379.   [267] D 2.   [268] D 11.

[269] S 342.   [270] 2. 371.

God's work, wait patiently for the hand of your artist, who does everything in due proportion, and in due proportion as regards you who are being made. Offer him your heart soft and pliable, and preserve the form which the artist forms out of you: preserve it by keeping yourself moist, so that you do not dry out and harden and lose the trace of his fingers. Keeping the form that has been impressed on you, you will move towards perfection, for the clay that is in you will be hidden by the artist. His hand has created the substance in you, and now it will cover you inside and out with pure gold and silver and beautify you so much that "even the king will lust after your beauty" (Ps 45.11). But if you despise his art and show yourself ungrateful to him because he has made you only human, you despiser of God, then you have forfeited both his art and your life. . . . If, however, you surrender to him what is yours, trusting faith in him and submissiveness, then you will receive his art and become a perfect work of God. But if you believe in him but still tear yourself out of his hands, the cause of your imperfection lies in your disobedience and not in him who called you.'[271] Life and art are thus won and lost together. 'Man's glory is to endure and persist in submissiveness to God, . . . the disciples did not glorify the Lord by following him, but because they followed him they were glorified by him.'[272] As they are, ' "all men need the glory of God," (Rom 3.23), but cannot justify themselves; they are justified by the advent of the Lord if they look towards his light.'[273] 'The glory of God is the living man, but the life of man is seeing God.'[274] 'Therefore you must first preserve the human order, so as eventually to participate in the glory of God.'[275] 'And whoever remains in his love and devotion and gratitude will increasingly receive greater glory from him by being formed into the likeness of him who died for him.'[276] 'The more we love him, the greater the glory we receive through him because we stand constantly before the face of the Father.'[277] But from the sight of the Father and from hearing his word Moses won such great glory that the others could not look him in the face.[278] This persistent standing before God is the sum of

[271] 2. 299. [272] 2. 184. [273] 2. 241; also 2. 192.
[274] 2. 219. [275] 2. 299. [276] S 342.
[277] 2. 183. [278] 2. 235.

Christian effort and virtue, and here the concept of glory incorporates the usual concept of 'merit' (which Irenaeus does not use) and gives it an aesthetic justification which is almost unquestionable: if goodness had been imparted to us by nature, 'what is good would not be sweet to us, or fellowship with God precious, ... and we would not conceive how beautiful (*pulchrum*) goodness is or delight in it . . . for what glory will be given to those who have made no effort to obtain it? What victor's wreath will be given to those who have not won the glory like the winner in the contest?'[279] And yet this glory of man who can do what God wants is always only 'the demonstration of the powers of God in him', who is only a 'vessel', and his growth is nothing other than 'grateful abiding in submissive love' of this active God,[280] who decrees everything for man out of love, even death, which puts an end to his sin and does not let him persist in undying transgression.[281] The golden gleam of Irenaean glory shines even into the dark powers of the world, for the world is *capax gloriae Patris*,[282] this world in its finitude, out of which God has still been able to make his work of art and his image, 'for he established it as a law that each thing should remain in its place and not go beyond the divinely decreed limit, but that each and every thing should bring its divinely ordained work to completion.'[283]

(b) But these are all categories of the temporal economy, which cannot itself become the mutual revelation of God and man until it unfolds to become God's art. It is the first great theology of the *kairos*, the *aptum tempus*, and in it the qualitative difference and uniqueness of every point in time in which a being or event is placed depends on the free decree of God, his revelatory will at any moment, and points to him. But the fact that the Son is in his essence the revealer of the Father's will and being and that the Spirit reveals to man the truth of the demand of the times means that the *kairos* in Irenaeus is from the start trinitarian. 'Thus it is from the beginning the Father's Son who

[279] 2. 290.   [280] S 342.   [281] S 392.
[282] 2. 246 [capable of receiving the Father's glory].
[283] D 10.

makes all known. He indeed was with the Father from eternity and made known the prophetic visions and the distributions of charisms and his ministries of service and the glorification of the Father to mankind in logical sequence (*consequenter*) and in harmonious arrangement (*composite*), at the appropriate time which would bring benefit in each case. For where there is logical sequence (*consequentia, akolouthia*) there is permanence, and where there is permanence there is opportuneness (*pro tempore*, Greek, according to Grabe, *kata chronon* or *epikairia*), but where there is opportuneness there is profit, and therefore the Word became the giver of the Father's grace for the profit of man, for whom he made such great dispositions of salvation by showing God to men but also by presenting men to God.'[284] The 'times' and their 'fulfilment' are 'appointed' according to the Father's 'pleasure' so that 'his art might not be in vain',[285] but this pleasure is always translated into the order of time by the Son and Spirit: 'and so, through this disposition (*taxis*) and by such rhythms (*rhythmos*) and with such guides (*anagōgē*) man, who has been produced and shaped, is led towards the image and likeness of the ungenerate God. In all this the Father approves and prescribes, the Son executes and forms, the Spirit nourishes and increases, while man gently advances and moves towards perfection, in order, that is, to approach the Uncreated.'[286] This is the *ordo promotionis* and the 'method of training for incorruptibility',[287] an essentially gentle, easy, quiet, patient order. These terms keep on recurring where Irenaeus wants to convey the authentic feel of the harmony of his spiritual world. He speaks of 'the mildness and peaceful calm of the kingdom of God',[288] of 'the Holy Spirit's having become accustomed to dwell among men and to rest in them',[289] of God's mercy spreading 'gently and slowly' in the world.[290] He tells of how for the sake of human freedom everything is ordained by God 'not to compel but to encourage free will',[291] of how he proceeds with *suasio*[292] and *suadela*[293] and *consilium*,[294] how man is destined through the

[284] 2. 218.
[285] S 382.
[286] 2. 296.
[287] 2. 411.
[288] 2. 221.
[289] S 302.
[290] S 392.
[291] 2. 285.
[292] 2. 230.
[293] 2. 315 (parallels in Reynders).
[294] 2. 289; D 55 (with parallels).

ages to offer God a *cor molle et tractabile*,[295] to fit himself with patience into the temporal sequence,[296] to 'await the time of growth' and 'not to transgress the law of human nature',[297] 'for Adam will never tear himself from the hands of God'.[298]

This original situation is described in terms of three ideas. The first is that man behaves like a child and acquires wisdom only slowly by experience. Adam in paradise is this child (the idea has appeared earlier in Theophilus of Antioch, *ad Autol.* II, 25): 'the intention was that, as he developed, he would reach adulthood and in order to feed himself and grow in pleasure (= Eden)' he was placed in the marvellous garden.[299] But the idea of development and education—where it is introduced into the Biblical dimension of time, the time of mankind—already includes the second idea. Just as the child gains wisdom through injury, so the great Adam, the human race, through *peira*, experience of the opposite, of the loss of God's grace, was to be trained in a true and definitive appreciation of it. Thus what has to be theologically justified and 'understood' is not just human freedom, but the whole dispensation of salvation which allows for the fall. If man had possessed all goodness from the beginning by nature, 'it would have not become sweet to him and he would not have valued the society of God as something precious, as a prize worth great effort. . . . The more we have to struggle for something the more valuable it becomes to us, but the more valuable it is to us the more pleasing it becomes to us too. What is given to us for nothing is not valued in the same way as what is won with great effort. But we were given the task of loving God more, and of winning this in a contest.' And finally, with all possible clarity: 'Sight would not be so desirable to us if we had not learned how awful it is not to see, and health becomes more prized by the sick as a result of experience, and light by comparison with darkness and life with death.'[300] Experience here is the key word, constantly recurring: *utrorumque experimentum*. 'Who could have acquired practice in the good without knowledge of the opposite? The concept of something acquired by experience is more solid and less open to

[295] 2. 299.   [296] D 3 (and parallels).   [297] 2. 297.
[298] 2. 317.   [299] D 12; 2. 292–97.   [300] 2. 291.

doubt than a conclusion from a hypothesis. Just as the tongue by tasting obtains experience of sweet and bitter and the eye by seeing distinguishes black and white and the ear by hearing perceives differences of sound, so the rational spirit, acquiring practice in good from double experience, is given a solid foundation for its test of obedience to God, . . . so that it is never again tempted to taste disobedience to God. But whoever flees the double knowledge and the double spiritual sensation is secretly destroying himself as a human being.'[301] The vehemence of this statement may be polemical, but it expresses nonetheless one of the positive achievements of this theology, which does not wish to maintain that the fall was inevitable, but acknowledges the profound necessity within God's free order of salvation: 'The generosity of God consisted in this, that man, by going through everything, . . . might learn by experience what he has been freed from and evermore remain grateful to God.'[302] Even for the spiritual man the experience of existence is close to the earth and the world of the senses. What Origen will later call the spiritual senses and, as a Platonist, sharply distinguish from the physical senses is for Irenaeus the man of earth's original and abiding sensitivity to the taste of things, the good and the bad. It is not until Claudel that a similar language reappears in Christianity.[303] The third idea develops directly from the first two; it is that of becoming accustomed. Man becomes accustomed to obey God, to bear his Spirit, to be a pilgrim in the world, to follow his word.[304] There is even, according to Irenaeus, an eschatological process of becoming accustomed to eternity, namely, the thousand-year kingdom of the just after the resurrection.[305] But God too has to become accustomed to mankind: at Jesus' baptism the Spirit of God descends on him to become accustomed, through him, to dwell among men.[306] And so it is finally the mediator who 'accustoms man to receive God and accustoms God to dwell in man'.[307] This process of accus-

[301] 2. 298; cf. 2. 323: peira mathontes.
[302] S 340.
[303] Cf. supra, vol. I, pp. 399–405.
[304] 2. 228; 2. 185.
[305] 2. 413.　　　[306] S 302.　　　[307] S 344.

toming takes place in the whole order of salvation, especially in the Old Testament, which is a preliminary adaptation (*praeaptatio*),[308] a preliminary formation (*praeformatio*),[309] a preliminary training (*praemeditatio, prosmeletan*)[310] of mankind for the coming of Christ.

This whole economy proclaims the pure goodness of the God who guides it.[311] In comparison, any kind of spiritualising does violence to man and in the end takes its revenge by turning into a new legalism. It does so because spiritualising of every stamp despises the *naturalia praecepta* and has to replace them with purely positive ones.[312] This has been confirmed time and again by the history of the Church and of dogmatics, and it is also the reason why Irenaeus' basic attitude cannot be assimilated by true Protestantism. The ancient Greek idea, also sanctioned by the Bible, of God's 'lack of envy', the idea that God is not jealous of created nature, but is able to guide it gently and, where necessary, even to crucify it, is dear to Irenaeus.[313] Such a theology does not find it difficult to answer the much-discussed question, why the redeemer came so late, not until the end of the ages.[314] Nor is it difficult for it to make credible the necessity of trials and temptation[315] nor, as already mentioned, to argue the usefulness of the 'chaff' in allowing the good seed to grow to maturity.[316] Such a theology will have a tendency to find even the most elevated teachings of the gospel traced somewhere in ordinary human nature, for example, the evangelical counsels in

---

[308] 2. 219; 2. 231.

[309] 2. 219; 2. 235; 2. 265: *multi unum praeformantes* [many prefiguring one]; 2. 355: *per temporalia praeformante (Domino) aeterna* [(the Lord) using temporal things to make a preliminary form of eternal ones].

[310] 2. 219; *in typo praemeditabantur* [they were trained beforehand in the type], 2. 251; in Abel, 2. 272; the earthly Jerusalem as preliminary training for the heavenly one, 2. 426.

[311] S 338.

[312] 2. 186 [the precepts of nature].

[313] 2. 1: *in Deo caritas, dives et sine invidia* [in God there is love, rich and without envy]; 2. 185. *Qui autem naturalia et liberalia et communia omnium auxit et dilatavit, sine invidia et largiter (= aphthonōs) donans hominibus* . . . [But he increased and expanded the things of nature which are free and common to all, making gifts to men without envy and without stint]; 2. 295.

[314] 1. 96.   [315] 2. 403.   [316] 2. 404.

man's general following of God.[317] It will everywhere stress the
congruence of grace and nature[318] and even in the order of grace
prefer the argument of congruences, which can be called an
aesthetic argument, but which for thinkers like Irenaeus expresses not just a vague appropriateness but bears the conviction
of absolute rightness.[319] And so the concept of justice becomes in
this view the concept of the deepest rightness and suitability,[320]
and there is not even a glimmer of an opposition or contradiction between the just and the good.

(c) The central exposition of the content of God's temporal
art takes place in the theology of the two testaments, and this is
where Irenaeus' theology too is centred and where his apologia
against Gnostic dualism is at its strongest. The economy of
salvation is the training of man by God to encounter the God-
man: the old Covenant is *paidagōgos eis Christon*. In a course of
instruction, however, everything must happen at the right time.
'With [Christ] nothing happens unplanned or at the wrong time
(*incomptum et intempestivum*), just as nothing inappropriate holds
sway in his Father. The Father knows all things in advance, and
then they are put into operation by the Son according to their
suitability, in their correct sequence and at the appropriate time
(*apto tempore*).'[321] Even the Son himself waits for his hour, which
only the Father knows, in order not to do anything too soon,
but to make the fulness of grace coincide with the fulness of
time. And this multiplicity of *kairoi* reveals the inner
multiplicity, the richness of the one God: *omnia ... ordine et
tempore et hora praecognita et apta perfecit Dominus noster, unus
quidem et idem existens, dives autem et multus.*[322] The idea of the
right *kairos* thus precludes a comparison between Old and New
Covenants as between imperfect and perfect: law and grace,

---

[317] 2. 189–90, 201.
[318] *Cf.* 2. 300, 302, and so naturally also the role of the Old Covenant as a
foundation for the New, which makes it easy for Jews to believe in Christ
because everything has been prepared for them down to the last detail (2. 231).
[319] S 364f.   [320] 2. 400.   [321] S 292.
[322] S 294 [our Lord brought all things to completion ... in order and at the
right time, at the moment he had determined in advance as suitable; he exists
always as one and the same, but is also rich and abundant!].

utraque apta temporibus.[323] To apportion them to two separate deities therefore means to undo all God's art and oneself 'to fall out of the saving dispensation': 'We, on the other hand, will show both the reason for the difference of testaments as well as their unity and perfect harmony.'[324] The unity consists in the fact that a single God both concerns himself with a single human race from beginning to end and maintains an association with it, 'now talking to what he has shaped, now giving it laws, now again reproaching it, sometimes exhorting it, finally freeing the slave and adopting him as a son, and at the appropriate time bestowing on him the inheritance of incorruptibility'.[325] It is the continuation of the first forming of man as a development towards the 'true man', Jesus Christ, 'for God repeatedly calls man to the fellowship with him through which we were to receive a share in incorruptibility. He who was announced by the law through Moses and the prophets of the Most High and Almighty, the Son of the universal Father, through whom all things exist, who conversed with Moses: he came into the world in Judaea, begotten by God through the Holy Spirit and born of the Virgin Mary, who is descended from David and Abraham.'[326]

Because in Irenaeus' trinitarian theology the creator Father creates the world through the Son and the Spirit, who are the visibility of the invisible Father, all the theophanies of the Old Covenant are the Son, just as the inspiration of the Old Covenant is the Spirit, so that the Son 'was with our humanity from eternity, announcing beforehand the things that were to happen later and instructing men in the things of God'.[327] This gives the Old Covenant in a hidden manner the same trinitarian structure which the New shows plainly, and the trinitarian faith of the New Covenant is the key which immediately unlocks all the riddles of the Old.[328] Because Christ is the goal of the whole development, he must necessarily be present even at the beginning.[329] The separate theological treatise which makes up the first part of the *Demonstration* therefore needs to do no more

---

[323] [each suited to its time], S 240.
[324] S 242.   [325] 2. 174.   [326] D 40.
[327] D 45ff.   [328] D 52.   [329] 2. 179.

than follow through salvation history, giving it a historical and theological interpretation, while the second part then fills out this outline with the parallels between promise and fulfilment.

It is typical of Irenaeus' approach here that he finds the totality of fulfilment in Christ promised and present in outline not only in Abraham as the father of all believers, Jews and Gentiles,[330] but already in the previous covenant with Noah, 'for after the flood God made a covenant with the whole world, especially with all the animals and men'.[331] He can do so because the order of salvation which starts with Abraham is not a different, purely supernatural one; no, through the Old and New Covenants the old world, the old creation of flesh was to be brought home. So also the symbolism of the 'two peoples' of Isaac and Ishmael, Jacob and Esau, is shifted back to the sons of Noah, one of whom continues the line of Cain's curse, while Shem and Japhet continue the line of blessing. Shem's 'blessing develops and reaches Abraham', while Japhet's blessing contains both the promise of 'enlargement' and that of 'dwelling in the house of Shem', which is a reference forward to the Church of today, which will inherit both the whole world and the covenant of Abraham.[332]

But Abraham is the father of our faith because he was the first to follow the call of God's Word, as the apostles did later, leaving all.[333] 'In Abraham mankind learned the Word of God in advance and was accustomed to follow it. Abraham followed the prescription of the Word of God in accordance with his faith when with a willing heart he gave his only-begotten and beloved son to God as a sacrifice, so that God too might be pleased, for the sake of all his descendants, to give up his own only-begotten and beloved Son as a sacrifice for our redemption.'[334] And if later the educational volumes of the Mosaic law were added, to prepare the people's faith for the unfettered freedom of Christ, we must still not forget that 'Abraham followed in generous faith freely and without ties and so became the friend of God,'[335] just as it is Abraham who later looks out

---

[330] *patriarcha nostrae fidei* [the patriarch of our faith], 2. 225.
[331] D 22.   [332] D 20–21, 42.   [333] 2. 156.
[334] 2. 157. Note the 'so that' (*hina*).   [335] 2. 183.

prophetically across the whole intervening order to Christ (Jn 8.56).[336] The 'natural' law (which for Irenaeus consists essentially in the attitude of following God in faith, hope and love) was alive in Abraham not least 'thanks to the blessing' of Shem, 'and because in the fiery zeal of his soul he roamed the whole world to find his God. . . . God had mercy on him, who sought him in loneliness and silence, and revealed himself to him through the Word as in a ray of light.'[337] So Mary is really Abraham's daughter and in her Magnificat inherits Abraham's longing and exultation.[338]

Because the Logos-Son has a personal association with Abraham, Moses and the prophets and gives them 'fore-knowledge',[339] a 'preview',[340] of his Incarnation and his Church, there exists between them and the Lord a direct relation of love:[341] they are at their point in time members of his mystical body.[342] Even the Old Covenant is a word about Christ, indeed 'the word of Christ', though still in a hidden way.[343] The two Testaments are made of the same substance.[344] The Old Covenant, with its prophecy and law, is directed wholly to-wards the New: originating in Abraham's free obedience, helping men to find the way to love through the law, and in the prophets rejecting all legalism and directly prophesying the New Covenant as an inner attitude of heart.[345] The signs and symbols are thus also set up purely in respect of the fulfilment which is to come and are fulfilled by Christ with literal faithfulness.[346] Of course, the Pauline perspective is not absent: the law as conviction of sin (*ostensio*),[347] as the establishment of a rule with the grace to keep it added only later,[348] the tightening of legal provisions as an antidote to concupiscence (the legal element of the New Covenant being also assessed from the same point of view),[349] the place of fear and punishment in the old righteousness,[350] while in the New Covenant free obedience based on gratitude predominates,[351] in short the historical

---

[336] 2. 157.   [337] D 24.   [338] 2. 163.
[339] 2. 174.   [340] S 189, 300.   [341] 2. 264.
[342] 2. 264–65.   [343] 2. 148, 172–73, 234.
[344] 2. 148, 168.   [345] 2. 193–95, 202; D 90, 93.
[346] 2. 189–91; D 25.   [347] S 326–28.
[348] S 340.   [349] 2. 187–89.   [350] 2. 240.   [351] 2. 181–83.

dialectic constituted by the two Testaments which ends the dogmatic section of Romans.[352] But the idea of the development and education of the human race is more important:[353] the fruit grows in the shell, the essential in the temporarily conditioned, which can then be left behind;[354] the law forms 'steps' (*velut gradus*) up to discipleship of Christ.[355] So direct does this development appear that a question is fully justified: If everything was literally stated in advance and laid down, what did Christ bring that was really new?

Irenaeus' answer is well-known and conclusive: *omnem novitatem attulit, seipsum afferens qui fuerat annuntiatus.* Everything new might have been announced, but it had not come; up to this point everything had been in the form of teaching, and now it becomes a person and so fulfilment.[356] The word 'new' in Irenaeus has itself a new sound, the exultant and youthful ring of the first Christian period.[357] It means the opposite of the Gnostic 'new'; it is that 'ancient truth' of God's intimacy in paradise which is now found again after all the estrangement, more welcome and better understood. It is not enough to note the absence of any contradiction between Old and New Covenant (it is only men and the misunderstanding of the law which introduce the opposition);[358] it is not even enough to talk about an 'intensification' or to demonstrate the reverence of the New Covenant before the Old.[359] What has to be seen is the creative movement of *fulfilment* (*adimplere*), which has already been described as the Christian temporal counterpart of the Gnostic pleroma.[360] In addition to the correspondence and the intensification there is Christ's divine quality and his efforts to transpose everything verbal and symbolic into living existence and so to recapitulate it by giving it concrete form in such a way

[352] S 342.
[353] 2. 150–52; 2. 230.
[354] 2. 151–54, 192.
[355] 2. 179.
[356] 2. 269–70.
[357] S 166; K. Prümm, 'Zur Terminologie und zum Wesen der christlichen Neuheit bei Irenäus', *Pisciculi* (1939), pp. 192–219; Reynders, s.vv. *novus, novellus.*
[358] S 240; 2. 169, 177, 181.
[359] S 251–53 (Peter), S 257 (Paul).
[360] For the numerous passages see Reynders s.vv. *adimpleo, compleo, impleo.*

that its reality is enhanced.[361] With this creative event in view the Father gave this 'hour' the character of the fulness of time.[362] In this fulness not only the Old Covenant but also all human and physical nature is fulfilled, because now the Word is present within the flesh.[363] Nor is this just in the one man Christ, because through him all hearts are really changed.[364] It is here that the Church with its timeless newness will makes its entry.[365] The roots of everything new always go back to the old and the primeval. So the universal priesthood of believers has its roots, not in Christ alone, but also in the priesthood of the Old Covenant;[366] anyone who is familiar with this will find it easy to understand what God means in the New Covenant.[367] The points of convergence are clearly indicated in the New Covenant, for example, in the incident between Peter and Cornelius.[368] But the Gentiles find themselves prefigured in the world of the Jews, Japhet in Shem, and Christ's fulfilment makes plain to them too why the old law was necessary and is now redundant.[369] Not for nothing did God's art place on the threshold of the New Covenant figures such as the Baptist, Simeon and Mary in whom the connection between the Old and New Covenants becomes, in persons and in conversation, a play between human beings: in them the relationship is presented as a tableau to our view.[370]

There is in this development an indissoluble mystery, which indicates the character of God's action in the present. On the one hand it is a 'ripening' towards fulness,[371] a growth (*profectus*)[372] until the 'flesh is ripe',[373] the tree of mankind bearing fruit,[374] but it is at the same time a return from all adulthood under the law to childhood,[375] because for us the Word of God was *made a child like us (coinfantiatum)*,[376] not now so that we could win back Adam's threatened childhood but, in Novalis's phrase, so that we might become the 'synthetic child'.

---

[361] D 37: 'fulfilment' and 'recapitulation' coincide in the incarnation.
[362] S 308.
[363] 2. 180–81.
[364] D 94.
[365] S 398.
[366] 2. 167–68.
[367] 2. 231.
[368] S 227–29.
[369] 2. 231–33; D 41, 96.
[370] S 162, 164; D 41; 2. 38, 85, 162.
[371] 2. 154.
[372] 2. 170–71, 291.
[373] 2. 353.
[374] 2. 175.
[375] D 46, 96.
[376] 2. 295.

Something of this paradox is also present in the life of the
Church, which is the mature product of salvation history and its
final form at the end of the ages. In Irenaeus the Church also
stands historically at the end of the early Christian era, the
splendour of which still surrounds it, and at the beginning of the
Catholic form of the world, the features of which it has already
assumed. It is the esoteric mystery of the world and of Christ
and yet the most public and anti-sectarian body known to
history. It is fully the pneumatic and charismatic Church,[377] as in
Tertullian; but Irenaeus avoids the dangers and disasters which
befell Tertullian, because at the same time in his view the
Church remains resolutely in the spirit of the apostolic kerygma
and *paradosis*.[378] The apostolic kerygma of the Church fills the
universe like the incomparable sun.[379] And the theological
integration of the *notae ecclesiae* reveals yet again the Irenaean
theological and apologetic method. 'It is inevitable that the
heretics, because of their blindness to the truth, should follow
the most diverse paths and that therefore the tracks of their
teaching lead hither and thither without direction or order. In
contrast, the path of those who are in the Church encircles the
world because it has its firm tradition from the apostles and
shows us that all possess one and the same faith because all
confess one and the same Father, accept one and the same order
of salvation based on the Incarnation of the Son of God, know
of the same gift of the Spirit, strive to keep the same command-
ments, preserve one and the same form of Church order (*eandem
figuram ... ordinationis custodientibus — to auto schēma tēs peri
tēn ekklēsian katastaseōs tērountōn* [Harvey]), wait for the same
coming of the Lord and hope for the same salvation for the
whole man, that is, for soul and body.'[380]

In the early books, Irenaeus' theology appears as nothing
other than an exposition of the Church's credo, and everything
he ventures to think or suggest clings tightly to the framework
erected by the *presbyteri* and previous theologians. Nevertheless
he pursues his theological work in the spirit of freedom and

[377] S 202–04.
[378] Reynders, s.v., *praeconatio, praedicatio, praeconium, trado, traditio*.
[379] I. 92.
[380] 2. 378. The strength of form and the intensity of this unity, 2. 236.

charismatic inspiration,[381] within that true and spiritual body
which in his eyes is the enduring incarnate beauty.[382] For it is
only in this body that the divine Spirit rests and remains,[383] only
from the body of Christ that the purest of springs flows—while
the others dig themselves stagnant cisterns.[384] For the Spirit
himself has created this body of the Church, and it is he who,
keeping the faith always fresh and youthful, 'constantly also
rejuvenates' his vessel the Church (dispositum juvenescens et
juvenescere faciens ipsum vas). . . . 'For where the Church is, God's
Spirit is, and where God's Spirit is, the Church is, and every sort
of Grace,'[385]

The eternally young beauty of the Church in its unity of
body and soul, which depends both on Christ's true bodiliness[386]
and on the fulness of his possession of the Spirit,[387] receives
concrete form anew in the sacraments, which match the nature
of man who is to be saved by being at once material and
spiritual, just as he is body and soul. 'So our bodies received the
unity which produces incorruptibility in the bath of baptism,
but our souls received it through Spirit,'[388] and similarly in the
eucharist body and soul must be fed on the heavenly food in
which the best of this earth combines with the best of heaven[389]
to produce the purest of all sacrifices.[390] The bread and wine
must come from the earth because the Church of Christ must
make the earth whole. So too the gospel has the fourfold
structure of the world with its four elements[391] and preserves in
its truth the distillation and quintessence of all that God wanted
to give and impart to men throughout the economy of
salvation: what remains as the fruit is its simplest form, the
attitude of Jesus, faith, hope and love,[392] which pick up the true
childlike fear of the Old Covenant, allowing it to develop and
grow.[393] This attitude does not in any way make the New
Covenant static, but just as the Lord 'has fulfilled all things by
his coming, so he continues to fulfil the New Covenant in the

---

[381] 2. 334.   [382] S 338.   [383] D 41–42.
[384] S 398–400.   [385] S 398–400.   [386] 2. 321–22.
[387] S 400.   [388] S 304.
[389] 2. 197–99, 204, 318; S 189.
[390] 2. 203.   [391] S 195.   [392] 2. 178.
[393] 2. 192.

Church until the end foretold by the law'.[394] Only in this way, in
the Christian life's constant newness, is it an abiding in the
fulfiller. But only in this way is the Church and existence in it
open to eternal life.

The goal of the process is not redemption, not the Church,
but the merging of both into eternal life. Accordingly, even in
Irenaeus' thought we find the Platonising perspective of the
letter to the Hebrews, in which the earthly is an image and copy
of the heavenly and is made perfect only eschatologically, when
the earthly Christ ascends through the heavens to the Father and
the heavenly Jerusalem descends to earth. Moses set up the tent
and the cult in accordance with the heavenly original on the
mountain, and John saw the same heavenly sanctuary in
Revelation: 'the whole earthly order of salvation corresponds to
the heavenly original, and both come from the same God. For
only so could he make the image like the spiritual things.'[395] The
heavenly is also the eschatological: 'the covenant tent was the
earthly imitation of the invisible spiritual things in heaven and
contained images of the Church, prophetic representations of
the things which were to come',[396] so that the one relation is
threefold, Old Covenant—heaven, Old Covenant—New
Covenant and New Covenant—heaven. To this ecclesiological
argument we must restore the human argument, the theology
of 'image and likeness', for then it will be seen that the
perfecting of the 'likeness', the unveiling of the original of man,
has itself an eschatological function.

At the same time Irenaeus remains a man of the present
Church, Catholic and Roman, attached indeed even to its
earthly form, the man of the pastoral letter to Florinus, of the
letter to Blastus about the schism, the bearer of the letter from
the persecuted church of Lyon to Pope Eleutherus, the author of
the impressive and effective letter to Pope Victor about the
urgency of settling the controversy over Easter. In this,
according to the tradition, he urged on the pope the very
practical view that the Church could be united in spite of

[394] 2. 270.
[395] 2. 210; cf. 2. 426. On Moses and the old liturgy, D 9.
[396] D 26.

differences of opinion and practice and so, as Eusebius says, well earned his name of peacemaker (*Eirēnaios*), since, moreover, he approached not just the pope 'but a very great number of church leaders with similar questions'.[397]

5. LIMITS AND STRENGTHS

Irenaeus' consciousness of the dazzling rightness of the dimension he has revealed gives him a self-confidence and sense of exhilaration similar to Paul's. This is vented in a long triumphal paraphrase of Paul's saying, 'The spiritual man judges all things but is himself judged by no-one.'[398] From the centre and unity which is the Church every deviation can be judged and its limitations exposed. Nevertheless no theologian will ever exhaust this unity. Every theologian's insight into the faith is limited, and it is in itself no small achievement if it does not prove contradictory, if it remains capable of development. Two such limits may be indicated for Irenaeus, the first Biblical, the second relating to his understanding of eschatology. The first is conditioned by his time and not specifically Irenaean. In the case of the second, which is usually the target for severe criticism, we shall have to ask how far such criticism is justified.

(a) Irenaeus' *Scriptural interpretation* of the saving economy of the Old and New Covenants is based, like that of his predecessors (especially Pseudo-Barnabas and Justin), wholly on the wording of the texts and on their literal correspondence. The clearest illustration of this is the arsenal of apologetic texts which makes up the second part of the *Demonstration*. This exegesis, which was to remain predominant down to Augustine's *City of God* and so through to the Middle Ages—though perhaps to a lesser extent in Origen and Cyril of Alexandria with their spiritualising tendency—impedes and obstructs the achievement of the very aim implicit in the structure of the system, a historical understanding of revelation. The texts are

[397] *Hist. Eccl.* V. 24, 11–18.
[398] 2. 256–63, 269.

taken as bare prophecies which, apart from their prophetic significance, have no content relevant to their own time or situation. So all that is compared and found to correspond is textual contents which are somehow timeless, rather than different periods, situations of the kingdom of God in different epochs, whose historical and existential contents in terms, that is, of life and experience, could have been brought to bear on each other. Even what Irenaeus regards as most important, the temporal value within the whole of each and every *kairos* of salvation history, remains in this way unrecognised and obscured. The elimination of this defect by modern historical exegesis is the removal of a defect which is accidental in Irenaeus; it is the true continuation and liberation of his basic purpose across the centuries. The premise of the ancient view is that a prophetic utterance remains unfulfilled and empty of meaning in the Old Covenant[399] and so can have a bearing only on the future. If one nevertheless wants to allow the prophet some insight into his utterance, he must be credited with a pre-vision or foreknowledge of the future event which is being prophesied. This is nothing less than a direct illumination from the New Testament (in much the way that Abraham, as a 'prophet', is supposed to have been able somehow to understand the encounter with the three angels in a trinitarian sense,[400] though not as clearly as the Christian faith enables us retrospectively to interpret the ancient events).[401] A further misunderstanding arises between the fulfiller, Christ, and the texts which are to be fulfilled by him. The fulfiller is tied all too materially to the wording of a text; too little allowance is made for the sovereignty of his freedom, precisely because the freedom of secondary causes, which would be presupposed by a thoroughly historical view of the prophetic events, also fails to emerge with sufficient clarity. Meaning attaches essentially only to the actions of the *auctor primarius*, the Word of God himself, who announces himself and lets himself be seen in advance.[402]

Also connected with this is the fact that in spite of the Pauline correction the curve of the development from the Old

---

[399] 2. 271.   [400] D 44.   [401] D 52.
[402] D 45.

Covenant to the New is presented too much as a single line, and not nearly enough in dramatic and dialectical form. The opposition between the two is underestimated because secondary causes are in practice given too little prominence. The Augustinian, and indeed general patristic, formula that the new is veiled in the old and the old unveiled in the new is a far too imperfect expression of the full truth. It implies that the problem is simply to 'understand' things which were there all along and could not be seen with sufficient clarity merely because they were obscured by signs and images. Here too modern exegesis will bring a significant enrichment of the theological dialectic of salvation.

(b) Irenaeus' eschatology must be seen first of all as the logical conclusion of his theological edifice, as the perhaps clumsy expression of his fundamental Christian, anti-Platonic endeavour to tie God's salvation to man, to the earth and to history. He develops the idea of the thousand-year kingdom of the just on earth after the resurrection because he takes seriously the Old Testament promises of a final, completely secure occupation of the land, promises not yet fully fulfilled by the missionary outpouring of the Church of Christ, by the pilgrim state of Christians (which corresponds to the nomadic state of the patriarchs and Mosaic Israel). Nevertheless the Church is essentially a re-entry into 'the inheritance promised to Abraham',[403] a return, *regressio*, not to be interpreted in Platonic terms as a return to the origin above the world, but that backward movement which is a main theme of the Old Covenant (down to the latest settlement in modern Israel) and whose eschatological counterpart would have to be the recovery of the original paradise. Irenaeus is the advocate of the new earth which constantly pales and vanishes in Christian eschatology in favour of 'heaven': that in the process he should clutch at the apocalyptic texts about the millennium is, in comparison with his aim, trivial. His insertion of this transfigured earth in between the resurrection and the judgment is admittedly awkward, and yet the anti-spiritualising tendency

---

[403] 2. 165; cf. D 46 (with parallel passages), D 91; 2. 420, 424–25.

in his eschatology (*nihil allegorizari potest, sed omnia firma et vera*)[404] is heartening. The new Jerusalem, the new earth, the new risen man, all of them *non in supercoelestibus possunt intelligi*.[405] All this is, in a triumphant working out of the great Irenaean theme, the last 'training' and 'accustoming' for the 'contemplation of the Father's glory'.[406] Another possible objection is that the distribution of the redeemed between three eschatological *mansiones in domo Patris*: the transfigured earth (the holy city), paradise and heaven, certainly points back to Valentinian eschatology. There the redeemed are distributed between three places; the psychics go to the residence of the demiurge, the demiurge to the previous residence of Achamoth on the edge of the pleroma, and wisdom with the pneumatic souls into the interior of the pleroma. But this suggestion does not determine the decisive element in Irenaeus' eschatology. Irenaeus' vision is that in the whole expanse between the new heaven and the new earth 'God will be seen everywhere, in each place according to the worth of the beholders',[407] and the whole pyramid of the eschatological universe will be yet another illustration of the fact that men are led by the Spirit and the Son to the Father by degrees.[408] In his eschatology Irenaeus produces an important counterweight to the flight from the world and the failure to take seriously the resurrection of the flesh which marks the Platonising Christian eschatologies of a later period and indeed the average Christian consciousness. It is of real importance to consider these statements well, if only for the sake of the dialogue with Israel[409] and in order to take account of the discussion of the picture of the world drawn by natural science and cosmic religion (Teilhard de Chardin).

In conclusion we must mention the great fidelity to the Bible in the way Irenaeus speaks theologically about judgment and its twofold outcome. What marks him out is that he allows the two lines in Pauline and Johannine theology to continue side by side

---

[404] 2. 426.
[405] [cannot be taken as referring to an upper, heavenly world] 2. 425.
[406] 2. 424.   [407] 2. 428.   [408] 2. 428–29.
[409] *Cf.* my book *Einsame Zwiesprache. Martin Buber und das Christentum* (Hegner, 1958); ET. *Martin Buber and Christianity*. (London, 1961).

without attempting to force them into a system—always
dangerous to the full breadth of truth. He maintains both the
line of a divisive judgment and the line of the unlimited
universality of the lordship and redemptive power of Jesus
Christ,[410] and at the same time always carefully juxtaposes God's
universal redemptive will and the mystery of his free choice and
the other mystery of human freedom. In the same way the
dogma of the eternal fire is also proclaimed in a truly biblical
way. There is no attempt to dissolve it as Origen does or to
justify it from the Old Testament. Instead it is established with
reference to Hebrews 6 as a specifically New Testament theologumenon, which did not have an adequate basis in the Old
Testament and has only received this through the final exposing
of God's love to men in Christ, through the far higher claim
made on the answer of human love.[411]

[410] I. 368; S 312; 2. 161; 162–64; 229; 249.
[411] 2. 244–45, 247, 280.

AUGUSTINE

Augustine's path, which we call his conversion and which comprises many stages, is, less than all the other exemplary 'turnings', one from 'aesthetics' to 'religion'; rather, in its crucial articulation, it is one from a lower to a higher aesthetics. No-one has praised God so assiduously as the supreme beauty or attempted so consistently to capture the true and the good with the categories of aesthetics as Augustine in the period during and after his conversion. And this was not just in words, but also in action: the *eros* with which he seeks the true and wants the good is, in both Christian and Platonic terms, an active enthusiasm which, even in the sobriety and humiliation of the later exercise of ecclesiastical office, does not cease to press back unswervingly towards the point at which God had unveiled himself to the enflamed heart of the young man as the supreme beauty: 'In a gaze and embrace of the highest chastity, without the interposition of any veil, you desire to look at her nakedness,[1] and to hold what she grants only to a chosen few of her admirers. If you were aflame with passion for a beautiful woman, she would refuse herself rightly if she found that you loved something other than her. ... '

Seeing, wanting to see and being able to see are for Augustine the essence of knowledge; just as he places the sense of sight high above the others, so the act of seeing spiritually becomes for him the act of cognition pure and simple. Reason (*ratio*) remains in itself *aspectus*, a looking towards, whose subjective power has no control over whether the object it is trying to catch sight of shows itself or not; it is only when the objects reveals itself by its own gracious pleasure that it comes into sight and so into knowledge.[2]

---

[1] The female figure is wisdom: *Soliloquia* 1.22. Augustine's works are cited in the Maurist edition. The texts on Augustine's aesthetics in the narrower sense are collected in K. Svoboda, *L'Esthétique de S. Augustin* (1933).

Abbreviations: S: *Soliloquia*; VR: *De vera religione*; LA: *De libero arbitrio*; DO: *De ordine*; QA: *De quantitate animae*.

[2] QA: . . . *ut ratio sit quidam mentis affectus, ratiocinatio autem rationis inquisitio, i.e. aspectus illius . . . motio. Quare ista opus est ad quaerendum, ad videndum. Itaque*

There is disagreement about when Augustine's questing reason 'saw' its all-important sight: at the time of his turning from Manichaeism and scepticism to the overwhelming light of Plotinus and to philosophical training for its ecstatic contemplation, or not until later, when the clear turning from 'philosophy' to Christian 'theology' took place. If the latter, when could this second shift have taken place? As early as the Cassiacum writings Augustine is fully conscious of himself as a Christian and a believer and, as Courcelle showed,[3] it was in Ambrose's sermons in Milan and in his contacts with the Christian Neo-Platonist, the priest Simplicianus, that he became acquainted with Plotinus. The two things come into his field of vision simultaneously, philosophical form and the content it frames and structures, Christian teaching; both are equally strongly attested by the early writings. And if later, especially in his counter-attack against the great heresies, the Christian content emerges ever more distinctly and strongly, it is never in the form of material additions, but as developments of parts and elements already clearly contained, albeit in outline, in the original conception. Things which were only implicit, which were in the air, come into full view, are given explicit formulation; single intuitions spark off whole series of books, like those on the Trinity and the city of God. Even among the early writings distinctions have to be made. Essays on subjects designed to overcome doubt (*Contra academicos, Soliloquia* with its sketched-out sequel *De immortalitate animae*, then *De quantitate animae*) are more introductory. *De beata vita* clarifies terms. *De magistro* is primarily defensive, constructive only in the short final section. *De musica* remains a fragment of the *Disciplinarum libri*, which were never written but were to have led men to the study of theology via the development of the

---

cum ille mentis aspectus . . . conjectus in rem aliquam, videt illam, scientia nominatur. [And so the reason is a sort of aspect of the mind, and reasoning an enquiry by the reason, *i.e.*, a movement . . . of that aspect. It is therefore needed for questioning and seeing. Thus when this aspect of mind is directed at something and sees it, that is called knowledge.] S 1.14: *Jam aspectum sequitur, ipsa visio Dei, qui est finis aspectus.*

[3] Pierre Courcelle, *Recherches sur les Confessions de S. Augustin* (1950), pp. 93f.

liberal arts; only in the sixth book does the treatise expand to take a broader view. *De ordine* remains for the most part playful and psychological. As the really central works there remain only *De vera religione* and *De libero arbitrio*. The latter was finished late (395) and, despite its broader horizons, is nonetheless specifically anti-Manichaean, while *De vera religione* (390), drawing together all the efforts of the early years and deliberately unpolemical, presents a sort of rational construction of sacred doctrine, not the credo itself (expounded four years later by *De fide et symbolo*), but its refraction in the temperament of a religious philosopher. It is here that we shall attempt to capture Augustine's basic intuitions (here and not so much in the *Confessions*, which shift the emphasis principally to subjectivity and precisely for this reason do not provide the key to theological seeing), though supplementing it as necessary from the surrounding early works.

The 'rational construction' of the Christian faith here has a very similar structure to that in Anselm. It is the thinker's question to himself, 'So what have you understood of what faith has presented to you?'. This leads to a bracketing-off of the object of faith in the interest of discovering how far what has been believed has been appropriated with intellectual integrity.[4] In this sense the form of reflection is the point around which all previous experience crystallises. We learn what made Augustine a Manichee and what made him stop being one, what made him temporarily a sceptic and what enabled him to overcome scepticism, and so on. *De vera religione* is thus a sort of *Pensées* ('I promised to write down for you my ideas on true religion'),[5]

---

[4] *Quamquam haec inconcussa fide teneam, tamen quia cognitione nondum teneo, ita quaeramus quasi omnia incerta sint. . . . Si quis ergo illorum 'insipientium', de quibus scriptum est, Dixit insipiens in corde suo, Non est Deus* (Ps 53.1), *hoc tibi diceret* [Although I accept these things with firm faith, since I do not yet possess them by knowledge, let us conduct our enquiry as though everything were uncertain . . . So, if one of those 'fools' of which it is written, 'The fool says in his heart, "There is no God," ' were to say this to you], what proof of the existence of God could you give him? LA 2.5. The task, as for Anselm, is *rationis vias pietate fretus ingredi* [to set out on the paths of reason leaning on piety], LA 1.14.

[5] *quid sentirem* (VR 12).

circling, unsystematic, but in secret drawn magnetically to its
true pole.

1. THE EYE, LIGHT AND UNITY

God is 'the true light without any darkness',[6] so John and
Plotinus agree and so too Augustine the Manichee and the anti-
Manichee repeats after them. He is the 'sun of minds',[7] of the
things that know and of the things that are known. But whereas
the physical sun is an object among others, albeit an exalted one,
which the eye can have before it as the object of its vision, God is
not an object in the same class as created things. It is true that
there are intellectual objects which can be seen only in the holy
sphere of his light, but while they may be divine in form,[8] they
are yet not God himself. He 'is light itself by which the soul is
illuminated to make it able to see everything either in itself or in
him with true understanding. . . . The soul is only a created
thing, though created with reason and understanding in his
image, and when it tries to look at that light it trembles with
weakness and faints. Nevertheless the light is the source of such
limited understanding as the soul has, so when it is swept up to
the light . . . , it sees, not spatially but in its own way, also what is
above it, which is the source of its power to see whatever it
perceives intellectually in itself.'[9] So the whole multiplicity of
both sacred and profane exists as a unity within this single light
which transcends all plurality,[10] and which consequently, for the
soul, lies rather in the extension of its illuminated subjective act
of seeing (inwards) than in the direction of the external multiplicity of objects, and therefore shines on the soul all the more to
the degree that it also purifies itself from the dross of the
multiplicity and corruption of the world and matter and rises
towards its own intellectual existence as light. The concen-

---

[6] VR 73; cf. esp. De Trin 12, c. 15.2; De civ Dei 10, c. 2; LA 2, c. 8.21; c. 9.26.
[7] VR. Jolivet, Dieu, Soleil des esprits (Paris, 1934) has the texts.
[8] In his early works Augustine still makes frequent use of the pagan
adjective divinus.
[9] De Gen ad litt 12.59.
[10] LA 2.27.

tration on the act of seeing, the purification and collection of oneself for unity: why should these not be taken ultimately as pointing in the same direction as Plato with his parable of the cave, Plotinus with his *epistrophē* and the Sermon on the Mount with its beatitude of the pure heart which will see God and for this encounter must shut itself in its inner room?

If God, as transcendent simplicity, is light, the soul will not be able to see him with a particular 'faculty', but only with its very substance, as it is collected and centred into a totality. As he proceeds, Augustine more and more sees the soul's visual power and penetration as its centre, the centre where soul-ground (*memoria*), soul-mind (*intellectus*) and soul-love (*dilectio*) coincide in substance. In this 'substantiation' of its faculties, the soul realises its true nature as mind, in which it becomes an image of the trinitarian light and so capable of seeing God. Certainly 'reason' already possesses light. The *oculus mentis*,[11] the *oculus interior*,[12] is as such the *lux mentis*,[13] and yet only a completely healthy and specially schooled eye is able to look into the eternal sun,[14] one which has learnt to make proper use of its acuity (*acies mentis*),[15] something which cannot occur without a general moral effort. Here, where theory and ethics converge, there emerges as a third term, almost as a product: aesthetics, the ability to see, *oculus quo cerni possit*.[16] 'Seeing the beauty of things must be left to those who as a result of a divine gift are capable of seeing it.'[17] This is true above all of seeing the beauty of God himself, access to which and passion for which will be given only to the person who, through having become himself pure and light, learns to see God's light. Such a person alone begins to have a 'taste' for God and 'an eye for the only true beauty',[18] that of 'the good and beautiful God, in whom and from whom and through whom everything is good and beautiful'.[19] If God's beauty is once seen as absolute, it becomes wholly obvious that

[11] [the eye of the mind], S 1.12; QA 6.
[12] [the inner eye], QA 23; DO 2.10.
[13] [the light of the mind], LA 2.21.
[14] S 1.23
[15] VR 57; 105–06.
[16] [an eye for things], LA 2.32.
[17] LA 3.36.　　　　[18] S 1.14.　　　　[19] S 1.3.

'God created all things in the most correct way, in the best proportions and with the greatest beauty,'[20] and also that all carping about providence (foreseeing) must be attributed to a failure to see oneself, a lack of aesthetic capacity. The argument Augustine mounts in his first theodicy against the Manichees (De libero arbitrio) involves the most broadly based proof of God's existence to be found in all his work: once one has seen (Book 2) that the glorious God exists, by that very fact every objection to him falls silent and turns into praise (Book 3). Certainly Augustine will also ascend from the beauty and order of the world to eternal beauty, but he far prefers to see in the light of God's beauty the beauty of the world revealing itself to the person who loves God: 'Whoever, on his way to wisdom, contemplates and considers the totality of creatures feels how wisdom kindly reveals herself to him on the way and goes to meet him with all forethought, and so his passion to walk that path will burn all the more fiercely as the path itself is beautified for him by that wisdom he thirsts to attain.'[21] Augustine is certainly familiar with the contemplation of the beauty of the world, but long before the vision at Ostia it is for him, much more than the theōria physikē was for the Greek Fathers, a means and a path: 'There is no lack of value or benefit in the contemplation (intueri) of the beauty of the heavens, the arrangement of the stars, the radiant crown of light, the change of day and night, the monthly courses of the moon, the fourfold tempering of the year to match the four elements, the powerful force of seeds from which derive the forms of species and numbers, yes, everything that preserves its own measure and nature in its kind. But such a consideration must not pander to a vain and passing curiosity, but must be turned into a stairway to the immortal and enduring.'[22] For that reason a sense of measure and proportion is no small advantage to the person who possesses it, and 'reason and truth' are very close, since even in the realm of the spiritual and the divine the important thing will be to see and to be able to judge proportions.[23] And this training in seeing also leads, when the soul becomes pure and open, to

[20] QA 80.   [21] LA 2.45.   [22] VR 52.
[23] VR 54.

that 'spiritual seeing' of God in his works of which Paul speaks in Romans (1.20): *invisibilia ipsius per ea quae facta sunt intellecta conspiciuntur*).[24] But this seeing succeeds only when the sight, leaving all finite things behind, has already reached the divine (*sempiterna ejus virtus et divinitas*) and looks back from there on what can become for it an entrance and an epiphany, when, that is, it is 'devout attention',[25] when the eye which looks has already been given strength and clarity by faith, hope and love.[26] Hence the detailed examination of conscience on which *ratio* embarks with Augustine at the beginning of the 'Soliloquies': how far have you got existentially with your love of God, with the quite specific desire to prefer God to all things?[27]

This means that the plurality of the world cannot be understood in any other way at all than in terms of God's unity and in its light. This basic theme of all philosophy, in particular of all Eastern philosophy (and the Egyptian Plotinus also belongs to the East) is used by Augustine right at the beginning of *De vera religione* both apologetically and theologically and as a proof of the truth of Christianity. All religion outside the Church, he says, is at best syncretism, to say nothing at all of polytheism;[28] the common worship of the Roman state is quite happy to allow everyone who participates in it, whether philosopher or not, to have his or her own opinion about God and gods. Plato, of course, had seen the unity of God, but he also saw that the soul cannot behold God's beauty without grace; if he had lived in Augustine's time, the direction of his thought would have made him a Christian. The philosophers too have been able to found only sects, while the Church is gradually bringing about the unity of mankind in practice and so revealing the reality of the unity it embodies.[29] It also does this theoretically, since according to its faith and teaching 'the first principle of human salvation consists in the fact that there is not philosophy, the quest for wisdom, on the one hand, and religion on the other,

---

[24] [His invisible things are seen in the mind through the things he has made], VR 101; *cf. Enarr in Ps* 41.6–8 (cols 467, 469).

[25] *pie attendere*, LA 3.70.

[26] S 1.12–13. [27] S 1.16f. [28] VR 1–11.

[29] VR 5–7.

for those whose teaching we do not approve of we do not admit to sacramental fellowship either'.[30] In this, in the exclusion and simultaneous polarisation of heresies, the Church demonstrates its true unifying power: all of them, the Jews too, are what they are as a result of a negative relation to the one centre which is the Church. The Church 'uses the pagans as material for its action, the heretics to test its teaching, the schismatics as evidence of its steadfastness and the Jews by way of comparison with her own beauty. . . . But the fleshly one in its own ranks it tolerates as chaff by which the grain is more safely preserved on the threshing-floor until it is stripped of such husks.'[31] The unifying power of the Church is thus irresistible even for everything which sets itself against it from outside or inside, and for this reason it is the complete manifestation in the world of the God whose order and providence no power, not even that of the devil, can oppose. Augustine's idea of the Church is already fully formed here. He sees its glory and also its unavoidably tragic character as an inherent element in the active presence of an absolute moment within time. There can, for example, be error in the exercise of the divine power of the keys: 'providence may very often permit that in the all too turbulent revolts of fleshly men even good people may be expelled from the Christian community'. If they die excommunicate, God in his mercy will look after them.[32] So far does the one God go in the hazardous venture of true religion, which in its unity is the most convincing sermon on the one, true God.[33] Only here is unity not just aimed at from afar or 'faked' in an illusion,[34] but displayed materially. In the world of plurality this is such a miracle that the individual miracles of the gospel and primitive Christianity could be brought to an end in favour of this miracle.[35] It can be said that Augustine's proof of the true Church is an aesthetic proof: anyone who cannot *see* the specific nature of this catholicity (as opposed to mere geographical extension or a syncretic, organisational unity) cannot be moved by it.

In the Church it is not a god or an idea of God which appears,

[30] VR 8.   [31] VR 10.   [32] VR 11.

[33] VR 46.   [34] VR 60.   [35] VR 47.

but the living God who is being, life and spirit in supreme unity, whose being must appear in a reality existing in history, whose life must appear in a sacramental organic life-*communio*, whose Spirit must appear in a spirit-filled community pressing forward towards the Spirit. All three aspects require an historical path and development from an external teaching to an inner appropriation, from a belief based on authority to a free understanding of what is believed, from an historical form (which is in itself prophetic, which is why *historia* and *prophetia* are mentioned together)[36] to a lived, integrated existence, and all this applies to the individual as well as to humanity as a whole.[37] However, since the individual will always have to start at the same point and have to struggle to the end of the same path (from the world and sensuality to God and the spirit), humanity's path too can be seen as a development only if the same movement away from the world and towards God is illustrated exemplarily in it as the one step from the old (covenant) to the new (covenant). But since Augustine sees principally the movement towards God ('I forget what lies behind and strain forward towards what lies ahead,' Phil 3.13), this historical step for him does not have a truly formal character. The 'old' is as such not an object of contemplation; it is either the jumping-off point for the new or the visible sign of the failure of those who fall back from the new into the old. What is decisive is the path taken; it alone in its movement is the image in saving history of the divine unity. The only interest of the parable is the truth it contains; of the obscurity of the old, what is revealed in the new. The kingdom of God, the *civitas Dei*, has existed in essence from the time of Abel; what occurs in Christ is only that it moves out of the shadow into the sunlight, though in the Church, 'for the sake of the fleshly and sensual ones', it still remains largely veiled.[38] And only 'the person who reads attentively discovers the articulations of the ages (*aetatum articulos*)'.[39] Indeed, it is the change itself which reveals more profoundly the unity of the

---

[36] [The historical and prophetic order of salvation must be believed so that subsequently (second stage) the way of life corresponding to faith can purify the mind and (third stage) fit it for the perception of spiritual things], VR 13.
[37] VR 19.   [38] VR 51.   [39] VR 50.

Testaments.[40] The movement is from 'body to mind' (Plato), from 'flesh to spirit' (Paul), and Augustine has deliberately equated the two terminologies.[41] In philosophical, Platonic terms, the movement is from appearance to being, in theological, Biblical terms, from being lost to redeemed existence in God. The direction decides everything, including the outcome of the last judgment. Already it divides humanity into 'two nations', 'two classes of human beings';[42] it 'divides the whole human race, which is like the life of a single person, from Adam to the end of this period of time, into two orders', into two 'kingdoms'.[43] This was what Manichaeism rightly saw, though it construed the division in terms of two substances whereas it should be seen in terms of the two different directions in which men strive; this is the starting-point for the *civitas Dei*'s theology of history. This is where the foundations of every ethics which divides people into defeated and undefeated are laid,[44] and where, at least in the early period, he constructs a parallel between the stages of an individual's development and the stages of the education of humanity as a whole. The path leads from above to below, from being to appearance, into death and damnation; from below to above it leads to the gathering up even of the realm of appearances into being, to the transformation of the meaning of death into no more than the transition to eternal life.[45]

All these movements of unity in the *oikonomia*, however, must be seen in relation to the unmoved unity of *theologia*, of the 'supreme and exalted and unutterable unity of the creator'.[46] This unity, which transcends every number and every form and essence and by transcending them makes them possible, is 'the one eternal essence in which there is no discord, no confusion, no transition, no defect, no death, but instead supreme harmony, supreme clarity, supreme persistence, supreme fulness, supreme vitality, in which nothing is lacking and nothing in

---

[40] VR 34.   [41] *De magistro* 39.   [42] LA 1.34.
[43] VR 50.   [44] VR 83–93.

[45] VR 49. Particularly in his early period, Augustine contructed several such stairways to God. Cf. the Ostia vision, QA 70–71, 79; *De Trin* 12, c. 15.25; *De doctr christ* 2, 7, 9–11; *De Gen contra Man* 1, c. 25.43.

[46] LA 3.69.

excess'.[47] Because it surpasses everything, this unity is free and creative, but because it inwardly makes possible the existence of everything, insofar as it exists at all, any discussion with it is ontologically impossible; it is always eternally right before we begin, and the only thing to do is for the creature to conform and bind itself to it—that is religion—and to look for a cause of the discords of the world outside this unity. Here Augustine in the first instance agrees with both Mani (and Marcion) and Plotinus; he then has to show as a second stage in the argument that this cause cannot be a subordinate god, nor an eternal opposed principle, nor matter devoid of being, but the abyss of creaturely freedom, for the misuse of which no primary cause can be made responsible. As Augustine observes with astounding profundity, 'The movement away from God does not come from God, so where does it come from? If you put the question like that, I must reply that I do not know. That may sadden you, but my answer is still right. There can be no knowledge of what is nothing.'[48] 'Why should one need to know it?'[49] It is the movement of alienation (*abalienatio*),[50] which Plotinus and Origen built into the foundations of their systems and then subdued by theological thinking, just as Hegel finally captured it in a system of dialectical necessities; Augustine, however, refuses to provide a final explanation for the yawning gulf of sin.

This is in all probability the reason for his lifelong refusal to offer a theory for the soul's origin in God and for the distance at which it is set from its maker: *anima vero unde originem ducat . . . , quantum distet a Deo, quid habeat proprium quoad alternat in utramque naturam, quatenus moriatur et quomodo immortalis probetur*: who can do justice to the philosopher's requirement?[51] Neither derivation from the parental soul nor individual creation by God, neither the insertion of the precreated soul into the body nor a pre-natal fall from the original unity, none of

---

[47] S 1.4. [48] LA 2.54. [49] LA 3.1.
[50] LA 1.2.

[51] [Where the soul originates . . . , how far removed it is from God, what property it has which allows it to alternate between two natures, how far it dies and how it can be shown to be immortal], DO 2.17.

these satisfied the searching mind.[52] Enough if the human being understands that he is always outside the unity, that his pro-gress from God (*progressus*) requires a re-gress (*regressus*),[53] a return home (*conversio, epistrophē*)[54] and a stretching out towards being[55] and towards the lost origin, and that this path in itself is already divine truth and guidance and order, whether it is called (as the essence of all true knowing, all *science*) *disciplina*[56] or *ordo*[57] or *lex*.[58] Enough that he strives to regain, in the spirit of the gospel, the principle, the origin from which he fell—how he does not know—to find himself in a strange land, by 'becoming a child for God' (*repuerescat Deo*);[59] enough if he opens the light of his eyes once more to the eternal light.

2. TRUE AND GOOD

What first gives the idea of this universal movement towards unity its distinctive Augustinian stamp is his anti-sceptical search for the true starting-point of intellectual reflection. The fundamental task of *ratio* is to find secure foundations for truth in the original pure act of the *cogito*.[60] But the evidential force of the *cogito* for Augustine includes, by contrast with Descartes, more than just simply the *sum*: 'Since it is obvious that you exist and since this cannot be obvious to you in any other way than from your being alive, your being alive is similarly obvious. . . . Consequently a third thing is also obvious, namely that you have understanding (*intellegere*)'.[61] Being, living and understanding (which means more than the Cartesian pure act of thought), are in the Augustinian *cogito* originally a unity of three

[52] LA 3.56f.; *cf.. De Gen ad litt* 10; *Ep.* 162 *ad Marcellinum,* 164 *ad Evodium;* 166 *ad Hieronymum; Contra Julian* 5.17; *Op imp contra Julian* 2.178; 4.104.
[53] DO 2.33.   [54] LA 2.29.
[55] S 1.2 (*omnia . . . tendunt ad esse*), *De morib. manich.* 2, 6, 8: *quæ tendunt esse ad ordinem tendunt* [Things which strain to be, strain towards order].
[56] LA 1.2; DO 1.24.
[57] DO 1.27–28: *ordo est quem si tenuerimus in vita, perducet ad Deum* [It is an order which, if we hold to it in life, will lead us to God].
[58] DO 2.25.   [59] QA 55.
[60] S 1.1; VR 73; *De Trin* 15, c. 12.21.
[61] LA 2.7.

in one. To say this is almost immediately to prompt the question, 'Which of these three seems to you the best?' and the answer, 'Understanding,' is justified as follows: 'because even a stone has existence and even an animal has life, but the stone is not alive and the animal does not think, so then if someone thinks, it is absolutely certain that he also exists and is alive'.[62] Nothing is more fundamental in Augustine than the hier-archical character of the primary intuition about being—even if the diversity of the levels is shown only by a comparison with the world. The point is not to establish an empty identity between being and thinking, nor an original 'tension' between subject and object; it is an attempt to find a place for the most fundamental order of being in the world within the original act of consciousness. This not only radically invalidates every dialectic between concept and existence, but also the unfruitful dialectic between thought and life whose divisiveness fills the history of modern thought. Rather, Augustine lays the foun-dation for a major thesis of Thomas Aquinas' when he says, 'I know that I can only know if I am alive, and I know this all the more certainly in that I become more alive by knowing.'[63] 'You did not prefer something else to life, you preferred a better life to a particular life.'[64] It is a law which determines both the intensification and the foundation of existence. 'To be in order to be alive, to be alive in order to understand.'[65] There is in the *cogito* that which is fundamentally self-evident to the eye of the mind: the recognition of precedence, a preference for the higher and better which entails a risk and a choice: *videt praeferendum*,[66] *audet se praeferre*.[67]

This core contains the whole of Augustinianism; it is from this original perception that everything else is developed, in agreement with and in opposition to Plotinus. 1. It contains a fundamental sense of quality or value, and correspondingly of hierarchy. 'No-one who has an eye for it (which is not a difficult art) will deny that living substance is to be preferred to lifeless,

[62] *Ibid.* [63] VR 97. [64] LA 1.17.
[65] S 2.1.
[66] [It sees that a choice has to be made], LA 1.20; 2.12.
[67] [It dares to put itself first], QA 73.

or that which bestows life to that which receives it.'[68] This all depends on being able to see, just as does all that immediately follows from it, which is called the Augustinian proof of the existence of God, the only one he produced but a comprehensive one, and one which Thomas set out schematically in the Fourth Way. The underlying assumption is that in *intellegere* the level of thought (*cogitatio*) is transcended and the level of the reality of being reached, an assumption which Descartes was never able to make fundamentally, *i.e.*, without reducing existence to the sphere of thought. 2. The triune experience of being in the intellectual act directly implies both freedom and order: freedom because preference presupposes the superiority of the higher level to the lower, and because such preferring becomes automatic in the mind; and order because the levels form a mutually supporting structure such that it is ontologically impossible to play freedom and order off against each other. 3. The same supporting structure in the human being shows his non-absoluteness. The hierarchical movement from being to life to mind (from stone to plant and animal to man), or psychologically from thing-consciousness via sense perception to intellectual reflection, compels thought to transcend this whole striving and potential realm of being in an unmoving and identical being which is the being of all beings, the life of all living things and the mind of all mind, and which must therefore be superior to the free human being as the free divine person. Plotinus too sees the hierarchical principle, but he ultimately turns to pantheism and absolutises striving human nature. Augustine goes beyond Plotinus by extending the Plotinian hierarchy to its logical conclusion, by crowning and perfecting the relative freedom of man, as exercised in human preferences by the creative freedom of the personal Biblical God. 4. In this way a path is opened up for the religious and aesthetic view of life to catch sight of God. It sees God in all things (which are what they are only by participation in an unqualified being, life and mind), and it can see them in no other way than in their participation in God; but equally it sees God over all things, since God can be the ground of all things only

68 LA 1.20.

because he is no one of them, which is why the supreme activity of human freedom is, when presented with the whole divinely established order of the world, to prefer God himself as the far better. When things reveal God, they point beyond themselves to him; that is, they conceal him in themselves to reveal him in himself. The inner order of being is thus perceived by the same vision which sees also the transcendent freedom of the creator and orderer. Contingency thus has its place within the necessity of the laws of being,[69] and from this it becomes apparent that the Augustinian proof of God's existence from the different levels of being does not go beyond the limits imposed by the structure of the proof itself.[70]

The analysis of the *cogito* (which, of course, is always performed under the stimulus of envisaging a not-I) can just as well be developed in terms of the triunity of power of thought, object of thought and act of thought,[71] but this schema is itself explained in terms of the first. The first reason for this is that the act of thought proves to be a judgment on what is presented to it and so demonstrates the superior position in the hierarchy of the mind-subject (and also of the animal subject of perception over the object perceived),[72] and the second is that the triad object–power–act reflects the triad being–life–mind.[73]

The structure of the *cogito* thus demonstrated requires for its completion what in Augustine's writing is usually called *illuminatio*. The only way in which finite mind can make judgments is in the 'light' of absolute mind: this light, in that it informs the mind, is the transcendental condition of the mental structure of finite mind, but at the same time, in that it is absolute and free, personal, it is its transcendent basis. The relation between finite and infinite mind must therefore be both necessary and free (this is the crux of Augustinianism): it must be both philosophically transcendental (in the sense of Kant's critical philosophy and

[69] Things could also be totally different.

[70] *Cf. e.g.* LA 2.46.

[71] LA 1.8.

[72] LA 1.10; 2.12.

[73] LA 2.13–14; 8–9: The external sense perceives the objective element, the internal sense (*sensus interior* in animals too) perceives the act of sensing, the mind registers and judges both.

Fichte and Hegel's 'mysticism') and theologically personal.[74] Thus the personal relation, that is to say, prayer and humility, the purification of the soul in its movement towards God, belongs fundamentally to the act of coming to know being, though it would be wrong for that reason to make prayer an instrument within that act, or to develop a methodology around it. The element of dialogue (in the *Confessions*) does not abolish the justified element of monologue (in the *Soliloquies*); it is impossible simply to reduce thought to 'dialogue' for the very good reason that God is not a finite partner but the ontological basis (*interior intimo meo*)[75] of the personal act of thinking. The temptation to resolve this tension must be resisted by anyone who wants to recapture Augustine's intention, as it must in the case of Origen's concept of the Logos (Logos as the absolute original structure of all mental acts and also as the personal Christ in the centre of our hearts as the one 'whom you do not know' [Jn 1.26], but who must be known for true knowledge).

Illuminatio coming from the truth which the Son of God is[76] therefore does not mean a vision of God's 'essence'. Augustine reserves this for the next life; here below it is granted only quite exceptionally and only in ecstasy (Paul, Moses). *Illuminatio* expresses in ancient language what moderns might describe as the fundamental openness of the kingdom of absolute truth (which as absolute belongs to God and is inseparably bound up with him), a truth therefore which, however profane it may appear, is in its source and ground sacred because it is part of the God who is never a thing, but always personal and alive. But this means that for this divine, absolute character of definitive truth, which bears eternity within it, to become visible at all to finite mind, certain requirements must be fulfilled. The truth which God is must spontaneously open itself to men, and consequently finite mind must be prepared subjectively to be

---

[74] Main texts on illumination: S 1.15; *De mag* 38–46; Ep 13 *ad Nebrid* (*De eo quod apud nos est Deum consulendo* [by asking instruction of God concerning that which is within us]); *De Gen ad litt* 12.59; *De pecc mer.* 1.38; *De civ Dei* 10.2; *De Trin* 12, c. 15.24; *Retract* 1, c. 8.2.

[75] [deeper than my deepest self], *Conf* 3, c. 6.10.

[76] VR 25; LA 1.5.

able to perceive this revelation for what it is: *aeternitate affici*.[77] Here, in passing, we find the starting-point for the whole of Augustine's later doctrine of grace and can see how wrong the Donatists were to appeal to Augustine's early writings. For already here the logic of his position requires him to state, 'Of himself man can by no means raise himself from earthly life to attain the image of God.'[78] The terms relating to truth's spontaneous opening of itself multiply: God's truth 'shows its face (*faciem*)', places itself 'at the ready' (*praesto*),[80] lets itself be 'embraced' (*amplectere*),[81] shows itself (*se ostendere*),[82] makes itself 'present' (*praesens*),[83] 'knows when to show itself' (*novit illa pulchritudo quando se ostendat*),[84] 'shows itself when it pleases' (*quando placet sese ostendit*),[85] 'lifts up to itself' (*sublevat*).[86] 'But it makes itself present in vain to stained souls, because spiritual blindness cannot see it.'[87] So the act of the mind again depends on the aesthetic capacity to perceive the quality of the eternal and divine in truth (something it can do only when it is collected and purified); otherwise, even if it draws the correct logical conclusions, it may miss the real experience of truth. The concluding truths of the secular sciences, whose laws rest in eternal truth, thus clearly have a profane and a sacred side, with the first extending further than the second;[88] further, 'between the intelligible majesty of God and the intellectual processes of reasoning there is a gulf no less wide than between heaven and earth'.[89] It is thus possible, without doing violence to the immanent structure of the human mind, to maintain the personal role of the inner teacher, Christ, who is 'the wisdom of God' (1 Cor 1.30). He is word and light at once: he is 'heard'[90] and 'he illuminates',[91] and anyone who 'is a disciple of the truth' and 'can see inwardly'[92] is 'instructed, not by my words, but by the things themselves, which God reveals within him'.[93] He has

---

[77] [to be sensitive to eternity], VR 19.   [78] *Ibid.*
[79] DO 1.23.   [80] LA 2.28.   [81] LA 2.35.   [82] LA 2.45.
[83] QA 77.   [84] S 1.25.   [85] S 1.26.   [86] S 1.30.
[87] *Div Quaest LXXXIII*, 12.   [88] LA 2.32.
[89] S 1.11.   [90] *De mag* 40.   [91] *Ibid.*   [92] *De mag* 41.
[93] *Ibid.* 40; LA 2.4; *summa magistra veritas intus docens*, [the chief teacher, truth, who teaches within us]; QA 81: *desuper Magister omnium* [the teacher of all on high].

passed from the external authority of teaching to the supreme authority of truth itself,[94] and to its 'hidden oracle'.[95]

This is the origin of the tension in Augustine between innatism (a position he never fully adopted), indeed the Platonic doctrine of anamnesis, and the idea (also never adopted) of the created mind as pure active potentiality for every intellectual content. 'Authentic' creaturely knowledge is something from which, in its pure spontaneity and freshness, each man has been estranged (by original sin); it is the simple knowledge of the presence of God, whose reality alone confers final reality and certainty on everything else: we are lighted towards this authenticity and reminded of it by the Son, whose will is to lead us to the Father. The renewal of men's ties (re-ligio) to this absolute origin, as distinct from man's bondage to idols of his own creation, forms the subject of the solemn conclusion to De vera religione.[96]

In this starting-point we can also see prefigured the later anti-Pelagian dialectic, which on the one hand must maintain that the structure of the human mind and, in consequence, of its freedom has not been destroyed by the Fall, but on the other that man, as a result of his alienation, must be incapable of a return to authenticity, of a free choice of the supreme God in love;[97] the analogy of states (status) cuts through the concept of nature.[98]

The transcendental and transcendent character of the sphere of divine reality is, finally, guaranteed by its supra-subjectivity. It escapes from the over-present 'mine' of the knowing and loving 'I'; in consequence, it needs, if it is to be grasped, a loving universalisation and fulfilling depersonalisation of the 'I', that lack of envy which the Greeks always regarded as a mark of the divine (but cf. also Mt 5.45), whereas all privatisation of the universal divine truth betokens a movement which is typical of sin and failure.[99] This universal character of truth must be taken

[94] VR 45.
[95] De mag 46.
[96] VR 108–113.
[97] LA 3.52.
[98] LA 3.54.
[99] VR 90; LA 2.53; 2.16f.; 2.28; 2.33.

together with its personal character.[100] Then, says Augustine, its divine character will become plain: only God can in fact be the love which is most personal to each individual and yet common to all. Augustine regularly relates the love command of the New Covenant to this realisation, and to the *regula*, the *ordo amoris*—including even love of enemy—as the 'understood' order.[101] This rule becomes light for the soul itself.[102]

Thus the good springs from the true in which it is already contained, just as, in the original intuition, freedom was already contained in order. Freedom contains the possibility of preferring, of choice (and the reverse), but freedom itself is free only in the measure that it rightly (*recte*) prefers the right and justly (*juste*) prefers the just.[103] It is sovereign in the measure that it conducts itself by the rule of the absolute: such conduct contains all virtue,[104] and fulfilling happiness (*vita beata*) supervenes both as its immanent result and as the freely given reward (*praemium*).[105] Only if a man sets a direct course to God is every possibility of error eliminated,[106] and the 'concept of happiness', like the 'concept of truth', imprinted (*impressa*) a priori on both rational and moral striving (the two are one), not as an 'innate idea', but as identical with the striving itself. The gracious restoration of this striving, however, takes place through faith, hope and love, which, in the end, where they are alive, are again one as humble submission and devotion to the divine true and good.[107] In such devotion we can already see how the concept of merit is, if not abolished, certainly surpassed. For in its devotion the loving soul knows itself more and more indebted to God,[108]

[100] LA 2.33: *miris modis secretum et publicum lumen* [a light in a mysterious way both secret and public]. This is Goethe's 'holy public secret'.

[101] QA 78; VR 87; 91; *cf.* S 1.17f.

[102] LA 2.52.

[103] VR 27–28; 44. Augustine quotes Christ's saying, 'The truth will make you free' (LA 2.37).

[104] LA 1.25, 27, 29.

[105] *Ibid.* 30.

[106] *Ibid.* 26. And so God, if he is sought, will infallibly be found (QA 24).

[107] S 1.13.

[108] LA 3.43, 45–46. This is where the image of the weight of love (*pondus amoris*) comes in, though Augustine occasionally has to be careful about the comparison between the weight of a stone and the downward pull of the weight of the will (LA 3.2).

though here Augustine takes every care to show that the encompassing freedom of God does not destroy human freedom.[109]

3. THE BEAUTIFUL

Discussion of beauty has been left to this point to show how far this basic category of Augustine's is built on well thought-out foundations. Elements of a doctrine of beauty have already appeared in plenty, in the basic experience of the self-manifestation of light-filled, light-giving essential truth, in the experience of its sacred and gracious character, in the demand that the vision of the experiencing soul should be purified and kept ready for this revelation. They have appeared too in the basing of revelation and the longing for it on love, but especially in the demonstration of the hierarchical structure of even the most primitive experience of being, which uncovers a pattern of levels of being in terms of form and matter. Alone, however, these would not be sufficient for more than a general dynamic from below to above, that movement of love whose Platonic and Biblical rapture is proclaimed by the *Confessions* and often too by the *Enarrationes*. What is still missing is the emphasis on the form in space and time which, again in Platonic terms, crystallises the enthusiasm and, in Christian terms, brings the striving of Jewish expectation to rest in the Incarnation of the Son of God. Only the one who loves finite form as the revelation of the infinite is both 'mystic' and 'aesthete'.

After the introduction dealing with the true unity of religion (contrasted with syncretism), Augustine begins the main part of his investigation into 'true religion' with the idea that the Christian dogma of the Trinity receives support from the fact that every created thing has its own structure, in that it exists (*esse inquantum est*), has a particular nature (*speciem suam habere*) and is placed within a perfect order (*ordinatissime administrari*). As an existent, the creature is an individual, as a member of a species it is distinct from others, but is as such caught within the order of things (*non excedat ordinem*).[110] Being inevitably includes being of a certain kind (species) or, what comes to the same thing, a form (*forma*), two words which imply both 'essence' and 'beauty' and are immediately understood by Augustine in this duality (*speciosus* and *formosus*, 'beautiful', 'well-formed').[111] To the question why this is so, we receive an answer on three levels: 1. Because everything that is and exists derives from a creative action by which the highest Being informs the 'nothingness' of matter; moreover this highest Being, as the supreme unity, is the absolute *fascinosum*, beauty as such. 2. Because the immanent structure of everything that is and exists displays this stamp and image of the unattainable unity. 3. Because all resemblances among created things point to a supreme, an absolute similarity and likeness in the triune God himself and are only adequately explicable by this.

Augustine thus explains the Biblical creation with the categories of Platonic participation. That something can exist outside the complete absolute unity is conceivable only if out of the quasi-nothing of matter, 'out of which God made everything,' the finite existing essences are formed by a creative irradiation from the forms which reside in God and are identical with him.[112] 'Shaped out of shapelessness' (*ex informitate formata*)[113] and 'created out of nothing',[114] these two dimensions, which Thomas and the Thomists will later carefully separate as a composite structure in the order of nature (matter and form) and in the order of being (being and existence), still coincide for Augustine because for him the supreme existent being is understood in Platonic terms as absolute unity, and contingency and creativeness are therefore adequately expressed in terms of the unity pertaining to things, which is only striven for and never attained. In terms of Thomas's thought, the setting-forth

[110] [does not go beyond the order], VR 13. Cf. *De mus* 6. 56: *Numerus autem et ab uno incipit, et aequalitate ac similitudine pulcher est, et ordine copulatur ... carissima caritate* [Number not only starts from one, but is also beautiful in equality and similarity, and combines in an ordered way ... with the most heartfelt love], *i.e.*, in a trinitarian way.
[111] VR 35.   [112] VR 35.
[113] *De Gen ad litt* 5.14.
[114] Cf. *Conf* 11.6–7.

of matter from God in Augustine must be regarded as the true act of creation, though real being is given to it only by the simultaneous action of form which calls it back to its origin.[115] Against this view it has rightly been argued that the formative moulding force of the ideas for Augustine must be seen as equally creative,[116] and this is indeed the only possible corollary of his 'essential ontology'. If being consists in unity, then the participation of created things in being also consists in a graduated participation in unity. And then matter itself (against both the Manichees and Plotinus) must be explained as the pure tendency and potentiality for form, as simply the capability of being formed.[117] In this way creation is seen as the art of the supreme artist and must be judged by his creative idea.[118]

Form and beauty, however, considered as immanent, can now be seen in purely numerical terms, for number is the pluralisation of unity which originated in unity and is explicable only in and through unity. This conception can and indeed must be developed in two ways, as the young Augustine saw in his lost first work *De pulchro et apto* ('On the Beautiful and the Suitable'): 'I defined and distinguished the beautiful as what looks good in itself and the suitable as what looks good when adapted to go with something else.'[119] The former expresses unity by the inner harmony of its parts or aspects, the second by fitting as a part into a larger complex. In the picture of the Trinity described above, these two aspects correspond to the Son (as *forma*) and the Spirit (as *ordo universi*), just as the Son becomes man and takes individual form while the Spirit brings the redeemed universe into harmony with that form. The idea that the nature of things is number was taken over by Plato in his later work from Pythagoras and incorporated by Plotinus into his system—and even Augustine allowed himself to be revered by his friends as a reviver of Pythagoras.[120] Nevertheless it

---

[115] Gilson, *Introduction à l'étude de S. Augustin* (3rd ed. 1949), pp. 266–67.

[116] Thonnard, in the French edition of Augustine, vol. 6 (1941), p. 509, and Gilson himself, *op. cit.* p. 267, n. 1.

[117] VR 36; *capacitas inchoata* [an inchoate capacity], LA 3.65.

[118] VR 57.

[119] *Conf* 4, c. 15.24.

[120] DO 2.53.

cannot be regarded as a mere quantification of being or merely a
translation into mathematics, because the unity which these
numbers and numerical relations reflect is, beyond all quantity,
the qualitative as such. Augustine consequently applies entirely
qualitative criteria to the numerical figures of geometry which
extend in space and to those of rhythm in music and speech
which extend in time, and arranges them in a hierarchy
according to various considerations which seem to him self-
evident.[121] But the question arises how these hierarchies are
related to the fundamental hierarchy of levels of being or
existence (being–life–mind), and whether they can be derived
from it. In spite of attempts which point in this direction,[122] this
is impossible if for no other reason than that it would run
counter to Platonic causality, which operates only from above
to below. Thus he can do no more than posit an analogy
between numerical figures and structures and the three levels of
existence (and the degrees which mediate between them), as the
theory of numbers shows, especially in Book VI of *De musica*.
By means of these analogies Augustine explains the possibility
both of sensory and of intellectual knowledge, which of course,
in Platonic terms, can never be explained by an action of the
external world on the senses and of the senses on the mind, but
only as an informing intuition of the mind into the senses and of
the senses into the external world, though such a process is
occasioned by the analogous numerical affection between the
lower and the higher faculties in the hierarchy. The observation
that geometrical phantasms are only an imperfect accompaniment of the exact mathematical laws perceived by the mind,
which the soul ultimately does not receive in itself, but (in
however veiled a form) by irradiation from the highest
'sanctuary of numbers', seems to confirm this epistemology.
Thus the concept of *numerus*, which applies to all levels of being,
can assume an internally analogous form: from the usual
mathematical sense in the material world through the sense of

[121] QA 13ff.
[122] Such as the speculations about the periphery and the centre, with the
centre as the qualitative centre of force, which somehow releases and controls
the periphery like a soul (QA 19 and 23–24), and the parallel drawn between
the centre of a circle and the pupil of the eye (QA 30 and 69).

proportion (in space) and rhythm (in time) within the world of souls (external and internal sense and memory) to harmony and intellectual correspondence in the realm of the mind, and finally to the harmonies we can only guess at in divine wisdom, from whose 'numbers' all form has flowed and in whose light it is seen and enjoyed as a beautiful copy of the eternal beauty. This explains Augustine's sense, as early as the *De vera religione* (where it is an ancient Platonic sense) of the harmony of finite form as the container of being, whereas he feels numerical infinity in time and space to be really a distorted product of the imagination, so overcoming in advance Pascal's horror of the quantitatively-infinitely large and infinitely small.[123] The aesthetic view of being found in the early works is expressed in the exaltation of measure and moderation, in which the term *modus* is applied not just to the Christian life as a whole,[124] but to God himself. '*Modestia* comes from *modus*, and *temperantia* from *temperies* (which is a harmonious combination). But where moderation and due proportion prevail, there is neither excess nor insufficiency. That is true fulness, which we oppose to "lack"—a far more significant opposition than between "lack" and "excess". For in excess there is an inflow and an altogether too turbulent overflow. If this occurs in greater measure than is required, then here too there is a lack of proportion; thus what is excessively disproportionate also displays signs of defectiveness. . . . The measure of the soul is therefore wisdom. That is what enables the soul to acquire a gravity which prevents it from

[123] [What is it in us which enables us to understand inwardly the relation of size between visible physical bodies and that every body, however small, has two halves and that each of its halves innumerable parts, and that consequently every millet seed seems to one of its particles as big as the whole world does to us; that the world as a whole is beautiful by virtue of the proportion of its forms and not of its size, and seems big to us, not because it is big but because we are small—that is, the creatures which fill it are small and in their turn, since they too can be infinitely divided, are not so small in themselves but only, once again, in comparison with others, especially with the universe? With the extent of the ages, too, the principle is no different. . . . We do not judge the beauty of this numerical succession and particular hierarchy of spaces and times on the basis of their spatial or temporal extent, but such beauty is the result of their ordered harmony, VR 80. No mass, whatever its nature, even if it glows with visible light, can be rated highly if it is devoid of life, VR 52.]

[124] DO 2.25.

running to excess or being restricted by a lack of fulness. . . . But what is wisdom if not the wisdom of God, God's son? . . . And wisdom is truth. "I am the truth" (Jn 14.8). But for truth to exist there must be a supreme measure, from which it proceeds and to which, when it is perfect, it returns. This supreme measure is subject to no other measure, for if the supreme measure is measure by virtue of the supreme measure, it is measure by virtue of itself. . . . So truth is never without measure, and measure never without truth.'[125] To this picture of God as self-measure there corresponds an ideal of the closed nature of essences even in finite mind: 'Everything that is conscious of itself embraces itself, but what is embraced is finite for itself. But mind perceives itself, and so is finite for itself. It would not even want to be infinite if it could be; for [it] wants to be known to itself because it loves itself.'[126] This un-Augustinian ideal is already paling in the emotion of the *Confessions*, which know that 'there is that in a man that even a man's own spirit does not know',[127] but this is also the same time at which the metaphysic of numbers recedes into the background.[128] True, Augustine cannot quite do without it; he takes it up again in his explanation of the creation story, since it is to the active force of numbers in potential being that he attributes the mysteries of the generation of animals,[129] and he relies on the *numeri efficacissimi* once again to explain how a unique creation always develops at its particular time.[130] And when, totally in the spirit of Plotinus, he describes time as an extenuation of the soul (the world-soul fallen from mind),[131] this non-identity[132] becomes for him an enduring basis for all the beautiful play of rhythm and melody which seeks in infinitely varied ways to imitate unity in the sphere of what is not-one. The element of painful melancholy which is present in all music because the totality can be grasped

[125] *De beata vita* 32-34.

[126] *Div quaest LXXXIII* c. 15.

[127] *Conf* 10, c. 5.7.

[128] But *cf. De civ Dei* 11.30, where the thesis on the significance of numbers is fully maintained.

[129] VR 74, 79.

[130] *De Gen ad litt* 5, c. 7.20.

[131] *Conf* 11, c. 23.30; 11, c. 26.33: *distensio animi*, the Neo-Platonic *diastēma*.

[132] *Enarr in Ps* 37.6; 62.6; 65.12; 89.6 (in the Vulgate numbering).

only in the flight of its parts becomes the complete expression of his temperament and a basic pattern of worldly ethics, which sins against the meaning of fleeting beauty when it tries to hold on to the individual note instead of allowing the quantitative to slip away as one sways to the rhythm of beauty.[133] Yes, the beauty of material bodies is real beauty:[134] there is nothing evil in it, but it is only a trace[135] and so a hint (*nutus*) pointing one away from the non-existent to the existent.[136] And the mature Augustine again uses numbers, this time taking them from the Church's tradition but giving them a justification at a deeper level in his metaphysics, to unlock the secrets concealed in the Biblical numbers.[137] Surely no-one would maintain that the many numbers of the Old and New Testaments were set down at random by the divine author, or even merely by Moses or John? They too are a hint which is in principle capable of being understood and yet can really be puzzled out only in rare cases.[138]

Nevertheless, none of these applications of numbers develops the original metaphysics any further. For this Augustine started from the identity of nature (*species* or idea = *ratio, sapientia*) and number, and even believed he had found confirmation of this in the Biblical books of wisdom.[139] However, it has to be said of this metaphysics that it does not uphold the original Pythagorean principle of the identity of countable quantity (of sounds in the monochord) and their qualitative counterpart as heard sounds in the soul. In Augustine's work there is a correspondence between various hierarchies of numerical systems, broadly speaking between material numbers and the

---

[133] VR 20; 40–42; 74; LA 3.42–43; *temporalis pulchritudo rebus decedentibus succedentibusque peragitur* [Temporal beauty is the result of the decline of things and their supersession, *Div quaest LXXXIII*, c. 44].

[134] VR 74.

[135] VR 75.

[136] LA 2.43.

[137] DO 1.24; S 7.14.

[138] *Cf.* the 'index generalis' of the Maurist edition (Migne, PL vol. 46, col. 464).

[139] Following the LXX: *et quaererem sapientiam et numerum* [and I would seek wisdom and number], Eccles 7.26. LA 2.24; 2.29, 30–31, 32.

numbers of the soul, but not between number and sound or number and colour. He does occasionally use the traditional definition of beauty as 'a correspondence combined with a certain sweetness of colours',[140] but he does not really make it his own. The reason for this peculiarity is to be sought less in his general Neo-Platonic approach than in a personal nervousness of Augustine's with regard to all sensible entities. He asks himself in the *Confessions* how he is to tear himself away from the spell of music, even of church music: it fans the flame of his devotion and touches the soul with 'some mysterious affinity', but, as sensual pleasure, must nonetheless be checked.[141] It is most revealing that in his treatise on music he deals only with one half of music, numerical rhythm, while melody is sent empty away. It only reappears in a lyrical and enthusiastic discussion of God's internal *melos*,[142] of a supernatural music which once again has nothing to do with Pythagorean music. His fundamental mistrust of the senses receives its most consistent metaphysical expression in his depreciation of the middle and mediating element of human and physical nature, the soul between body and mind, the imagination between the bodily senses and reason. (This will be discussed later.) This, the true seat of the aesthetic sense, because also the seat of the production of the world of images, is constantly accused by Augustine of untruth and falsehood, emptiness and pretence. And even though he does say on one occasion that 'what is of first importance is to know in itself the living nature which senses all this (the beauty of the world) and which on any account, since it gives life to the body, must be better than the body,'[143] the firm rejection of the senses and especially of the imagination continues to be a basic feature of his philosophical attitude. In terms of Plotinus' theory this is justified because the higher level

[140] *Ep* 3 *ad Nebrid* 4. But *cf.* also *De mus* 6.38. On the Stoic origin and wide currency of the formula and on its history, *cf.* H. Krug, *De pulchritudine divina* (1902); Svoboda, *op. cit.* pp. 53–54.

[141] *Conf* 10.49. On the psychological distraction from the contemplation of the eternal numbers caused by the different forms of sensuous rhythms and their pleasure *cf. De mus* 6.39–41.

[142] *Enarr in Ps* 41.9; 42.7.

[143] VR 52.

contains the goods of the lower eminently within itself and has no essential need of the latter in order to reproduce them in itself, but for a Christian incarnational and (so to say) resurrectional view this idea lacks certain necessary qualifications. It appears first, in an eschatological and theological context, at the end of the *City of God*, where it is said of the risen that they will see God with their glorified bodily eyes, not directly, since he is spirit, but also not indirectly in the way that we infer God from the order of the world, but in a similar way to that in which we, living among other living human beings who express (*exserere*) their life in vital movements, 'immediately *see*, and do not just believe, that they are alive'. In an analogous way, the transfigured universe and especially transfigured souls, our own and those of others, will be a direct expression of the living and all-controlling God.[144] However, this eschatological indication of imagination and sense comes too late to make up for the illusory status ascribed to sense on earth.

The only slight adjustment of the balance comes in the theological culmination of the system. For here the image character of substances is justified by reference to the original image in God himself, the Son who is identical with the Father in nature and who yet stands in relation to him as his image. But for this crowning idea, all the Platonism could only veer tragically between the mystical dissolution of all images in the imagelessness of unity and the aesthetic idolisation of finite form as it is worshipped and absolutised. The further Augustine penetrates into Scripture and theology, the more detailed and the richer become not only the figure of the Son as eternal wisdom and original likeness, through which and by participation in which all things can be traces and images of God,[145] but also the figure of the incarnate, humble and humiliated Christ, disfigured to the point where no image is left. The Incarnation is now no longer for him simply (Alexandrian) 'milk' instead of solid food, an introduction for 'children' and the 'immature'.[146]

---

[144] *De civ Dei* 22, c. 29.6.
[145] *De Gen ad litt liber imperfectus* 16.57.
[146] VR 45; 51; DO 2.27; LA 3.30.

Rather, just as he saw the temporal void as the medium of beauty, he now sees Christ's *kenosis* as the revelation of the beauty and the fulness of God: 'the path itself is beauty'.[147] All the inexhaustible wealth of Augustine's ideas about Christ, about the mystical Christ, about the kingdom of God on earth, about the humility of Christ and the Christian, about longing for God and the long pilgrimage towards God's light, is now permeated by a trembling and blazing rhythm of beauty which owes no more to the philosophy of numbers than the *Retractationes* allow it, namely, the role of a preliminary training which has to be abandoned again when the real work comes. And so even that 'hidden sanctuary' of the eternal numbers (*quasi cubile ac penetrale, quasi habitaculum quoddam sedemque numerorum,*[148] [*in*] *secretari veritatis*)[149] is drawn back up into heaven like the linen cloth in Peter's vision, and being swept up in ecstasy to the heavenly numbers gives way to the simple following of Christ.[150]

4. THE REALITY OF THE IMAGE

There runs through Augustine's thought the contradiction which, ultimately, is the contradiction of all Platonism. Regarded statically, it is a dualism of world and God, sense and mind, not mediated as in Aristotelianism, and yet it is at the same time a monistically descending outpouring of the One truth-and-beauty and a monistically ascending eros moving towards this One. What remains dualistic when static is, however, brought together when dynamic. Consequently, where Platonic and Augustinian thought loses its erotic dynamic it necessarily disintegrates into Cartesianism, Idealism and mathematicism. The fact that in Augustine the picture of the world does not fragment is due to the Platonic and Biblical enthusiasm of the heart, which brings together, not only in appearance but also in reality, what the schematism of the

[147] LA 2.45; *Enarr in Ps* 123.2.
[148] LA 2.30; DO 2.14.
[149] LA 2.42.   [150] LA 2.30.

thought very deliberately sets out to leave unconnected. It is enthusiasm which has to fill the theoretical gap, and it can only do this, to put it briefly, by looking at the world in an aesthetic way. Precisely because the world lacks the theoretical status of an image, it has paradoxically to be viewed aesthetically as a world of images, as an aesthetic world in the narrow sense. This paradox must be explained in more detail.

Since, in Platonic theory, there is no receptivity of the human mind to that which lies below it, the mind contains eminently, exactly, and as truth, that which is suggested inexactly, in rough transcription in the senses and the imagination.[151] No sensible circle attains the precision of the concept of the circle. The whole world of images therefore lacks truth. Nevertheless, whereas sense impressions are 'true' at least to the extent that they announce states of affairs in the material world (which in turn are only striving for unity in time and space), the internal image-world of the imagination—and so human art as part of its domain, and also metaphysics in so far as it is dependent on imagination and as it is un-Christian—is the source of all deception and the true *fabrica idolorum*. Naturally, Augustine knows that it is not the imagination which sins, but the free rational person, but the sin lies in taking the buffoonery of the imagination for truth and in becoming attached to it. The speculations of Manichaeism—ultimately on the same level as the sensual fantasies to which Augustine was attached in that period—were nothing other than the imagination become images,[152] 'the illusion created by the shadow-figures of the imagination'.[153]

As far as human arts are concerned, Augustine does want to distinguish fiction from lies; art is based on the former,[154] and it can be said that deception is the truth of art.[155] In this Augustine is more Platonic than Plotinus, who had tolerated art as the imitation of nature, since does not nature itself imitate the

---

[151] S 2.34: *vera figura in intellectu* [a true outline in the mind] as opposed to *phantasia sive phantasma, quam sibi fingit cogitatio* [a phantasy or phantasm produced by the imagination for itself].

[152] VR 96; cf. 68, 108.

[153] VR 40.

[154] S 1.16–18.   [155] S 2.18; 31.

Idea?[156] Plotinus sees the connection with the Ideal, Plato and Augustine the unreality of artistic images.[157] The roots of this rejection, particularly of the plastic arts (music seems to him more intellectual, closer to the order of the world) include a deep-seated and almost traditional Christian suspicion, and, not infrequently, Old Testament ideas (such as that the drive to produce images derives from the cult of the dead and leads from that to idolatry).[158] Whereas Augustine almost everywhere vigorously rejects the theatre, in *De vera religione* he develops a profound and illuminating theory about the pleasure contained in the movement between illusion and its unmasking ('getting behind it' to see 'how it's done') in theatrical performances, in conjuring displays and feats of dexterity.[159] But the pleasure of seeing through such performances ultimately rests on curiosity, which, as the *Confessions* show, is the opposite of true pleasure and intellectual rapture.[160] 'The attraction of the theatre and entertainment lasts only as long as we realise what truth is being compared to to make us laugh. And so we are refuted by our own judgment and out of our own mouths, since we simultaneously approve the one thing with our reason and pursue the other in our vanity.'[162] We should therefore 'banish ... the figments of our madness from the stage of reason' as a 'valueless and deceptive pastime' because 'they turn our whole life into an empty dream'. We should set out on the road from poetry to philosophy as on the path from appearance to being, a way Augustine describes in the little myth of the two birds Philocalia (love of beauty) and Philosophia (love of wisdom). Philocalia, unconscious of her origin, sits trapped in the cage of the earthly world, while Philosophia flies free and soars to heaven; she recognises her imprisoned sister, but can only rarely free her.[163] Suspicion of imagination made Augustine in *The City of God*

---

[156] *Enarr in Ps* 5.8; 1.

[157] *Div quaest LXXXIII* 78: the rejection of poetic fiction is very common in Augustine; *cf. De civ Dei* 2, c. 8; 2, c. 14.2; 4, c. 10.17, *etc.*

[158] *Sap* 14.15; *cf. Contra Faustum* 22.17.

[159] VR 94–95.

[160] *Conf* 10. (35) 55.

[161] VR 95.   [162] VR 98.

[163] *Contra acad* 2.7.

the final demolisher of the ancient myths;[164] but it also cast its shadow over his theology of mystical experience, in which he firmly and remorselessly demythologises all forms of 'manifestations', whether they be natural, praeternatural or supernatural, and reduces them to the same psychological level.[165] This theology continues to have very significant effects even in the eschatology of De Genesi ad litteram, where the damned finally lose possession of true being and are consequently hurled into the being-less world of the impressions of sense and imagination, which constitutes eternal hell (in this respect the pure opposite of the true eternity of heaven).[166]

The Platonic dualism between the higher real, intellectual world and the lower material world of appearance also has serious implications for the question of the status of earthly culture, the state and its order and authority. If for Augustine all genuine truth is transcendent and so determined by religion, any earthly truth which is indifferent to the connection with the living God can a priori only belong to the sphere of appearance. Long before the decisions of The City of God, Augustine takes it for granted that 'no true freedom' can prevail in this whole area (since such freedom can be set free only in a loving relationship with God).[167] The most that can exist is an apparent, civil and political freedom, although there is naturally nothing to stop the legislator of the earthly state from seeking advice on the framing and application of the temporal law from the eternal law.[168] Connected with this is the negative teaching of De magistro, according to which no pupil really learns from a human teacher but is stimulated by his words to find the truth in himself.[169]

And yet again the Platonism in Augustine's thought here should not be construed in terms of a vulgar dualism, as though the world were divided horizontally into two parts, the sphere

[164] Cf. esp. the chapters attacking the 'political theology' of Varro and the Roman state in general: De civ Dei 6, c. 5.3; 9, cs. 4ff.

[165] De Gen ad litt 12.49.

[166] Ibid. 12.61–63; VR 104–05.

[167] libertas, quae quidem nulla vera est, nisi beatorum et legi aeterni adhaerentium [a freedom, which, however, is no true freedom unless it is that of the blessed (i.e., the truly wise) and those who cling to the eternal law], LA 1.32; cf. 2.25f.

[168] VR 58; LA 1.15.

[169] De mag 39.

of the senses and of appearances and that of the intellect and truth. The true cause of the lower world's lack of being is merely that it is not understood and construed in terms of the upper, as is required for truth, for in fact the truth of being is not restricted to the upper world, but embraces the whole, though the whole as viewed from above. This true world consequently includes, not just the material, temporal and sensible as its emanation, but, as Augustine emphasises most forcefully against the Manichees, also sin, alienation and even the abandonment of hell. It is at this point that the great final vision comes, the vision which enabled Harnack to speak of Augustine's 'aesthetic optimism'.[170] It is a contemplation of the world-totality from the supreme vantage point of divine providence, which enables us to survey the 'whole pattern of the mosaic floor' and not just an isolated section.[171] It is the world seen in the light of the God 'through whom the universe, even with its left side, is complete' and 'who does not allow even the slightest discord to arise, since the less good is in harmony with the better'.[172] 'Just as in a painting the black becomes beautiful in the context of the whole, so too immutable divine providence presents this whole contest for our instruction', to show us that even 'the imperfect' contributes 'to the perfection of the whole', to 'the beauty of the universe'.[173] It is mistaken to argue here that in that case sin was willed by God 'because without it an element of perfection would have been lacking',[174] or to object that it would have been a simple matter for God to create us sinless and perfect from the beginning,[175] mistaken because sin depends on the free will of the creature, not on God. However, God is powerful enough to find a place for immanent disorder in his transcendent order and to fit it into the higher harmony. Augustine has to press his argument against the Manichees into the finest points of detail, and, tentatively but also firmly, he makes no exception for the sufferings of the irrational creation,

[170] *Lehrbuch der Dogmengeschichte* (3rd ed.), vol. III, p. 106.
[171] DO 1.2; cf. *De civ Dei* 16, c. 8.2. Someone who is within an encompassing order as himself a part of it cannot get a view of the whole, or only with difficulty: *De mus* 6.28–30; VR 43.
[172] S 1.2.   [173] VR 76.   [174] LA 3.26.
[175] *Ibid.* 24.

not even for the sufferings of innocent children,[176] for suicide nor finally for the existence of hell.[177] The same images which Plotinus and Origen had used to justify the existence of the ugly and base, of physical evil and finally of medicinal punishments are extended by Augustine to moral evil and the eternal punishment of pure justice.[178] The weighting of the formulation varies between the simple statement that God's unshakable order includes equally good and evil,[179] that even lies have to serve truth,[180] that the 'rightness' of God's love and of its order does not become a punishing justice of itself, but as a result of human sin, in order to remain faithful to itself,[181] and that in the process the faithful human beings have to fill the gap left by the fallen angels,[182] and the much more extreme statement that beauty even requires its opposite,[183] and that in the harmonious universe no level can be omitted.[184] The darkness in the world 'seasons' it, just as a solecism in a high-flown speech provides a 'highly pleasurable spice'.[185] This slight variation in formulation between the assertion of the ethical non-necessity of sin and its consequences and that of its aesthetic necessity is not just important for Augustine alone; its significance for the millennium which follows him can hardly be overestimated. It will be this aesthetic justification, and not primarily Scripture, which will be the source of the shadows which from Gottschalk onwards darken the middle ages and, from Calvin and Jansenius, the Christianity of the modern period. We can say that Augustine's concluding aesthetic theodicy represents a two-fold reduction of the Biblical data, first by interpreting its existential statements in aesthetic and systematic terms and again because this interpretation, in which immanent evil, considered transcendently, becomes good, is then used to close a gap left open by philosophy. The Greek Fathers, who follow Plotinus and Proclus, never opened up the abysses in the same way (on

[176] LA 3.68f.   [177] LA 3.20f.   [178] LA 3.27.

[179] DO 1.16–17.   [180] DO 2.11–13.   [181] DO 2.23.

[182] LA 3.35.

[183] DO 1.18; 2.13; cf. De civ Dei 11.18.

[184] LA 3.24–25.

[185] DO 2.13; on the aesthetic justification of evil, cf. also Enarr in Ps 7.19; Ep 140.4.

the one hand Manichaean, on the other markedly Western) as Augustine, who then, as a last resort, has to call in the Eastern theodicy and throw it like a cloak over the tragedy. The return of the Italian and German idealists (from Ficino via Bruno to Hegel) to the pure contemplation of Plotinus provides, for the Christian, no escape from the dilemmas of Augustinian aesthetics; only a deeper Biblical theology promises a solution, and this can naturally not be a renewed, still less a higher, 'systematics'.

5. THE DYNAMIC AND DEVELOPMENT OF THE IDEA OF BEAUTY

The dilemma we have outlined is not Augustine's last word. It is possible to be true to him without accepting the tragic consequences of his static model of the world, since all that is really positive in his thought is contained in the dynamic of the light of truth and love: this is a dynamic which both creates connections and is itself creative, a light which not only combines the separated fragments but even creates them in order to combine them. It would thus be a mistake to take the harmony of the world, which is built on fixed numerical relationships in space and time, as an ultimate, static entity from the passive contemplation of which the contemplating mind receives aesthetic sensations. On the contrary, for Augustine this beauty itself is only a dynamic striving towards a unity which can never be attained,[186] but which at least is intellectual (and ultimately divine) and which thus makes it possible ontically to transcend numerical beauty.

Our original starting-point was the intellectual light which is primarily the light of God himself and secondarily the light of created mind and as such truth itself. 'That by which you recognise that these things are not the true things is the true light.'[187] This light of God, which is the simplest of all light, original truth, is also original beauty: but, if so, what is its

[186] VR 60–61; LA 2.22.
[187] VR 64.

relation to the plurality of number? Surely it is in the search for this relationship of light and number that the key to Augustine's whole aesthetic must lie, assuming that such a key exists at all? If it does not, his whole religious aesthetic is open to the usual criticism that the concept and domain of beauty in the strict sense—the harmony of number in the cosmos—is determined by a transcendental ideal. It is not clear how beauty in the strict sense can be attributed to this; to do so nevertheless is the unscientific dogmatism of mystical enthusiasts. The path by which Augustine demonstrates the unity of his aesthetic must therefore be retraced step by step and shown to be a Christian and a theological path.

1. That we love only what is beautiful was self-evident in the ancient world. It was a belief which Augustine took as the basis of his argument as early as *De pulchro et apto* and again in *De musica*.[188] But if the beautiful is what is rhythmical and harmonious, how can we love the simple beauty of light? The first answers which suggest themselves incorporate simple light into the numerical network of relations itself. The senses, and even the soul itself, derive pleasure from functioning: the soul loves to receive what is appropriate to it, while rejecting and fleeing unsuitable sensations.[189] But the action of light on the eye—as Basil, making use of Aristotelian and Stoic ideas (Posidonius), had already remarked in his commentary on the creation story—is beneficial. This assumed harmony between light and the sense organ of the soul is itself based on a further Stoic assumption which Augustine also adopted: in the eye, he says, there is a sort of light-like matter, in the ear, an airlike, in the nose a steamlike, in the mouth a moist sort, in the fingertips an earthlike sort.[190] This is a Stoic variant of the general ancient theory that like is known by like, Stoic because a background assumption is the pantheistic conception of the intellectual and material world-soul.

By contrast with this horizontal parallelism, the Augustinian

[188] *De mus* 6.38.
[189] Svoboda, *Esthétique*, pp. 37f., 80.
[190] *De mus* 6.10, possibly taken from Varro; *cf. De civ Dei* 7, c. 23.1.
[191] *De mus* 6.2f.

movement does not begin until the point where the phenomenon of number, as outlined above, forms itself into a hierarchy
and at the same time becomes interiorised. Its only element of
intellectual originality (after the first five books of the *De musica*,
which draw on Varro) is the psychological theory of numbers.
According to this, numbers lead upwards in stages from the
'material' numbers in the external object, via the rhythms of the
senses and the rhythms of the memory to the bodily rhythms
actively produced by the soul, such as breath and heartbeat, and
the rhythm of the *judicium sensibile*, which for its part is
subordinate to the judgment of the mind and the intellectual
rhythms which God inspires in it.[191] Although Augustine gives
it no special weight—and this is a matter of regret—the
physiological rhythm of heart and breath seems particularly
interesting here as a biological phenomenon expressive of the
soul; it would have been a point which would have given a
purchase to the Aristotelian and Thomistic idea of the unity of
sensible and intellectual worlds.

2. Augustine, however, develops this idea of the interior-
isation and consequent simplification of rhythm in another
passage, where he applies his doctrine of rhythm to the soul and
its virtues. The virtues are the way in which the soul gives itself
back to itself,[192] returns from alienation from self to authenticity
and subjectivity by being *transformed into its own likeness*. And
that is what virtue is, the coming together of life in unity and
likeness as it comes to agree in all respects with reason (*aequalitas
vitae rationi undique consentientis*).[193] Virtue is thus the eurhythmy
of the soul, goodness and beauty at once ('everything in the soul
that is beautiful is virtue').[194] Augustine demonstrates this in
respect of the individual virtues, especially of justice and
wisdom. Justice is the order and rightness of the soul's direction;
it 'consists in loving the better more and the worse less'[195] and so
'giving to each his own'.[196] 'For we say that justice is nothing

[191] QA 55.
[193] QA 27.
[194] *Enarr in Ps* 58.18.
[195] VR 93.
[196] DO 1.19; 2.22.

other than equity (*aequitas*), and equity seems to get its name from a sort of equality (*aequalitas*).'[197] Such subjectivity as it comes to itself is, however, itself inner light (the great Eastern theme from Plotinus to Gregory of Nyssa, from Evagrius to Symeon), of which it is sufficiently clear that for Augustine it is only light by virtue of its transcendent and transcendental relation to God's eternal light: as the rhythm of the process whereby created unity, by gradually simplifying itself, comes more and more to resemble the uncreated absolute unity, in which every attribute is identical with the substance. 'For everything predicated of God is himself. In God power is not one thing and wisdom another, courage one thing and justice or chastity another. Whichever of these you predicate of God, it makes no difference, and you do not predicate them according to its degree of dignity because they are all things of the souls which as it were that light envelops, making their attributes stand out, rather as when the sunlight rises over the material world. When it sets, all objects become the same colour or, better, colourless. If that light lights them up, it sprinkles them with different kinds of brightness according to their constitution.'[198] What Augustine is trying to convey through the image is the mystery by which every soul which unifies itself in an attempt to approach God's unity receives from God its unity and at the same time its relative uniqueness and personality. God, as the only unity, is at once the giver of unity and uniqueness; since, as the absolute light, by his light–giving action he both creates unity and bestows individuality, he is at once creative justice and absolute beauty: *justa pulchritudo*.[199] And the soul's rhythmic entering into relationship with this light is not distinct from its simplification; in fact it is what makes simplification possible. Here, then, qualitative number and light (to which the primary 'colours' always belong) have simply become one. It is in this realm that are heard the 'inner melodies'

---

[197] QA 15. The beauty of justice is mentioned in Plato (*Laws* 9.859 D) and Plotinus (*Enn* 1.6, 4), but the Christian fathers also praise the beauty of the virtues (Basil, *In Hex* 3.8; Ambrose, *De offic* 1.67; 2.64).

[198] *Sermo* 341, n. 8.

[199] [a just beauty], QA 80.

(*melodia interior*)[200] whose praises Augustine sings with such longing; that there can be seen 'a certain light, a certain voice, a certain fragrance, a certain food, a certain embrace',[201] 'the beauty above all beauty',[202] the 'indescribable beauty',[203] 'the true, unique beauty, beauty itself',[204] seen moreover with an insight which is at once enthusiastic and totally lucid, 'philosophical'.

3. This divine beauty is in Greek philosophy the 'captivating' beauty of that intellectual light which itself makes everything light (*lucifica lux*),[205] which confers truth and existence on everything. This light's lack of envy makes it supremely lovable and ethically most worthy of imitation; already in Plato it is what provokes the supreme human attitude, eros. When, in Christianity, this overflowing light names and reveals itself as freedom and love, creaturely love for this God is once more drawn more deeply into the rhythm of unity. This is where the fundamental Augustinian category of *frui* is to be located; here, in relation to God, the relation to truth becomes a relation to love, and this grows into the settled and blossoming enjoyment not granted in one's relations with fellow creatures in the world of original sin. The appropriate relation to a being in the world, subordinate to the soul, is the sobriety of *uti*, right use, but the movement of *frui* goes inwards and upwards to God: *veritas sapit*.[206] Augustine's anxious caution about the sensual and this-worldly enjoyment of beauty cannot therefore be described in the strict sense as asceticism, since it is no more than a preparation for true enthusiasm. That God's offer of himself for the definitive enjoyment of the purified soul is only eschatological may not yet have been so clear to the young Augustine as to the older, but that is not the issue here, since even the God of the suffering Son of man and of the Church is

---

[200] *Conf* 4, c. 15.27.
[201] *Conf* 10, c. 6.8.
[202] *Conf* 3, c. 6.10.
[203] *Enchir* 5; *De civ Dei* 9, c. 22; *Sermo* 12.4, 4.
[204] S 1.14; DO 1.26.
[205] *Contra Faust Man* 22.8–9; *In Joh tr* 14.1.
[206] *Conf* 4, c. 12.18.

never present for the believing soul in any other form than in the relationship of *frui*.

4. The culmination of this equation of number and light, however, is the mystery of the transcendent Trinity which is nevertheless immanent in the whole world of creation and redemption. In the mystery of the *lumen de lumine* which is constituted by subsistent love in its union with the Father, the relatedness (of the persons) is crowned as identity (of nature). Light is now no longer just the interiority of absolute subjectivity, become one with its being; it is now absolute love, which transcends and flows over into the world only because it is already love in itself. Augustine's psychological images of the Trinity in the created soul, which cannot be expounded in detail here, form the conclusion not just of his metaphysics, but, expressly, of his aesthetics. It is only in the light of such considerations that the beauty of all being is fully justified, because here for the first time the inner vitality and dimensionality of being as such fully emerges and gives being the fulness and richness which neither the hierarchical pyramid alone nor the dynamic of eros alone was able to give it. Here also the defects of Platonic-Augustinian essentialism are to some extent counterbalanced, since though the trinitarian structure is also treated as a question of form, indeed of the *image*-character of beings, it nonetheless reaches, in intention, the ground of being itself. And when Augustine, in the last book of *De Trinitate*, rubs out again the pictures he has drawn and gives the last word to the greater unlikeness, this is, after all, inevitable since we are dealing with the God *qui scitur nesciendo*;[207] indeed, we can say that a glimmer of infinity and unintelligibility thereby falls on the image itself.

5. It would have been strange if the effects of this exploration of the *mysterium* of the Trinity had not been felt in Augustine's theological aesthetics; they are visible in his sermons, the *Enarrationes, Sermones* and the *Tractatus in Johannem*. God's eternal beauty becomes a man, enters the fallen, alienated world

---

[207] [is known by not being known] DO 2.44.

of space and time; it appears as humility, veiled. Is Christ beautiful? Is the category 'beautiful' applicable at all to this manifestation of eternal beauty? Two scriptural texts seem to conflict in the writings of the Fathers, the saying from the Psalms (45.2), which greets him as the fairest of the sons of men, and the one in Isaiah which denies him any beauty or attractiveness (53.2).[208] Relying on the former, Chrysostom[209] and Jerome[210] assert Christ's physical beauty, while Justin,[211] Clement of Alexandria,[212] Tertullian[213] and Ambrose[214] deny it. Origen argues that Christ was without beauty for the unpurified, the 'fleshly', but to the purified and 'spiritual' (at least when he himself wished, as on Tabor) he could appear in his eternal beauty.[215] Augustine puts this idea, which is typical of Origen's approach, into his own idiom: a person must love Christ and have pure eyes to see his inner spiritual beauty,[216] because for those who stand at a distance, and certainly for his persecutors, he is veiled to the point of ugliness.[217] But his veiling of his beauty was not just inspired by his wish to be like us, who are ugly, in all things, but also by his desire to make the ugly beautiful by his love (*qui et foedos dilexit, ut pulchros faceret*).[218] With this statement Augustine moves away from his first assertion that only beauty is lovable. This Platonic statement, whose audacity culminates in the idea that the lover, the eros of beauty, need not himself be beautiful, gives place to the Christian view that love for beauty in Christ creatively produces beauty. How could it not when the love of Christ is the manifestation of the all-creative divine love? This is argued at length in the exposition of the first letter of John: ' "Let us love one another because he first loved us." He loved us and

---

[208] Cf. *DThC* VIII.1, col. 1153.

[209] *In Mt* 27.2.

[210] *Ep* 65.8.

[211] *Dial* 14.8.

[212] *Paed* 3, 3.3.

[213] *Adv Jud* 14; *De carne Christi* 9.

[214] *In Luc* 7.12; 183.

[215] Origen, *Serm in Mt* 35 (Klost.-Benz. 11.65).

[216] *Enarr in Ps* 127.8.

[217] *Enarr in Ps* 43.16; 44.14; 103, I.5; *Sermo* 138.6.

[218] *In Joh tr* 10.13.

gave us the power to love him. Through love we became beautiful. What does a crippled man with a hideous face do if he loves a beautiful woman? What does an ugly, crippled, dark-haired woman do if she loves a handsome man? Can she somehow become beautiful by loving? Can the man become well-proportioned by loving? Will he wait until beauty comes to him? If he waits he will become old as well, and uglier than ever. There is no escape; there is no good advice you can give him. But our souls, brothers, are ugly because of their wrong-doing: by loving God they become beautiful. What sort of a love is it that makes the lover beautiful? But God is always beautiful, never deformed, never liable to change. He, the beautiful one, first loved us, and what were we like when he loved us? Ugly, deformed. And it was not to leave us ugly, but to transform us and turn us from ugly creatures to beautiful ones. But how do we become beautiful? By loving him back, him who is eternally beautiful. The more love grows in you, the more beauty grows, since love is itself the beauty of the soul. Listen to Paul: "God showed his love for us in that while we were yet sinners Christ died for us," the just man for the unjust, the beautiful for the ugly. By taking flesh, he took to himself, as it were, your ugliness, to make himself like you and suited to you, and to spur you to love inner beauty. Where do we find it said that Jesus was beautiful? "You are the fairest of the sons of men; grace is poured upon your body" (Ps 45.2). Where do we find it said that he was deformed? Ask Isaiah: "And we looked at him, and he had no form nor beauty" (Is 53.2). They are like two flutes with different sounds, but the one spirit blows in both, the one fills both, and together they produce no dis-cord.'[219] Here too, everything follows the path of love which leads inwards. 'Christ's beauty is all the more lovable and wondrous the less it is physical beauty.'[220] In the *Enarrationes* and the sermons the theme is firmly switched to that of marriage. The Bride-Church is the ugly woman who is endowed with beauty by the love of the Bridegroom;[221] for her, who was ugly,

[219] *In 1 Joh tr* 9.9.
[220] *De civ Dei* 17, c. 16.1.
[221] *Enarr in Ps* 44.3.

he made himself ugly too out of love (*deformis factus est*) 'for he emptied himself and took the form of a slave (Phil 2.6) so that the people rightly shook their heads at the sight of the cross and said, "Is that the Son of God?".'[222] But the Bride becomes beautiful by confessing her guilt; the psalmist mentions *confessio et pulchritudo* together.[223] Christ is thus the ugly root from which the beautiful tree of the Church rises,[224] and the ugliness of earthly birth is the condition for the glory of the resurrection.[225] Christ loved ugly sinners to make them lovable.[226]

What needed to be done, and what Augustine, once he became a bishop, could no longer do, was to revise his early aesthetics on the basis of these new principles or—since not much in it could be altered—to let the new christological principles work themselves out in it in all directions. The crucial area for this, of course, is eschatology, and Augustine himself was anxious to see development here. Eschatology—and for him that means the resurrection of the body—is the only place in his theology where man is safe from the fear of the *posse peccare*. The Greeks regarded the end as a return to the beginning; Origen, in his early systematics, did not shrink from including the original *posse peccare* in the eschatological situation; Augustine, however, from the beginning saw, as Kierkegaard later even more sharply, a shadow in the possibility of sin included in the paradisial state, despite that state's excellence; the good beginning hides uncertainty and indifference.[227] Only at the resurrection will the difference between *frui* and *uti* be abolished, will 'enjoyment' be permitted to include not just the spiritual God but also his material creation, in which he will henceforth be openly reflected. Only then will the analogical hierarchies of rhythmical systems be

---

[222] *Enarr in Ps* 103, I.4–6.

[223] [confession and beauty], *ibid.* and *in Ps* 95.6–7.

[224] *Sermo* 44.1f.; *cf. Serm.* 62.8; 95.4; 138.6f.; 285.6.

[225] *Sermo* 254.5.

[226] *Sermo* 142.5. Similarly, it is necessary to have spiritual eyes to see the real beauty of the Church, the beauty, for example of the martyrs running with blood, the beauty of faith and all the other virtues of the soul. *Enarr in Ps* 33, I.6; 33, II.15; 64.8.

[227] LA 3.64–65; 71.

able to vibrate through the whole, as was plainly the creator's intention. And if Augustine all along admitted that a disinterested aesthetic contemplation even of material beauty, its form and colour, was possible, and certainly distinct from concupiscence,[228] if even now during our contemplation of the divine things bodily rhythms often vibrate harmlessly in sympathy, how much more after the resurrection, 'when we shall see the one God and truth made plain, will we feel the rhythms with which we animate our bodies without disquiet and with full joy?'[229] Until then, however, it is none other than the virtue of discipline, imposing as it does a rhythmic harmony (*temperantia*), which draws us away from the love of lower beauty, and courage which enables us to rise above it.[230] But the extent to which the action of the soul's vibrations on the body and its beauty is originally and eschatologically the natural state is shown by the statement that what prevented Paul, when caught up into the third heaven, from seeing God with final abandonment (like the angels in heaven) was the fact that his soul in one final point was still scattered and disturbed by the defective harmonisation of his body.[231] This is a notable victory of Christian thought over Platonism, and is confirmed at the end of *The City of God*, where (as we have already seen) the bodily senses are promised a share in the soul's vision of God. Nor is it pure souls, but risen human beings, which are called to fill the gap left by the fallen angels, by 'contemplating the eternal artist who has formed all things in measure and number and weight'.[232]

---

[228] *Contra Julianum* 4.65–66; 75; cf. *De civ Dei* 22.24.

[229] *De mus* 6.49.

[230] *Ibid.* 50.

[231] *De Gen ad litt* 12.68: *quia inest ei (animae) quidam appetitus corpus administrandi; quo appetitu retardatur quodammodo ne tota intentione pergat in illud summum coelum, quamdiu non subest corpus, cujus administratione appetitus ille conquiescat* [There is in it (the soul) a sort of appetite for administering the body, and this appetite holds it back, as it were, from concentrating all its energy on entering that highest heaven, until the body no longer exists to be administered and satisfy that appetite].

[232] *Enchir* c. 29.

6. HARMONY AND ANALOGY

The unique balance between the pathos of rhythmical proportion and the pathos of infinity which dominates Augustine's
aesthetic theology does not derive simply from the encounter of
a burning African soul with the culture and conceptuality of
Hellas and Rome; this balance of apparent irreconcilables is
fought for and finally achieved in the inner battle of his
Christian and personal existence. And if nevertheless Platonic
and even Manichaean dualisms and personal rejections of certain
levels threaten to cloud the harmony (and in certain forms of
Augustinianism they have produced terrible destruction), in
spite of everything harmony remains predominant. In
Augustine—as again later in Pascal, Soloviev and Newman—
the certainty of the ultimate rightness of the *vera religio* does not
rest in mere intuitions of heart and conscience or of faith, but
resides in a seeing of the rightness which in the broad sense must
be called an aesthetic vision and yet which stands up to rational
examination and which can even be made visible to the person
who purifies his mind's eye. The doctrine of hierarchical
number, the highest level of which rests in God and forms the
ideal world of the Logos, is the clear expression of this
conviction. This hierarchy cannot be translated into the
quantitative terms of a mathematical picture of the world (in
which identity, and no longer analogy, would have to
predominate) without first banishing the soul of
Augustinianism. On the other hand, neither can it be portrayed
as a mystical monism, because Augustine was constantly aware
of the always greater dissimilarity between God and his
creatures, and indeed right to the end (in the struggle against the
Pelagians) continued to become increasingly aware of it. Once
these dangers are excluded, his hierarchical world-picture
becomes a secure and open framework within which a whole
Christian millennium was able to develop the rhythms of its
thought and life in all directions.

The harmony between God and the world exists as a result of
this relationship of the original numbers, which are displayed in
the being and nature of everything in the world, though always
only in approximation and by way of participation. It exists also

at a higher level because even the infinite God is not without measure,[233] but has been fully measured by the Son as his exact image and because this point in God is the source of the possibility and reality of a measured world. 'First comes the form of all things, which, without any dissimilarity, is the image and likeness of unity ... and completely fills the unity from which it derives so that the other things which exist, to the degree that they are like the One, can come into being through this form.'[234] Image, word and light of the world are thus one and the same.[235] And to prevent this image and emanation from being dissipated into infinity as in Plotinus, in Christianity the relation between Father and Son is completed in the Holy Spirit to give an eternal, infinite, but personal and free 'form', which bestows freedom and selfhood on the created person as a 'gift'.[236]

There is therefore not just the analogy of divine and created being, but also that of divine free personal being and created free personal being. This is where the Biblical and Christian content bursts out of the Platonic frame. God is the one who freely chooses; man is the one who freely ratifies or rejects this choice. And these personal relations do not form a higher storey above natural relations, because the natures themselves are personal and free, and God's decisions always express his essence, just as all human and historical decisions always coincide with the laws and rules which govern the nature of man and the world. God's law is both positive and natural. Man is never rewarded or punished purely from outside, but by the operation of his nature itself.[237] Augustine therefore attaches vital importance to the harmony between providence and personal development. His thesis is that nothing is guided by God purely externally without at the same time being guided internally,[238] though this involves him in a much more audacious bridging operation than the one required of the Stoic and Plotinian doctrine of providence. The *dispensatio temporalis* of providence is described with

---

[233] VR 81.

[234] *Ibid.*; *cf.* 66. This is where the final answer is given to the question *quemadmodum sit anima similis Deo, cum Deum a nullo factum esse credamus* [how the soul is like God since we believe that God was not made by anyone]. QA 3.

[235] *Ibid.* 66.   [236] VR 112.   [237] *Cf.* LA 1.31.

[238] LA 3.31.

almost organic categories chosen to suit the development and
education of man and the human race, with the final unity
between natural and supernatural order and control provided
once more by aesthetic categories.[239]

Here Augustine goes back to the aesthetics of the Christian
era for which Irenaeus laid the foundations and extends it by
integrating the periods of personal life into the massive construction of the ages of salvation history. 'The scale shows, for
anyone who takes the trouble to examine it, the significance of
the intervals of beauty and appropriateness which seem to be as
it were simply scattered through the universe. . . . Sacrifice, as
prescribed by God, was appropriate for the earliest periods, but
now it is no longer appropriate since God has ordained something else to be appropriate for this period. He knows much
better than man what is suited to each period and what it needs,
what he should bestow, add, take away, withdraw, encourage
or check. He is the unchanging working for the changing. As
creator he also guides the ages until the beauty of the universe,
whose individual parts consist of things appropriate to each
period, combines in the great song of an incomparable
composer: *velut magnum carmen ineffabilis modulationis.*'[240] So it is
an idle question why Christ appeared so late. The answer runs:
'Because all beauty derives from the supreme beauty which is
God, but the beauty of the ages from the appropriateness of the
sequence of things. Even in the individual human life each age,
from childhood to old age, has its particular beauty. How stupid
therefore would be a person who wished that man, who is
subject to time, should always be young—they would be
missing the other beauties which succeed each other in due
order in the other ages. And it would be just as stupid to long for
the whole human race to be the same age. Mankind as a total
man also has its tides.'[241] Number and beauty thus rule even the
apparent void of time.

Once this is seen, the relationships and analogies within the
universe will, despite all the gaps, no longer be difficult to see.

[239] VR 48.
[240] *Ep 138 ad Marcell* 5.
[241] *Div quaest* LXXXIII c. 44; cf. *Contra epist Man* 47.

Those between soul and body are created by the system of bodily and mental rhythms, which are connected by physiological ones. There is a closer relationship between bodily organs and the organs of sense, between sense and memory, between the soul which is linked (in whatever way) to the physical elements and the soul as pure spirit. Where the relationships in Augustine are not relationships of information, and so of expression, they are still hierarchical relationships of inclusion and control, which often strain the analogy but never to breaking point. They may have a real existence, but this does not mean that they will necessarily be seen; the image does not force a vision of the essential form on a person, although that form alone makes it intelligible. The beauty of the body does not force people to notice the beauty of the soul, though the former derives totally from the latter.[242] Only the person who already enjoys the spiritual vision of the higher realm, or finds that he has it unconsciously 'buried' in him and 'digs it out', can see,[243] looking down from above, where the image is pointing. Philocalia sits imprisoned; beauty alone cannot fly up to the true and living God. If Augustine regards all 'love of beauty' (as an ultimate) as pagan, we can nevertheless say that he also regards all objective beauty in nature or mind as consciously or unconsciously Christian, and believes that only a Christian aesthetics can be true. Plato and Plotinus may have said amazing things about beauty, 'but it does not immediately follow from the fact that what they said was true that they really knew what they were talking about.'[244] Truth in any area exists only when a person looks up from below and penetrates to the one true, living God. Art is thus either untrue, where the light does not penetrate to the higher realm, or it receives truth by looking down from above through God. In this vision, which is at once religious and aesthetic, the character of appearance and emptiness which all beautiful things necessarily retain without the God who is disappears, and they come to share in the reality of his ordering of the world. In the kingdom of being there are

[242] De Gen contra Man 1.43; Mor eccl 1.7.
[243] QA 5.
[244] S 1.9.

thus only two movements, that upwards towards truth (*caritas*)
and that downwards from truth towards appearance (*cupiditas*):
all being in time and history is tied to these two. Nothing else in
world history, salvation history or Church history interests
Augustine. It is a constant astonishment to find how much *The
City of God*, which laid the foundations of Western philosophy
of history, is an essentially unhistorical work, original and
creative only in those places where it abstracts the eternally
unchanging existential conditions of historical existence from
the historical process. Not even the great aesthetic turning-point
of Christian salvation history, the dialectic of the Testaments,
receives full justice from Augustine, since from Abel to the last
day the kingdom of God is always present, veiled, unrecognised, both before and after Christ, but present. In
Augustine everything becomes transparent; through the flow of
history he perceives always the relation between time and
eternity, the pilgrimage through the night of faith, hope and
love.

DENYS

1. THE PHENOMENON

With Denys we have a unique case in theology, indeed in all intellectual history. A man of the foremost rank and of prodigious power hid his identity not only from centuries of credulity but also from the critical acumen of the modern period, and precisely through that concealment exercised his influence. That for our modern, and above all German, scholarly world is unforgiveable. After their tank-formations have laid waste his garden, there is for them not a blade of grass left: all that remains is PSEUDO-, written in bold letters, and underlined with many marks of contempt. Not only is he branded as a forger, but, with a reference to his dependence on Plotinus[1] and Proclus,[2] any originality of thought is stripped from him. Indeed, scholars declare, what has real substance in the Neo-Platonists is with him detached and without any proper foundation,[3] so that in the end he stands forth as a wretched mongrel:[4] a corpse beneath the triumphal car of modern philology, which by the same token and without noticing it also discredits his commentators, the greatest minds of late Antiquity, of the Middle Ages, of the Renaissance and even of the Baroque period.[5] This explains why in Germany

---

[1] H. F. Müller, *Dionysios, Proklos, Plotinos. Ein historischer Beitrag zur neuplatonischen Philosophie* (BGPhMa XX, 3–4, 2nd ed., Münster, 1926).

[2] Hugo Koch, *Pseudo-Dionysius Areopagita in seinen Beziehungen zum Neuplatonismus und Mysterienwesen* (Mainz., 1900). (For Koch's earlier writings, see Völker's bibliography.) J. Stiglmair, SJ: *Der Neuplatoniker Proclus als Vorlage des sogenannten Dionysius Areopagita in der Lehre vom Übel.* (Hist. Jhb. d. Görresges. 16, Munich, 1895). Further details of Stiglmair's work in Völker's bibliography.

[3] E. von Ivánka, 'Inwieweit ist Pseudo-Dionysius Neuplatoniker?', *Scholastik* (1956), 393ff. (reprinted in his *Plato Christianus* [1964] 262–289).

[4] For different, more recent judgements of this sort see Walther Völker's introduction to his book, *Kontemplation und Ekstase bei Pseudo-Dionysius Areopagita* (Wiesbaden, 1958).

[5] On the commentaries, commentators and translators and their history, see the many works of G. Théry (listed by Roques), and then Ph. Chevallier (and

there has been scarcely any theological work on Denys since the researches of Koch and Stiglmair,[6] whereas today France, in continuation of the great Catholic tradition, produces not only distinguished tools for research and critical editions[7] but also, leaving on one side the question of authorship, has devoted itself to serious theological research.[8] It is a pity that since Koch and Stiglmair, who established the date of the composition of the *Corpus Areopagiticum* as between 480 and 510, there have been

others), *Dionysiaca*, 2 vols. (Paris 1937 and 1950), in which all the Latin translations are printed line by line with the Greek text and are discussed in the introduction. The first detailed examination of the whole influence of Denys in the East and the West can be found in *DSp*, art. Denys l'Aréopagite (many contributors), vol. 3 (1954), 244–429.

[6] Exceptions to this are the three scholars: E. v. Ivánka, who has concerned himself with the proper relationship to the sources (bibliography in Roques, to which should be added the article mentioned in n. 3 and the selection of translations, *Von der Namen zum Unnennbaren* [Einsiedeln, 1958]); O. Semmelroth, SJ, who has wrestled with the philosophical and theological structure of his thought in seven articles (especially in *Schol*, 1949 to 1954); and Walther Völker, who in his unwearying studies of the ethics, ascetics and mysticism of the Alexandrine and Cappadocian Fathers has now reached Denys and applied to him the method thus developed (see n. 4). Though very worthy, none of these works has really succeeded in infusing any new life into the figure of the Areopagite.

[7] The already mentioned *Dionysiaca* of Chevallier contains, beside the synopsis of the translations, an index of Greek and Latin words. Something similar, but more convenient, was produced at about the same time by A. van den Daele, SJ, *Indices Pseudo-Dionysiani* (Louvain, 1941). After protracted preparations (see Roques' introduction) *Sources Chrétiennes* have been able to begin a critical edition. The first volume has already appeared: *La Hiérarchie Céleste* (*SC* 58, 1958) with an introduction by René Roques, critical text by Günther Heil, and translation and notes by M. de Gandillac. The last mentioned had already in 1943 (Ed. Montaigne, Aubier) brought out a complete translation (not indeed unexceptionable, but very readable).

[8] The most important theologically constructive works are those of V. Lossky, 'La notion des analogies chez Denis le Pseudo-Aréopagite', *AHDL* 5 (1930), 279–309, and 'La théologie négative dans la doctrine de D.', *RSPhTh* 28 (1939), 204–221; of H. Ch. Puech, 'La ténèbre mystique chez le Ps.-D. et dans la tradition patristique', *EtCarm* 23 (1938), 33–53; and of René Roques, *L'univers Dionysien, structure hiérarchique du monde selon le Ps.-D.* (Paris, 1954), which contains a bibliography of his other writings up to 1954. Roques' important short article, 'De l'implication des méthodes théologiques chez le Ps.-D.', *RAM* 30 (1954), 268–274, is among the most significant work that has been done on Denys in modern times.

recently fantastic and indefensible attempts at redating that are scarcely worth the trouble of refutation.[9] All these untenable hypotheses are signs of a certain spiritual 'colour blindness' which prevents them, for all their individual scholarship (which Stiglmair, Pera, Honigmann and the rest doubtless have), from grasping the general flow of the Areopagitic handwriting. That goes especially for their attempts to identify him with personalities otherwise already well-known (such as Severus of Antioch): as if a Severus (or a Peter the Fuller) could have 'on the side' worn Denys' mask too, or *vice versa*: as if the writer of the CD[10] could conceivably also have been someone other than himself, or have written another style than his own![11]

[9] For a general view of these theses: Stiglmair (Severus of Antioch), Schepens (time of Athanasius, Egyptian), Quadri (an Egyptian friend of Apollinaris), Pera (a disciple of Basil), Elorduy (Ammonius Saccas), Honigmann (Peter the Iberian), and their refutation, see Völker, *op. cit.* 5–11, and Roques' introduction to the new edition of the *Celestial Hierarchy*. For an account of more recent attempts and a critique, see Jean-Michel Hornus, 'Les recherches Dionysiennes de 1955 à 1960', *RHPhR* (1961), 22–81. The most recent hypothesis has been advanced by Utto Riedinger, OSB, 'Petros der Walker von Antiochia als Verfasser der pseudo-dionysischen Schriften', *SJP* (1961/2), 135–156.
    A critical account of all the recent literature on Denys can be found in: Jean-Michel Hornus, 'Les recherches récentes sur le Ps.-D. l'Aréopagite', *RHPhR* 35 (1955), 404–448; *cf.* also Eugenio Corsini, 'La questione areopagitica, Contributi alla cronologia dello Pseudo-Dionigi', *AAST* 93 (1958–9), 1–100.

[10] CD = *Corpus* of the Dionysian writings which we as usual cite as: CH = *De Coelesti Hierarchia*, EH = *De Ecclesiastica Hierarchia*, DN = *De Divinis Nominibus*, MTh = *De Mystica Theologia*, Ep = *Epistolae* 1–10. The works will be cited according to Migne's edition, PG 3, in the case of CH taking the critical text of the *Sources Chrétiennes* edition as a basis, which follows the numbering of Migne and keeps to the lines of Migne's text.

[11] Nor can there be any question of identifying Denys with the extravert and erudite humanist John of Scythopolis, as I must have 'indirectly suggested' (according to Hornus' comment, *op. cit.*, 446). I had simply made the suggestion ('Das Scholienwerk des Johannes von Scythopolis', *Schol.* 15 [1940], 16f.), a suggestion which, I later discovered, had already been made by Irenée Hausherr ('Doutes au sujet du Divin Denis', *OrChrP* [1936], 484–490), that the personality of Sergius of Reshaina should be investigated more closely. That has meanwhile been done by Polycarp Sherwood ('Sergius of Reshaina and the Syriac versions of the Ps.-D.', *Sacris Errudiri* 4 [1952], 174–184), and seems to have produced in respect of his personality yet another negative result. It only remains to say that the unknown author, on account of

But if anyone should set aside all bias (and equally the bad humour and resentment with which the CD is often approached) and allow this astonishing work to exert its influence upon him, he will in the same glance recognize two things. First, that this writer, like no other, is 'indivisible' and that his person is wholly identified with his work; in other words, that there is nothing 'made-up' about him, that he is no 'pseudonym' for another. And then, that such power, such radiance of holiness streams forth from this unity of person and work—as the Middle Ages sensed immediately—that he can in no case be regarded as a 'forger', not even as a clever 'apologist' pulling off a trick. From the first it follows that it is this indivisibility that has made the theology of Denys, whatever the influences are— Neo-Platonic or Christian, Alexandrian or Cappadocian—into an original whole of such character and impact that none of the great theological thinkers of the following ages could avoid him, could escape a fascination to which the supposed august authorship may have contributed something, but which could scarcely have had less influence, had there been no claim to apostolic authority. Or is one to say that Scotus Eriugena, the Victorines, Bernard and his followers, Albert, Bonaventure and Thomas, Eckhart, Tauler and Ruysbroek, Gerson and Nicholas of Cusa, the Spanish mystics up to and including John of the Cross, Bérulle and Fénelon have all fallen victim to a crass forgery without which the theological substance and power of the CD would never have had any influence? All one needs to do to be convinced of this explosive and yet constructive originality is to listen to the unmistakable sound of gifted self-consciousness which, in union with the deep humility of the author, echoes throughout the *Corpus*, above all in the letters, where the man appears most strongly as he responds to questions and doubts raised in the course of the systematic work: a tone the genuineness of which has nothing to do with so-called literary fiction. One may, with Richstätter, deplore the 'fateful influence' of the 'father of Christian mysticism';[12] one can, on

his christological language, must be set in a Monophysite ambience, without having himself to be accused of Monophysitism.

[12] 'Der "Vater der christlichen Mystik" und sein verhängnisvoller Einfluss' (note the quotation marks!), *Stimmen der Zeit* 114 (1928), 241–259.

the other hand, welcome the way in which the modern psychological trend is being replaced in spiritual theology by the ontology of CD: but one cannot deny the influence of this spiritual theology. It is on the whole scarcely less than that of Augustine (if we include Boethius as part of the received wisdom), and one can see virtually all medieval philosophy up to the Aristotelian renaissance and the whole of theology up to Thomas as derived from the fecundity of these two. And even with Thomas himself: if Aristotle supplies the exact categories, Denys supplies not just the great frame for the plan of the *Summa*, with procession and return[13] and many essential adagios, but also the fundamental structure of the doctrine of God, of the angels, of a 'sacred' cosmos (with structures based both on function and rank), of the ecclesiastical hierarchy. He gives atmosphere, a sense of the spiritual, he gives a deep peace and blessedness which Augustine could not have provided to the same extent and which is and remains perhaps the most important evidence of the presence of Asia in the heart of Western theology. He gives a sense of the sacral and the sacramental, without its developing into an ecclesiastical seclusion from the world (one thinks of his first impact on Eriugena!). But above all he gives, and in this we see his deepest influence, the clear, realized synthesis of truth and beauty, of theology and aesthetics, which was never wholly lost even in the driest realms of the scholasticism of the schools.

So the second question is to be approached only with the greatest circumspection: is Denys a forger? If one proves that he was not the convert and disciple of Paul, that he was not in correspondence with the Apostle John, nor with Titus or Polycarp, nor present at the death of Mary, that he did not send his writings to Timothy, nor experience in Egyptian Heliopolis the eclipse of the sun at Christ's death, has one really done him the slightest injury? Is one telling this Syrian monk in 500 A.D. anything new, if one proves to him that he was not converted by the speech on the Areopagus in 50 A.D.? Or does not the whole phenomenon exist on an utterly different level? On the

---

[13] M.-D. Chenu, *Introduction à l'étude de S. Thomas* (Paris, 1956). Turbessi in *DSp* III, 349f.

level, that is, of the specifically Dionysian humility and
mysticism which must and will utterly vanish as a person so that
it lives purely as a divine task and lets the person be absorbed (as
in the Dionysian hierarchies) in *taxis* and function, so that in this
way the divine light, though ecclesially transmitted, is received
and passed on as immediately (*amesôs*) and transparently as
possible? The identification of his task with a situation in space
and time immediately next to John and Paul clearly corresponds
for him to a necessity which, had he not heeded it, would have
meant a rank insincerity and failure to respond to truth. One
does not *see* who Denys *is*, if one cannot see this identification as
a context for his veracity. And one can only rejoice over the fact
that he succeeded in vanishing behind the Areopagite for a
millennium, and that now afterwards, in the age of the opening
of graves, he has been brought out, he stubbornly hides his face,
I suppose, for ever. Could he ever have said more than his work
has said?

Nothing is more characteristic of Denys than his rejection of
apologetic: why engage in controversy? To do so is only to
descend to the level of one's attacker, 'but if the truth is rightly
developed, it simply offers no openings to any possible attack.
Everything that is not wholly in accord with it is cast out by
itself through the unconquerable presence of genuine truth.
Knowing this, therefore, as I say, I never argued against the
Greeks (the philosophers) or against any others.'[14] One cannot
therefore assume with Ivánka that the author has adopted his
system and his pseudonym and the enticing and suggestive
language of the mysteries from essentially apologetic motives,
in order to make Christianity palatable to his Platonising
contemporaries by the use of fashionable language.[15] One can at
most regard his Christianizing of the Neo-Platonic *milieu* as a
side-effect of his own properly theological endeavour, for
Denys disposes of the objection that he is a 'parricide' because he
uses the teaching of the Platonists against themselves with the
unruffled reply that they themselves turn 'the divine weapons

[14] Ep 7. 1077C–1080A.
[15] E. v. Ivánka, 'La signification historique du "Corpus Areopagiticum" ',
RSR 36 (1949), 5–24; and also in his introduction to *Von den Namen zum
Unnennbaren*, 20–22.

against divine realities when they try to destroy the reverence that is due to God by means of the wisdom that they have received from God'.[16]

Now indeed someone with a mission is never alone, and Denys, as his writings show, was certainly not that. He could not situate himself in the apostolic period on his own; he must transfer to that period his relationships, his theological and spiritual acquaintances. The person of his much-lauded teacher whom he calls Hierotheus and whom he regards as a disciple of Paul and to whom he maintains that he owes everything of importance is undoubtedly a real person: perhaps the man who had converted him from Neo-Platonism to Christianity, perhaps the abbot of his monastery.[17] And the other personalities to whom he often attributes very contemporary opinions or accusations or from whom he pretends to have received letters containing enquiries about particular theological problems, are surely to be found in his own surroundings, only their names are transferred into the apostolic age. So the 'philosopher Clement' (DN 5.9) who has nothing to do with the Alexandrine, or 'Saint Justus' (DN 11.1), or 'Saint Bartholomew' (MTh 3) who expresses his opinion in a way reminiscent of Origen and Nazianzen; 'the mad speeches of Simon' who 'imagines that he is wise' (DN 6.2) may in name be modelled on Simon Magus, but the denial of the resurrection has nothing to do with the historical Simon; rather, we may suppose, we have a reference to an Origenist-Evagrian contemporary. Similarly with the scoffing reference: 'That is something the wise Elymas has not understood' (DN 8.6) whose sophistical objection that there are things of which God is not capable again has nothing to do with the Elymas of the Acts of the Apostles. The letters to Sosipater, to Polycarp, to Titus reflect quite real encounters, not to speak of the great letter to Demophilus, the elevated tone of which is unique in the CD and surely reflects a historical occurrence. The wonderful last letter to the apostle John may, on the other hand, be the immediate

[16] Ep 7. 1080AB.

[17] He stands in relation to Denys somewhat as Socrates did to Plato, or, if one wants a modern example which is strangely apt, as Scheuer did to Maréchal.

fruit of prayer and contemplation, a loving homage, which stands at the close of the work to seal it, and to express, as through a veil, the family likeness of the Dionysian to the Johannine theology.

All these personal relationships find their place in a form, a picture, a pure, immediate relation to the original, which only the apostolic age possessed. So a monk, dying to the world, assumes the name of a saint, and lives in his encompassing reality; so too the disciples of the great prophets, living centuries later in the tradition of this particular calling and continuing it, unconsciously attribute their own sayings to the founder: and one speaks rightly of a Deutero- and a Trito-Isaiah, but not of a Pseudo-Isaiah. It even seems as if, long before Valla and Erasmus, in the early and high Middle Ages, there was already a sense of this mystical relationship, without this in the least upsetting the reverence in which the author was held. Hausherr has gathered together a whole collection of expressions of such knowledge or suspicion.[18] One can even ask whether Thomas of Aquinas himself did not know of this relation, or at least suspect it, when he recognized the dependence of the *Liber de causis* on Proclus' *Stoicheiōsis Theologikē* (which William of Moerbeke had recently translated), and in his commentary on it repeatedly speaks of the relation between Proclus and Denys: *hanc autem positionem (Proculi) corrigit Dionysius*.[19] Thomas hardly thought that Proclus belonged to the pre-Christian period.

The CD presupposes by its whole attitude a great distance, both spiritual and temporal, between many of the movements and struggles of the first three centuries of the Christian era and its own situation. The completely untroubled way in which he appropriates and uses thought-forms which a century earlier were still deeply controversial, and whose rejection or use in those days still had an actual, temporally conditioned, polemic and apologetic character, means that most of those storms have now passed and that such thought-forms are henceforth at the disposal of the Christian thinker without any recrimination or

---

[18] 'Doutes au sujet du "Divin Denys" ', *OrChrP* (1936), 484–490.

[19] [Denys however corrects this position (of Proclus)]: In 1. d. causis, lect. 3 (ed. Mandonnet, 208).

bother: the concepts and patterns of ancient Gnosis, of the Mystery cults, of Manichaeism and of the religion of Mithras; but above all the language and the realm of feeling of the early Church's *disciplina arcani* and of the Gnostic secret tradition, the images of the Platonic and Neo-Platonic mythic world, the religious-aesthetic idea of the cosmic eros (which Denys expressly equates with Christian agapē, both God's and men's), Iamblichus' language of theurgy, the quasi-pantheistic, emanationist language of Plotinus, and finally the triadic ontology of Proclus. All that is used with an easy, lucid carelessness and dogmatic sureness of touch: a few corrections from time to time suffice to avoid any dangers. What was once historical, temporally conditioned reality becomes for Denys a means for expressing an utterly universal theological content. The dimension of history and Church history interests him not at all; only the eternal, only the divine concerns him. And each thought-form of which he makes use will, at his touch, be liberated from its historical context and exalted into eternity.

To give an example: take the *disciplina arcani* we have just mentioned. He makes use of this not only in relation to the sacraments of the Church: there indeed it is much emphasized in the exclusion of the catechumens, the possessed and the penitents before the eucharistic prayer. But he makes use of it too in relation to the theological doctrines of the divinity, of the holy angels, Scripture, Tradition, and the Christian life: everything is essentially holy and therefore essentially secret, it can only be misunderstood, fundamentally and necessarily, by the profane, the uninitiated, and greeted by them 'with roars of laughter'.[20] What idiom is adequate for the divine mysteries as a whole? Denys asks. And his reply is that it can only be an idiom in which every sentence, indeed every part of each sentence, is appropriate to the character of the content as mystery, is indeed the unique form of the unique content. The theological structure of the CD is not only an outer, but also an inner, structure: an idiom which no-one has ever used before him or since, an

---

[20] EH VII.3.1 (556D–557A). Stiglmair, who finds Denys' style tedious, can find only 'flowery language' and 'stylistic decoration' in this continual recalling of the significance of mystery: see his notes to the translation of EH (Bibliothek der Kirchenväter, 1911) on pages 100, 102, 137.

idiom which springs not from a queer, affected mulishness, but from an inward commitment to the divine character of God and all his saving revelations. The Christian *disciplina arcani* and the Hellenistic mystery-language provide only a philological and aesthetic tool for this unique creation of theological form. For this Denys needs both the atemporal and what belongs to all time. The revelation of Christ is finished, the divine mixing bowl has been emptied out into the world. There remains only to drink the drink of wisdom,[21] to breathe in the divine scent that forever pours forth,[22] through the sacred veil of the temporal revelations to perceive in rapt contemplation the eternal mysteries disclosed to the initiated.[23] Denys, who for the sake of this *theoria* withdraws from all doctrinal polemic, can feel only constraint where the contemporary doctrinal struggles over Christology—it is the period of Neo-Chalcedonianism— impose precisely on him, the irenical discerner of the whole in all partial formulations, a reserve, a way of thinking and speaking that leaves such matters undecided.[24] In such a deeply believing thinker, who maintains moreover that all his wisdom is drawn from Holy Scripture, the conscious timelessness of this Dionysian theology might appear to present a problem, though in reality it is a consciously willed way of proceeding: precisely not to follow through in thought the Biblical history of salvation, but from the viewpoint of timeless *theoria* to contemplate the essentially timeless (and only lately temporal) outflow of the eternally good God, or rather, as Denys never tires of saying, to celebrate it. The actualisation of the divine mysteries as in ecclesiastical celebration they assume forms which are supratemporal is what we mean by liturgy: the whole theology of the Areopagite is for him a single, sacred liturgical act. To the extent that liturgy is a human, ecclesial act which, as a response of praise and thanksgiving, seeks to echo the form of the divine revelation, the categories of the aesthetic and of art will play a

[21] Ep 9.3 (1109B).
[22] EH IV.3.1–4 (473B–480A).
[23] DN I.8.
[24] Roques, *L'univers dionysien*, part 4, 305ff. Also, Grillmeier-Bacht, *Das Konzil von Chalkedon* I (1951), the contributions by Lebon and Charles Moeller.

decisive role in it, and there has hardly been a theology so deeply informed by aesthetic categories as the liturgical theology of the Areopagite.

2. THE STRUCTURE OF THE WORK

If Greek thought from Plato to Plotinus has an essentially aesthetic, religious structure—for the cosmos is experienced as the representation and manifestation of the hidden transcendent beauty of God—then it is no sacrilege, but rather a fulfilment, if Christian theology, following Philo, first in Alexandria and Cappadocia, then in the Egypt of Synesius and Nonnus, then in Latin hymnody from the time of Hilary and Ambrose, Juvencus, Ausonius, Prudentius and Sedulius, and with the Greeks from the time of the Nazianzene, and in the great forms of the Greek liturgies—if in all these manifestations, Christian theology takes over this aesthetic and metaphysical schema. But in all this, nothing approaches in power and will to achieve expression the theological composition of the Areopagite. In order to grasp his intention in its fulness, the numerous hints as to the complete structure must be followed up, whether the parts of it we do not possess have been lost, or were perhaps never written, or only sketched. It will not do at all to take these references, as is usually done nowadays, as a merely literary device making for further mystification. There are most telling reasons for believing that at least three of these missing works actually existed: not simply the repeated references, not only the assignment of an adequately described and quite indispensable place in the complete work, but above all the same kind of summary recapitulation and indication of content, and at the same time the graphic evocation of other works in a phrase or two in one or other of the surviving works, as for example the *Celestial Hierarchy* is summarized in outline both in the *Divine Names*[25] and in the *Ecclesiastical Hierarchy*.[26] Roques[27] and

[25] DN IV.2.
[26] EH I.2 (372C); IV.3.6 (481AB).
[27] In *DSp* III. 257ff.

Ivánka[28] have therefore rightly again put some weight on the declarations of the author about the general plan of his works, thus departing more than a little reluctantly from the usual disparagements.

If one counts the ten genuine letters as a single work (which fundamentally they are not) and the *Mystical Theology* likewise as a single work (although it could be regarded as a 'letter to Timothy', for even the longer works are in the form of such open letters), then the author mentions eleven works of his own, as well as both a theological and a hymnic work by his teacher, Hierotheus. The *Divine Names* presupposes the existence of five works: *Theological Outlines, On the Properties and Orders of the Angels, On the Soul, On Just and Divine Judgement*, and on the *Symbolic Theology*. The *Mystical Theology* refers to the *Divine Names*, the *Outlines* and the *Symbolic Theology*; the *Celestial Hierarchy* likewise refers to the *Symbolic Theology* and to a work *On the Divine Hymns*; the *Ecclesiastical Hierarchy* refers to the *Celestial Hierarchy* and to a work *On the Objects of Spiritual and Sensible Perception*; Epistle 9 refers once again to the *Symbolic Theology*. These references are logical and enable us to deduce the order of appearance of the surviving works, with the exception of a single obscure point: the *Divine Names* presupposes a treatise on the angels, but it is not clear how this treatise can be the same as the treatise we now have, as this presupposes unequivocally the *Divine Names*. Both writings could have appeared at the same time, or perhaps there was an earlier form of the *Celestial Hierarchy*, and one might also bear in mind that dates of publication would not have the same precision then as now. Other 'contradictions' that are sometimes referred to simply do not exist.[29] Of the six works referred to that have not survived we can form a clear picture of at least three which equally have an indispensable place in the whole structure: the *Theological Outlines*, clearly the first, basic work that defines the structure of the whole, the *Divine Judgement*, the content of which can be clearly inferred, and the *Symbolic Theology*, to

---

[28] In the introduction to his translation (*Von den Namen zum Unnennbaren*), 16.

[29] *E.g.* Bardenhewer IV.286–7, which also gives the detailed references.

which reference is made with such emphasis and so much detail as being the decisive work in the whole system: it is logically linked to the *Divine Names*,[30] of which it is the indispensable counterpart. It is perhaps less important to reconstruct the content of the lost works, for Denys has the characteristic already mentioned of continually recapitulating what he has said and reminding us of the all-encompassing nature of his vision. Rather, must we grasp the significance of the works within the grand structure of the whole *Corpus*, something which is quite possible with so systematic a writer and which is also illuminating, regardless of how many of the works now lost ever existed (for they all subsisted in the mind of the author, and probably also in outline).

A word first about the two works of his teacher: the *Elements of Theology* and his *Hymns of Love*, both of which are generally consigned to the realm of fable, because they remind one of no-one but Denys, whose style is quite unmistakable. But the citations from both works (DN II.10; IV.15–17) prove just the opposite. The doctrine of the Logos in II.10 contradicts quite decisively the Areopagite's doctrine of the Trinity, both in its content and in its strongly Stoic formulation, for Denys strictly denies any distinction between the functions and spheres of the three divine Persons in this world. There is contradiction too in the teaching on love in IV.15–17, which is much closer to Proclus than the more cautious account that Denys gives in the hymns. As Denys explains his relationship to his teacher and the reasons why he has dared, despite the existence of the *Elements of Theology*, to put pen to paper himself, there emerges a humanly very credible relationship: Hierotheus had the gift of 'drawing much together in comprehensive definitions in a single sentence' for his disciples; he had also given his favourite pupil the 'task' of expounding his 'closely packed summaries' (*synelixeis synoptikas*) more comprehensively to his fellow pupils.

---

[30] Since Denys represents the *Symbolic Theology* as still unwritten in the *Divine Names* and in the last sentence declares his intention of making a start on it, it is sheer absent-mindedness on Stiglmair's part (unfortunately not the only example) when he translates DN IV.5: 'which we have dealt with in the *Symbolic Theology*' (where it only says: *alla tauta men tē symbolikē theologiā*—all this belongs to the *Symbolic Theology*).

Hierotheus is the surpassing genius, his work 'is like a kind of second sacred scripture which discloses itself immediately to those who are divinely inspired', his 'vision, self-witnessed, of the spiritual revelations' and his 'synoptic manner of teaching' presupposes a spiritual power that stands (*presbytikē*) closer to God.[31] Denys therefore interprets, and indeed he takes great care not to touch what his teacher had made perfectly clear from the Scriptures and to limit himself to unfolding his teacher's 'synoptic' statements. Only the imperative missionary task implicit in Christian truth has enabled him to overcome his 'exceeding reverence' and become a writer.[32]

His first work which sets out the framework of the whole is the *Theological Outlines*.[33] Its content is the unknowability of the triune God (DN I.5), the 'detailed discussion' of his 'shared names' (which are basically identical with those treated in DN). Beyond that, he deals with the use of the 'differentiated designations' for the individual persons in God himself and in his Incarnation (something briefly mentioned at the beginning of DN as not belonging to its theme and then excluded: DN II.3; in II.4 there is again a reference back to the first work). In II.7 a twofold theological method is distinguished in the *Outlines*, corresponding to the twofold mode of communication in Sacred Scripture, both in plain speech and in hidden yet suggestive figures: on the one hand a peaceful contemplation of the mysteries presented to man's view and on the other a being caught up into the mysteries presented, beyond any active knowledge, in mystical union. According to XI.5 the *Outlines* dealt with the Biblical names of Jesus, which indicate his

---

[31] DN III.2 (681BC).

[32] DN III.3 (684BD). Certainly the title, *Theologikai Stoicheiōseis*, reminds one of Proclus himself and of his technique of definition in his *Stoicheiōsis Theologikē*. Nonetheless they cannot be the same, because Hierotheus' *Elements* is said to have been an exposition of Scripture. It is also probable that Denys in his account of his teacher's lectures tended to impose his personal style on them.

One might compare Hierotheus' doctrine of the Logos (DN II.10) with that of Denys (DN VII.4), where the Logos is a name held in common by the Trinity and not, as formerly, designated as 'Jesus', *i.e.*, as one of the usual designations for the eternal Son in Monophysite circles.

[33] DN I.5; II.1; II.3; II.4; II.7; XI.5; MTh III.

'supernatural gifts', as when he is said to be our 'Peace' (one must think here of the Fathers' frequent treatment of the names of Jesus, such as Shepherd, Door, Resurrection, Light of the World, something which is sadly missing from the surviving *Corpus*), names which are to be clearly distinguished from the philosophical divine names dealt with in DN. MTh III arranges the *Outlines*, the *Divine Names* and the *Symbolic Theology* in a logical order, according to which the *Outlines* dealt with the unity of God (*De Deo uno*), his threefoldness within the abiding unity (*De Deo trino*), the Incarnation of Jesus (*De Deo incarnato*), 'and other such matters drawn from Scripture as are celebrated in the foundations of theology.'

The *Outlines* is followed (MTh III) by one of the surviving works, *Of the Divine Names*, the centrepoint of which is the theology of creation as a communication of God (*De Deo creante*), expressed Platonically as the theology of the God who allows creation to participate in himself, who proceeds forth into multiplicity.

Now this can be properly expressed only if the relationship between the communicable and incommunicable in God is everywhere presupposed. God's 'becoming the world' can be described only if it is understood that the immutable one, exalted and transcendent over all, is the one who, in different degrees of intensity, gives to the realms of creation a share in himself while safeguarding the immanent order of all things.

In relation to this, the complementary book of the *Symbolic Theology* is very clearly defined: 'In the book on the *Divine Names* (we have discussed) how God is called good, existent, life and wisdom and power, and the other spiritual names of God. In the *Symbolic Theology*, in contrast, (we have discussed) the meaning of names whose application is changed from sensible things to the divine; what are the divine shapes, what the divine figures and parts and organs of the body, what are the divine places and divine worlds, what the passions, what the griefs and wraths, what the drunkenness and intoxication, what are the oaths and the curses, what the sleep and the awakenings and the other similes belonging to the symbolic depiction of God, sanctioned in the divine oracles.'[34] Letter 9 to Titus answers

---

[34] MTh III (1033AB).

exactly to this description, for it is directed to his inquiry in what sense we can speak of the 'House of Wisdom', of her 'mixing bowl', of her 'food' and her 'drink'. After his explanation Denys concludes in these words: 'For the rest we send our complete book, the *Symbolic Theology*, in which you will find explanations of the other expressions that designate Wisdom: house, seven pillars, solid food divided into offerings and loaves; all that concerns the mixing of the wine, the divine drunkenness and intoxication, and other similes that we have just explained: which is there developed further'.[35] Similarly DN I.8 tells us that in contrast to the intelligible divine names treated in DN it is the sensible names that Scripture ascribes to God which are to be dealt with in the *Symbolic Theology*: human forms and shapes, fire or electron, eyes, ears, hair, face, hands, wings, arms, back, feet. Crowns, seats, drinking-cups, mixing-bowls, and a number of other mystical objects which express something of God are also dealt with.[36] There too the meaning of light and the sun (DN IV.4–5) is explained, which Denys indeed celebrates among the intelligible names. The distinction is not very exact. When he (DN IX.5) deals with the divine name of the 'other', he introduces the spatial dimensions of 'breadth, length and depth' and interprets them as God's procession, his limitless power and his incomprehensible secrecy: 'But lest in this exposition of the various shapes and forms we should unconsciously confuse the immaterial divine names with those drawn from sensible symbols, these latter will be dealt with in the *Symbolic Theology*.'[37] CH XV.6 makes reference to the theological treatment of the four elements in the *Symbolic Theology*, and in different places in the two *Hierarchies* there is

---

[35] Ep 9.6 (1113BC—following Gandillac's tr. which amends the Greek of Migne). Already at the beginning of the letter (1104B) it is said that symbolic theology justifies and explains those expressions Scripture uses of God which appear to us 'monstrous' and give 'an impression of dreadful absurdity'.

[36] DN I.8 (597BC).

[37] DN IX.5 (913B). *Cf.* XIII.4 (984A). Identical distinction between DN and symbolic theology in CH III (1033AB), where it adds that the *Symbolic Theology* needs many more words than the *Outlines* and the *Divine Names*, for the more spiritual the object, the more synoptic the method.

worked out an interpretation of fire, wind and water, as applied to God.

Mention is made, more incidentally, in EH I.2 of a book, *On the Objects of Spiritual and Sensible Perception*, which was to have constituted, on the one hand, the crucial link between the *Divine Names* and the *Symbolic Theology*, and, on the other, that between the *Celestial Hierarchy* and the *Ecclesiastical Hierarchy*, as well as concerning itself with the central object of any 'aesthetics'.

Further, CH VII.4 once mentions a tractate on the *Divine Hymns*, in which the songs of the angels mentioned in Holy Scripture such as the *trisagion* in Isaiah, the calls of the angels in Ezekiel (3.12), and the thunderous hymns of the Apocalypse, were made to yield their meaning: something of decisive importance for Denys, because all theology is for him a glorious celebration of the divine mysteries and therefore has its arche-type and pattern in the liturgical songs of heaven, as DN I.3 declares: 'Submitting to the yoke imposed by the Thearchy, which governs all the sacred orders of the choirs beyond the heavens, we wish to join in honouring the secret mystery of the Thearchy, which is beyond intellect and being, and, abandon-ing all attempts to penetrate the mystery, in the silence of humility to worship the ineffable in acts of spiritual reverence. Reaching out to the rays that illuminate us in the sacred oracles (Holy Scripture), we receive from them the light which leads us to the hymns of the Thearchy, and illuminated by them (the Holy Scriptures) in a supernatural way and patterned after the sacred hymnology, we are enabled to contemplate the lights given us through them (the Scriptures) according to our capacity by the Thearchy, and to hymn the generous source of all sacred manifestation of light, as it is handed down to us in the sacred oracles.'[38] The 'hymnic' is therefore for Denys a methodology of theological thinking and speaking.

There is also only passing mention made of a book, *On the Soul*, the content of which, manifest in outline from DN IV.2, would in a Plotinian context have had its proper place after the tractate of God and his processions, and of the Nous (that is, the

[38] DN I.3 (589AB).

intelligences, the angels)—but which in the CD remains shadowy. Denys admittedly avoids speaking in a Plotinian way of a world-soul, he simply sets 'nature as a whole' over against the individual soul (DN V.7). This is indeed one of the most striking deviations from the Platonic world-view, a deviation that even Augustine did not dare to carry through with complete decisiveness, although the individual personality receives much greater emphasis with him than with Denys. But for that reason the metaphysical place which the latter could have allowed the soul in his cosmos is somewhat opaque. For soul is for him, in a much clearer way than for Origen, Gregory of Nyssa or Augustine, a spirit bound to the body with ways of perception conditioned by the body, which therefore appears in a 'symbolic' hierarchy, ecclesially and socially ordered. But for Denys the individual and social orders (*taxis*) are inseparable, as will appear. A *Peri psychēs* can only be systematically conceived as the individual complement of the social *Ecclesiastical Hierarchy*, even though this relationship does not appear to have been fully thought through by Denys; this not least in view of the fact that he offers no final explanation of the relationship of the *Mystical Theology*, as the highest personal event, to the ecclesiastical hierarchy (which appears more clearly as a social structure than as the 'Bride of Christ' and bearer of the mystical life). This is something which will have consequences for the history of Western mysticism.

It is otherwise with the last of the lost works, the *On Just and Divine Judgement*, whose place in the system is immediately manifest if one considers that *krisis* is inseparably bound up in the Alexandrine-Evagrian theology with the concept of providence (*pronoia*), and that therefore everything is conceived in terms of this double concept, *krisis-pronoia*, from the creative distribution of the destinies of beings and essences, to the preservation of beings within their own limits and specific natures, to the apportioning of 'worthy' rewards and 'worthy' punishment. It will become plain just how indispensable this concept is for Denys, who here perfects and transcends the Origenist *krisis* in the creation of the cosmos in that he rejects the idea that it is based on a precosmic fall due to sin, and makes the justice of God coincide with his election conceived as an allotting to each being of a particular and limited existence. The occasion of this work was the 'sophistical objection that charges God with injustice and falsehood and is to be vigorously dismissed as foolish and empty talk.'[39] DN VIII therefore expressly lists power, justice, salvation and redemption as divine names, whence it follows that 'all those who impugn the divine justice themselves unwittingly pass judgement on their own open injustice.'[40] For Denys, as little as for Augustine, evil and sin cannot upset the divine ordering of the cosmos to salvation; at best they contribute to its clearer revelation. If the Platonic *tyrannis* is for Denys the essential image of the perverted, demonic 'order' of sin, divine power and justice is characterised, on the contrary, by its complete freedom.[41] What folly and arrogance, then, when Demophilus takes it into his head to 'avenge God'.[42] So the tractate becomes a justification of the ways of God, a theodicy.

Significantly, there is no mention of a treatise on the Incarnation, although Denys composed two splendid letters (4 and 5) on the *Mysterium Christi* as the veiled unveiling of the unknowable God and often spoke of Christ as the appearing God. It may, on the one hand, be due to the christological controversies: if one was to speak systematically there was no possibility of adopting an irenical position. On the other hand it may be, as we shall see, because of the difficulty posed by the very design of the Dionysian cosmos. In Roques' systematic account, christology appears as a kind of appendix.

If we organize the total oeuvre, which existed at least in outline, according to its essential aspects and with abbreviated titles (with the surviving works *underlined*), we get the following picture:

[39] DN IV.35 (736B).
[40] 896A.
[41] CH VIII.1 (237CD), and Gandillac's note *ad loc.* in the *Sources Chrétiennes* edition. Similarly EH III.3.11 (441B), and Stiglmair's note in his translation. EH VII.3.1 (557B), EH VII.3.6 (561B).
[42] Ep 8.4 (1096B).

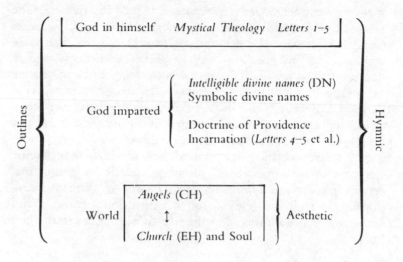

The schema is for many reasons inadequate. For one thing, it does not enable one to bring out the fact that the imparting of God is not a realm on its own between God and the world, but that movement of God in creation and grace, which on the one hand with regard to what is imparted coincides with God himself, and on the other (as to its goal) with the world. The symbolic divine names (and indeed the intelligible names) are identical, as far as content goes, with the material and spiritual structure of the cosmos. The doctrine of providence is discerned partly in the immanent, ontological rightness of things, and partly from the equally 'worldly' Holy Scriptures. The Incarnation fulfils this, for it is in unity both the unknowable God and also God made known as man. CH and EH are then not an immanent ontology of creatureliness (a doctrine of the cosmos), but—because it is a matter of theology—a doctrine of the structure of the world conceived as having God completely and utterly as its goal, indeed even its formal object; and in this respect one may observe that for Denys no other creaturely ontology could in fact ever seriously come under consideration. Therefore, between the content of the 'aesthetic' (*On the Objects*

of Sensible and Spiritual Perception) and that of the two treatises on the 'divine names' there can be no sharp distinction, as little as there can between the doctrine of providence and the hierarchies. The 'hymnic', however, makes contact with the doctrine of the angels, as far as content goes, because in heaven the praise of God appears archetypally perfected, and, as a concept, can serve as the ideal of the hymn of all creatureliness, especially of the Church and within it of the individual, and can therefore also serve as theological method.

So finally, according to Denys, all is in all in accordance with the great flowing movement of being itself as procession and return, *proodos* and *epistrophē*, so that what is ultimately important is to trust oneself to the direction of this flow, recognizing in the procession the source, and in the return the goal.

3. AESTHETICS AND LITURGIOLOGY

But what is the meaning of this movement? It is the manifestation of the unmanifest. Manifestation is the aesthetic expression for communication and word. Manifestation conceived of in the Greek, not the Indian, sense, as becoming visible in reality—not as *maya*, mere seeming illusion, but always as (real) manifestation of the unmanifest, of the ever greater and ever more hidden God who can never be changed into simply comprehensible appearance. As *manifestation* of the unmanifest, the movement is procession, *proodos*, and as manifestation of the *unmanifest* to which every manifestation refers (and which it discloses as it conceals it), it is return, *epistrophē*. Indeed, every manifestation, even within this world, is such a manifestation of the unmanifest: were the external splendour of the beautiful and of order not the splendour of a mysterious depth—of being, still more of life, still more of spirit—then it would not be the beautiful and would not awaken reverence before the 'sacred mystery made manifest'. But in the world there is a proportion suitable to the creature between the manifestation and what it is that (unmanifestly) is manifest, even

if there is a gradually increasing transcendence of the
comprehensible relation. This proportion (between spirit and
what is perceptible to sense), which is the real centre of the
aesthetic, is, without being simply ruptured, infinitely transcended and, as it were, stretched out, when it is a matter of the
relation between God and the world. If, on the one hand, any
manifestation makes itself known as the manifestation of the
One-and-Only not merely contingently (as is often the case
with members of a class) but rather of necessity, then indeed this
One is truly visible, everywhere announced, in the all which is
his manifestation, but only as the eternally One and therefore
eternally mysterious, hidden One who can never be fully
comprehended in any of his manifestations; and therefore the
wondering admiration of his beauty as manifestation, as
relation between manifestation and non-manifestation—is
grounded in the worship of what is not manifest. The more
deeply our wonder experiences the unmanifest God, and does
not simply know him (*ou monon mathōn alla pathōn ta theia*, DN
II.9), the more the aesthetic relationship is transcended, the
more it is possible to discern in the manifestation *what* is really
manifest, the more the truth of the aesthetic emerges. This
relationship between negation and affirmation was laid down
by Plato and determined the mysticism of Plotinus and Proclus
as also of Gregory of Nyssa and Augustine; but only with Denys
did it receive its balancing counterpoise: in that the tremendous
ascending movement of negation, often rising to a pitch of sheer
frenzy,[43] which sets the apophatic (rejection of names) over the
cataphatic (affirmation of names), is kindled only—and ever
more brightly—by God's movement of descent as he imparts
himself in manifestations. The proper attitude to these manifestations of God (this is perhaps the most characteristic thing
about Denys) is neither disdain nor aversion, because such
behaviour would necessarily have its effect on the relation to the
self-manifesting God. For any 'entanglement' in the manifestation itself mistakes its essential language which declares only the
truth of the One and the Good and the Beautiful; and it is this
alone which is essentially esoteric and imparts to all its

[43] So at the end of the *Mystical Theology*.

manifestations something of this esoteric character. If no one has emphasized so strongly as Denys the transcendence of God, nor has anyone upheld so decisively the givenness of the essential boundaries and hierarchical ordering of the creation (because no one has thought through or applied so consistently the consequences of this apophaticism). As a result, Thomas of Aquinas had no need to draw his conception of *ordo* directly from Aristotle, because here it was already thought out for him. The objective, hierarchical *taxis* (already we are moving towards the Byzantine and Carolingian world-order!) is the form of God's self-manifestation; the Church is the heart of the world and the earthly representation of the heavenly court; and any flight from the world is unthinkable, even for the most exalted mysticism. And if the earthly manifestation, the actual Church, is defective, then this never becomes for Denys (as it did for Augustine) an opportunity to distinguish between the carnal manifestation of the institution and the spiritual core of the 'pilgrim people of God'. Rather, the spiritual lies definitely in the form of manifestation, in hierarchy and sacrament; what is and what should be, the 'physical' and the 'moral', must, in accordance with God's will (which is decisive for theology), simply coincide, in proof of which the orders of the angels are forever set over the Church, who must see herself as their earthly translation. Therefore the mystics' praise of God is none other than the expression and development of the Church's praise, and is in this way also liturgy. The form of words of this hymn is a marvelling, rising to worship, at the beauty which appears in every manifestation of the unmanifest, and which is therefore the sacredness of everything apparently profane. Everything lies in the circular movement between procession and return, the cataphatic and the apophatic, nothing can find fulfilment except by entering into this movement. No explanations can help him who does not see the beauty; no 'proof of the existence of God' can help him who cannot see *what* is manifest in the world; no apologetic can be any use to him for whom the truth that radiates from the centre of theology is not evident.[44] And it is not as if something good is to be effected by the

---

[44] Ep 6 and 7 (1077A ff.)

theologian's looking restlessly back and forth between the needs of his age and the apparently so uncontemporary divine truth in the Church; but 'just as with earthly pictures, if the painter looks constantly at the archetypal form, not distracted by any visible object, nor divided at all in himself, then what is to be depicted is (if one can speak thus) duplicated, and he can show forth the truth in its likeness, the archetype in the image, and each is in the other, only the substances remaining different. So too for the lovers of (the divine) beauty, whose image they inscribe in their minds, the constant and intent contemplation of fragrant and secret beauty is rewarded by that manifestation (*indalma*)[45] which is unerring and most godlike.'[46] By 'divine artists' Denys means of course the saints, who look to God alone with undeviating gaze and reflecting him are 'little concerned to attract the attention of men' or indeed to display the likeness publicly at all (as also the Church veils her sacraments). But what has been said applies just as much to the theologian who, on this view of the world, can be such only if he is involved in the business of the saints. Only he who can show the truth as a whole is beyond refutation—this is the teaching of the Sixth Letter. But the truth is both single and mysterious (*kryphios*), and so in refuting something from polemical ends one does not thereby demonstrate the truth of the alternative. For if it is proved that something is not red, it does not therefore follow that it is white.[47] But if someone gets in a passion of zeal about a partial lack of order, he shows by that fact that he does not possess the calm of order, and therefore cannot reveal it.[48]

Because the object can only be grasped by a movement—a circling movement—it is right to speak of the mutual 'implication' of the methods (Roques).[49] The mystical method is for

[45] Hapax with Denys, from *indallomai*: to appear, to come before the eyes (in order to be seen, *eidenai*). Cordier: *impressio scil. imaginaria, i.e., imago interior . . . impressa et expressa* (1159). [an impression, presented, that is, to the imagination, *i.e.*, an interior image . . . impressed and expressed].

[46] EH IV.3.1 (473BC).

[47] Ep 6 (1077A).

[48] Ep 8 (1084A ff.)

[49] *Cf.* n. 8.

Denys by no means a renunciation of the aesthetic method, and in that too he is far removed from Plato's 'conversion' from art to philosophy. Indeed Denys can be regarded as the most aesthetic of all Christian theologians, because the aesthetic transcendence that we know in this world (from the sensible as manifestation to the spiritual as what is manifest) provides the formal schema for understanding theological or mystical transcendence (from the world to God). For just as, when we form an idea of the soul, we give it a bodily likeness, and surround with bodily parts that which is without parts, so we interpret these bodily parts in a different way, suitable to what is without parts—so the head signifies the mind, the neck opinion (which is between the rational and the irrational), the breast the passionate part (*thumos*), the belly the desiring part (*epithumia*), and the bones and feet the nature—thus using the names of the parts as symbols for the soul's powers. Much more, then, in the case of the one who is transcendent over all, it is necessary to purify utterly (*ana-kathairesthai*, to lift up to a purer understanding) the forms and shapes of all otherness so that they may express (*anaptyxis*, unfolding) what is holy, fitting to God and mystical.'[50] But this ascending 'much more' cannot be developed to the point where one altogether abandons the relationship between the form and what it expresses, because viewed from above the relation of likeness and beauty between spirit and the sensible within this world is itself a reflection of the relationship between God and the world (the *analogia entis*). But not for a moment is the singularity of this analogy, its irreversibility, forgotten: things are both like God and unlike him,[51] but God is not like things.[52] Already there is a pointer to this expressed in the fact

[50] DN IX.5 (913A). *Cf.* DN I.1: 'Just as the intelligible can neither be grasped nor seen by the sensible, ... so by the same law of truth what is boundless and beyond all being transcends all beings.' [Trans. note: B. sees in the prefix 'ana-' an overtone of ascent (which 'ana' can mean, though not necessarily), so *anaptyxis* is taken to mean an unfolding that *elevates*, and *anakathairesthai* purification that aids one's ascent (*auf-klären*—to raise to a purer comprehension).]

[51] DN IX.7 (916A).

[52] DN IX.6 (913CD). From such a Platonic point of view it can also be said that 'things which are caused carry within themselves as far as possible the image of their causes; these causes themselves, however, are transcendent over

that God is in all things in his immanence and yet in himself is independent, transcendent over them, and therefore even his immanence is comparable with none other.[53] If then the concept of image (*eikōn*), in all its forms (as *theāma*, object of contemplation, drama, or, using the language of the mysteries, as *agalma*, sacred idol or image of the gods), is applied to the manifestation, through which, for those who can see, 'the blessed beauty of the archetype shimmers through (*apostilho*) clearly',[54] then only this qualification is needed, that between manifestation and what is manifest there is no sort of link of natural necessity, and that even where the divine is imaged, the more sensible the representation, the more it is a concession to human weakness,[55] and so the more it reveals the more it conceals.[56] Indeed, images can be interpreted in different ways, the ordinary people remaining standing in front of the symbols while the priests and the contemplatives penetrate more deeply to their spiritual meaning;[57] but a more penetrating (*optikōteros*) gaze could discern in the same images something still deeper and more revealing.[58] The same knowledge of God demands both a deeper penetration *into* the image and also a more sublime transcendence *beyond* it, and the two are not separated one from another but are the more fully integrated, the more perfectly they are achieved. For if it is true that God goes out of himself 'ecstatically'[59]—because all things really are, and would not be if God were not in them all in all[60]—then it is also equally true, and even more true, that he need not go outside himself in order to know the world,[61] for he knows it in himself in an archetypal fashion, which is the same as to say again that God does not

their effects': joy and pain create the feeling of joy and pain, but they themselves feel neither joy nor pain (DN II.8; 645CD).

[53] DN III.1 (680B).
[54] EH III.3.2 (428C).
[55] EH VII.3.5 (560B).
[56] See below, n. 156f.
[57] EH II.3.2 (397C) and often.
[58] EH VII.3.11 (568D).
[59] DN IV.13 (712AB).
[60] DN V.10 (825B). Often expressed in the Pauline formula: from him and in him and to him are all things.
[61] DN VII.2 (868C–869C).

simply—as creative *causa efficiens*—set a 'second thing' alongside himself, but that the mystery of creation because of its intimacy cannot dispense with the category of participation; that God, like the sun, imparts being through his being and is present to every being, so that now no being or form can be—or may be—excluded from those which can help us to find him.[62] Here it is already clear that, just as in God rest in himself and going out from himself are held together, so also with the creature: its movement towards God in ecstasy, a movement that reflects God's movement and answers it, is held together with its nature as established and complete in itself:[63] the creaturely understanding in its movement to absolute unity is already unifying in itself (*gnōsis* as *henotikē*, unifying, of the knower and the known). Only here Denys would not speak of a 'synthesis', but rather of (certainly active) participation in the unifying and reconciling power of God, who as pure peace quietens the 'immanent war' (*emphylios polemos*) of limited and opposing things, without robbing them of their own being.

Theology is exhausted in the act of wondering adoration before the unsearchable beauty in every manifestation. It is knowledge, *gnōsis*, but knowledge that answers to the mystery of beauty in a beautiful fashion, which is to say in a manner fitting, apt, poised (*symmetrōs, en symmetriā*).[65] While for Gregory of Nyssa *eros* overthrows all limits as it hastens after the ever-greater God, with Denys the self-same *eros* is contained in its striving after infinity within two limits: the possible (*hōs ephikton*)[66] and the permitted (*themiton*, strictly speaking: what can be attained without sacrilege).[67] Theological thought and speech here finds in measure the optimum. Boldness of thought is not at all decisive, for it can impair the awe and the reserve,[68] restraint,[69]

---

[62] DN I.5: 'whence as the subsistence of goodness, by his very being, he is the cause of all beings . . . ' (593D).

[63] See below, 'Theological Mysticism'.

[64] DN XI.2 (949D–952A).

[65] *Indices* (van den Daele) 128.

[66] *Ibid.* 70: the word occurs 42 times. Also *hōs dynaton*, 35 times.

[67] *Ibid.* 75: the word occurs 33 times (see Gandillac on CH X.3).

[68] *eulabeia*: DN I.3 (589B), DN III.3 (684B).

[69] *sōphrosynē*: DN I.1 (588A).

and holy reverence[70] demanded by the object of its thought. Two things upset this measure: love of evil, which makes the eye of the soul apprehend the divine rays in a squinting and short-sighted way, and presumption, which 'oversteps the limits that have been wisely set for vision and pretends that it can in itself behold the light immediately'. If the beholder is blinded, the fault lies not with the light, which gives itself in a bounty innocent of envy, but with the beholder, who has not kept to the proper relation set down for him.[71] The divine light raises to contemplation of itself and to contact with it all those 'who eagerly desire it in a way permitted, suitable to such sacred things, and do not insolently presume to something more exalted than the divine manifestation thus harmoniously offered them, nor because of a weakness for what is worse slip downwards.'[72] This methodical *harmonia* is an *analogia*,[73] an appropriate relation, a proportion between revelation and the capacity for receiving it, set by the one who reveals himself with regard to the particular nature and comprehension of the subject. Providence itself, both as creating and as communicating salvation to the creature, is analogous,[74] in that it guarantees to each being a primordial 'worthiness' (*axia*) to receive God in accordance with its rank and imparts its divine self-expression in accordance with this 'worthiness'.[75] All this in such a way, however, that the ontological worthiness connected with rank always includes the ethical self-realisation of the being that has received such worthiness.[76] But because this ethical moment is only included as a consequence, it would be a mistake to translate *kat' axian* as 'according to merit'.[77] The

---

[70] *hosiotēs: ibid.*

[71] EH II.3.3 (397D–400A).

[72] DN I.2 (588D–589A).

[73] *Cf. analogia, analogos, analogikōs* in v.d. Daele, 18–19; and Lossky's article on the analogies (*cf.* n. 8).

[74] *analogos pronoia*: CH XIII.3 (301C).

[75] *kata tēn hekastou tōn hierōn noōn analogian*: CH III.2 (165B) [according to the analogy of each of the sacred minds].

[76] On this problem of *axia, cf.* Roques, *Univers dionysien,* 61, where *axia* is quite properly discussed together with *symmetria* and *analogia.*

[77] In the places where the concept of merit obtrudes, e.g. 557C, 560C, Denys does not in fact use the word *axia.*

apportionment of divine grace is not a matter of reward, but of symmetry and harmony between the giver and the receiver, whereby the being and nature of the receiver is always already grounded in the allotted grace, and God primarily crowns his own gift, while correct (symmetrical) human behaviour is taken up into this divinely established harmony secondarily and as a response to God's giving. This Patristic use of *axiotēs* and *meritum* occurs otherwise almost only in liturgical and hymnic formulas such as the address to Mary: *tu quae meruisti portare* (you whom God made worthy to bear). But with Denys such use is thorough-going and fundamental.[78] Because grace is participation in the infinite God and because the assimilation of man to the proper measure laid down by God is equally a matter of infinite approximation, there is, even in the Dionysian theology of fittingness, room for endless striving.

If the manner of theology is 'holy measure', its sound is 'holy celebration'. Because God is in all things and above all things, being and knowing can only be a festival and a 'dance', [79] a continuous 'celebration' of the glory that communicates itself and holds sway in all things and above all things, a 'hymn', a 'song of praise', which has its own laws which must be followed in everything from its basic conception, the choice of point of view, right down to the least form of expression. Everything that antiquity had at its disposal by way of sacred forms is included and adapted. The style strides along so consciously loaded, draped with so many sacred garments, that it makes any haste impossible and compels us not only to follow him in his train of thought but also to join with him in his mood of celebration. Nowhere do we find the lyrical-subjective mood,

[78] The divine righteousness is therefore true, 'because it administers to all creatures what is fitting in accordance with the worth of each, and preserves the nature of each in its own rank and power' (DN VIII.7; 896B). *Cf.* EH I.2 (373B): all beings strive after the same good, 'but it is far from being the case that all participate to the same degree in that good, rather each participates in accordance with the rank it has been divinely allotted.' *Cf.* CH III.1 (164D); EH II.3.4 (400D), II.3.7 (404C), IV.3.4 (477D). In the last text the creature's working together with God is stressed.

[79] Ep 8 (1088A). On festival and feast: Dumézil, *Le festin d'immortalité* (1924). On the theme of the festal dance in Denys and in antiquity: Gandillac, on CH VII.4, p. 118.

DENYS 173

as with Augustine, but nowhere the decline into theoretical
dryness either—except in the often-noticed (because clearly so
dependent on Proclus) and much-despised treatise on evil and
wickedness. 'The style,' says Stiglmair, 'now becomes very
sober and dry and loses the exuberant intensity and moves in
short, dialectical formulae':[80] certainly, for should one 'celebrate' the evil and the wicked? Can one in such a theology do
otherwise than speak of it tunelessly? But where it is a matter of
God and the divine, the word *hymnein* almost replaces the word
'to say';[81] for what is at stake is that 'the divine mystery should
be honoured by spiritual and invisible knowledge and kept free
from any contact with or contamination by the profane.'[82] So it
is a matter always and above all of vision, of looking and
striving after vision, but ever only (at least on earth) of vision
through veils that protect and conceal.[83] All is a sacred veil: the
world as much as the Church and her sacraments, the hierarchies
in heaven and on earth. But it veils only in order to initiate one
more perfectly, so that ascending the steps of the shrine one can
draw yet nearer to the mystery. Theology is essentially
initiation, *myesthai*.[84] But the mystery entrusted to the initiate
(even the expression *thiasōtēs*, participant in the cult of
Dionysus, is used for him[85]) is none other than that of the divine
being of God, whose minister (*leitourgos*[86]) he is to be. Theology
in an all-embracing sense is—as in the pictures of the
Apocalypse—the concentric arrangement of heaven and earth,
angels and men, in praise around the throne of the Invisible: the
Word, that is repeated in an ever louder echo, around the silent
centre; sounds around the essential stillness, unapproachable,
hidden.[87] First the angels are 'called to proclaim the divine
silence, set up as manifest lights, so to speak, interpreting what is

[80] In his translation of DN, p. 80, n.
[81] It occurs, together with its derivatives, 108 times.
[82] EH I.1 (372A).
[83] CH I.2 (121B).
[84] DN I.8 (597AC), DN III.1 (680B), III.2 (681AB), CH II.5 (*entheos entheōn
en myēsei ginomenos*, 145C), VI.1 (200C), and particularly CH I.5 (376D–
377B), where the whole of Christianity is described as a mystery religion.
[85] CH II.1 (136D); III.2 (165A); EH I.1 (372A).
[86] Denys only uses the word for the ecclesiastical and hierarchical office.
[87] DN XI.1 (949A).

in the sanctuary (*adyta*).'[88] This central silence is for Denys not at
all the empty silence of non-Christian mysticism, but rather that
unique, primordial Word which transcends all the sounding
words. The further its echo sounds, the more words are needed
to realise it. For even the angels fall short of expressing it
adequately,[89] and men need many words indeed. This is 'why
the latest, most remote, works are much longer than the first
and highest. The fundamental concepts of theology and the
explanation of the divine names must be much briefer than the
Symbolic Theology, for the higher we ascend, the more the realm
of words narrows—in proportion as our spiritual perspectives
expand. Just as now, on our entry into the darkness that is
beyond understanding, we find not even brevity of words, but
complete wordlessness and failure of the understanding. . . . In
the end speech is rendered utterly inaudible, and becomes
completely one with the Inexpressible.'[90] The word that proclaims to those outside must, therefore, if it is to be a true word,
itself embrace the divine stillness: in other words, the theological
liturgy must be essentially contemplative. The aim of the
sacramental liturgy is the spiritual enactment of that which is
celebrated in symbols—*ut quae sollemni celebramus officio,
purificatae mentis intellegentia consequamur*[91]—but the spiritual
insight is 'more hidden and more unified, more unifying'.[92]
Theology must therefore take care not to multiply interpretations infinitely, lest it lose its symmetry with the one
Word, just as Denys, in his short treatises, 'was concerned about
the symmetry of his expression and about honouring the
transcendent hiddenness of the divine with silence.'[93] Earthly
liturgy makes this unconditional demand that the celebrating
hierarch (bishop) be perfected in the contemplation of the
divine and be still, so that while he does indeed go forth into the
congregation, in imitation of God's going forth, in his actions,

[88] DN IV.2 (696B), similarly IV.22 (724B). Koch, *op. cit.* 131.
[89] DN XIII.4 (981C). Stiglmair's translation does not give this sense.
[90] MTh IIIe (1033BC).
[91] *Postcommunio* for the Mass of the Epiphany [that what we have solemnly
celebrated, we may apprehend with the understanding of a purified mind].
[92] CH X.1 (272D).
[93] CH XV.9 (340B).

speaking and consecrating, he nevertheless during this moving out in action still holds fast to contemplation—like God himself—and leads all his activity back to it.[94] But if the unity of the sacrament and the 'insight of purified spirit' is the very meaning of the liturgical enactment, then it becomes clear why Denys will have nothing to do with an isolated consideration and treatment of *opus operatum*: the moral enactment is not a second act alongside the sacramental which merely occasions it, it must be one with it or it is nothing at all. If Denys affirms the principle of Tertullian and the Donatists that only he can mediate who himself possesses, only that can shine which 'has itself in a measure become the sun',[95] then this is said from no sectarian zeal,[96] but from the ideal of his theological perspective, from which he refuses to stray. The priest and theologian who does not live out of the grace of his office departs from the law of being which demands the unity of essential and moral 'worth'. For Denys it is pointless for a theologian to speak from any other perspective than that of purifying, illuminating and unifying grace. The realm of sin, apostasy and rejection can concern the Christian liturgy only insofar as it provides the raw material for the Church's activity which sets forth liturgically the salvation wrought by Christ. It is the Church which thus transforms the chaos of the realm of sin, by the inclusion of the 'embryonic'[97] existence of the catechumens, the possessed (that is, hardened sinners), the only half-converted and the penitents in the structure of the hierarchical liturgy—whereby we must remember that the liturgy embraces more than the three sacramental ceremonies of water, bread and wine, and of chrism.

As with the anarchy of sin, so too Denys considers the realm of human life and humanity in general only under this form. The meaning of the Fall and of the ordering of man's existence towards death, the meaning of the cross and redemption and of human hope and of correct human action: all this is declared to

---

[94] EH III.3.3 (429AB), III.3.10 (440A). A notion which made a deep impression on the medieval understanding of vocation.

[95] EH III.3.14 (445AB).

[96] Although Denys is not afraid of drawing practical conclusions: Ep 8.2 (1192BC).

[97] EH III.3.6; VI.1 (432C–433B; 532A).

us by the 'divine utterances' (for it is of such that Denys speaks, rather than of the 'Scriptures') in Epistle and Gospel.[98] Indeed the whole scriptural revelation is taken up as the 'reading' into the liturgical action—it is portrayed in this distinctive perspective from Genesis to the Apocalypse[99]—it is so to speak raised to a liturgical potency, it is moulded into the theology of the celebrating Church, to which the 'holy songs' of Scripture (Psalms and alleluia) already provide the bridge. The only consideration of the relation between the Old and the New Testaments in the whole work of the Areopagite is in this place, a purely liturgical one. In this context it is a matter of the mystery of the Incarnation as also of the following of Christ,[100] but the Incarnation has to be seen in a measure in the context of the other theophanies[101]—as their consummation—and the following of Christ in the context of the 'imitation of God' (*mimēsis theou*).[102] All history is, as it were, aesthetically set at a distance, forming an eternal, sacred picture (*agalma*),[103] for the Church has no longer any proper history, or, if one prefers, its history forms a kind of heavenly concert, like the great polyphony of Josquin or Palestrina, the roots of which stretch back to the cosmic music of the Pythagoreans. 'It is certainly true that his writings represent a bold attempt to provide a series of intelligible settings for the various acts of the Christian history of salvation; so, for example, the whole earthly life of the Lord appears as it were swallowed up in the timeless contemplation of the sacrament of the eucharist. Yet it cannot be said that Denys destroys the meaning of history; the world and its contents are

[98] EH III.3.11 (440C–441C); IV.3.10 (484B); VII.3.8–9 (565AC), etc.
[99] EH III.3.4–5 (429C–432B).
[100] EH II.3.2 (401D–405A); III.3.12 (444B); V.3.4 (512AB): 'The sign of the cross means the destruction of all fleshly desires, and a life in imitation of God, unwaveringly contemplating the human and most divine life of Jesus who, in accordance with the sinlessness laid down by the Thearchy, went to the cross and death, and those who thus live, imprinted with the sign of the cross, become like him and bear the image of their own sinlessness.' Ep 8.4 (1096AB) portrays the ethic of the monk and the priest as an imitation of the Good Shepherd.
[101] DN I.4 (592BC).
[102] EH III.3.12 (441C).
[103] *Cf.* v. d. Daele.

not given once for all as in Greek wisdom, rather the divine truth is inscribed as an event in the very bosom of space and time.'[104] And the union of the world and God, which is already philosophically the only possible justification of its multiplicity and its existence, is brought to completion precisely in the Incarnation, the efficacy of which is continued in the sacraments, above all in the eucharist.

As the dogmatic hymns of the Western Fathers are taken up in the liturgy, as are indeed those of the later Byzantines, so it is a mark of the purity of style of the Dionysian theology that as a work which is overall hymnic in character it assumes, on occasion, the tone of great poetry. As for example in the last chapter of the *Divine Names*, which praises God with a wealth of titles:

'The many-named God is called Pantocrator, because he is the all-ruling seat of all things, embracing and penetrating everything, giving it stability and foundation in himself, and binding all together. He perfects everything in himself so that it shall not be moved, and everything comes from him as proceeding from an almighty root, and all things are drawn into himself in return, as to an almighty trunk which bears and supports all, and he embraces all things as the sovereign throne of all. All embraced find security in him in accordance with a single transcendent embrace; sent forth from him and driven from this all-perfecting hearth, they may not perish. The Thearchy is also called Pantocrator, as both ruling over all and as holding sway, yet without confusion, within all things, as being desired and loved by all, and imposing a voluntary yoke on all and the sweet pangs of a divine, almighty and indissoluble longing for its own goodness.'[106]

Such language, too, which can be distinguished from the rest only by degrees, is meant to reveal the symmetry, the appropriateness to its object; it is in its way a much more exact expression of the vision of the divinity of God than most of what a theology that works by definitions can say about God.

[104] Roques, *L'univers dionysien*, 123.
[105] EH III.3.12–13 (444AD).
[106] DN X.1 (936–937A). *Cf.* the hymn to God as peace, DN XI.2.

There can be no doubting that Denys was a monk: that much is clear enough from his humble[107] placing of the monastic state in the last hierarchy below the priestly state[108] and his blazing censure of Demophilus. His theology too, like everything in the West that stems from Benedict, is a theology of monasticism,[109] which in its structure is to be contrasted sharply with a theology of the priestly hierarchy (the Roman) or a lay-theology, whether medieval or modern. It is noteworthy that the genuine, inwardly hierarchical theology has not been created by the Romans but by a Greek, in whose ecclesiastical hierarchy the papacy is indeed not mentioned: his hierarchy is concerned with degrees of consecration which correspond from the first with the degrees of authority.

4. THEOLOGICAL SYMBOLISM

We must now attempt to give an outline of the three stages of this theology: the material stage (of symbols), the intellectual stage (of predominantly affirmative expression) and the divine stage (of predominantly negative expression). The methods are distinguishable, but they condition one another and are complementary, at least for us men. For example, we can understand the material symbol only if we see its spiritual content, but only if we also grasp the complete inadequacy of this spiritual content as applied to God.[110] It cannot be said that the symbolism and the spiritual conceptuality express God's immanence, while mysticism expresses his transcendence, for the symbols and

---

[107] Cf. DN III.2 (684A); XI.1 (949B).

[108] EH VI.1.1 (532A); VI.1.3 naturally depicts the ideal state of the monk, but equally in its subordinate rank (*deuterōs*) (533A). Monks do not have, as do priests, an apostolic commission and mission to lead others; they remain in one place in their holy unity, obey priestly directions, and follow the priests like faithful fellow-travellers on the road to divine apprehension of the mysteries which have been committed to them (VII.3.1; 533C).

[109] As most recently Dom Jean Leclercq has developed it in his balanced work on the theology of monasticism in the Middle Ages (*L'amour des lettres et le désir de Dieu* [1957]; ET. *The Love of Learning and the Desire for God* [1962]).

[110] Cf. O. Semmelroth, 'Die Theologia *symbolikē* des Ps.-Dionysius Areopagita', *Schol* 27 (1952), 1–11.

concepts can only be interpreted as referring to God, who in all analogies remains the 'Wholly-Other', while the mystic negations have no other goal than to express the contact, encounter, union with God, as he really is. In other words: the whole tension between cataphatic and apophatic theology runs right through symbolic theology, as Denys continually emphasizes. For in the sensible symbol, in its necessity and impossibility, there is exposed not only the dialectic of the doctrine of God, for God is and must be both all in all and nothing in anything, but also the doctrine of man, for man is 'indivisible' as regards his soul and 'divisible' as regards his body, and a divine revelation to him therefore naturally needs both levels, that of the 'simple, inward pictures' and that of the external 'symbolically fashioned figures, which have been artistically fashioned beforehand'.[111] It is the greatness of man and his tragedy to embrace both without being able to bring them into a final synthesis: to be immersed in the aesthetics of the world of images and at the same time to have irresistibly to dissolve all images in the light of the unimaginable. Perhaps never in the history of theology has the unity of the two been more strikingly visible than here. By no means is Denys just the advocate and architect of negative theology, the mystical iconoclast, as he is generally thought to be. He is not even, like Origen, the unflinching allegorist, for whom the 'letter' is pre-eminently a pointer, an appeal to search for the deeper, spiritual meaning; rather, with Denys we characteristically find of allegory neither the word nor the thing. In his attempt to elucidate and explain the text, Origen's concern with the literal meaning (*historia*) is no more than philological, whereas Denys contemplates the divine symbols in creation and the Church with an aesthetic delight. Things are not simply the occasion for his seeing God; rather, he sees God in things. Colours, shapes, essences and properties are for him immediate theophanies, and if he gives up the veil for the sake of what is veiled, then he gives up something that he has embraced and loved. He can give dialectical expression to this state of affairs, as when he speaks of an 'unlike likeness',[112] or says that 'the same things can be both

---

[111] *Promemēchanēmenois tōn typikōn symbolōn anaplasmois*: Ep 9.1 (1108A).
[112] CH XV.8 (337B).

like God and unlike him: like, in virtue of the possible imitation of the inimitable, and unlike, because of the difference between effects and their cause, because they fall short in an infinite and incomparable degree of their origin.'[113] But he knows too that this dialectic is nothing other than the unravellable phenomenon of the 'significance' (sēmainein) of a 'manifestation'.[114] If, then, Denys expounds his theory of 'like unlikenesses and unlike likenesses', that is, of those images of God and the angels which seem to make immediate reference in themselves to God, such as light, fire, water, and a sweet smell, and those others, so frequent in the Scriptures, which by means of their striking inappropriateness invite us to reject them in order to lift ourselves from the picture to what is meant, and indeed precisely in these pictures to see the 'protective shields' that guard against any confusion of sense and spirit, or the world and God, then he clearly knows that both functions are ultimately complementary and at their limits pass without a break into each other, 'because the ineffable and what can be uttered are inextricably entwined (sympeplektai)'.[115] 'The reflective spirit' must always 'regard the manifestation of beautiful things as reflections of a beautiful form not made manifest, sensible odours as the expression of an intelligible emanation, and material light as an image of the diffusion of immaterial light, and the discursiveness of sacred instruction as a pointer to the fulness of contemplative reason.'[116] Indeed, were it not for the 'stimulus' of unsuitable pictures—which represent to us angels as stones and beasts, and God himself as angry, grievously affected, as cursing, deceiving, war-mongering, and so on— were it not for the 'perfect inadequacy',[117] then there would be a great danger of resting content with the affirmations, of imagining angels as 'golden, radiant forms',[118] and ascribing an elementary beauty to God himself. This inappropriateness applies just as much to the symbols of the cosmos as to those of the Bible or the Church's sacraments, so there is no question with Denys of 'demythologizing' Scripture or the Church in order to contemplate God more purely in nature, nor of

[113] DN IX.7 (916A).   [114] DN IX.5 (912D–913A).
[115] Ep 9.1 (1105D).   [116] CH I.3 (121D).
[117] CH II.2 (137D).   [118] CH II.3 (141B).

devaluing the images of nature in favour of Scripture and the Church (as with many spiritual writers of the Middle Ages), because the Bible and the sacramental order depend on the images drawn from creation, for example on the symbolic power of water, of bread and wine, light and oil, used in the administration of the sacraments. Nor can one say that Denys in his interpretation of the cosmic language of essences is determined by his own age. His art of interpretation betrays only a loving and deeply absorbed gaze into the elements, forms and processes, which is characteristic above all of the artist. Nor can one say, finally, that he projects the sensible into the spiritual (the negative theology should be sufficient protection against this), but one must rather notice that his penetrating contemplation of the symbols makes it possible for him to receive an utterly different—and quite concrete—picture of God from that found in predominantly abstract and conceptual theologians. An example: the image of fire, for which the Scriptures have a particular fondness:

'The sacred theologians many times describe that being which is beyond being and any form in terms of fire, which contains many images of the nature of the Thearchy—if it is permitted to say this—in sensible terms. For sensible fire is, so to say, in all things and shines through all things without confusion and yet is at the same time quite distinct from all things; it is both wholly luminous and yet also secret, unknowable in itself, if there is no combustible material in which it can manifest its peculiar energy; it cannot be mastered or banished, having power over all and assimilating everything it penetrates to its own essence and activity; communicating itself to everything that approaches it in whatever manner; renewing and rejuvenating with its vital warmth, illuminating by its irresistible rays; unvanquished, unmingled, dividing and unchangeable, tending upwards, attacking vigorously, blazing up, not open to flattery and pandering; eternally on the move, self-moved, moving others; circumscribing and uncircumscribed, needy of nothing, increasing itself secretly and manifesting its own greatness to those substances that receive it; active, powerful, invisibly present to all things, not seeming to exist if neglected, but suddenly revealing itself as indwelling things and yet as obedient

to its own nature when rubbed—which is a way of seeking it—
and then again flying away from men's grasp; undiminished by
all its joyful bestowals of itself. And many other properties of
fire can be found that provide a visible image of the thearchic
energy.'[119]

One can only with difficulty resist the temptation to quote
profusely the theological portrayals by this poet of water, wind
and clouds, and particularly of the fragrance of God, the
delightful interpretations that go right to the heart of such
things as bodily eating and drinking and the assimilation of
food, sleeping and waking, and also the drunkenness of God (as
the 'ineffable measurelessness of the divine perfection').[120] Particularly noteworthy are his accounts of the spiritual significance of the colours,[121] of the essential properties of the beasts—
the might of the ox, the sublime untameability of the lion, the
majesty, powerful ascent, swiftness, watchfulness, inventive-
ness, and sharp-sightedness of the eagle, and so on[122]—of the
power of symbolic expression found in the human body and its
individual organs[123]: this gives one an idea of what natural
contemplation (*theōria physikē*) can mean in Greek theology.

The same thing recurs in the Holy Scripture, which, although
in contrast to nature it is throughout regarded as the Word of
God, is as a whole a symbolic cosmos which is to be read as such
within the tradition of 'spirit to spirit'.[124] And because Scripture
provides a better education in the things of God than does
nature, it is here that are to be found especially images that
startle because of their discordance. They are found much less in
the mysteries of the Church, in the *theamata* (contemplations,
remarkable dramatic presentations) of her liturgy, which are
regarded more as divinely ordained, appropriate[125] translations

[119] CH XV.2 (329AC).
[120] Above all Ep 9; CH chaps. 2 and 15; in EH in the contemplations
concerning the sacraments and ordinations.
[121] CH XV.8 (337AB).
[122] *Ibid.* (337A).
[123] *Ibid.* XV.3 (329C–332D).
[124] EH I.4 (376BC).
[125] EH II.3.6: *akribēs eikōn* [exact image] (401C); III.3.1: *en taxei* [in order or
rank] (428A); II.3.7: *oikeiotēs tōn symbolōn* [properties of the symbols] (404B);
II.3.1: *ouden aprepes ē anhieron* [nothing unsuitable or profane] (397A).

of the spiritual into the sensible. In particular the *theoria* of the
bishop and priest must pass through all these sensible signs in
order to fix itself directly on the spiritual sense;[126] indeed, the
spiritual understanding must precede the sensible celebration,
which is why the liturgy of the Word and the eucharistic prayer
come before the consecration and communion.[127] The symbolism of the sacraments is naturally not to be construed in our
modern attenuated sense: it is quite clear that the mysteries
continent et causant quae significant.[128] One ought rather to extend
this realism to the other holy symbols, the cosmos and the Holy
Scriptures: even if they do not cause, at least they contain what
they signify. Therefore the pictorial character of the liturgical
ordinance belongs unconditionally to the sacramental effectiveness: the ever-present fragrance of the holy oil, the sweet smell
and the rising movement of the incense, the movement of the
celebrant from the altar to the people and back again, the sign of
the cross in baptism, confirmation and hierarchical consecration, the dipping of the baptizand in imitation of Christ's
descent into death, the tonsure of the monk, the breaking of the
host, the assimilation of the bread and wine in communion, and
whatever else the purifying, illuminating and perfecting
mystery-rites contain. Their holy forms are finally the content
of all true form-ation: only through them does the material,
embryonic man attain his divinely ordained form.[129]

In the Church's liturgy the Platonic dialectic of the image is to
a certain extent stilled: its emphasis on the image as 'holy myth'
together with its destruction of the image for the sake of the
pure concept and finally of mystical union. As little as the great,
final image of God in the world, Jesus Christ, can be dissolved
and thus rendered null and void (no more than can be the
Transfiguration and the Resurrection), as little are the divinely

Therefore too the sacraments and ceremonies are only 'visible images of the
invisible, as has been shown in the treatise on sensible and spiritual objects'
(397C).
    [126] EH IV.3.2 (476B).
    [127] EH III.3.12 (441CD).
    [128] [contain and cause what they signify]. As is clear in the way the Eucharist
fosters unity as a *proodos* of the one Christ into multiplicity and the return of
the many into his unity: III.3.12 (444AB). *Cf.* Semmelroth, *op. cit.* 8–9.
    [129] EH III.3.6 (432CD–433A).

ordained images of the Church, its hierarchy and liturgy to be spiritualized away. A true theology of images can be achieved only in a Christian context, as the next methodical step will definitively show. It belongs to the Areopagite to have caught up the whole spiritual energy of the Alexandrines and the Cappadocians in his work and at the same time to have banished definitively their tendency to threaten the Incarnation, the visible Church and the resurrection of the flesh.

5. THEOLOGICAL EIDETIC

Only through the mediation of an understanding spirit can the sensible symbols speak of God. What such a spirit understands of God are those 'names of God' in the cosmos, which are the expression of his true communication and self-explanation. But the understanding spirit is first the pure, creaturely spirit, the angel, and only secondly the spirit bound to a body, man. It is for the sake of this spirit that God has spoken of himself in the world and Scripture (*theo-logia* as God's speech), that there are inspired heralds of God's word (*theo-logoi* as prophets, apostles, those inspired, the commonest use of the word in Denys), that there is finally a theo-logy in the Church, in the modern sense of the word. The spirit of angels and man can theo-logically understand the whole communication of God in which he, the created spirit, is a part. But he would not understand if, in so doing, he failed to discern that all his understanding is an understanding of the incomprehensible, because it is an understanding of God. All the divine names together produce nothing less than a system of God: that is indicated in the introduction to the treatise on the 'divine names' which, after some preliminary remarks on the holy tradition of revelation (chap. 1), goes on immediately to treat of the central content of revelation (chap. 2): of the three-in-oneness of God, which is clearly expressed in dogmatic-liturgical form, but as a whole is consigned to the darkness of the unsearchable *mysterium*. In this way any theology of an *imago trinitatis* in the creature is strictly rejected: whether an Origenist 'sub-division' of the 'realms' of the Father, the Son and the Spirit within the created order

(Father–being, Son–life, Spirit–reason, or Father–being, Son–reason, and Spirit–holiness), or a Tertullianist-Joachimite partition of saving history amongst the three persons, or an Augustinian indication of *vestigia* and *imagines* in the structure of the individual creature. And this rejection is the work of a pupil of Proclus for whom the whole structure of being and the world has a triadic structure! One senses what sort of ascesis the Areopagite imposed on himself with this constant renunciation. The mystery within the unsearchable unity has nothing to do with number and cannot be translated into numbers.[130] Only by directing our gaze upwards to the transcendent unity do we look in the direction of the trinitarian mystery. And it is not that some aspects of God are comprehensible while others are not: in this way the theological schematism found in Philo and Proclus is transcended in a Christian way. It is not that one can 'only' know the powers of God *ad extra*, but not the underlying essence; rather, for Denys what is Incomprehensible is to be found in what is really comprehensible, for it is in every case the incomprehensible God in his totality who makes himself comprehensible in his communications. Nowhere is there any trace of the Gnostic and Hegelian *Ungrund*, whose obscurity ultimately gives way to universal comprehensibility: in its stead we find everywhere the consciousness that even in the most comprehensible we are concerned with the mystery and in the most incomprehensible we are embraced by the supreme light of the Godhead. This is the sphere of Christian thought, marked out once for all with the utmost precision and lucidity—even for thinkers who will think in quite another way, perhaps much more biblically or 'existentially', than Denys.

This spiritual theology has two areas. The one is the interpretation of the world as the *act* of divine communication (*proodos*): that is the content of the theology of the 'divine names'. The second is the interpretation of the world as the *result* of this communication, that is, the divinely ordained 'holy order' (*hier-*

---

[130] DN I.4 (589D); II.2 (640A) and particularly II.4 (640Dff.); II.5 (644A): 'Participation is for the whole Godhead something common, united and one, so that each of the participants participates in the whole and complete essence, and not only in a part'; II.8 (645Cff.).

archia), which can be seen as the result only as the return of the creature to God (*epistrophē*). We shall deal with these in turn.

The act by which God allows creation to share in his being, through which the world comes into being and in which it consists, is God himself, in whom each creature participates, as does each radius in the centre of the circle, or each mark of a seal in the original. But as a radius only subsists because of the centre and the mark only because of the seal, and yet the centre is not a radius, nor the seal a mark, we must speak of 'participation, while not participating': God's primordial reasons are 'participated in for all that they cannot be shared' (*amethektōs metechomena*).[131] The multiplication and differentiation of the participants is primarily a matter of 'closeness' and 'distance'— that is admittedly a picture that reminds one of both Origen and Plotinus and yet is understood in the sense of neither—it is, always allowing the necessary deficiency of all being that is not divine, also a matter of the determination and positioning of beings by God, who allots to each its being and essence 'analogously'. The deliberate turning of God towards the creature is equally that in which it participates (the communicated God) and the truth of the creature; the ideas or paradigms are equally the predestinations.[133] Because the creature participates in that 'which cannot be shared' and yet not, as for example in Spinoza, as an accident in a substance, it participates in God's *allowing* it *to share* and as a creaturely being necessarily possesses within itself the ontological difference between Being and being—put in general terms—or between that in which it participates and that which participates (*metocha* and *metechonta*). This distinction, which is the very basis of the ontology of creatureliness, was already repeatedly misunderstood in Denys' time, so that, towards the end of the book, he explains it yet again to some rather slow-witted person who had asked him about it in a letter (Chap. XI.6)—and yet even today he is

[131] DN II.5 (644A).

[132] But in a genuinely aesthetic way, because the picture of nearness and distance makes perceptible the *taxis* and hierarchy of the graded structure of the world.

[133] DN V.8 (824C).

persistently misinterpreted. His teaching is as simple and luminous as possible, as he himself says: 'We are convinced that this is not an intricate problem but rather the most direct and simple explanation.'[134] One must simply guard against hypostatizing the *metocha* (the participated) as any sort of 'gods' or 'world demiurges' or 'angelic essences' (as did Proclus and the Gnostics)—in Denys' theology they have therefore nothing to do with the angelic hierarchies—but nor are they simply the archetypal 'thoughts' of God (as Augustine interpreted the Platonic ideas); rather, they are the genuine reality of the world itself, in so far as it consists of principles which share their reality with the individual essences that participate (*metochonta*), of which principles Denys indeed says that among themselves they stand in a relationship of participation, because Life Itself participates in Being Itself, and Wisdom Itself participates in both.[135]

'And so before everything else first Being Itself is brought forth (*probeblētai*). And Being Itself is prior to Life Itself and Wisdom Itself and Divinisation Itself and so all the others (scil. *metocha*) in which things participate in Being before anything else,'[136] which can be best understood in terms of Thomas Aquinas' *actus essendi*. Denys does not want to make a real distinction between it and Life Itself, Spirit Itself and even Divinisation Itself, but only to distinguish it in terms of the *metechonta*'s degree of intensity of participation. But Thomas does not in any way designate his *actus essendi* as a 'creature', rather creatures are for him only the *metechonta*; no more does Denys, who is at the same time careful not to equate the *autometochai*[137] with God in himself. We see him first of all ranking goodness (*agathotēs*) above the *actus essendi* because goodness embraces in its sphere not only being, but also not-being (by which is meant any kind of subjective or objective potentiality), so that therefore the act of being is always already embraced by the absolutely primordial determination: the Good. This most sublime and pious of all metaphysical thoughts, which later Christian ontology was hardly able to do

---

[134] DN XI.6 (953C). [135] DN V.5 (820A).
[136] *Ibid.* [137] *Ibid.* (820C).

justice to, finds its true resonance in Denys, because with him the *metocha* are no longer emanations of the One but those world-principles that effect and mediate participation in the living God. But where the Good can be seen as the embracing principle of all divine communication, God himself is rightly raised above all the principles of his communication (otherwise there would be no participation in him) and is always designated as beyond being (*hyperousios*: 115 times), beyond the cosmos, beyond the heavens, super-abundant, beyond perfection, supernatural (*hyperphyēs*), and finally beyond the divine (*hypertheos*), because 'God' is that in which the creatures can by grace participate through the principle of 'divinisation'; but that in which they participate is itself precisely that in which they cannot participate, for were it not that, they would not be participating in God.[138] He who does not keep that in mind at every stage of his thought has, in Denys' opinion, no understanding of creaturely being. But he neither intends to develop an immanent ontology of the creature, nor to offer a doctrine of God as he is in himself; rather he wants (in the *Divine Names*) 'to celebrate providence manifested as creative of good, most excellent goodness and the source of all good, as being, life and spirit, as the source that makes being and life and grants spirit to all those who participate in being, life, spirit, reason and feeling.'[139] Therefore God is called in the world 'by all names', while he remains in himself (and therefore for us too) nameless;[140] he is 'of all forms' without himself possessing a form;[141] he who creates and releases from himself every relationship and each opposite in the world is therefore necessarily beyond identity (*tautotēs*) and otherness (*heterotēs*), equality (*isotēs*) and inequality (*anisotēs*), likeness (*homoiotēs*) and unlikeness (*anomoiotēs*),[142] and also something that will interest Nicholas of

[138] 'If we call the hiddenness (*kryphiotēs*) which is beyond being 'God', or 'life', or 'being', or 'light', or 'word', then we mean by that nothing else but the powers which come forth from it to us and effect divinity, or make being, or beget life, or grant wisdom'; DN II.7 (645A). Same teaching in DN II.11 (649CD); DN XII.2 (969C), CH XIII.4 (304C).

[139] DN V.2 (816C).

[140] DN I.6 (396AB); XII.1 (969A): *apeironymos* (of boundless names).

[141] DN V.8 (821B).

[142] DN VIII and IX; cf. *Indices*, v.d. Daele.

Cusa—beyond greatness and smallness, and—something that had fascinated Gregory of Nyssa—beyond movement and rest.[143] As God in his radiance makes himself available as gift and fashions the world,[144] two things happen: the gift takes on a graduated form and therefore brings forth the different realms of being (*proodos*), but also at each level the whole God communicates himself and presents himself and therefore draws everything back to himself as a unity (*epistrophē*). So the structure of the treatise on the Divine Names becomes clear:

I. Introduction

1. On theological knowledge and manner of expression (chap. 1).

2. On unity and distinction in God: a. the Trinity, b. creation, c. Incarnation (chap. 2). In what follows neither the Trinity nor the Incarnation will be dealt with, but creation as God's communication.

3. On the methods of theology: prayer, holy Tradition, relationship between the master and his disciples (chap. 3).

II. The names of the act of creation (as names of the stages of being, names of distribution, *proodos*).

1. The name that transcendently embraces all being, that of the *Good* (beside which, of equal rank and the same meaning, stand the names of light, beauty and *eros*. Evil, discussed from the point of view of the embracing good.) (chap. 4).

2. The act of *being* which underlies all stages. The fundamentals of being, idea and *metochē* (chap. 5).

3. *Life*, as a particular form (intensity) of being (chap. 6).

4. *Intelligence* (*nous*), as the highest intensity of being. And in relation to this, spiritual accomplishment (reason, faith) and truth (chap. 7a).

III. The names of the act by which things are brought back to

---

[143] DN IX.8–9 (916BD).

[144] The affirmation of true creation by Denys is no problem; Stiglmair refers to it many times, and it is to be postulated from his Christian understanding of God without more ado, exactly as with Augustine, even if both of them use Platonic vocabulary for it.

their home or of controlling providence (names of union, *epistrophē*).

1. *Wisdom* (*sophia*) (chap. 7b).

2. *Power* (*dynamis*) as ordered (justice), salvific (salvation, preservation, redemption), apportioning equally (*isotēs*) (chap. 8).

3. Apropos the equality of God in the inequality of things (which proceeds from God) the names of contraries are dealt with: great–small, identity–difference, likeness–unlikeness, rest–movement, and comprehensive likeness (chap. 9).

4. Names embracing time and space: Pantocrator, 'Ancient of Days', Time and Age (aeon) (chap. 10).

5. Peace (*eirēnē*). Appendix to chap. 5 on the meaning of the *metochai* (chap. 11).

IV. The Names of perfected Union and Transcendence.

1. The potentiated names (of power): Holy of Holies, King of Kings, Lord of Lords, God of Gods (chap. 12).

2. Final name: Perfection and *Unity*.

Endre von Ivánka[145] has argued that we have here a structure consisting of the names of procession and distinction, dealt with in accordance with Proclus' schema (II), and then of the names of providence drawn from the triad of Constantinian theology, in which the names of the three churches founded by Constantine in Constantinople appear: Hagia Sophia, Hagia Dynamis and Hagia Eirene, interlarded with the names of contraries applied to the One, mentioned in Plato's *Parmenides* (and discussed by Proclus in his *Parmenides* commentary!). The last-discussed names complete the series by reverting to the beginning and so set at the very end the Biblical and Platonic names of unity. Denys does not want the transition from II to III, or from III to IV, to appear too obvious, so intelligence and wisdom are dealt with under the same heading, and the chapter on peace forms a hinge between the third and fourth parts. Any

---

[145] 'Der Aufbau der Schrift De Divinis Nominibus des Ps.-Dionysios', *Schol* XV (1940), 386–399 (reprinted in *Plato Christianus*, 228–242). Ivánka can demonstrate references to the Constantinian triad in Gregory of Nyssa.

sharp disjunction would have obscured the complementary immanence of the points of view. The One is not placed at the beginning, as in Plotinus and Proclus, but at the end, together with concrete totality (*teleion*), which rules out any suspicion of an idealist unfolding in 'procession' or a mere filling-up of the abstract. The One belongs to the realm of the good, of beauty and of *eros*, which express the power of the primordial Godhead in radiance and affirmation that underlies any concrete form of being and fundamentally shapes any real or possible creation. This primordially divine power of affirmation, in which all created things participate in every respect, and to which all the great theological images of the cosmos in the West from Eriugena to Hegel are indebted, may never be attenuated, in Denys' theology, in favour of the expressions of negative theology or relegated to the second rank. The 'yes' to the world that issues from God and is repeated at every level of being is just as original as the knowledge every creature has that it is not God, either as an individual or generically. And that must equally be dealt with.

But first two concluding remarks. The first is about the wholes (*hola*; the word *holon* occurs over 180 times). In the Dionysian cosmos they are neither bare generic concepts or 'ideas', nor hypostases or demigods; rather, they are, as we saw with the highest *hola* (being–life–wisdom), genuine aspects of concrete reality, which contain the participants in themselves without endangering their individuality and only together with them form the all: *meros kai holon* is *pān*.[146] Perhaps the neglect of this aspect of reality in Christian theology has provoked the repeated reactions of pantheism, but these for their part did not notice that according to Denys the Godhead is certainly truly immanent in the *hola* (just as it is in the *pān* as such), but only because it transcends the *hola*, the *merē* and the *pān*.

The second point touches the hierarchical structure of the world as a concentric formation around God: from the greatest closeness—the highest angels stand *amesōs*, immediately, before God[147]—through all the ranks of the angelic and ecclesiastical

---

[146] DN II.10 (648C). [part and whole is the all.]
[147] CH VII.3 (209C) and frequently.

hierarchies to the beasts, plants and the 'most distant echo' of the
divine names, to material things and the 'not-being' of pure
matter.[148] Now this is certainly a vision of the greatest aesthetic
power, but it is not without its problems. For with this
'distancing' the light, the power, and also the Word of God are
'weakened',[149] because the medium in which the revelation is
'refracted' becomes thicker and less transparent,[150] because further the intervening levels become more numerous, and because
by the same token even the Incarnation of God falls under this
'general hierarchical law',[151] which means that Christ is, as man,
necessarily subject to the angels.[152] Is this law of a gradual
'lessening' and 'darkening' acceptable in a Christian theology? Is
it not trying to express in a single form two irreconcilable
points: the truth of the right ordering of the cosmos and the
truth of the sinful fall from God?[153] Against that one can
immediately say with Ivánka that the system of mediation
found in Gnosticism and Neo-Platonism is undermined in a
Christian sense by Denys with his assertion of the immediate
relationship of all creatures, especially man, to a personal God of
love.[154] One can also make the opposite and therefore
complementary point that, in a splendid passage in the
Ecclesiastical Hierarchy, Denys condemns those who despise the
prayers of the saints and think themselves capable of ascending
to God by their own efforts alone.[155] Here hierarchy is understood as the communion of saints, which is one way of
conceiving it for Denys: if with the angels there is no sin and
therefore no error in the passing on of the spiritual light, then
just as little is it the case in the ecclesiastical hierarchy as such,
considered as the divinely-ordered arrangement.

But there is yet a third aspect to consider. God is essentially
kryphiotēs, unified depth of mystery, which as such is hidden.

---

[148] *E.g.* DN IV.2–3 (696–697).
[149] *amydroū* (CH VIII.2: 240C).
[150] DN IV.4 (697CD).
[151] CH VIII.2 (240D).
[152] CH IV.4 (181A–D, esp. C).
[153] *Cf.* Gandillac on CH IX.3 (critical edition, p. 135).
[154] 'Inwieweit ist Pseudo-Dionysius Neuplatoniker?' *Schol* (1956), 393f.
[155] EH VII.3.6 (561BC).

Revelation of this mystery is necessarily double-sided: it will be clearest to the highest creatures, who as the most unified will receive it most immediately; in this way its mysterious character will be most truly preserved. The further revelation penetrates, the more it will need words of interpretation, the more 'public' and 'expounded' (*emphanēs*) it will become, and just to that extent the weaker in meaning. The theophany and theology of the angels is '*kryphiotera*, more secret, because more intellectual and simple and more unified, and *phanotera*, clearer, because the first gift and the first manifestation, because poured out more universally and potently, into this transparent order.'[156] The more expounded (*emphanesteron, ekphanesteron*), more discursive theology of the lower levels, even that of men, is therefore a sign of distance:[157] there is a shift here in the understanding of revealedness and therefore in another way—in that of mystery, for with increasing interpretation the mystery is veiled still more, 'and the Thearchy as it were reduces its radiance so as to uphold the oneness and unknowability of its own mystery.'[158] The nearer a creature stands to not-being (and the boundary between being and not-being is pure matter), the darker is God's revelation of himself in it, or the more God reveals in it his darkness. If God is in the beings as that which is beyond being, he is in nothingness as that which is beyond nothing,[159] and in this way the sudden radiance of God can shine into the darkness of human existence (suddenly—*exaiphnēs*) in the Incarnation of the Son, because here what is the more revealed is the more hidden: 'He who is beyond being has come forth from his secret place, clothed in being in a human form, to manifest himself among us. And yet he is hidden even after his manifestation, or to speak more divinely, precisely in his manifestation. For this mystery of Jesus is veiled and cannot be explained or understood as it is in itself in any way, but even when spoken remains ineffable, when thought unknown.'[160] One can therefore from this point reject criticisms of Denys' manner of expression when

---

[156] CH X.1 (272D).
[157] CH IX.2 (260A).
[158] CH XIII.4 (305B).
[159] DN IV.3 (697A).
[160] Ep. 3 (1069B).

he refers to the descent of the angelic hierarchies to the lower as also a completion (*apoperatōsis*),[161] for the increasing darkening, in its way, reveals anew the true nature of God, and so the high and the low, the great and the small, light and darkness in the world compensate for one another.

Now to the structure of the creatures themselves, of the *metechonta*. The first thing that strikes one if one comes to Denys from Alexandria, from Origen and Evagrius and Gregory of Nyssa, and the more so as Denys is seen as the theologian of the divine limitlessness, is the emphasis he places on limits. Limit (*peras*), holy law of being (*thesmos*), rank (*taxis*), ordering (*diacosmēsis*), measure (*metron*), symmetry (*symmetria*), analogy (*analogia*), holy gradation (*hier-archia*) are the perpetually recurring categories. Because God is beyond rest and movement, beyond finitude and infinity, there is no direct opposition between him and anything created; and therefore the latter is set forth in its limitedness and finitude, and as such affirmed and sustained. Not only the equal, but the unequal too, comes from God and is a name of God.[162] Still more important: because God's unity is beyond the unity of wholes (*hola*) and that of individuals (*hekaston*), the unity of both—for they are equally his image—is set up, safeguarded and assured by him: the particularity (*idiotēs*) of the individual is just as positive and final in its unlikeness (*anisotēs*) as the relatedness, the harmony of the parts as a whole and the common breath (*sympnoia*) that penetrates everything. No pantheism, not even of the Stoic sort, could give such positive significance to finitude and limits, and even with Plato the finite form remains questionable and is threatened by a spiritualistic doctrine of man. Denys, however, safeguards his cosmos with the theological doctrine of the resurrection, through which the sustaining of individual form is finally assured:[163] 'Its whole being will be saved and live forever in fulness.'

Here the Chalcedonian concepts press forward powerfully

[161] CH IV.5 (196B) and Gandillac's note, *ad loc.*
[162] DN VIII.9 (897BC).
[163] EH VII.1.1 (553A).

and broaden their range from christology to the whole conception of the world, the whole sense of being. 'Unconfusedly'
(*asynchytōs*), 'unchangeably' (*atreptōs*), 'indivisibly' (*adiairetōs*)
and 'inseparably' (*achōristōs*): thus was each of the two natures
preserved (*sōzetai*) in its individuality in Christ.[164] The concept
sōzein takes on with Denys an undreamt-of wealth of meaning.
God is above all *Soter* already as creator, in that he affirms and
safeguards the natures in their particularity and the individuals
in their individuality and preserves them as such from
destruction, the tendency to blend with others and to yield
before the superior power of the all, and protects 'each one in
the position allotted to it in accordance with its rank and
power'.[165] For that God is celebrated especially as the righteous
God: 'because he keeps (*diasōzein*) everything free from mixture
(*amigē*) and confusion (*asymphytos*) with all else and gives to each
what is suitable in accordance with its worth.'[166] In this God is
primarily salvation (*sōtēria*), and it is only because he wills the
individuality of each being that he draws it up again and thus
saves it (*sōstikōs*) from its tendency to sink down away from
itself into non-being; thus he becomes the 'redeemer', 'who
paternally forgives frailty and re-establishes it when it falls
victim to evil, or who rather by setting it firmly in the beautiful,
restores to it its lost goodness, putting its disarray to rights and
adorning it and bringing it to perfection.'[167] This unity between
preservation and redemption as the work of the righteousness of
God is for Denys the perfect 'beauty, even measure and right
ordering'.[168] All things are drawn into an 'unconfused union'
with one another and with God, 'in which union nothing of
their clarity or purity is lost'.[169] And everywhere protection is
afforded by the 'bolt' (*kleithron*) which is pushed home lest the
world dissolve into a material or spiritual chaos, 'and things fall
apart and sink into the indefinite and limitless, and lose their

[164] Denz.-Schön. 302.
[165] DN VIII.7 (896B).
[166] DN VIII.7 (896A).
[167] DN VIII.9 (896D–897B).
[168] *Ibid.* 896D.
[169] DN XI.2 (949C). In detail in the discussion of the name 'beauty' (*kallos*):
DN IV.7 (701C–704C).

structure, and forsake their foundation, and be deprived of their
own unity and be chaotically confused with one another.'[170]
Limit is not an evil thing; even privation is not evil as such.[171]

The thought of being allotted a finite position leads to the
thought of the divine election (*eklogē*), particularly developed in
connection with the priesthood. Denys sees here a conjunction
of three factors: suitability for the function, calling by God and
the conferring of orders by the bishop, so that the bishop makes
himself the 'interpreter' of this divine election.[172] Such a calling
(*klēsis*) exists more generally for all the baptized and redeemed,[173] and in the most general sense (according to an
etymology which derives *kallos*, beauty, from *kaleō*, to call)
everything is 'called'[174] to its place in the beauty and harmony
fashioned by God.

And with that the way is open for an understanding of the
concept of 'station', which for Denys, long before the development of the medieval estates, is always a 'sacred estate', a
hierarchy. This is, according to Denys (*kat'eme*), not primarily
what we imagine by this term, an ordered arrangement of
functions. First of all it is an individual station (as being situated
in a particular spiritual place), which is determined by its place
in the order of being (*taxis*), by the allotted insight (*epistēmē*) and
activity (*energeia*): these three serve 'for the attaining, as far as is
possible, of likeness to God and ... imitation of God', and
because 'the beauty that befits God is simple and good and the
cause of all initiation ... it causes each being to participate in its
own light so far as it is worthy and perfects it harmoniously to
itself ... in an unchangeable form.'[175] Thus the determination of
this threeness of being–knowledge–action has its basis and goal
in the transcendent, and the order of being itself, together with
its acts of knowing and doing which build it up and express it,
has its immanence only by virtue of such a basis and goal. This

[170] DN XI.1 (949AB).
[171] DN IV.29 (729C).
[172] EH V.3.5 (512B–513B). The determination of office by God is also
designated as judgement (*krisis*): EH III.3.13 (445B).
[173] EH II.2.3 (393C, *cf.* 513B).
[174] DN IV.7 (701D).
[175] CH III.1 (164D).

dynamic will now inform the twofold schema of God and the world: that of creation, rest–procession–return (*monē, proodos, epistrophē*) and that of redemption, God–fall–purification, which have both an active, communicating aspect and a passive, receptive aspect. Knowledge is primarily the reception of spiritual light from God (*ellampsis*); activity is primarily the giving back of this light in imitation of the God who goes out from himself and communicates himself. But because the outgoing creature is equally the fallen creature, the turning to God demands as its presupposition a 'purification' (*katharsis*).

From the viewpoint of the individual, the movement is on the one hand the strictly complementary response to the articulation of revelation: the 'purification' corresponds to the movement of in-gathering (*epistrophē*), the 'illumination' to the self-revelation of the inner light of God (*proodos*) and the 'perfection', the goal, is the 'union' (*henōsis*) with the immovable God, ever abiding in himself. In this ecstatic movement towards God the creature finds itself and perfects its order of being (*taxis*). But the movement is not only a 'passive' response to the active God; it is an active search for the divine. The creature's return becomes of itself its own going forth (*proodos*) as communicating, apostolic movement. As God 'humbles himself', so does the spirit, as it ascends above itself to God, 'humble itself', seeking out those who as yet are lacking in order to mediate to them what it already possesses. This communicating activity necessarily assumes the same threefold character that holds between the creature and God: the spirit can now purify others for God, because God purifies it; it can enlighten in respect of the divine, because it has been enlightened; it can contribute towards union with God, because it is thus united.

This active-passive pattern has its original context in a metaphysical-ethical psychology and expresses the threefold holy ordering (*hierarchia*) of the religious progress of the individual, the 'way of enlightenment'. It is therefore the religious way for society, which the Church lays down for man: purifying conversion, illuminating instruction, perfecting and consecrating union. Only if this personal hierarchy is established (which Denys everywhere recognizes and presupposes) could it be sensible to require that the individual moments be stressed and assigned to particular functions of the individual, and even then only in such a way that these prevailing emphases do not threaten the inseparable unity of the three moments. And also in the sense that one who has the function (say) of unifying therefore possesses *eminenter* the other two functions and must exercise them, and that always includes as a presupposition the passive movement of being oneself one who is purified, enlightened and unified. But he who has the predominant function of being purified has therefore not only the task of striving after enlightenment and union, but also already, as far as he can, of helping to purify others.

So there develops a subtle net of relationships, extending in all directions and universally applicable, which, through the stressing of each respective function, can be unfolded to a static yet versatile structure of respective stations, but in which, because everything rests upon everything else and each remains in need of the other, function remains transparent to that nature which expresses itself identically in all things: a most spiritual, most Greek product, which adapted itself to being a tender and inspiring soul for the more rigid and more external social structures of the Romans and the Germans. If one now observes the dimension of the 'aesthetic' (that is, of the relationships between the sensible and the spiritual), then the hierarchy once again possesses a threefold structure: as hierarchy in the realm of pure spirit—the three times three orders of the angels; as hierarchy in the realm of the purely sensible symbol, still unenlightened in the spirit—the hierarchy (only mentioned by Denys and not more closely described) of the Old Testament;[176] and as hierarchy 'standing in the middle' between symbol and spirit, as sacramental and in the strictest sense 'hierarchical' hierarchy, that of the Church, which seeks as far as is possible to become like the heavenly.[177] If the angelic hierarchy has the advantage of being constructed throughout in accordance with the pattern (in three times three orders), so that it forms a clear, if somewhat pale, archetype of the Church, then it presents this

[176] EH V.1.2 (501CD).
[177] CH VIII.2 (241C).

difficulty, that the function of 'purification' can be used only in an inauthentic sense (the removal of a relative ignorance through a higher enlightenment[178]). The ecclesiastical hierarchy has the advantage of a much greater closeness to reality and experience: here the functions can really be grasped, but for that reason the triadic system is either incomplete or rendered viable only at the cost of being forced. Because of his faithfulness to reality, the Areopagite has set up only two triadic structures in the Church: that with the active function of initiating—high priest (= bishop), offerer (= priest), server (= deacon), and that with the passive function of being initiated—monks, holy people and catechumens (with which are included sinners and penitents). Within the two triads the first function corresponds in each case to unification, the second to enlightenment, and the third to purification.

Denys, in fact, also attempted to provide these two ecclesiastical hierarchies with a third, that of the sacraments, which he likewise makes threefold (but without however forcing the scheme, for he adds further sacred initiations): the sacrament of water (baptism) as conversion and divine birth, that of bread and wine (the synaxis) as union with Jesus who proceeds (himself in the Incarnation, sacramentally in the host), imparts and returning enfolds in himself, and that of the oil (confirmation, priestly ordination, extreme unction).[179] But an assignment of the three functions to the three sacraments was not possible, because even baptism, which must properly be union, is called 'illumination' in the Church's tradition, and if the synaxis is claimed as 'union', then no particular function is left for the *myron* and its properly initiating function.

If Denys withstands the temptation to find a thorough-going external pattern in the Church, he also resists the temptation, which attracts him even more and is ready to hand, of a trinitarian or christological derivation of the order of triads. He does admittedly explicitly state: 'The origin (*archē*) of this

[178] CH VII.3 (209CD).
[179] If 'confession' is included in the conversion of baptism (for it is a matter of self-knowlege, renunciation of the devil and shame over sin, EH III.3.4), then there is missing from the 'seven sacraments' only marriage, of which as *theomimēsis* Denys can find in himself nothing to say.

hierarchy is the fountain of life, the essential goodness, the one cause of all beings, the Trinity, from whom flows through goodness both being and well-being to all that is. To this most thearchic blessedness, transcendent over all things, to this truly triple monad belongs that will, incomprehensible to us though known to itself, which is the rational salvation for us and for all beings that transcend us,'[180] something that, as he then works out, is realized through the equally threefold turning of the creature to God. But nowhere is there any attempt to set out the hierarchical functions in terms of the personal relationships within the thearchy. The same reserve can be clearly seen when, although every hierarchy both of angels and of men is declared to be ordered from and to the incarnate Son—for 'he is the *archē* and being of every hierarchy and sanctification and theurgy, and the most thearchic active power',[181] and 'every hierarchy finds its completion in Jesus', as it does in the complete God-head[182]—there is yet no suggestion that the individual functions can be derived from the functions of the incarnate Redeemer. As soon as God comes into view—and Jesus is God—then any comparison of orders, any discernible analogy, ceases. Enough, if the beauty of the order of the world points to God, who is, in a way beyond our comprehension, 'primal order'. Therefore the final meaning of the hierarchies is not, in a Christian context, designated as the knowledge of God or even the representation of God, but love: as 'the perpetual love for God'[183] to which all three functions raise us, but also, in the game of give-and-take between the creatures, the imitation of God in mutual love.

And here appears, as already mentioned, a gap in the absolutely continuous and inexorable intermediary order, in that from each step there opens up an immediate way to God, which love always wants and which every world-order intends and reflects immediately. For if the hierarchy does not reflect the trinitarian in God, then 'it is nevertheless an image of the order and distinction in the divine activities. . . . For the Thearchy purifies first those intelligences to which it is closest, and then

[180] EH I.3 (373CD).
[181] EH I.1 (372A).
[182] EH V.1.5 (505B).
[183] EH I.1 (376A).

illuminates them, and then perfects those whom it has illuminated to a godlike, consecrated activity.'[184] This image-likeness
is, to put it more accurately and comprehensively, true natural-
supernatural secondary causality, for, to give an example, the
priestly hierarchy has, on the one hand, nothing to com-
municate but what is divine, and on the other hand a priest, as a
fellow-worker with God, must without question himself also be
purified, enlightened and unified, in order to hand on the graces
of God in an appropriate way.[185] So the motive of mediation is
reduced   to   the   double   motive—both   Christian   and
ecclesiastical—of the sacramental structure of the Church (in
which the familiar three 'offices' of the Church are expressed)
and to the clearly defined thought of the missionary character of
all Christian grace: whoever receives must in turn pass on; he
who has been made personally worthy by God must live in his
worth (*axia*) as if it were a rank (*taxis*) which makes its claim on
him, a claim that reaches to what is most deeply personal. This
objectivity of sanctity, which includes and does not exclude
personal piety, prayer and mysticism, will be passed on to the
Middle Ages not by Augustine, but by Denys. There is yet
another point to notice: the care with which Denys describes the
hierarchy (the astonishing definition of which we have given
above) as a single order in three functions. What is important for
him is not that the angels form nine choirs, but three hierarchies,
within which the three functions are of equal rank.[186] And if

---

[184] EH V.1.7 (508CD).

[185] How true that is and how wrong are those who suspect Denys of a kind
of occasionalism is shown by his angry reproof of Demophilus and his equally
strict requirement that the priest must both possess and be what he mediates
and what he requires of others (EH III.3.14; 445A). A sign of how little Denys
can begin to be numbered with those who dissolve the *opus operatum* in
existential factors is his answer to the objection to infant baptism and infant
communion: he justifies these by their upbringing in a Catholic spirit (EH
VII.3.11; 565D–568C).

[186] CH IV.3: *homotagēs* (181A); VI.2 (201A); VIII.1 (240A); IX.2 (257C);
more explicitly: EH IV.3.7 (481A). If this moment of equal rank is underlined
more firmly in the case of the angels than of the Church, it applies here too—
indeed, the structure of the heavenly is strictly read off the model of the
ecclesiastical hierarchy—and it can be said that the 'holy people' belong to the
hierarchy (in the defined sense) (EH VI.3.5; 537A).

there is then gradation, it is not in the sense of a simple subordination, but of an order of foundation. One can therefore ask what the word-structure *hier-archia* really means, especially if one sets it alongside the concept continually used for the divine, that of *the-archia*. If thearchy means the principle of all divine being, or of all divinization, then hierarchy can only mean the principle, foundation, effective form of holiness and sanctification. Holiness (or simply the holy order) certainly demands as elements both the ordered sequence of the three stages and the active-passive reciprocal working of the three functions; but this is only a first deduction. Hierarchy is not primarily graded subordination, but order within the individual person as within the community, a divinely ordained divine order, which leads to God and consists essentially of bounty and grace.

This whole spiritual and yet visible order is, as is said eloquently and ever again, the cosmic beauty, in which the thearchic, surpassing beauty is manifest.[187] The hierarchical principle in the defined sense is for Denys simply the world-principle. He has taken over this fruit of late Neo-Platonic wisdom in its, for him, unquestionable self-evidence, but has given it a Christian *point de départ*—what a moment, when he discovered that the revealed names of the angels were really nine and of the ecclesiastical ranks twice three!—and a most deeply Christian sense. If the triadic image of God applies now also to the structure of the Church, it remains still for Denys—if in a different way from Proclus—the structure of the world and the structure of being. Not only is philosophy in a non-Christian sense derived for him from the true, revealed Wisdom, but he makes the historical economy of salvation include the whole of history in an all-embracing way. Thus he will have nothing to do with the theologumenon, according to which the nations have their archontic 'angels', but Israel alone is immediately under divine rule. Like the others Israel has its own revealing,

---

[187] CH XIII.3 (301A), *ibid.* (301C); X.1: *tēs eukosmou taxiarchias thesmon en harmonia theia kai analogia pros tēn hapasēs eukosmias hyperarchion archēn* ... (273A) [the law of the principle of well-ordered structure, established in divine harmony and analogy with the principle beyond all principle of all good order].

hierarchic angel (Michael); the same providence rules over all the nations; and the question is only how the nations hearken to this illuminating and guiding providence.[188] This liberal view is strengthened by the exceptional position accorded to Melchizedek: with Abraham's homage to him the legal hierarchy is subordinated to him as the 'hierarch of all the nations and the immediate type of Christ'.[89] These not completely harmonized motives testify, at least, to a tendency towards an historical universality, which is in any case realised in the conception of the Church as the heart of the world, the source of all form and life. As in the great peace of God among all created natures the 'natural war' of all limited beings one with another is overtaken and softened, so at a much higher level the Church of Christ is the place of peace and reconciliation and union of all being with God.

It is hard to say what Denys, the disciple of the Alexandrines and of Nyssa, thought about eternal damnation. He repeats in his letter to Demophilus the vision of Carpus, who, in the face of open heaven and open hell, must reach his decision about love:[191] but this vision is related with the express intention of warning and frightening. If the *Ecclesiastical Hierarchy* treats of the fall of the angels and their being assigned places within God's good cosmos,[192] it is as little a matter of Origenist *apocatastasis* as it is of an Origenist pre-temporal fall: Denys in no way belonged either to the professed or to the secret Origenists.[193] His picture of the world remains pre-eminently a 'picture', in the realm of the now appropriate liturgical thinking such that any attempt to penetrate eschatologically beyond this picture would endanger the *symmetria*. It is only with Maximus that the Dionysian world will at this point again be channelled into an Alexandrian course.

[188] CH IX.2–3 (260AD).
[189] CH IX.3 (261A).
[190] DN XI.1 (948D–949B).
[191] On this Koch, 18–27: dependence on Plato; and Stiglmair, 'Die Eschatologie des Ps.-D.' (ZkTh, 1899, 1–21). (The vision occurs already in Nilus, who repeats it as an 'old story'.)
[192] EH III.3.3 (397D–400A).
[193] EH VII.1.2 (553C). And Stiglmair, *ad loc*. The same in the above-mentioned article.

6. THEOLOGICAL MYSTICISM

Mystical theology is the high-point of the whole theology of
the Areopagite. It is present secretly or openly in all his
theological utterances and it is systematically necessary to the
whole. It is called for as much by his doctrine of God as by his
doctrine of the Church, and is therefore no 'appendix' for the
'chosen few'. But for just this reason it is not so much the centre
of his theology, such that his symbolic and intellectual theology
might be relativized and even called in question. There is no gulf
between exoteric and esoteric theology; each needs the other
and they compenetrate one another:[194] there is not even any
tension between dogmatic and mystical theology. Each dogmatic decree, even the sharpest conciliar definition, must be seen
in the light of the ever-greater unlikeness of God,[195] of his ever-
deeper mystery. To all eternity we know God only in his self-
communication, though it is really God in his self-communication. But even the communicated divinity and goodness of
God is an 'inimitable imitation of what is beyond divinity and
goodness', which, 'being beyond any principle of divinisation
or any ground of goodness, is as such inimitable and un-
graspable and transcends every imitation and every attempt to
comprehend it as it transcends all who imitate it or participate in
it.'[196] So the old principle is called to mind: 'If anyone sees God
and understands what he has seen, then he has not seen him at all
but rather something of his that can be known. But he is
transcendently enthroned beyond intelligence and beyond
being, and only by virtue of not being known in any way at all
and by not being does he exist beyond being and is he known
beyond understanding. And this perfect ignorance, understood
positively, is knowledge of the one who is beyond all that can be
known.'[197]

That is a dogmatic, not a psychological, utterance, although
it would be ridiculous to deny (as people have) that Denys had
experienced what he expressed. The correctness—both philo-

[194] Ep 9 (1105D).
[195] DN IX.7 (916A).
[196] Ep 2 (1068A–1069A).
[197] Ep 1 (1065AB).

sophical and theological—of his utterance, which again could be doubted only by one who has no sense at all of what is intended here, is certainly no objection to such realization. Certainly it is true that according to Denys the essence of each being is itself ecstatic towards God (something that so little threatens its individuality that this movement itself determines it at its deepest level); indeed, that this ecstasy of creaturely *eros* is itself an imitation of the ecstatic divine *eros* which out of love goes out of itself into the multiplicity of the world;[198] that therefore mystical experience represents a philosophical and theological realization of that which *is*, an experience which the hierarch of each hierarchy should have undergone in order to be able to 'purify' and 'illuminate', to say nothing of being able to 'unify'.[199] In this sense the mystical experience is for Denys no 'exceptional experience', which does not prevent it being such on the psychological level (as is, for example, the case with Spanish mysticism).

The God of the 'dazzling darkness', whose 'simple and absolute and immutable mysteries of theology are hidden' (or according to another reading 'are revealed') 'in the dazzling darkness of most secret silence', mysteries 'that dazzle with a light of the utmost clarity in deepest darkness, and—in a way completely beyond our grasp and utterly invisible—overpower blinded minds with a splendour surpassing beauty':[200] this God is the Johannine God, in whom is no darkness at all (1 Jn 1.5). Only the transcendent brightness of this inapprehensible light, which immeasurably transcends the power of spiritual sight, may in no case be taken as a quantitative or relative superabundance. But this relationship of the creature to the ever-greater God is not, in the end, a complete denial of all relationship, but is rather that of a relation established by God through creation, a relationship which the creature itself can realize by peeling off all the concealing veils of creaturely being and knowing, and of which the apophatic method is only, so to speak, the negative impression or hollow reverse. Obviously for

[198] DN IV.12–13 (709–712).
[199] *Cf.* EH III.3 and V.1.3ff.
[200] MTh I.1 (997AB).

Denys this method of continuing negation and of peeling off the veils of sensible symbols and intellectual concepts can never be adequately separated from the positive mystical experience (which stems from God); the concrete whole that he continually has in view is not a method of thought, but an always experienceable encounter, something that takes place in the presence of the mystery of the living God, known through faith. And therefore the often-mentioned 'third step' beyond affirmation and negation, the transcendence (*hyperochē*),[201] not a cognitive 'method', but the proof that there is, beyond anything that a creature can either affirm or deny, only the objective superabundance of God,[202] so that the last word of 'mystical theology' can only say that God is not only beyond all affirmations but beyond all negations too.[203] The expressions, handed down in part from Plotinus and Proclus, which describe the mystical act—'union without knowledge' (*henōsis agnōstos*), 'throwing oneself against' (*epibolē*) the dark ray (*aktis*), 'contact' (*epaphē*)—remain descriptions, which are again meant theologically not psychologically, and yield the positive meaning (*kata kreitton*) of the negations.

All this presents no fundamental difficulty. There is perhaps a difficulty only in the relation of this assertion to the eschatological vision of God. An immediate vision on earth is denied even to Moses and Paul—somewhat in opposition to Gregory of Nyssa and several texts of Augustine: there is only

---

[201] Cf. *hyperechō*, *hyperochē*, *hyperbolē* in v.d. Daele.

[202] CH XIII.4 (304C); DN IV.4 (697C); IX.2 (909C); XI.2 (952A); XII.3 (972C); XIII.2 (977C); MTh V (1048B); Ep 9.3 (1109C); 9.5 (1112C). God is himself causally superior to any transcendence (including, therefore, that of the understanding mind): DN II.7 (645B). Any measure (*taxis*) and anything beyond measure (*hyperochē*) is from him: DN IV.10 (705C). The application of negative names (such as unreason, lack of feeling) to God is possible *kath' hyperochēn*, and implies therefore an objective content, *viz.* the 'transcendence of the light of God over anything visible' (*ibid.*). His lordship is not only 'superiority' (*hyperochē*) over what is subordinated, but simply total possession (DN XII.2; 969B). DN VII.3 (872A) is therefore to be interpreted in accordance with all these texts, where it is a matter of a methodical ascent '*en pantōn aphairesei kai hyperochē*' [in negation and transcendence of all things]: the last word means here nothing else than the objective superabundance of God.

[203] MTh V (1048B).

mediated knowledge of God.[204] In accordance with the law of hierarchy, the angels of the first hierarchy can see God immediately (*amesōs*).[205] Does this law cease to be valid eschatologically? At first sight it can appear so, for the vision of God now 'through the sacred veil', through 'form and image', is contrasted in Scripture and Tradition with the coming vision at the resurrection, when 'we shall be with the Lord for evermore, filled with the purest contemplations of his visible theophany which will surround us with most luminous splendours as [once] it did the disciples in that most divine Transfiguration' on Tabor. But at once the following sentence describes this eschatological vision with expressions belonging to' mystical vision.[206] And indeed Denys could not possibly speak in any other way according to all his presuppositions: he can emphasize the illumination of the 'dazzling rays', the blessedness of contact with them, but only in the context of a general emphasis on the overall continuity of the epistemological structure. And this leads one to ask whether the '*amesōs*' of the highest angels is not something conceded to a philosophical system of thought rather than something due to the influence of the specifically Areopagitic conception of God—unless, that is, one takes the '*amesōs*' to mean only that the first hierarchy has no need of a further intermediary between itself and God, which need not, however, imply that because of this it possesses an 'essential vision' of God. Naturally this 'union' between God and a creature freed from all forms and categories of sensible and intellectual knowledge is something utterly positive, fulfilling beyond any hope, because in it there is something that as it were corresponds to the inexpressible: but why attempt once again to express this with finite categories?

The theology of the Areopagite was seen and used for a thousand years and longer as one of the basic forms of the Church's theology. He remains, with Augustine, *the* classic

---

[204] CH IV.3 (180C–181A).

[205] CH IV.2 (201A) and frequently.

[206] DN I.4 (592BC). And already Tabor is certainly the transfiguration of 'the veil' of Christ's humanity, but not at all its rending (of which Denys never speaks). The greater assimilation to the knowledge of the angels likewise need not point to immediacy.

representative of theological form in the West. If nowadays the
'myth' of his person has been demythologized (at least, in part),
nothing is thereby said about his achievement. The proof that
the influences on his thought are not only ecclesiastical (the
Alexandrines and Gregory of Nyssa), but also Jewish (Philo)
and Hellenistic (Plotinus and Proclus) says—in his case as little as
in the case of any other Christian thinker—nothing against the
genuinely Christian substance of his theology. His dependence
on Neo-Platonic forms of thought is so obvious that it was
already turned against him in his lifetime. But he turned the
tables himself, and retorted, 'the Greeks had made an impious
use of the divine in relation to the divine, trying by means of the
wisdom of God to destroy the fear of God.'[207] And by that is
certainly intended not only the traditional idea of the
borrowings of Greek philosophy from the Bible, but something
much deeper and truer, which relates to post-Christian Gnosticism and the (likewise post-Christian, and not uninfluenced by
Christianity), philosophy of Plotinus and Proclus, and perhaps
more fundamentally still the relation of all Greek philosophy to
what we nowadays call natural theology or primordial
revelation: the misuse of true religious thought for the purpose
of Promethean speculation. Denys therefore does not want to
borrow, but rather to return what has been borrowed to its true
owner.

His stupendous knowledge of Scripture may not be overlooked; he does not quote much, but when he does it is with
exactness and with sovereign mastery.[208] Often he only hints,
and leaves it to the initiate to understand. He places himself on
another level than that of scriptural theology, as indeed the
fashioner of a theological liturgy must do. What appears to be
missing suddenly emerges in a secondary passage, so that one
must conclude that what was presumably quite consciously not
expressed was always to hand. So for him the mystery of the
God-man, his humiliation, his suffering, death and descent is
perfectly present, but it is contemplated in the context of God's

[207] Ep 7.2 (1080AB).
[208] One need only go through Gandillac's index of scriptural citations and
allusions in the critical edition of CH.

descent into the world as a whole and only comes to the fore as a
theme when he treats of following Christ in the case of those
who are called, the priests and the monks. The bearing of sinners
by the Good Shepherd, his prayer for his enemies on the cross,
his condemnation of all thought of revenge by his disciples, his
compassion for our weaknesses, his soft and gentle manner, his
offering of himself for our wickedness,[209] all that ought to have
been in the mind of the rebellious monk, Demophilus. But
everyone anointed with the holy oil must behold the 'divine
humiliation' of Jesus who, 'that we might be divinized, himself
died on the cross, in order to snatch away from the abyss of
death any who have received the baptism of his death.'[210] Should
one hold it against Denys, if he relates this sacramental dying
(Rom 6.3) to martyrdom, and also to the Christian's life of
witness, the Christian who 'dies for the truth daily', in that he
'bears witness, as is fitting, with each word and deed',[211] and
beyond that especially to the dying to the world that happens
both as a sign and in actual fact in the ordination of monks? If
finally he interprets the actual death of the saints who are
commemorated in the Mass as the 'consummation of their
holiness',[213] namely as the inner conclusion of their death with
Christ, which already has taken place, and on account of which
the death of the believer is at every stage contrasted with the
death of the unbeliever?[214] In the face of such a theology, what
would be the use of referring to the fact that the Greeks (or the
Buddhists) also see 'philosophy' as a daily learning to die? What
force has this observation in the face of Jesus' saying (reminding
one of Pascal) in the vision of Carpus? For the Lord, descending
from heaven, takes the side of the two sinners persecuted by
Carpus and says to their avenger: 'Raise your hand and from
henceforth beat me, for see, I am ready to suffer afresh for the

---

[209] Ep 8.4 (1096A–C).

[210] EH IV.3.10 (484B).

[211] DN VII.4 (873A). As here it is especially a matter of the apostles,
martyrdom is certainly included in this witness.

[212] EH VI.3.3 (536A).

[213] EH III.3.9 (437C).

[214] EH VII.1.2 (553B–556B).

salvation of men, and I would do it gladly if thereby I could stop other men from sinning.'[215]

For Denys the sanctity of Christians is the result of the harmony of hierarchical order, the knowledge of revelation and apostolic activity (*taxis–epistēmē–energeia*). In this divinely-arranged triple harmony man becomes transparent to God and amenable to the proclaimed will of God. That is true typically of the hierarchy, which is called in the following of Jesus to be a 'herald of the counsels of God'. In the realization of this thought Denys' doctrine of prayer[216] (Neo-Platonic, it is said) is drawn into the Christian realm at the deepest possible level. Through putting himself completely at God's disposal in purification, illumination and union and through assimilation to the divine will, the hierarch comes to the point of 'no longer willing anything that is not completely pleasing to God and in agreement with the divine promises'. As a sacred minister he utters no petition which he does not know corresponds to the saving will of God. Therefore he chooses nothing in his own power, but rather places his will as a tool within the divine will, just as Peter, to whom has been given the power of the keys, the power to bind and loose even in heaven, did not utter the 'holy theological words' confessing Jesus' Godhead on his own impulse or through revelation from flesh and blood, but 'in virtue of an initiation by God'. Prayer is therefore resignation to God, but in order to be 'moved' or 'inspired' more effectively by the divine will. Here for a last time office and spirit have become one.

[215] Ep 8.6 (1100C).
[216] The main section on prayer, DN III.1 (680AD), seems to say that prayer only moves men to God, in accordance with which it would appear that as God moves himself to himself, prayer moves something in God.

ANSELM

Anselm's slender work, radiant and perfectly balanced, realises in the purest form the concerns of theological aesthetics. His reason is monastic, like that of the Areopagite, but it is Benedictine, and that means both communal and dialogic at the same time. Its monastic form is contemplative, beholding, transparent; its Benedictine content is manifest in the consciousness of freedom and in a form of life stamped by freedom. These yield a common fruit in the acme of Christian aesthetics. Anselm contemplates the highest rectitude (*rectitudo*) of the divine revelation in creation and redemption; he discerns its truth from the harmony, from the faultless proportions, from the way in which it must be so (*necessitas*), something at once dependent on the utmost freedom and manifesting the utmost freedom, and this vision reveals to him absolute beauty: God's beauty in the freely fashioned form of the world. When he asks by what reason or necessity God was made man (*qua ratione vel necessitate Deus homo factus est*), the question appears to him 'very difficult, but in its solution it is intelligible to all and delightful both on account of its usefulness and on account of the beauty of the reason (*rationis pulchritudinem*).'[1] This beauty appears to the

---

[1] Anselm's works are cited according to the critical edition by F. S. Schmitt, OSB, six volumes so far (1938–61), the final volume of which, consisting of fragments and apparatus, has yet to appear. To that there should be added the incomplete work, *On Ability and Inability, On Possibility and Impossibility, Necessity and Freedom* ('Ein neues unvollendetes Werk des hl. Anselm von Canterbury', ed. with comments by F. S. Schmitt, in *BGPHM* Vol. 33.3, 1936); Anselm's lecture in Cluny, 1104 taken down by Eadmer: *De beatitudine coelestis patriae* (*PL* 159, 587–604); Eadmer's biography (*PL* 158, 49–118) and his *Historia novorum* (*PL* 159, 347–525). Finally the collections of similes (*De similitudinibus*) which Anselm was accustomed to use in his lectures to his monks and novices, but also on other occasions, collected by the monk Alexander of Canterbury (*DSp* I.694), which includes another version of the lecture given in Cluny, and repeats material known elsewhere; meanwhile the neglected work remains very illuminating for Anselm. The older literature is cited in *DThC*. Important new contributions of the International Anselm Congress, 1959, in *Spicilegium Beccense* I (1959) (= *SpicBec*). The edition of Schmitt is cited by work and chapter, and then in brackets: volume, page and line, *e.g. CDH* (*Cur Deus homo*) I.1 (II.48.8–9).

one who beholds it so ineffable (*inenarrabilis pulchritudo*[2]) that he hardly dares attempt its human imitation; the master does not want to accede to Boso's pressing requests, 'for the subject matter is not only precious, but is fair with a reason (*speciosa ratione*) above human understanding, just as it has to do with him who is "beautiful above the sons of men". I am always indignant with poor artists when I see our Lord himself painted with an ugly form, and I am afraid that I may find myself in the same position if I dare to set out such a beautiful theme in rude and contemptible language.'[3] However, the problem of expression remains secondary to the problem of thought: the decisive thing about this monastic contemplation is that it is not ecstasy, nor feeling, but contemplative reason (*rationis contemplatio*[4]), contemplation albeit of a reason on a pilgrimage of longing, between earthly faith and eternal vision (*meditetur . . . esuriat . . . desideret tota substantia mea*[5]). It is the contemplation, above all, of a praying reason which only hopes to find insight in dialogue with the eternal truth, and therefore ever again passes over from the form of meditation to that of prayer.

Anselm's work has two sides: form and content, method and subject matter; and if both exist in tension with one another, too little attention is usually paid to their unity and their mutual interdependence. The method is that of *rationes necessariae*; it appears as a prevalent philosophical method, and this presupposes that the subject matter is to a significant degree also philosophical. In spite of this the subject matter is the free dealings of the free God with a mankind freely created and brought anew into freedom by Christ, that is, a predominantly theological subject matter, which will be shown to be reflected in the method. The 'philosophical' meditation is unfolded predominantly in the first two works, the *Monologion* and the *Proslogion*, while the theological questions concerning the freedom of God, of the angels, and of men, their presuppositions, conditions and their dramatic outworking, are the concern of all the following systematic works: *On the Freedom of the Will, On the Fall of the Devil, Why God Became Man, On the*

[2] *Ibid.* I.3 (II.51.12).   [3] *Ibid.* I.1 (II.49.17–22).
[4] *De ver.* 11 (I.191.11–12).   [5] *Prosl.* 26 (I.121.22–122.1).

Virginal Conception and Original Sin, On the Concord between the Foreknowledge, Predestination and Grace of God and the Freedom of the Will. The polemic against Roscelin (*Letter on the Incarnation of the Word*), the discussion with the Greeks at the Council of Bari (1098), *On the Procession of the Holy Spirit*, overarch the problem of freedom at the level of the trinitarian relations, while the wonderful *Prayers and Meditations* bestow on it the indispensable ecclesiological and existential form. Although, then, the method and subject matter completely interpenetrate one another, we may, beginning with considerations of method, treat them one after another, because in this way what is peculiar to Anselm, even over against his great master, Augustine, comes into prominence.

1. AESTHETIC REASON

Contemplative Christian reason, whose subject matter is the truly real, grows organically—if one sets on one side all polemical deviant strands—out of the ancient contemplation of Being. The gnostic, as Clement and even more Evagrius Ponticus conceives him, thinks not only the content of Biblical revelation which is believed by the pistic, he thinks it necessarily as the perfection of the philosophical theology of the 'pagans'; as the authentic—theoretical and practical—philosopher, he brings the wisdom of the world to its final state. The *monachos* (*i.e.*, a solitary and unified man, enfolding everything in himself and turned towards the One) brings the ancient *theoria* to perfection; he is therefore the philosopher in the Christian realm.[6] The question whether Anselm is a philosopher or a theologian is therefore quite superfluous and fundamentally misconceived: the anti-pagan polemic of the Fathers is no longer relevant, nor is the separation of disciplines which began in the period of high scholasticism yet acute: Anselm stands in the *kairos*, for the Biblical revelation can be understood simply

[6] Dom Jean Leclercq, *Etudes sur le vocabulaire monastique du MA: Monachus, Philosophia, Theoria* (Stud. Anselm. 48), 1961.

as the transcendent consummation of ancient philosophy, which never was philosophy in the modern sense but was rather in its fundamental concerns theology: speech about God, about the eternal, about the being of the one who is. That all earthly existence is rooted there, whence it has proceeded and whither it seeks to return, this the Greeks knew, but Christians know something they hardly guessed: that God is a person, that he is free, that he is therefore creator and loving, loving in the inner freedom of his life. Here philosophy, without any discontinuity, finds its authentic self, and thus it is pointless to ask whether these last expressions are 'theology' or the fruit of reason illuminated by the light of revelation. In face of the overwhelming depths of reality it would be irrelevant and uninteresting to ask what reason might do without revelation, but it would also be unthinkable to want to dispense with reason so as to live from 'faith alone', for the revelation of God means his causing himself to be beheld and therefore appeals unequivocally to the understanding of the believer, to the eye of his reason.

In so far as the free God expresses his inner being in freedom, everything begins with the acceptance of his word, and therefore with faith; the humble acceptance of the free and absolute word, in the form in which it offers itself, is the fundamental meaning of *credere*, which, because this presupposition always remains the same, can never be set aside by understanding. It is in particular also the reception of the word in its churchly form; the ever-new sowing of the word, 'or more exactly of the sense which is perceived through the word', in the heart, and the wearisome cultivation (*laboriosa cultura*) of this grace which is allotted to the believer, is the ever-new foundation for any understanding.[7] But the word in the gospel itself continually demands of the hearer understanding, insight, apprehension. Therefore *credo, sed intelligere desidero*.[8] *Credentem me fecisti scire quod nesciens credebam*.[9] So it is a matter of *fide stabilitus in rationis*

---

[7] *De conc.* III.6 (II.270.21–24; 271.11).
[8] *De lib arb.* 3 (I.211.1). [I believe, but I desire to understand.]
[9] *De cas. diab.* 16 (I.261.25). [Make me, believing, to know what without knowing I believed.]

ejus indagine se exercere,[10] *ut non solum fide, verum etiam evidenti cognoscant ratione.*[11] This understanding has its place, as we have said, between faith and vision (*inter fidem et speciem intellectum esse medium intelligo*[12]), although no sort of immediate transition from the one to the other is intended.[13] The earthly character of this understanding is made even clearer if we consider its twofold intention: from below it is a defence against unbelief, whose grounds are hereby removed; from above it promotes contemplation and the Christian life.[14] The understanding of the total (philosophical-theological) truth demands—as the wise men of the ancient world knew—the total commitment of a man: 1. a life established on the truth and set free for it, to which life there belongs for the Christian the wrestling of prayer; 2. the struggle for conceptual understanding so as to achieve in-sight, *intel-lectus*; 3. the pure joy and blessedness (*delectatio, beatitudo*) in the truth thus found, which accrues to man through grace and merit alike. Each of these moments yields an aesthetic moment, from which the Anselmian *pulchritudo rationis* attains its unity.

1. Life for the sake of the truth (such as Pythagoras, Plato, Epicurus demanded of their disciples) means a loving devotion to the thing itself: for this is *tanta res*, that is, it wills to be embraced not only with 'most certain faith', but also with all love, even with life-giving love.[15] In Christian terms it means purity, freedom from sin, for how should the spirit understand the things of God 'when it is so estranged from itself by the enormity of its dullness that it is scarcely aware of the seriousness of its sickness'?[16] This 'deathly insensibility'[17] must be removed

[10] *CDH, commend.* (II.40.1–2). [established in faith, to exercise oneself in investigation by one's reason.]
[11] *Ep de Inc. Verbi* (second version) 6 (II.21.5–6). [that not only by faith, but also by evident reason, they may know the truth.]
[12] *CDH,* commend. (II.40.10–11).
[13] As, above all, Henri de Lubac has shown in *SpB* 295–312.
[14] Both are named together: *Ep. de Inc. Verbi* (second version) 6 (II.21.1–2); *CDH, commend.* (II.39.3–6); *ibid.* I.1 (II.47.8–11). Often the two goals are also mentioned separately.
[15] *Mon.* 78 (I.84.16–17).
[16] *Or.* 5 (III.13.13–14).
[17] *Or.* 10 (III.37.129–30).

by living faith, but also we 'must carefully detach ourselves from the inclinations of our own will, which often and greatly hinders the mind from the understanding of rectitude.'[18] For certainty concerning the things of God comes only to those who are willing: *omnibus est volentibus advertere perspicuum.*[19] This will in relation to a free God means prayer, *ut Deus aperiat quod prius latebat,*[20] means to be free and to be still in the presence of God,[21] to wait patiently for understanding, 'worshipping by loving and loving by worshipping with all one's powers'.[22] On the other hand, it does not mean 'raising up the horns of a knowledge that trusts in itself', rather: 'if I am able to understand, then I say thank you, if not, then I bow my head in reverence.'[23] The demand of 'purity of heart', of 'humble docility before the testimonies of God', of 'becoming a child' and before all else of the exercise of 'firm faith, serious virtue and wisdom' is the ancient demand of the Fathers, which Anselm repeats against Roscelin: it is only when one is perfected in *praktike* that one can undertake *theoria*; between faith and insight comes the experience of life: *qui non crediderit non experietur, et qui expertus non fuerit non cognoscet.*[24] This experience yields the 'spiritual wings', with which alone one can 'ascend to the loftiest questions of the faith', and without which an 'untimely ascent' (*praepostere*) can lead only to one's being 'cast down into manifold error'.[25] But what is this experience of life? It is a rising above the level at which mere thinking is simply confronted by what is merely thought; it is the realization that a free, created person—who moreover knows himself to be lacking in

[18] *Conc. virg.* 23 (II.165.1–2).

[19] *Mon.* 1 (I.14.9). [it is open to all who are willing to turn to what is clear.]

[20] *CDH* I.1 (II.49.4). [that God may reveal what previously he had concealed.]

[21] *Prosl.* 1 (I.97.6–10).

[22] *Mon.* 80 (I.87.9–10).

[23] *Ep. de Inc. Verbi* (first version) 4 (I.283.24–5).

[24] *Ibid.* (I.284.27–31). [who will not believe will not experience, and who has not experienced will not know.] The second version (II.9.6–8) adds, more sharply, that through a lack of humility and virtue an 'insight already granted may be again withdrawn, indeed even faith itself may perish, if the purity of the conscience is neglected' (*ibid.* 9–11).

[25] *Ibid.* (I.283.30–284.3).

freedom due to sin—faces the infinite, free, personal God, whom he can neither control nor command for a double reason: because he is created, and because he is lost and sinful. *Experientia*, as the intellectual result of *praktikē*, consists precisely in the *sensorium*, that each finite and fallen creature is entirely bereft of the *sensorium* appropriate to the living God. Both moments, the philosophical (the *major dissimilitudo* of God) and the theological one of the fallenness of the creature from God, belong together for Anselm; the prayer at the beginning of the *Proslogion* testifies to this, when it bewails the 'absence' of a God who is yet believed to be present, while it cannot effect of itself the act by which he would be made present, because it is 'man's unhappy lot to have lost that for which he was made', to have fallen 'from his native land into exile, from the vision of God into our blindness'.[26] 'Grant me to behold your light, even if only from afar, from the depths.' The one praying appeals to his knowledge of the *analogia entis*: 'I do not try, O Lord, to penetrate your depths, because I do not at all compare my understanding to that, but I desire to understand in some measure (*aliquatenus*) your truth, which my heart believes and loves.' But he appeals equally to the grace of God, which can renew and restore again the image of God which has been buried and blackened in the sinner.[27] And yet when once the proof of God's existence and the consideration of his nature have been given, there returns, at a deeper level, the same prayer of lament: 'if you have indeed found him, why do you not feel (*sentis*) what you have found? . . . O Lord my God, my maker and remaker, say to my soul in its longing what else there is than what it saw, that it may see purely what it desires. It strains itself to see more, and yet it sees nothing beyond this thing that it sees except darkness; or rather it does not see darkness, which does not exist in you, but it sees that it cannot see *more* on account of its own darkness.'[28] The formula for the analogy between God and the creature so characteristic of Anselm (*videt se non plus posse videre propter tenebras suas*) makes the philosophical one

[26] *Prosl.* I (I.98.2–3, 16–17; 99.5–6).
[27] *Prosl.* I (I.100.8, 12–17).
[28] *Prosl.* 14 (I.111.14, 22–112.1).

with the theological, not only in the sense of the Areopagitical contemplation in dazzling darkness, but equally in the realization of the loss of any perception as a result of original sin, something that goes beyond the Augustinian prayers and contemplation in the *Confessions*. Following Denys and Augustine he can say: 'my spirit is darkened through its short-sightedness, and overwhelmed by your infinity ... your light is too strong, the eye of my soul cannot long behold it.'[29] But then, in contrast to Augustine, comes the lament: 'I do not feel you ... my soul looks around, but it sees not your beauty. It listens, but does not hear your harmony. It smells, but does not perceive your fragrance. It tastes, but does not know your savour, feels but does not sense your gentleness. For all these, O Lord God, you have in yourself in an ineffable manner, for you have given them to things created by you in their sensible manner, but the senses of my soul are hardened, stupefied and blocked by the ancient malady of sin. And again behold what trouble, what sadness and lamentation meets one who seeks joy and happiness. ... I had thought that I could eat, and behold I hunger for more.'[30] So faith's starting-point, when taken seriously, brings reason to this realization: that it is not only—in the experiencing of reality—overwhelmed by God's being ever greater, but beyond that it perceives in the personal encounter how out of tune with all-purity and all-love is man, subject as he is to original sin. It is certainly the 'inexhaustibility for mortals of the *ratio veritatis*',[31] the 'incomprehensibility of the divine Wisdom',[32] and the one who seeks 'should endure the fact that there are things in God that his understanding cannot penetrate',[33] should also understand that, if he does find reasons, there 'are always still higher reasons that remain hidden',[34] and that man never deals with God as an equal and can never ascend above God even in his thoughts.[35] But beyond all this it is the

---

[29] *Prosl.* 14 (I.112.3–4), 16 (I.112.24–5).
[30] *Prosl.* 16–18 (I.113.4–114.2).
[31] *CDH, commend.* (II.40.4–5).
[32] *Ibid.* II.16 (II.117.4).
[33] *Ep. de Inc. Verbi* (second version) 13 (II.31.3–4).
[34] *CDH* I.2 (II.50.12–13).
[35] *Prosl.* 3 (I.103.4–6); *Ep. de Inc. Verbi* (second version) 4 (II.18.6–7).

realisation that there is a dependence on the freedom of the God of grace, which proves itself gracious to the sinner only in the irreducible situations of the history of salvation. Only on this level can the next step, the effort of conceptual understanding and the methodological bracketing (*epochē*) which subserves it, be made comprehensible.

2. This effort of the understanding is what is decisively Anselmian in the universal Christian demand of *intelligere fidem*. Anselm, who much more than Augustine emphasises the freedom of the creature, experiences this effort as an obligation of gratitude in response to the word of revelation: 'It seems to me to be negligence, if, after we have been established in the faith, we do not make the effort to understand what we believe.'[36] The bracketing[37] of faith grounded on authority, of the simple acceptance of the facts presented in the Bible, is intended above all to disturb the untroubled and comfortable way in which the pistic relies on mere facts which a man does not need to answer for to transcend theological positivism and nominalism. If it is truly the Logos who became man, then it can only be the case that in this, his highest manifestation, the whole meaning of Being is made manifest, and to grasp this, at least in outline, belongs to the dignity of a Christian. To that can be added that the reason, which operates here within the methodological bracketing, is no 'pure' reason, but a reason sinful and redeemed and coloured by the historical dimensions of existence, and that it demonstrates from historical reality the conditions of its possibility and therefore reduces to silence those who deny and scoff.[38] Moreover this reason, which produces a kind of freehand copy, retains a continuing contact with revelation: whatever in it contradicts the evident decisions of authority is acknowledged as false.[39]

[36] *CDH* I.1 (II.48.18).

[37] *Remoto Christo, quasi nihil sciatur de Christo* [Putting Christ on one side, as if nothing was known of Christ]: *CDH, praef.* (II.42.12–14), *cf.* I.10 (II.67.12–13), I.20 (II.88.3–7), *necessariis rationibus sine scriptura auctoritate* [by necessary reasons without the authority of Scripture]: *Ep de Inc. Verbi* (second version) 6 (II.20.19); *Mon. prol.* (I.7.7–8).

[38] *CDH* I.2 (II.95.1–3; 96.10–12).

[39] *CDH* I.2 (II.50.7–9), I.18 (II.82.8–9); *De conc.* III.6 (II.272.1–6).

But these are simply preliminaries, for still nothing fundamental has been said about the character of Anselmian reason.
This reason has such a unique character that it can be determined
neither by relating it back to the Patristic *intellectus* nor by seeing
in it a foreshadowing of the *ratio* of High Scholasticism. Reason
is for Anselm the spirit's capacity for sight in a quite original
way. To think means to make something visible spiritually.
Because the introduction to this vision often happens in
dialogue between the master and the disciple, the teacher is the
one who brings about vision, who draws the truth out of
hiddenness: *Aperias!*[40] *Ostende!*[41] is what one demands of him.
The result of his pointing is sight: *non video cur, nisi mihi
ostendas.*[42] *Videre* is the fundamental word for understanding, in
each case as the result of an explanation or pointer[43] which, in its
simplicity and clarity, has something evident about it,[44]
something beyond contradiction.[45] *Video nunc aperte quod
hactenus non animadverti.*[46] *Nihil corrigendum esse video.*[47] This
continually repeated *videre*[48] also relates to cases of difficulty
(*quiddam inexplicabile video*,[49] *non video cur*,[50] *nondum video*[51]); it
gives the *videtur (mihi)* a quite specifically eidetic colouring (*nec
mihi nunc videtur*,[52] *quamvis mihi videar intelligere, apertius
ostende*;[53] finally: *si videtur quomodo Christus huic subjacere non
potuit, palam erit . . .*[54]). Instead of *videre* Anselm can use any verb

[40] *CDH* II.15 (II.116.11), II.16 (II.116.17). [Open!]
[41] *De ver.* 13 (I.197.14,30); *CDH* II.17 (II.126.5). [Show!]
[42] *De cas. diab.* 3 (I.237.31). [I do not see why, unless you show me.]
[43] *De ver.* 5 (I.181.15): *video quod dicis.* [I see what you say.]
[44] *De ver.* 13 (I.198.17).
[45] *De gramm.* 13 (I.158.22): *sic consequi video.* [I see it follows thus.]
[46] *De ver.* 9 (I.189.26). [Now I see clearly what up to now I had not noticed.]
[47] *De ver.* 12 (I.194.29). [I see that nothing needs to be corrected.]
[48] *De gramm.* 4 (I.148.29–31), 5 (I.149.29), 7 (I.151.11), 14 (I.160.26), 15
(I.161.9), 21 (I.168.6), etc.
[49] *Mon.* 63 (I.74.5). [I see something inexplicable.]
[50] *Mon.* 67 (I.78.2). [I do not see why.]
[51] *De gramm.* 9 (I.153.32), 13 (I.153.10), 14 (I.159.16). [I do not yet see.]
[52] *De gramm.* 21 (I.168.8); *cf.* 8 (I.152.11,19). [it does not now appear to me.]
[53] *De ver.* 9 (I.189.8–9). [Although I seem to understand, show me more
plainly.]
[54] *De conc. virg.* 1 (II.140.5–6). [If it appears how Christ cannot be subjected
to this, it will be clear. . . .]

for beholding: *intueri*,[55] *cogitando intueri*,[56] *inspicere*,[57] *speculari* (with the clear connotation of mirror and sight),[58] *contemplari*,[59] whence one passes without a break to *considerare* and *meditari*. Much is made of the transparency of what is true *liquida vera*,[60] *liquidissime pervisum est*,[61] *liquet*,[62] *liquido*,[63] *liquidissimum est*.[64] Truth or *ratio* is *perspecta*,[65] *pervisa*,[66] *conspicua*,[67] *perspicua*,[68] *manifesta*.[69] It is revealed, made known: *patet*,[70] *palam est*,[71] it is seen *patenter*;[72] it appears, *apparet*.[73] Continually there surface the words: *aperire*,[74] *apertum*,[75] *ratio aperta*,[76] *apertissimum*,[77]

---

[55] *Mon.* 49 (I.64.17), 59 (I.71.3), 62 (*sed ne forte repugnet huic assertioni quod intueor* [but lest perhaps what I behold is inconsistent with this assertion.] I.72.6).

[56] *Mon.* 63 (I.73.11).

[57] *De ver.* 5 (I.181.30).

[58] *Mon.* 6 (*si cui forte quod speculor persuadere voluero*, I.19.19), 67 (*Ipsa* [anima] *sibimet esse velut speculum dici potest, in quo speculetur* ... *imaginem* [Dei], I.77.27–8).

[59] *De ver.* 5 (I.181.18; 182.20).

[60] *Mon.* 21 (I.38.8).

[61] *Mon.* 44 (I.61.7–8).

[62] *Mon.* 48 (I.63.18), 69 (I.80.4).

[63] *Mon.* 48 (I.63.21).

[64] *Mon.* 80 (I.87.8–9).

[65] *Mon.* 16 (I.30.12), 18 (I.32.11), 62 (I.72.20).

[66] *Mon.* 21 (I.38.17), 44 (I.61.8).

[67] *Mon.* 16 (I.30.15).

[68] *Mon.* 41 (I.58.11), 55 (I.67.9).

[69] *Mon.* 4 (I.17.32), 37 (I.55.14), 50 (I.65.10), 56 (I.68.4)

[70] *Mon.* 7 (I.20.27), *ibid.* (I.22.5: *certissime patet*), 50 (I.65.7); *De gramm.* 16 (I.161.23); *De cas. diab.* 13 (I.258.4); *De conc.* I.6 (II.256.27), I.7 (II.259.29), etc.

[71] *Mon.* 50 (I.65.3).

[72] *De cas. diab.* 21 (I.269.7).

[73] *Mon.* 48 (I.63.19); *De gramm.* 21 (I.168.1).

[74] *De cas. diab.* 26 (I.274.5).

[75] *Mon.* 7 (I.22.7), 55 (I.67.7); *De gramm.* 14 (I.159.29), *De ver.* 5 (I.181.27), 8 (I.188.8), 9 (I.189.9); *De lib. arb.* 5 (I.216.11); *Ep. de Inc. Verbi* (first version) (I.286.26); *CDH* I.21 (II.88.28); *De conc. virg.* 7 (II.148.1); 13 (II.155.23), 22 (II.161.24), 26 (II.161.24), 26 (II.169.22); *De conc. virg.* I.6 (II.256.16); I.7 (II.259.29), II.3 (II.261.17).

[76] *De gramm.* 19 (I.164.16); *CDH praef.* (II.42.14); *De conc.* III.6 (II.272.1); *Medit.* 3 (III.87.79).

[77] *CDH* II.14 (II.114.20), II.18 (II.129.22); *De conc.* I.6 (II.257.2–3), I.7 (II.258.8).

apertissime probare,[78] and this opening up of the truth and its grounds causes it to appear in its incontrovertibility: *inexpugnabiliter*,[79] *ratio* (or *necessitas*) *inevitabilis*,[80] *irrefragabilis*,[81] *indubitabilis*,[82] in a *robur inflexibile*,[83] finally as *ratio evidens*,[84] *evidentissime*.[85] In an openness or revealedness which spiritual vision cannot withstand: *non possum apertae consequentiae resistere*,[86] *non potest aliud esse*,[87] *resistere nequeo rationi tuae*,[88] and which compels agreement: *cogit*,[89] *velit nolit sentit*.[90] The radiant obviousness of the truth (*claritas veritatis*,[91] *nihil clarius*,[92] *claret*)[93] is something that convinces so persuasively (*persuadet ratio*)[94] that finally it must be described by using the keyword, as 'necessity', that which must be so: as *ratio necessaria*,[95] *rationis necessitas*,[96] *necessitas veritatis*,[97] as that *quod supra rationabili et perspicua necessitate claruit*.[98] The interchangeability of *perspicuum* and *necessarium*[99] points to the true character of the latter: it is that made apprehensible to spiritual sight, realizable, unavoidably

---

[78] *CDH* II.18 (II.127.7).

[79] *Mon.* 29 (I.47.12), 18 (I.33.10); *De Inc. Verbi* (second version) 6 (II.20.15); *CDH* I.24 (II.94.21); *De proc. spir.* 1 (II.185.16, 27), 14 (II.212.11).

[80] *Mon.* 22 (I.40.16); *CDH* II.9 (II.105.26–106.1), II.19 (II.130.22).

[81] *De proc. spir.* 1 (II.183.15).

[82] *Mon.* 54 (I.66.21).

[83] *Mon.* 29 (I.47.8).

[84] *Ep. de Inc. Verbi* (second version) 6 (II.21.5–6).

[85] *Mon.* 55 (I.67.6–7).

[86] *De gramm.* 13 (I.159.1), 21 (I.166.1). [I cannot resist a clear consequence.]

[87] *De gramm.* 21 (I.167.3). [It cannot be otherwise.]

[88] *CDH* I.12 (II.69.31). [I do not know how to resist your reason.]

[89] *Mon.* 33 (I.52.2, 8).

[90] *Mon.* 4 (I.16.31).

[91] *Mon. prol.* (I.7.11), 33 (I.53.20).

[92] *De ver.* 13 (I.198.21); *De cas. diab.* 13 (I.257.32).

[93] *De cas. diab.* 23 (I.273.28).

[94] *Mon.* 4 (I.17.4), 6 (I.19.19); *De gramm.* 17 (I.163.1).

[95] *Ep. de Inc. Verbi* (second version) 6 (II.20.19); *CDH* II.18 (II.126.27).

[96] *Mon.* 18 (I.33.6).

[97] *Mon.* 17 (I.31.21).

[98] *Mon.* 21 (I.38.4–5); *CDH* I.25 (II.96.10). [which is manifest beyond rational and clear necessity.]

[99] *Mon.* 16 (I.30.15), cf. *Mon.* 41, *perspicuum* = *certissimum* (I.58.11–12).

perceptible as true (*intellectus sentire per rationem constringitur*[100]). From such apprehensibility there arises certainty (*certa ratio*,[101] *certa veritas et verta certitudo*,[102] *certissimum*,[103] *indubitanter*,[104] *nihil consequentius*[105]), the opposite of which is absurd (*stultissimum*,[106] *absurdissimum*[107]).

The Anselmian process of thought is, at the level of spiritual demonstration, true thought, which can never cease to protest against 'modern dialectic'[108] which plays with unclear concepts (*dialecticis sophismatibus*[109]) and just for that reason, as Anselm sees it, remains bound to the realm of sensible imagination without being able to rise to the level of aesthetic reason.[110] In order to think, there is needed a *simplicem intellectum et non multiplicitate phantasmatum obrutum*.[111] But what is here spoken against Roscelin can elsewhere be used against a theology that is pleasing but devoid of thought, which thinks it sufficient to compare image with image and set up 'fitting parallels'— comparing the disobedient woman Eve with the obedient woman Mary, the tree of paradise with the tree of the cross—in order to fashion thereby a 'wonderful beauty'. 'It must be admitted that all these things are beautiful and can be accepted as material for the imagination. But if they do not rest on something solid, they are hardly enough to convince unbelievers. . . . For when a man wants to paint a picture, he selects

[100] *Mon.* (I.30.33–31.1). [the intellect is constrained by reason to be aware of it.]

[101] *CDH* II.17 (II.126.5).

[102] *Prosl.* 14 (I.111.13).

[103] *Mon.* 63 (I.73.5).

[104] *Mon.* 54 (I.66.21).

[105] *Mon.* 48 (I.64.2), 71 (I.81.19–20).

[106] *Mon.* 70 (I.81.2).

[107] *Mon.* 69 (I.80.2). All these keywords in Anselmian language are missing from F. S. Schmitt's new Anselm dictionary.

[108] *Ep. de Inc. Verbi* (first version) 10 (I.289.18).

[109] *Ibid.* 3 (I.282.23).

[110] *In eorum quippe animabus ratio . . . sic est in imaginationibus corporeis involuta, ut ex eis se non possit evolvere . . . nec ea quae ipsa sola et pura ratione contemplari debet, valeat discernere. Ibid.* 4 (I.285.5–11).

[111] *Ibid.* 10 (I.289.10). [a simple understanding, not overwhelmed by the multiplicity of imaginations.]

something solid to paint on, so that his painting will endure. . . . *Monstranda ergo prius est veritatis soliditas rationabilis, id est necessitas. . . .*'[112] At the end of his proof Anselm will take up again the images of fittingness with which he began; their rightness and fittingness (*convenit valde*) has now been demonstrated, and it can be said: *valde pulchrae et rationabiles sunt istae picturae.*[113] Now are these things 'established on the firmness of truth, as on a solid foundation, which, with the help of God, we have to some extent perceived.'[114] Neither playing with concepts nor looking at images is in itself to be equated with thought. *Monologion* 10 enumerates four steps: (1) the mere ostensive naming of a significant name, such as man; (2) the inward thinking of the name (*nomen cogitare*); (3) the spiritual apprehension of the thing itself through a sensible image (*imago*); (4) The spiritual apprehension of the thing itself by reason (*ratio*). While the *imago* only represents the *figura sensibilis*, reason grasps the *universalis essentia.*[115] *Proslogion* 4 emphasizes once more the second and the fourth steps: 'the thing is thought in one way when the word signifying it is thought, in another way when the thing itself which it is is understood.'[116] For the understanding of the thing itself there stands the traditional expression *universalis essentia*, which in the first place need mean no more than that the insight into the essence of the thing, the philosophical intuition of its essence, is the unconditional presupposition of any, even of theological, thinking. 'How can someone who does not yet understand how several men are one man in species comprehend how in that most mysterious and lofty nature several persons, each one of whom is perfect God, are one God? Or how can someone whose mind is so dark that he cannot distinguish between his own horse and its colour, distinguish between the one God and his several relations? Finally, he who cannot understand that

[112] *CDH* I.3–4 (II.51.5–52.4). [First, therefore, there needs to be demonstrated the rational basis of truth, that is, necessity.]

[113] *CDH* II.8 (II.104.24, 28). [these pictures are exceedingly beautiful and rational.]

[114] *CDH* II.19 (II.131.9–10).

[115] *Mon.* 10 (I.25.4–9).

[116] *Prosl.* 4 (I.103.18–19).

anything except the individual is man will only be able to understand "man" as referring to a human person. For every individual man is a person. How, then, will he be able to understand that manhood, but not a person, was taken by the Word . . .?"[117] In all theological thought philosophical thought is implicit, but nominalist philosophy (for which nothing universal can be intuited) is for Anselm a contradiction in itself.

For Anselm the process of thought moves unmistakably towards the point where the subject studied appears with such clarity that one can speak of an immediate in-sight, towards the making present of the subject matter, whereby the attempt to achieve such a making-present proves whether the subject matter can be achieved and is therefore true or not. To give an example:

> Anselm: Can you suppose that a man who has once sinned, and has never made satisfaction to God for his sin, but is simply let off unpunished, is equal to an angel who has never sinned?
> Boso: I can think and say the words, but I cannot think their real meaning any more than I can suppose falsehood to be the truth.[118]

This making present before the mind (*cogito hoc, velut ante nos sit*[119]) will not be achieved by the unexperienced at the first stroke; the pure beholding (*puro rationis intuitu*[120]), the simple conceptual vision (*simplex intellectus*[121]) is accomplished in a process of analysis and synthesis of the components (*intellectus dividens et componens*, as Thomas will say), each of which is a partial view (*quasi cogitando intueri, cogitantis inspectio*[122]), which to begin with appears to be quite irreconcilable with any other view (*ne forte repugnet huic assertioni quod intueor.*[123] *Sic tua disputatio . . . necessariis rationibus concatenatur, ut nulla ratione . . .*

---

[117] *Ep. de Inc. Verbi* (second version) 1 (II.10.4–13).
[118] *CDH* I.19 (II.84.17–21).
[119] *Ibid.* (II.85.10).
[120] *De conc. virg.* 13 (II.155.15).
[121] *Ep de Inc. Verbi* (first version) 10 (I.289.10).
[122] *Mon.* 63 (I.73.11–12).
[123] *Mon.* 62 (I.72.6). [lest perhaps what I behold is inconsistent with this assertion.]

dissolvi posse videam, *nisi quia* video *aliquid consequi . . .*[124]), Thus
the foremost task for the thinker is to develop and use this power
of synthetic vision, the capacity to gather together what is
separated, which is the root meaning of *legere, logos: opus est ut tu
ea quae dicam non sis contentus singula tantum intelligere, sed omnia
simul memoria* quasi sub uno intuitu colligere.[125] This power of
uniting in the *intuitus*, which raises one from a particular view to
a universal vision, is judgement: *judicium animae*.[126] Anselm will
have recourse to this same unifying judgement for his proof of
the existence of God: *nullus intelligens id quod Deus est, potest
cogitare quod Deus non est.*[127]

Such unifying vision—as *speculatio*,[128] *meditatio*,[129] and particularly *consideratio*[130]—judges what belongs together, what
unites in the correct way (*concatenatio*,[131] *contextio*,[132] *convenientia*,[133] *congruentia*,[134] *consequentia*,[135] *concordia*[136]) what forms a
unity in spite of the initial impression (*quomodo convenient
contraria*[137]) and produces a *concors veritas*.[138] It can take place as a
calculating hesitation (*mihi magis videtur convenientia quam*

[124] *De cas. diab.* 20 (I.264.22–4). [Your disputation is so bound together by
necessary reasons that I *see* it can be dissolved by no reason, unless because I *see*
that something follows. . . .]
[125] *De cas. diab.* 12 (I.252.2–4). [The task is that you should not be content to
understand the things that I say one by one, but that you should collect them
all together at once in the memory *as if in a single intuition.*]
[126] *De ver.* 6 (I.184.30).
[127] *Prosl.* 4 (I.103.20–1). [no one who understands what God is can think that
God does not exist.]
[128] *Mon.* 67 (I.77.24).
[129] *Mon.* 6 (I.19.16).
[130] *Mon.* 64 (I.75.11); *De ver.* 5 (I.182.26–7); *CDH* I.19 (II.85.2,5), I.21
(II.88.18), II.11 (II.111.6).
[131] *De cas. diab.* 20 (I.264.22–3).
[132] *Mon.* 19 (I.34.27); *CDH* II.19 (II.130.2).
[133] *Mon.* 19 (I.34.27), 22 (I.41.1), 39 (I.57.12), 45 (I.62.5), 78 (I.85.7); *De cas.
diab.* 14 (I.258.31); *CDH* I.7 (II.57.9), II.8 (II.104.7, 24), II.9 (II.105.19–20).
[134] *Mon.* 76 (I.84.1); *Ep. de Inc. Verbi* (second version) 10 (II.27.16).
[135] *De lib. arb.* 1 (I.209.6).
[136] *Mon.* 22 (I.41.18).
[137] *Mon.* 22 (I.39.3).
[138] *Mon.* 22 (I.41.18).

inconvenientia,[139] *magis convenit*[140]), a preference on balance, so that his words here are often in the comparative (*congruentius*), granting rather than requiring (*non incongrue*[141]), marking the perception of a suitability (*decet*[142]). So there arise degrees of compellingness with which the subject matter thrusts itself upon the *intuitus* (*non solum conveniens, sed etiam necessarium*[143]).

This notion of degrees, however, so far as it is concerned with the divine work of salvation, does not apply to the subject matter itself, but rather its more or less central manifestation of itself to the subject. Where, on the other hand, the subject matter is concerned, there are in God's free dealings no degrees of necessity. Just as his creation proceeded from the fullest, unconstrained freedom from which developed an order determined by law, so his self-revelation is unfolded in the history of salvation and in Jesus Christ equally in unsurpassable freedom and ordered necessity. The God who allows himself to be seen (even if through a veil) shows himself with a logic nothing can surpass, the inner consequence of which is the most compelling that there is, in the objective structure of which there is no room for any distinction between the necessary and what is simply fitting and suitable. It is only that the vision of the whole structure is something that transcends human, even believing, reason; what it can perceive of necessity within it is only a fragment which nevertheless clearly contains within itself a guarantee of the meaning of the whole. With this we stand once more before the Anselmian form of the *analogia entis*, in which *evidentissime comprehendi potest* that the manner of God's knowing and fashioning *ab humana scientia comprehendi non posse.*[144] This is again the *videt se non plus posse videre.*[145] Nevertheless God's revelation of love is presupposed, and there is no

[139] *De cas. diab.* 23 (I.270.19). [To me there appears to be fittingness rather than unfittingness.]

[140] *Ep. de Inc. Verbi* (second version) 10 (II.26.10). [rather it is fitting.]

[141] *Mon.* 46 (I.62.16); *De conc. virg.* 20 (II.160.19).

[142] *CDH* I.12 (II.69.9, 15) and often.

[143] *CDH* II.16 (II.119.14). [not only fitting, but also necessary.]

[144] *Mon.* 36 (I.54.16–18). [It can be comprehended most evidently . . . (that it) cannot be comprehended by human knowledge.]

[145] *Prosl.* 14 (I.111.25–112.1). [It sees that it can no longer see.]

harsh barrier set in the path of the one who seeks and longs, but rather just as the being of existents is disclosed to the philosopher in an incomprehensible manner, so the inner ground of the freedom and love of God is opened to the believer in an incomprehensible manner: *miro modo apertissimum est.*[146] There is a necessity which 'compels' us to posit within God, the free creator, a *pluralitas, ineffabilem certe*, and which 'can be expressed in no way';[147] there reigns *quaedam tam ineffabilis quam inevitabilis pluralitas* in the highest unity.[148] After Anselm has taken a few more steps into the *mysterium*, he breaks off: 'For I hold that it must be enough for the one who seeks to understand an incomprehensible matter if by reasoning he arrives at the conclusion that he knows most certainly that it is, even if he cannot penetrate by his understanding how it is. . . . For what is so incomprehensible and so ineffable as that which is above all? If, then, those things which up till now have been disputed concerning the highest being are asserted on the basis of compelling reasons, although they cannot be so penetrated by the understanding that they can be explained in words, in no way is the sure foundation of their certitude shaken. Such consideration understands rationally that it is incomprehensible . . . *rationaliter comprehendit incomprehensibile esse.*'[149] The solution of this paradox lies in the human mind, which can only understand itself, its rationality and freedom, in the inner opposition of ground (memory), spirit-word (understanding) and will; but this structure can be understood only as a reflection of a quite other archetype and so that in itself it 'reflects' as in a 'mirror' the obscure archetype (*in speculo speculari*).[150] This is good Augustinianism; only it should not be overlooked that here too the theological act is rooted in the philosophical, and that, as the existent is distinguished from Being, in which it is rooted, and the creature from God, so the free spiritual being understands itself in the contrast with absolute Spirit, in which it is rooted just in its being spiritual and its being free.

---

[146] *Mon.* 38 (I.56.11).
[147] *Ibid.* 15–17.
[148] *Mon.* 43 (I.59.15–16). [a certain plurality as ineffable as it is inevitable.]
[149] *Mon.* 64 (I.75.1–12).
[150] *Mon.* 65–7 (I.75–8).

The way of the *Monologion* (beside which the *Proslogion* can be seen as an epitome) is this steady ascent from philosophical (or a classical-theological) vision to the vision of (Christian) theological reason, in which the theological element lies rather in the light of faith which falls on the divine being than in an object of faith of its own; this last is already methodically bracketed off, for the sake of understanding. The change is accomplished as imperceptibly as possible—through the equation of *per ipsum* with *ex* in chapter 5: what comes forth from God is also created by him, and indeed, as the continuation shows, necessarily out of nothing or out of his creative idea, from which there follows God's freedom and personality and finally his being as spiritual word. Thus one of the standing titles of God is henceforth *creatrix essentia (substantia, natura)*,[151] and the 'ideas' are deduced not primarily from below, from the contingence and the degrees of worldly qualities, which are ascending degrees of perfection, indeed of reality, and which persuade (*persuadet*)[152] of the existence of something most perfect and most real in their sphere, but rather from above: from the free self-expression of God, who plans and 'imagines' what he wills. And with that the category of expression (*exprimere*) is given its place, which will become so important for Bonaventure; and the *ars divina* will be less *in facto esse*, in the order of the universal, than *in fieri*, in the free discovery of essences, seen in the power of expression of the divine 'fancy' and located in the 'place' in God, where the power of generation within the divine itself is engaged in its trinitarian work.[153] All this is certainly a continuation of Augustine's trinitarian thought, but from the outset there is an emphasis on God's total freedom and therefore on the spontaneity of his self-disclosure; also the philosophical categories of infinity, of God's transcendence over space and time, his invulnerability (*apatheia*) and therefore his immanence in everything finite are filled out in a personal way: impassibility must be one with God's mercy,[154]

[151] *Mon.* 8 (I.23.32), 11 (I.26.17), 18 (I.32.7), 20 (I.35.7), 22 (I.39.27), 36 (I.55.6), 37 (I.55.17–18), 66 (I.77.14).

[152] *Mon.* 1–6 (I.14.9–18.3), 31 (I.49–50).

[153] *Mon.* 10 (I.24–5), 29–35 (I.47–54).

[154] *Mon.* 60 (I.70–1); *Prosl.* 8 (I.106), 10 (I.109.3–4).

his immanence is equivalent to his personal presence.[155] The striving after happiness, which the Greek philosopher sought to satisfy through contemplation of the highest good, assumes in virtue of the personal freedom of God the mode of an aspiring after God, who both graciously gives himself and himself comforts him who exerts himself on his account and recompenses (*retribuit*) him in accordance with his effort.[156] And if already with Plato thought gains admittance 'suddenly' (*exaiphnēs*), then this is even more true with Anselm, where the granting of the decisive encounter depends on the very decision of God in his freedom. Anselm was already close to giving up in despair his efforts to find a synthetic proof of the existence of God (*desperans volui cessare*) when that for which he was seeking suddenly 'presented itself' (*se obtulit*),[157] as earlier in the *Monologion*: '*ad magnam et delectabile quiddam me subito perduxit haec mea meditatio*'.[158] From this the *appetitus naturalis ad Deum* emerges in clarity and without caesura as the Christian stance of faith, hope and love, and indeed this is characteristic in that from the recognition of God as the highest good 'there follows with utmost certainty that each man has to love and long for this God with all his heart, all his soul and all his feeling', something that equally includes the fact that no-one can strive for this without the hope that he may one day attain to it. 'No-one, however, can love or hope who does not believe.' Anselm characterizes this faith as *credere in summam essentiam*, because the 'in' expresses both the movement towards God and the acceptance of all that which is a presupposition for such a thrusting forward (*intentio*). 'For it would not seem that he believed in that if he believed something that did not belong to this striving, or if he did not strive for that through what he does believe': the content of faith is specified by the pressure of love and derives both its measure and its title to existence from it. In every way is this remarkable: not only in respect of the sequence love–hope–faith, but also in the way the Christian faith is incorporated without break into

---

[155] *De ver.* 13 (I.199.19–20).

[156] *Mon.* 70 (I.80–1).

[157] *Prosl. proem.* (I.93.12, 18).

[158] *Mon.* 6 (I.19.15). [This my meditation suddenly led me to something great and delightful.]

the classical eros in its movement towards God, even though Anselm naturally knows that the content of faith is God's freely revealed reality and truth, which is presupposed even for the striving itself. Thus, even though he does indeed equate *credere in* with *credere ad*, it is the former expression that he prefers, because he goes on to say that whoever 'believes in God' already moves within the sphere of God (*intra illam permanebit*) and, in the light of faith and its object, participates in God.[159] This whole conception culminates in a theology of the human spirit as *imago trinitatis*, as spiritual ground, self-possession and will of love, which is presupposed in the act of trinitarian revelation and is actualized as the answer to the Word of God. What spirit finally is is only clarified in the personal dialogue between eternal and created spirit, whose answer is comprised in and made possible, both essentially and personally, by the word of eternal love.

The *Proslogion* with its 'ontological argument for the existence of God' presents itself as a tautened condensation of the *Monologion*[160] and must therefore contain in a tightly argued form the thought of the earlier work. If, then, the proof derives God's existence from the speculative characterisation of God as *id quo majus cogitari nequit*,[161] because what exists is more than what is merely thought, then the first point to make is that according to the *Monologion* God can be attained by no concept drawn from the world,[162] indeed that a 'concept of God' is a contradictory form of words, because God is essentially what cannot be conceived, and that this indeed is what finite reason can grasp: *comprehendit incomprehensibile esse*.[163] The *id quo majus cogitari nequit* is thus exactly translatable by *quiddam majus quam cogitari possit*.[164] No more than being is a concept, though it is the presupposition for any formation of concepts, no more, indeed far less, is God a concept, although he is the presupposition for all being (and any being) and all thought (and any thinker). If

[159] *Mon.* 74–6 (I.83).
[160] *Prosl. prooem.* (I.93.4–6).
[161] *Prosl.* 3 (I.102.10). [that than which no greater can be thought.]
[162] *Mon.* 15 (I.28.11–12).
[163] *Mon.* 64 (I.75.11–12).
[164] *Prosl.* 15 (I.112.14–15). [something greater than what can be thought.]

the negative formula (*id quo majus* . . .) could be taken at most as designating a limiting concept, then the comparative (*majus*) clearly expresses the fact that it is in no sense a static concept, but rather points to a dynamic movement of thought, and within that to a never-attained horizon of thought, which yet contains all thought, a horizon indeed which the positive formula (*quiddam majus* . . .) then expressly represents as transcendent. But in Anselm's doctrine of thought each statement about essence is primarily a function of a statement about existence; if the function of indication or meaning can indeed be considered or understood for itself, abstracted from existential correctness, then it can be so only in its applicability to the real.[165] If reality or unreality or any condition of being is to be predicated of something which we conceive, then we must at least initially posit the act of thinking as the existing 'cause' (*causa*) or active bearer (*facere*) of the property of being or essence which is predicated.[166] Thinking owes (*debet*) this effective cause, on the basis of which it makes its claims (*affirmatio*[167]), a statement which rightly characterizes reality (*recta = vera significatio*[168]). Thus it follows that thinking owes the final bearer of the whole order of designation and expression the declaration of reality, because this logical bearer is by definition also the ontological bearer, in so far as every conceptual order is founded on the order of existence; the judgement S = P is reduced in this case to the tautology A = A: being is being. This is not to deny that for the aesthetic, intuitive thought of Anselm this highest

---

[165] *De ver.* 2 (I.179).

[166] *Cum dicitur quia homo est aut homo non est, prius concipitur in mente significatum hujus nominis, quam dicatur esse vel non esse, et ideo quod concipitur causa est ut dicatur de illo esse. Si etiam dicimus: homo est animal, est homo causa ut sit [ipse] animal et dicatur esse animal. . . . Hoc enim nomine significatur et concipitur totus homo, in quo toto est animal ut pars. . . . Hoc igitur modo de quocumque dicitur esse sive simpliciter, ut: homo est, sive additamento, ut: homo est animal, aut: homo est sanus: praecedens ejus conceptio est causa, ut dicatur esse vel non esse, et ut intelligatur quod dicitur. Quoniam ergo de quacumque re aliquod verbum pronuntietur, praedicta ratione dicitur facere, quod eodem verbo profertur, non sine omni ratione . . . omne verbum facere dicitur.* (*Ein unvoll. Werk* . . . pp. 27–8).

[167] *De ver.* 2 (I.178.8).

[168] *Ibid.* 18.20.

intuition,[169] achieved after a long struggle, presupposes the conventionalities of thought of the *Monologion*: on the one hand the manifestation of the highest reality from the attempted comparison of degrees of being of ever-ascending reality, and on the other, and as part of that reflection, that philosophical experience of thought about the existent itself, which the letter against Roscelin calls *experimentum*. A 'deduction' of existence from a concept, or even the notion that we can think God as a concept, can only be for Anselm a caricature of a philosophical act. In contrast, the full realisation of the true philosophical act is to be found in that theological experience of the revelation of the mercy of the Father in the suffering Son, in which in an incomprehensible manner all righteousness is satisfied, *ut nec major (misericordia) nec justior cogitari possit*:[170] herein lies nothing less than the overwhelming of the aesthetic reason of faith by the incomprehensibility of the divine love, an incomprehensibility radiating in the form of revelation as it is exhibited: *rationabiliter comprehendit incomprehensibile esse*.[171] This structure of thought is final, it applies even in the heavenly vision: *Sancti Dei in gloria sua Deum videbunt, sed magnitudinem divinitatis ejus sive immensitatem potentiae illius comprehendere nequibunt. Non enim immensus esset, si intellectu alicujus comprehendi potuisset.*[171a]

3. It is precisely from this structure of aesthetic reason that the third moment emerges: joy, *gaudium, delectatio*. It is joy at the

[169] Apart from his own testimony in the *Prooemium, cf.* the version, exaggerated into myth, in Eadmer's *Life: PL* 158, 63–4.

[170] *CDH* II.20 (II.131.29). Anselm Stolz, in particular, has emphasized the presupposition of the proof from degrees ('Vere Esse im Proslogion des hl. Anselm', *Scholastik* IX [1934], 400–9); on *experimentum* as a mediating concept, Henri Bouillard in *SpicBec*, 191–207. The way in which our interpretation differs from that of Karl Barth (*Fides quaerens intellectum. Anselms Beweis der Existenz Gottes*, 1931) is self-evident. [That (mercy) can be thought neither greater nor more just.]

[171] *Mon.* 64 (I.75.11–12).

[171a] *Simil.* 167 (*PL* 159. 692C). [The saints will behold God in his glory, but they will not be able to understand the greatness of his divinity or the infinity of his power. For he would not be infinite if he could be comprehended by anyone's intellect.]

'utmost beauty' of God,[172] which to begin with certainly, again in the sense of classical contemplation, is read off from the glory of the world-order (*multitudinem tam formose formatam, tam ordinate variatam, tam convenienter diversam*[173]) but is much more to be seen in the supernatural beauty of the order of salvation, which is *propter rationis pulchritudinem amabilis*[174] and makes possible a *valde pulchra contemplatio*.[175] But because the joy of finding the harmonies hidden in the history of salvation presupposes the grace of faith and therefore supplicating prayer, it will at the same time be both satisfaction of the reason through the evidence that is offered and, at a deeper level, thankfulness for its being given in grace: thus the theological blessedness is found in the philosophical and beyond it. Both moments are inseparable in the *delectabile quiddam*, at which the contemplation suddenly (*subito*) arrives,[176] in the *delectabiliter intueri*[177] of the inner mysteries of God: *valde mihi videtur delectabile retractare saepius tam impenetrabile secretum*.[178] This joy breaks out at the end of a wearisome train of thought, which as such has been sustained wholly by an ascetic concentration of thought which allows itself not so much as a glance to the side, a pause for rest. For the joy breaks out really in the moment of reaching understanding: *ut eorum quae credunt intellectu et contemplatione delectentur*.[179] It is the *gaudeo invenisse*.[180] But it is not without cause that this joy breaks forth unhoped-for just at the point where despair at ever being able to attain a solution (*desperans volui cessare*), even indeed where an erosion of one's resistance to such a pressing and dominating problem (*cum vehementer ejus importunitati resistendo fatigarer*), has gone before:

[172] *Mon.* 16 (I.31.5).
[173] *Mon.* 7 (I.22.8–9). [a multitude so beautifully formed, so varied in an orderly way, so fittingly diverse.]
[174] *CDH* I.1 (II.48.8–9). [loveable by reason of its beauty.]
[175] *De cas. diab.* 25 (I.273.3–4). [exceedingly beautiful contemplation.]
[176] *Mon.* 6 (I.19.15–16).
[177] *Mon.* 49 (I.64.17).
[178] *Mon.* 43 (I.59.17). [rather it seems to me delightful to withdraw more often into so impenetrable a mystery.]
[179] *CDH* I.1 (II.47.9). [that they might be delighted by the understanding and contemplation of the things which they believe.]
[180] *Prosl. prooem.* (I.93.20). [I rejoice to have found.]

for the evidential form of the truth which offers itself to the despairing (*se obtulit quod desperaveram*)[181] shines out of the abyss of ever-deeper incomprehensibility, indeed it is and remains the manifestation of just this: the incomprehensible.

Creation, and even more the order of salvation, is radiant in the order of its beauty as the revelation of God's freedom and therefore of the wholly other and infinite blessedness which belongs to the realm of the divine.[182] Therefore the joy communicated through the grace of God not only stands in no relation to human effort or to human joy in discovery, but neither does the joy which is granted through God's grace in this life of faith stand in any relation to the promised joy of the eternal vision face-to-face, in which the shared joy of all redeemed and loving creatures will be fulfilled at the same time. Henri de Lubac[183] has shown that the line of the *Proslogion* is thus deeply broken: the intellectual satisfaction at the discovery of the proof of God's existence is not at all the joy in God promised by Christ: the light of truth which streams forth from God does not bestow the vision face-to-face, and therefore the book ends with faith's reflection on the eschatological joy, in which alone the full satisfaction and the full overwhelming by the eternal blessedness of God will take place. The model of heavenly joy also makes clear what the vision face-to-face can mean for Anselm: nothing other and nothing less than the final and most positive fulfilment of the *comprehendit incomprehensibile esse*. 'O human heart, O needy heart, O heart experienced in suffering, indeed overwhelmed by suffering, how greatly would you rejoice if you abounded in all these things! Ask your innermost soul whether it could comprehend its joy in its so great blessedness? But surely if someone else whom you loved in every respect as yourself possessed that same blessedness, your

[181] *Ibid.* 12, 16–18.
[182] *Prosl.* 24 (I.117–18): 'For if there are many and great delights in delightful things, what sort of a delight, and how great a delight, is there in him who made the delightful things themselves?'
[183] *SpicBec* 295–312. His distinction is supported by *Simil.* 164: *Tribus modis sentitur Deus: videlicet intellectu, amore et usu. Per intellectum sapimus, per amorem justificamur, per usum beatificamur. Inquantum quis Deum intelligit, sapiens est; inquantum vero amat, justus; ... inquantum utitur, beatus* (PL 159.691D–692A).

ת!33

joy would be doubled, for you would rejoice as much for him as for yourself.' But there are not just two or three but innumerable souls, 'no one of whom will love another less than itself, and each will rejoice for every other as for itself. If, then, the heart of man will scarcely be able to comprehend the joy that will belong to it from so great a good, how will it find space for so many and such great joys?' And because each one will love God and God's own happiness infinitely more than itself and than the others, it is clear 'that their whole heart, their whole mind, their whole soul, will not suffice for the grandeur of this love'. Therefore, deduces Anselm, the joy of God will not enter into the heart, but the hearts of the blessed will enter into the ever-greater joy of God: *intra in gaudium Domini tui*. Meanwhile there remains, rising up in a great wave to meet overwhelming joy, the greater longing and hope, the thirst of love for the stilling of love's longing.[184]

And then there comes a final thought. The joy of the aesthetic reason, which contemplates the harmony of God's work of salvation, is founded on the suffering of the Son of God. This casts a shadow over the whole theological aesthetic, at least so long as it is the aesthetic of faith, of the mortal life. 'But Thou, O Lord, Thou, that I might live, hast taken death upon thyself. How can I rejoice at my freedom, which would not be were it not for thy chains? How can I be thankful for my salvation, which would not have been except for thy sorrows? How can I rejoice at my life, which would not have been except for thy death? Or should I rejoice at those things which thou hast suffered, and at the cruelty of those who did these things to thee, for unless they had done them . . . this my good would not have been? Or if I grieve for those things, how can I rejoice for these things which would not have been, if those had not been?'[185] In this reversal, which explodes every perceptible proportion and finally casts the one who beholds together with his joy out of himself into the ever-greater love of God, there lies the overwhelming nature of Christian joy, which here can no longer be

---

[184] *Prosl.* 25–6 (I.120–1); *De beat. coel.* 14 (PL 159, 599C–600B); *Simil.* 71 (643A).
[185] *Medit.* 3 (III.89.137–44).

in any wise a human achievement, but which, because in spite of
all it is offered, is given in grace as Christ's Easter present.

2. THE RADIANCE OF FREEDOM

Anselm's most important dogmatic treatises revolve round the
problem of freedom: the early work, De veritate, points up the
ethical element in truth, De libertate arbitrii sets out the basic
principles of freedom, De casu diaboli their application to pure
spiritual being, De conceptu virginali et de originali peccato their
application to mankind; Cur Deus homo demythologizes the
doctrine of redemption and grounds everything in the unforced
freedom of the death of the Redeemer and the consequent
liberation of the constrained freedom of men, and De concordia
answers the objections against freedom drawn from the foreknowledge, predestination and grace of God. Freedom is the
central concern of a Christian understanding of reality which
(bracketing the historical–positive under revelation) contemplates the relationship of absolute and relative being in the
light of the self-disclosure of the absolute. Anselm's inquiry is,
moreover, timely, for 'in our times there are many who
completely despair of the freedom of man.'[186] From time imme-
morial, and in particular since the Augustinian doctrine of sin
and predestination, freedom has been the playground for all
short-sighted and corner-cutting philosophers.

Everything springs from an utterly simple vision of the
analogy between God and the creature as an analogy of freedom. For the creature, freedom can only mean being allowed to
enter into communion with the other (and thus participation in
God's independent personal being), something, however,
which can only be perfected as, through grace, creaturely
freedom is drawn ever more strongly into absolute freedom, to
the point where the creature achieves its final freedom, when it
is free with God and in God, and simply wills, in freedom and
not through being overpowered, what God wills: 'God's will
itself will no longer be different from yours, for as you will will

[186] De conc. III.1 (II.264.9–10).

what he wills, so will he will in all things what you will . . . you will almightily dispose of your willing, because the Almighty himself will in all things be in accord (*concordantem habebis*) with your will.'[187] But because 'perfect *concordia* will reign only where this unites to become an *identitas* and a *unitas*', namely, in the divine triunity,[188] the eschatological analogy of freedom between God and the creature can be realised in no other way than in grace as participation in the triune life, because 'the Father has joined us to his almighty Son as his body and as co-heirs with him, and made us who are called in his name to be gods. But God is the one who divinises; you on the contrary will be the one who is divinised.'[189]

It is this eschatological orientation which renders everything intelligible: the whole way that created freedom has to go before it can be realised and be freed for its own freedom. Looked at from this goal it may 'not be part of the definition of freedom to be able to sin', because such a definition would 'lessen freedom, while its rejection would increase it';[190] at best the power (*potestas*) which originally constituted freedom can in part be defined as being unable to be constrained to sin by any power on earth,[191] even the power of temptation.[192] 'If it succumbs, then not to any alien power, but to its own.'[193] Freedom is therefore power (*potestas sive libertas*[194]), and this can be so powerful that either there simply is no question of powerlessness to resist temptation, as in the case of God and also in the case of Christ,[195] who is the only creature who is God, or there is no longer such a question, as in the case of the angels after the temptation which established them, or in the case of holy men—in both of which cases, because they are not God, this

[187] *De beat. coel.* 10–11 (PL 159, 596C, 597B); *Simil.* 68 (641C).
[188] *Ep de Inc. Verbi* (second version) 15 (II.33.21–3).
[189] *De beat. coel.* 12 (598A).
[190] *De lib. arb.* 1 (I.208.10, 209.4–5).
[191] *Ibid.* 2 (I.210.3–4).
[192] *Ibid.* 5 (I.214–17).
[193] *Ibid.* 5 (I.216.26–7).
[194] *De conc.* I.6 (II.257.24).
[195] *Possumus itaque dicere de Christo quia potuit mentiri, si subauditur: se vellet.* CDH II.10 (II.107.6–7). [Thus we can say that Christ was able to lie, if we understand: if he willed.]

final freedom could only be attained with a great effort.[196] To
have seen the necessity of having to attain by one's own efforts
the state of created freedom is one of Anselm's greatest achievements, and governs his whole doctrine of freedom.

The non-necessity or contingency of the creature carries the
implication that, if God gives it creaturely freedom, the ground
for such freedom cannot lie in itself but can only be attained in
the ground of divine freedom which is creaturely freedom's
ultimate ground. As a guide to the creature's achievement of its
freedom by its own efforts, God's freedom comes to it
necessarily in two ways: as law and as grace. Both together
inseparably form the initial gift given and required by God
himself for man's realisation of his freedom. To make this
intelligible Anselm works out, first in the treatise De veritate, the
concept of rectitude (rectitudo) as a governing concept for the
true and the good (and therefore for the beautiful, too): 'true'
refers to the thought or proposition that rightly engages with an
existent, or to that faculty which is able to express the sense of an
existent according to its natural determination; 'true' refers also
to the existent itself in so far as it corresponds to the highest
norm of God's knowledge and will. This ontic truth then leads
into the ethical and in this way the right being (just or lawful
being) of created freedom is subordinated to the norm of
absolute freedom. Thus 'truth and rectitude and justice are
mutually defined',[197] to which it is necessary to add in the case of
justice that the free will may embrace the right norm for the
sake of no other good or goal than rectitude itself,[198] something
that for freedom leads to the final definition: 'freedom of the
will is the power of preserving the rectitude of the will for the
sake of rectitude itself.'[199] This firmly-held definition[200] has
meaning only within the context of a theistic and theological
thought, in which the opposition of autonomy and heteronomy
has been already overcome: rectitude, which is fitted for and
empowered to preserve creaturely freedom, is nothing other

[196] CDH II.10 (II.108.20–1).
[197] De ver. 12 (I.192.9).
[198] De ver. 12 (I.194.23–4).
[199] De lib. arb. 3 (I.212.19–20).
[200] Ibid. 13 (I.225.10–11); De Conc. I.6 (II.256.15–16).

than the initial gift of divine autonomy and therefore of the promise of participation in it. The self-orientation of *rectitudo propter se servata* is the way in which freedom is grounded in itself: *voluntas non est recta quia vult recte, sed recte vult quoniam recta est.*[201] Thus we can see why Anselm, when considering his aim, never fills out the content of the law (in terms of 'natural law') but rather determines it only formally as the will of God. This will is, by definition, identical with absolute freedom, which God is, no matter how it is made concrete for the creature, and submissiveness in relation to it is therefore the only way in which the creature can achieve its freedom. This will be better understood through a look, first, at God's freedom, and then at the freedom of Adam, or, indeed, of the angel before its establishment in the good.

God is truth, because everything that regulates itself according to his idea is true; he is goodness, because everything that regulates itself according to his will is good. He himself regulates himself according to nothing: 'his rectitude is his own will', and 'if rectitude must be preserved for its own sake, then this can be said so fittingly of no other rectitude than of God's. For just as it preserves none other than itself, ... so also it is not for the sake of any other, but only on its own account.'[202] What was more difficult to see in the case of truth, namely, how God, if truth is defined through a right *relation* to God, can be himself the highest truth,[203] is clearer in the case of freedom, because it emerges clearly that an identity of being and self-being (self-possession, freedom) does in fact occur, in which the moment of God's being a rule—which is presented to the created will—exists in God himself. If God owes (*debet*)[204] no-one anything and needs (*eget*)[205] nothing, if he is free from within himself (*a se*)[206] and observes no superior will;[207] if further his will can be

[201] *De conc.* III.3 (III.265.28–266.1). [A will is not upright because it wills rightly, but it wills rightly because it is upright.]

[202] *De ver.* 12 (I.196.1–8).

[203] *Ibid.* 10 (I.189.31–2).

[204] *Ibid.* 8 (I.186–7), 12 (I.192.1–5).

[205] *Medit.* 3 (III.86.65–6).

[206] *De lib.arb.* 14 (I.226.6).

[207] *De cas. diab.* 4 (I.242.5–6).

broken by no foreign will, then this would appear to lead right
to the limits of a pure voluntarism: 'Any necessity or impossibility is subordinate to his will, for his will is subordinate to no
necessity or impossibility. Nothing is either necessary or
impossible, except because he wills it so.'[208] However, 'this must
not be taken to mean that if God were to will something
unfitting, it would be just because he wills it . . . thus it is only
true to say: If God wills this, it is just, of those things which it is
not unfitting for God to will.'[209] 'God's will is never irrational.'[210] But this again does not mean that God's will is
governed by norms laid down by a reason prior to him; rather
his freedom penetrates and upholds his being through and
through, and in this self-mightiness of being his truth is illuminated as the power of the total illumination of self and self-
presence. 'This insurmountable power and might'[211] of God
over himself and over all real and possible being keeps his being
free from anything coerced or prohibited, 'two necessities
which are as closely interrelated as necessity and impossibility'.[212] *Voluntatem vero ejus nulla praecessit necessitas*,[213] and for
this very reason this will, for the creature, is truth beyond any
court of appeal.

And now the 'dignity and power and beauty'[214] of Adam in
his original dowry of freedom becomes understandable. If God
wished man to be free, then in creating him he had to give him a
threefold endowment to set him on his way: the act of willing,
which obediently wills the divinely-ordained good; in this very
act the rule, which lies both in the act (in so far as it is morally
good) and beyond the act (in so far as he obeys); and grace to
enable man to keep himself in the freedom of this obedience.
God must impart the act of willing (*i.e.*, not only possible, but
real, freedom), for without God's act of freedom our ability

[208] *CDH* II.17 (II.122.26–8).
[209] *Ibid.* I.12 (II.70.15–17, 24–6).
[210] *Ibid.* I.8 (II.59.11).
[211] *Ibid.* II.17 (II.123.12).
[212] *Ibid.* 23–24.
[213] *Ibid.* (II.125.29–30). [Indeed, no necessity precedes his will.]
[214] *De conc.* III.7 (II.273.24).

(*potestas*) will not come to the point of acting.[215] In this notion Anselm will root his profound doctrine of the abiding freedom of the sinner: he possesses the *potestas* and is so far free,[216] and the sinner remains indebted to God for being free in the act of freedom,[217] 'for he is always by nature free to preserve rectitude, if he once possessed it, even when he no longer has that which he is to preserve';[218] he retains the *aptitudo intelligendi et volendi*,[219] the *naturalis dignitas*,[220] but the ability remains idle (*otiosa*).[221] Thus God has created Adam in the act of freedom: *in ipsa datione facta recta*.[222] But this means that the rule (which is God in his will) must at the same time be imparted to this will at creation, and, in so far as this rule was once one with the freedom and self-possession of the creature, it cannot be withdrawn from it by God without contradiction.[223] But this handing over of the personal will of God to the created will in the form of a rule to be followed is grace,[224] whence again it becomes conceivable at a deeper level why the sinner's *rectitudo voluntatis*, which was lost in the Fall, can no longer be won back by the sinner himself, but can only—through a miracle!—be restored by God.[225] For 'the will wills rectitude only because it is upright. For the will it is the same thing to be upright and to have rectitude. Thus it is clear that it can only will rectitude when it has rectitude. I do not deny, therefore, that the upright will can will rectitude which it does not yet have, *viz.*, when it wills a greater than it has; but I say only that it can will no rectitude unless it has the rectitude by which it can will it.' But the will cannot bring it forth out of itself, nor can it borrow it from any other creature. 'Grace alone' can give it to the creature 'without preceding merit'; if then the

[215] *De lib. arb.* 3 (I.212.30–1).
[216] *Ibid.* 4 (I.214.4–5).
[217] *De conc. virg.* 2 (II.142.3–4).
[218] *De lib. arb.* 11 (I.223.10–11).
[219] *Ibid.* 12 (I.224.15).
[220] *De cas. diab.* 16 (I.260.14).
[221] *De conc.* III.13 (II.287.6).
[222] *De cas. diab.* 9 (I.246.27–8); *CDH* II.1 (II.97.17–18); *De conc. virg.* 1 (II.141.3–4).
[223] *De lib. arb.* 8 (I.220–1); *De conc.* I.6 (II.256.27).
[224] *De lib. arb.* 3 (I.221.19); *De conc.* III.2 (II.265.22–3).
[225] *De conc.* III.14 (II.287.3–8).

one who wills justly merits a higher rectitude or a reward, that is 'all fruit of the first grace'.[226] And 'even if rectitude is preserved through free will, it is not so much to be imputed to free will as to grace, for free will possesses and preserves rectitude only through prevenient and subsequent grace.'[227]

In all this Anselm speaks only of the final freedom of the creature, which serves it for the attainment of salvation.[228] But the character of this freedom is such that it can only be understood in terms of that most intimate and incomprehensible penetration of human freedom by divine freedom, which makes the whole relation of man to God dialogical; it is personal obedience to the free personal God, and through the appropriation of the will of God to its own free being this obedience becomes the incomprehensible mystery of the taking of God into its own being. Anselm, who always speaks only of *rectitudo* and obedience (and firmly avoids the Augustinian language of a *delectatio spiritualis* for the good, which was later misused by Jansen[229]), can here, where he deals with the depths of the concepts of *rectitudo* and *justitia*, no longer avoid that of love. Thus the *propter se servata* can be illuminated in a *solo amore*.[230] And similarly the meaning of free will and the ability to discriminate is that it 'should love the good and choose it, and still more love and choose the better'.[231] Indeed 'this choice, which can also be called judgement, is free, because the reason, by which rectitude is understood, teaches that that rectitude should always be preserved by the love of the same rectitude.'[232] The fact that freedom cannot be coerced, its incomprehensible spontaneity—*sponte* is the key-word of the Anselmian doctrine of redemption—gives to its applications that costliness which belongs only to love and which determines the meaning of what

[226] *Ibid.* III.3 (II.266.2–267.1).
[227] *Ibid.* III.4 (II.267.15, 19).
[228] *De conc.* I.6 (II.256.5–7).
[229] There is only one suggestion of the doctrine in citations of Rom 7.22 (*condelector legi Dei secundum interiorem hominem*): *De conc. virg.* 4 (II.144.17); *De conc.* III.12 (II.284.26); *Simil.* 163 (691C), 171 (694A).
[230] *Simil.* 169 (693B).
[231] *CDH* II.1 (II.97.10–11).
[232] *De conc.* I.6 (II.257.13–14).

takes place between God and the world. *Memoria* and *intellectus* are in the service of *amare*;[233] all natural *rectitudo* refers in the end to the *rectum cor*,[234] which is created in order to 'love and to choose God, who is subsisting love',[235] 'above all else, for no other reason than for his own sake'.[236] So it is significant that the 'Book of Similitudes', both at the beginning and again at the end, goes beyond Augustine in depicting creaturely freedom in the language and thought-form of Origen, admittedly in a terminology which betrays a uniquely Anselmian character:[237] 'the power of willing . . . occupies a position between God and the devil like that of a woman between her lawful husband and an adulterer. . . . If she unites herself only with her lawful husband, then she is lawful herself and bears legitimate children, but if she unites herself with the adulterer, she is adulterous and bears illegitimate children. If it unites itself to God, by receiving the prompting of the Holy Spirit, like a good seed, it is the lawful spouse and bears legitimate children, that is, virtues and good works, for straightway at its command all the organs (*sensus*) of the soul and the body are opened to fulfil the command of God: the power of willing itself is opened to the inclination (*affectio*) to virtue and to the (actual) willing of what it longs for, [similarly] memory, power of reflection, insight, the mind is given courage to love, is made ready for humility, is steeled for patience, and is opened to the bearing of the other virtues. Similarly the bodily senses are opened. . . . The one power of willing bears all that, when in love it has united itself to the will of God. The inclination or the use (*usus*) of the will is called the pleasing will or obedience, for, hearkening to God's will, it has him for a defender (*advocatam*) when it is asked why it does this or that.' Things are quite otherwise in the case of the pact with the devil, in which the soul opens itself to evil and gives birth to pride, that is 'the overstepping of its obligation', which is to say of its subjection to God's will. 'Each sin springs

[233] *Mon.* 68 (I.79.5–9).
[234] *De conc.* III.2 (II.265.1–9).
[235] *Prosl.* 23 (I.117).
[236] *CDH* II.1 (II.97.15).
[237] The distinctions between will as *instrumentum quo*, as *affectio* and as *usus* answer exactly to those found in *De conc.* III.11 (II.278–9).

from such [pride]. And because man has this pride from himself and will not endure above himself the will of God as that to which he must owe obedience, therefore he withholds from God something that most properly and uniquely belongs to him. For it must belong to God alone to will from his own will, without owing obedience to any will set over him. . . . As God's own will is the source and origin of all good, so is man's own will the origin of all evil.'[238] This passage sheds light on the otherwise strange *Meditation 2*, in which the *virginitas male amissa* is bewailed: 'You were a virgin, betrothed to Christ . . . you have become an adulterer to him; freely you have cast yourself down miserably from the sublimity of virginity to the abyss of fornication, . . . you have become a stubborn harlot, a shameless whore . . ., you have deserted your chaste lover in heaven, and followed your odious seducer into hell!'[239]

Only against the background of this mystery of marriage are Anselm's final intentions perceptible. For him the philosophical *analogia entis* becomes the *analogia personalitatis* or *libertatis*, and correspondingly the perfection of the creature is found in its perfect liberation in the absolute divine freedom as it is taken up into the divine will: *haec est enim perfecta et liberrima humanae naturae oboedientia, cum voluntatem suam liberam sponte voluntati Dei subdit, et cum acceptam bonam voluntatem sine omni exactione spontanea libertate opere perficit.*[240] The good will is 'received', *accepta*, as the seed of God and of eternal freedom in the womb of human freedom, and the 'opening' of this womb to God—as obedience—is precisely the reception of freedom. Indeed, the *De concordia* compares the union of grace and created freedom in the begetting of the redeemed man with the union of father and mother in the begetting of the child.[241]

This further sheds light on the central concept of *debere*. God is simply free; he owes no man anything. The redemption of the

---

[238] *Simil.* 2–8 (605B–607C); cf. 70–2 (693C–694C).
[239] *Medit.* 2 (III.80–1.ll.8–19, 29–31, 33, 39–40).
[240] *Medit.* 3 (III.88.118–21). [For this is the freest and perfect obedience of human nature, when he submits his free will freely to the will of God, and when by this work he perfects the good will which he has received by spontaneous freedom without any compulsion.]
[241] *De conc.* III.5 (II.270.6–9).

sinner by Christ is not a ransom, as if the devil had any rights over man which he could assert against God.[242] Not the least necessity saddles God's freedom if he decides freely (*sponte*)[243] to save lost mankind.[244] And the whole obedience of the incarnate Son depends entirely on the spontaneity of his love and simply unfolds the inner necessities of this free love,[245] including the very mystery of Gethsemane, the heavy bearing of the guilt of the world and the death. The whole trinitarian mystery between the Father and the Son—that the Son obeys really and to the end, and on the other side that the Father compels nothing but allows the Son's way of sacrifice—however one contemplates it, is such a mystery of spontaneous, unforced love.[246] And just this absolute, because divine, spontaneity in the sacrifice of the Son determines its utmost costliness, which outweighs infinitely all the guilt of the world.[247] The sacrifice consists, however, in the fact that God of his free love really enters worldly destiny, really humbles himself to be included in the lineage of Adam, in that he becomes the son of Mary, and yet thereby, because all depends on freedom, does not fall under the sway of Adam, as did all the others who are included in his seed as members of his lineage.[248]

This assumption of worldly necessities into the free will of God which is not inwardly affected by them, that is, the assumption of worldly necessities into the necessities of intra-divine love, now raises the question: how far is God's plan of creation affected by the sin brought about by man's free will? If God owes nothing to any creature, does he owe it to himself, in view of his responsibility for the consequences of the world he has undertaken, to intervene and redeem, and indeed in just such a manner as is demanded by the linking of the necessities of the world order with those of his divine freedom? Man has violated God's glory in that 'he has taken away from God whatever he

[242] *CDH* I.6–7 (II.53–9); *Medit.* 3 (III.85.46–9).
[243] *Or.* 6 (III.16.3); *Medit.* 3 (III.87.95, 99).
[244] *CDH* 12 (II.70.6–7).
[245] *Ibid.* I.8 (II.60.12–13).
[246] *Ibid.* I.9–10 (II.61–7), II.11 (II.111.23–5), II.16–17 (II.122–6).
[247] *Ibid.* II.18 (II.128.1–2); *Medit.* 3 (III.87.89–90).
[248] *CDH* II.17 (II.126.5–6); *De conc. virg.* 8–13 (II.149, 155).

has planned to make out of human nature'.[249] 'For the wisdom of the artist is praised and declared according to the success of his work. As human nature, then, the precious work of God, on account of which he is to be glorified, diminishes or soils itself, so does it by its own fault dishonour God.'[250] There has then been withheld (*subtrahitur*) from God what is 'justly owed'[251] him.

But this withholding of honour must first be made good in the right measure: 'When the creature wills what it ought to will, it honours God—not because it bestows something on him, but because it willingly submits itself to God's will and direction, and keeps its own place in the universe of things, and maintains the beauty of that same universe, as far as in it lies.' But if it does not do this, then it 'disturbs the *universitatis órdinem et pulchritudinem*, as far as lies in it, although of course it cannot injure or diminish the power and dignity of God.' For, Anselm continues in the working out of an Augustinian meditation, the beauty of the world-order and therefore the glory of God are in any case intact, because God's distributive justice sees to it that order is preserved even in the event of an insurrection, so that no *ex violata ordinis pulchritudine deformitas* can develop; as little as any creature can escape any part of the canopy of heaven, except by approaching it at another point.[252] However, this aesthetic justification of evil, which has eschatological significance for Augustine, has only a limited place in Anselm's scheme of thought, and he will attempt to pass beyond it from various directions. The reflections immediately following on the 'perfect number' of the elect, that is, of the eschatological *civitas Dei* with its constitution of angels and men, attempt to take him beyond Augustine in a subtle chain of reasoning: if the purpose of the elect human beings were to fill up the number of the fallen angels, then each one of them would have to rejoice over the fall of the angel whose place he was taking—but this would be

[249] *CDH* I.23 (II.91.8).

[250] *De conc.* III.7 (II.273.26–274.1).

[251] *Or.* 7 (III.25.2–3).

[252] *CDH* I.15 (II.73.3–24). Thus already Boethius: 4 *De cons. prosa* 6: *licet in alium, tamen in ordinem [homo] relabatur. Cf.* Augustine, Ep. 140.2.4. And later Bonaventure: *Brevil.* 3.4 (Opp. V.233).

unbearable in Christian terms.[253] So the full number of the angels can in no way have made up the full, eschatological number of the elect, and men were elected for their own sake and not simply as stop-gaps; and further, the material creation is not simply a replacement for the spiritual, but was originally created with a view to the perfected cosmos, which should consist of both spirit and matter.[254] So Anselm does not stop, in what concerns the injured honour of God, at a consideration of the *ordo congruus universitatis rerum*:[255] no matter how intact God's honour remains because of his punitive justice, his love still suffers loss which dishonours it and which must ultimately be made good. The insubordinate will deprives God of his own most proper good: *ipsi Deo aufert quod proprie et singulariter debet habere*.[256] And as all the angels and just men, as the whole *civitas Dei* and God himself are grateful (*gratiosi*) to the lover who helps to build up the city of God, so contrariwise are they all wounded by the fact that the wicked banish (*extorres*) themselves from the holy city. 'Just as any man sorrows and mourns if he in any way loses what he has acquired for his needs and his advancement, so, as it were, does God sorrow and mourn too, when he sees how man, whom he created for himself, has been abducted by the devil and is to be lost to him for ever. So indeed are the damned designated lost, because they are lost to God, for whose kingdom and glorification they were created.'[257] And so the tender thought can find expression, that the just man confers a benefit on God himself (*beneficium praestabit*),[258] is in a certain way profitable to him (*quadam ratione prodesse videtur*),[259] that God himself is grateful to the lover for his love (*Deus ei scit gratias*).[260] Love indeed is conceivable only as a mutual occurrence, and

---

[253] *CDH* I.18 (II.78–9).

[254] *Ibid.* (II.79–81).

[255] *De conc. virg.* 6 (II.147.19). [the harmonious order of the universe of things.]

[256] *Simil.* 7 (607B). [he deprives God himself of what he [God] most properly and particularly ought to have.]

[257] *De beat. coel.* (601–2).

[258] *Simil.* 44 (624C).

[259] *Simil.* 43 (623A).

[260] Eadmer, *Vita* I.41 (*PL* 158.73B).

that *rectitudo*, which Anselm erected into the supreme concept embracing the whole of logic, ethics and aesthetics, ends in this mutuality: 'God must be loved . . . from rectitude (*rectitudine*), because he gives us everything that we have, even our very being. And so must we love him all the more than ourselves, the greater he is who gave himself for us and himself wills to keep us for himself.'[261]

So much may lead us to suspect, indeed to see, that Anselm's doctrine of redemption, his so-called doctrine of satisfaction, will have about it nothing of the 'juristic'. On the contrary, he is at pains to defend himself against any idea of a God of justice, 'who would so delight in or stand in need of the blood of the innocent that apart from his death he would not pardon the guilty'.[262] But this would be the clear implication if God were to let himself be reconciled through the sacrifice of his Son in such a way that he 'reckoned' the merit of this death to the guilty and therefore let them off their punishment. It is not a matter of reckoning, but of inner, ontological union: no one will willingly add a blemished pearl to his treasure.[263] If God were therefore to forgive man, because man, in the powerlessness he brought on himself by his sin, cannot pay his debt, 'surely that is to say that God remits what he cannot get; but it is mockery to ascribe such mercy to God';[264] and besides, man would be in heaven eternally one who could not pay and therefore one who is needy (*egens*) and thus deprived of blessedness.[265] 'Therefore Anselm used to say, to the astonishment of many, that he would prefer to be free from sin and to bear hell innocently than to go to the kingdom of heaven polluted with the stain of sin.'[266] The moment of 'rectitude' in the Christian explanation lies therefore not so much abstractly in the fact that guilt must be expiated, that for an infinite guilt an infinitely valuable penance must be made, as in the fact that it only happens justly (*juste*), when man, on whose side the guilt lies, can pay for himself, which means on

[261] *Simil.* 182 (697D).
[262] *CDH* I.10 (II.66.24–6).
[263] *Ibid.* I.19 (II.85.11–23).
[264] *Ibid.* I.24 (II.93.18–20).
[265] *Ibid.* I.24 (II.93.11; II.94.3).
[266] Eadmer, *Vita* II.22 (90A).

a deeper level: 'when of himself he rises and again lifts himself up'.[267] If the accent were placed only on the divinity of the Son, then the whole would remain an inner-trinitarian concern, and man, who is meant to be the object of the whole business, would remain outside. But the accent is placed on the covenant between God and man and on the obligation God has placed on himself by his decision that man should remain an authentic partner. That is the undertaking of grace, which 'he undertook for our sake and not for his own, since he is in need of nothing. For what man was going to do was not concealed from him when he made him, but despite this, in creating man of his own goodness, he freely bound himself, as it were (*sponte se . . . quasi obligavit*), to complete the good work once begun.'[268] For this reason nothing less costly is required than a God-man as redeemer; man had indeed to become free for the convenant with God, that is, free for absolute freedom. A merely sinless man would not have sufficed here, for 'if any other person had redeemed man from eternal death, man would rightly be reckoned eternally as his servant. But in that case man would in no sense have been restored to the dignity he would have had if he had not sinned, that is, to be the servant of God alone, and equal in everything to the good angels.'[269] Christ is not an (Arian) instance of mediation, but rather the effectiveness of the covenant itself (*pacti efficacia*[270]); on him, therefore, the whole human race founded in Adam can converge as its centre.

On the level of debt (*debere*), the reckoning cannot be settled, and therefore Anselm's theory cannot be understood juristically. For in what way is man not 'indebted' to God? 'When you pay what you owe to God, even if you have not sinned, you must not count this as part of the debt you owe for sin'; the highest exertion of love would be demanded to meet God's covenantal promise, and in this highest exertion it would always have to be weighed 'that you do not possess what you give of yourself, but from him whose servants both you and he to whom you give are. . . . As for obedience, what do you give

[267] *CDH* II.8 (II.103.9).
[268] *Ibid.* II.5 (II.100.16–20).
[269] *Ibid.* I.5 (II.52.19–23).
[270] *Ibid.* II.16 (II.118.18).

God that you do not owe him, to whose command you owe all
that you are and have and can do?'[271] From this point it becomes
only negatively clear that the freedom of the sinner, despoiled as
it is of its capacity to act, restores to God nothing of what he
owes him—but has even Christ in his work of redemption not
simply done what was owing? For if his work was well-pleasing
to God, then 'he had to do what was better, especially since the
creature owes to God all that it is and knows and can do.'[272] The
answer to this can only be to point to the impetus of ever-
greater love, how, beyond all calculable proportions, it is carried towards the ever-greater God and how, in the human
realm, it finds its expression in the freely-offered vow: 'Even
though the creature possesses nothing of itself, when God
permits it either to do or not to do something he puts both
alternatives in its power, so that, although one course may be
preferable, neither is definitely required. Thus, whether a man
does what is better or does the other, we can always say that he
does what he ought to do (*debere facere dicatur quod facit*). . . .
Although celibacy is better than marriage, neither one of them
is definitely required from a man. . . . Thus, when you say that
the creature owes to God what he knows is best and is able to do,
this is not always true, if you interpret it as a true debt (*ex debito*),
and do not understand: if God commands it.'[273] Thus the inquiry
has suddenly moved forward into the realm of the vow, and
only here does it find its true solution. Anselm's aesthetic reason,
which considers the mystery of salvation, is ultimately monastic
reason. Here is found the profound justification of the vow of
obedience against secular men who uphold the opinion that it is
more meritorious again and again to do what is right
spontaneously (*spontaneus*) than to give up one's free disposal of
oneself and 'to suffer oneself to be compelled to serve against
one's will'.[274] This would be, replies Anselm, as if a slave were to
say to his master: 'Lord, I want to serve you with my whole
heart, but that I should remain faithful to you I do not wish to
promise. For if I promised it and afterwards sinned, then would

[271] *Ibid.* I.20 (II.87.23–4).
[272] *Ibid.* II.18 (II.128.8–12).
[273] *Ibid.* 13–25.
[274] *Simil.* 81 (653A).

I, guilty of a more serious sin, be due a more severe punishment. I want to serve you as well as I can, but if I fail, then judge me as one who did not promise at all to remain faithful to you.' The monk, by contrast, is that slave who has given up to his lord his whole person and his whole freedom. If the first slave fails, he will be judged by God as one who does not belong to him (*alienus*), but the second will be improved that he may genuinely belong to him (*ut proprius emendatur*).[275] The former offers his works but not his person; the latter gives, together with the fruits, the whole tree and its roots: 'he loves God so, that he offers him his whole self, while he says: Lord, hitherto I have disposed of myself and done according to my own lights good and evil. But because I must (*debeo*) be wholly yours, I deliver myself wholly to your disposing power (*potestas*), in order, in the future, to bear fruit for you alone. In order to be able to do that the better, I submit myself to an ecclesiastical superior, who watches over me and teaches me to do only those works which he knows are the more pleasing to you. But also I will strive, as much as I can, to watch over myself.'[276] In this *suscipe* there lies for Anselm the absolute spontaneity of human freedom, and his doctrine of redemption is conceived after this pattern. It is loving, creaturely freedom, which wholly gives itself up to eternal freedom, and on its side finds a model in the trinitarian freedom of the Son, whose spontaneous loving obedience to the Father is necessitated by nothing, but in the splendour of his absolute freedom is that which is most acceptable to God and, to that extent, most necessary: *debuit facere, quia quod voluit fieri debuit; et non debuit facere, quia non ex debito.*[277]

To this there corresponds the inner construction of freedom, as Anselm gives it apropos Lucifer's fall. The presupposition of freedom is a dualism between two scales of value: that of the moral (*justitia*) and that of the agreeable (*commodum*).[278] Were

[275] *Ibid.* 82 (653B–654B).
[276] *Ibid.* 84 (630A–C).
[277] *CDH* II.18 (II.129.6–8). [he ought to do it, because what he wills ought to be done; and yet he does not have to do it, because it is not required of him as a debt.]
[278] *De cas. diab.* 12 (I.255.5–11).

the mind presented with only one scale, then there would be no freedom; each time it would have to choose the better. Because the scales can be considered separately, there is the possibility of a choice, which then necessarily leads to the alternative: to prefer God in obedience to his command and so to stake oneself on the Absolute, or, choosing rather the *commodum*, to prefer oneself and reject absolute freedom. But how can Lucifer, who has been fashioned in willing the good, turn his will? To that there can be only one answer: because he wills it. He has a motive, but that he follows it through has no other reason than the abyss of his freedom.[279] 'Why, therefore, has he willed? Only because he has willed. For this will . . . is itself the efficient cause and the effect.'[280] Over against this diabolical *sponte* there stands only the *sponte* of the eternal love of God in Christ.

3. THE VICTORY OF PRAYER

The final illumination of his whole work stems from Anselm's prayer. This is properly directed to the eschatologically fulfilled form of freedom, it aims exactly at the point where the free will of men—in the Church and her saints, supremely in Jesus Christ—is made one with the free will of God. What is (this is the initial question) the character of fulfilled freedom? The answer lies in the doctrine of the establishment of freedom in the good, both for the steadfast angels and for the saints in heaven; God's reward for their steadfastness is a fulfilment such 'that they are granted whatever lies within the sphere of their willing, so that they see nothing that lies beyond their desire, and thus can no longer sin because of it.'[281] Already at the end of the *Proslogion* the transcendence, beyond any fulfilment, of heavenly blessedness had been depicted, because the heart not only acquired whatever it wished but infinitely more beyond that; the creature's mental capacity was simply swamped, and it was not that the freedom and joy of God entered into the

[279] *Ibid.* 3 (I.239.11).
[280] *Ibid.* 27 (I.275.30–3).
[281] *Ibid.* 6 (I.243.20–2), 25 (I.273.29–30).

creature's heart, but that the heart entered into the freedom and
joy of God.[282] In thus transcending themselves, the hearts attain
the freedom of God and are in concord (*concordia*) with him,
'henceforth almighty in their wills, as God is in his'.[283] In this
concord of the divine-creaturely omnipotence of love Anselm
puts down his roots. It is the place where the New Covenant,
the Church, is at its most real.

The place from which he prays is the place where one is lost,
hell as existential reality. He has considered *quanti ponderis est
peccatum*.[284] The man without the grace which rectitude bestows
on him is conceived of as moving away from God, falling into
that which is bottomless, *in abyssum sine fundo, nisi misericordia
retineatur*.[285] As God's enemy, he has made enemies of all beings
which were created good, so that they can hardly endure him.[286]
His place lies *in descensu super irremeabile chaos inferni*,[287] in the
threefold abyss of God's judgement, of his own sin and of the
eternal state of being lost which thus threatens him.[288] Again and
again without hesitation Anselm takes up his position there, as it
is to this place that Christ descends in his Passion, as grace too
descends to save mankind.[289] 'God did not need to suffer anything so wearisome, but man needed to be reconciled in this
way. Nor did God need to suffer such humiliation, but man
needed that he should thus be saved from the depths of hell.'[290]
'O hidden strength: a man hangs on a cross and lifts the load of
eternal death from the human race; a man nailed to wood looses
the bonds of everlasting death that hold fast the world, a man
condemned with robbers rescues those damned along with the

[282] *Prosl.* 25–6 (I.118–21).

[283] *Ibid.* 25 (I.119.7–9).

[284] *CDH* I.21 (II.88.18). Temptation insinuates to man: *nec tanti ponderis est
peccatum, quanti facis illud* [nor is sin of such great weight as you make it]. *Simil.*
115 (672A).

[285] *De conc.* III.8 (II.275.13). [into the bottomless abyss, unless restrained by
mercy.]

[286] *Simil.* 102 (666AB).

[287] *Medit.* 3 (III.89.153). [in descent through the chaos of hell from which
there is no return.]

[288] *Or.* 14 (III.60.1–2).

[289] *Ibid.* 7 (III.21.77–8).

[290] *Medit.* 3 (III.86.65–8).

devils.'[291] 'O glorious cross! . . . The cruel ones could do nothing but what he in his wisdom permitted. . . . They worked to condemn the Redeemer, he to redeem the condemned.'[292]

But if the saving love of God vicariously descends into his abyss, has Anselm still any claim on this love? Has he not finally gambled it away? Here is the place of the appeal to the *concordia* of the city of God—between Son and mother: 'For if I have sinned against the Son, I have hurt the mother, nor can I offend the mother without injury to the Son. . . . Whither therefore will you flee, sinner? For who will reconcile me to the Son, if the mother is my enemy? And who will pacify the mother, if the Son is angry? But if you have both been offended equally, may you not both show clemency? Let the one therefore who is guilty before the righteous God flee to the kind mother of the God of mercy. Let the one who is guilty of offending the mother take refuge with the kind Son of the loving mother. Let the one who is guilty before both thrust himself between them both. Let him cast himself between the kind Son and the kind mother. . . . Let me who cast myself between two of such great kindness not fall upon two so severe in their power.'[293]

Still more imposingly in the great (the third) prayer to Mary, which Anselm subjected to a series of revisions, until his final thought was brought to expression: 'For if you, Lady, are his mother, are not your other sons his brothers? . . . For he caused it to happen that he should be of our nature by his birth from a mother, and that we by the restoration of life should be sons of his mother: he invites us to confess ourselves his brothers. Therefore our judge is our brother! The Saviour of the world is our brother. Indeed our God has, through Mary, made himself our brother. With what certitude then ought we (*debemus*) to hope, with what consolation can we fear, we whose salvation or damnation rests on the will of a good brother and a kind mother? . . . The good mother may pray and implore for us. . . . The good Son may hear his mother pleading on behalf of his brothers. . . . Perhaps I speak presumptuously, but it is your

[291] *Ibid.* 84.22–85.3.
[292] *Or.* 4 (III.11.10–19).
[293] *Ibid.* 6 (III.16.41–50).

goodness that makes me bold. . . . Lord and Lady, is it not much better that you should freely give to him who seeks what he does not deserve, than that you should be withheld what is justly owing to you? . . . Show me therefore your mercy, which is profitable to me and becoming to you.'[294]

Or between Christ and Peter: 'Good Shepherd, Peter, before you there lies groaning a sick sheep. . . . But although it has erred, it has not denied its Lord and Shepherd. . . . Recognize its confession of the name of Christ, who, three times asking you whether you loved him, said to your threefold confession: Feed my sheep. . . . As you confessed his love, so this one confesses itself to be his sheep. How therefore can you, his shepherd, despise the sheep? Peter, shepherd of Christ, gather up the sheep of Christ.'[295]

Or between Christ and Paul: 'O Saint Paul, have you not called yourself the nurse of the faithful, cherishing your sons? And for which children do you lie in travail, which do you nourish, unless those whom by teaching you cause to grow and educate in the faith of Christ? . . . Behold, this your son is dead. . . . Mother, you are again in travail with your sons, offer to him your dead Son, who is to be raised again, who, with his death, raises his servants. . . . But you, Jesus, good Lord, are not you mother? Were you not mother, when, like a hen, you gathered your little ones under your wings? . . . For what others are in travail with and give birth to, they have received from you. For unless you had been in travail, you would not have endured death; and unless you had died, you would not have given birth. . . . You are both, therefore, mothers. . . . Thus you are fathers in your effectiveness, but mothers in your tender feeling. . . . And if you are unequal in the amount of your care, in its quality you are not dissimilar. . . . In will, however, you are at one (concordantes). . . . You declare yourselves mothers, I confess myself your son. . . .'[296]

Or between Christ and John: 'Therefore, blessed John, make it that he who loves you may also love me through that breadth

[294] Ibid. 7 (III.23.130–25.176).
[295] Ibid. 9 (III.30–1).
[296] Ibid. 10 (III.39–40).

of love, which you teach and possess, and because of which you envy no one, but wish that good in which you rejoice to be common to all. Make it, through that mutual love which you owe him, that you may tax for him my love too together with yours, for in return simply for his love you owe him not your love only, but that of many. For, blessed John, you have experienced in your blessedness itself that just as no one can offer God anything before he ought (*debeat*), so no one can ever pay him more than he ought. If therefore all who love God, your lover, through you cannot requite him, then I pray, O Lord, that you reject not him who would be numbered among them. ... Jesus, Lord, whom I choose to grant my requests, John, whom I put forward as intercessor, my desire so compels me, that my heart desires to compel you, not truly as if you were reluctant, but of your own free will (*spontaneos*). ... Be patient therefore and forgive, if my heart devises something in order to extort love. ... Lord, and lord, I believe and I know that you love one another; but how may I experience (*experiar*) this, if on account of your mutual love you do not grant that for which I seek? ... Do not shut up among yourselves for your own enjoyment such a great good, but let something of it overflow to us. ...'[297]

Or between Christ and the Magdalene: ' "Woman, why weepest thou?" O ardour of grief! ... But why, at all events, do you, her sole joy, excite her sorrow? ... Indeed faithful love can no longer bear either her sorrow, or to remain hidden. ... The Lord names the familiar name of the maiden and the maiden recognizes the familiar voice of the Lord. ... "Mary!" ... But what should I, unhappy man without love, presume to say about the love of God and of the blessed friendship of God? For how should my heart bring forth a perfume which it has not savoured within itself? Truly you are my witness, truth ... that I desire that your love should be kindled in my heart. ... Hear me for the love and the dear merits of this your beloved Mary and those of your most blessed mother, the greater Mary. ...'[298]

As Anselm puts down his roots everywhere in the manifest

[297] *Ibid.* 12 (III.47–8).
[298] *Ibid.* 16 (III.66–7).

almightiness of love, which stands open and is approachable in the perfection of the *analogia libertatis*, so in his letters he draws his correspondent ever again into this *concordia* of love, which, overcoming all distance, makes him present to the beloved: *nostrarum conscii sumus conscientiarum de invicem*.[299] There is a strange logic of fate in the fact that the same man, who had to defend Christian freedom against all the gloomy clouds of an unbiblical doctrine of foreknowledge, predestination and original sin, had to spend his best efforts in struggle for the freedom of the Church in the English investiture controversy. For this reason it is important that, in all his unswerving and crystal-clear loyalty to the Holy See, he always saw the office and the *concordia* of the Mystical Body, the objective and subjective holiness of the Church in a perfected unity.[300] The Church is for Anselm essentially the Bride, who through the new marriage-bond with Christ is chosen and enabled for the freedom of love. 'God loves nothing in this world more than the freedom of his Church. And those [kings] who would rather control it than further it are doubtless to be handed over as opponents of God. God wills to have his bride free, and not as a hand-maid. Behold this queen whom he has been pleased to choose from out of the world as his bride. Her he calls "beautiful" and "friend" and "dove".'[301] If *concordia* characterises the uncompelled freedom within the Church, Anselm has no other word to characterise the relationship between Church and state: the king is *advocatus*, *defensor*, but in no way *dominator* of the Church; over both there rules uniquely the free God.

The older and the more experienced Anselm becomes, the more the accent on aesthetic reason of his early works (*Monologion* and *Proslogion*) with their, as it were, immediate ap-

---

[299] *Ep.* 4 (III.104.21); *Ep.* 6 (III.106.5–8); *Ep.* 12 (III.117.1–3), etc. [We mutually bear witness to our consciences.]

[300] For the whole subject see Y. M.-J. Congar, 'L'Eglise chez S. Anselme', *SpicBec* 371–99, esp. p. 380, where *Ep.* 162 (IV.35) is cited: *Sicut enim episcopi servant sibi auctoritatem quamdiu* concordant *Christo, ita sibi eam adimunt, cum discordant a Christo.* Also p. 382 for a presentation of the presence of Peter, the door-keeper of heaven, and his authority in his successors, which is worked out more in a mystical way that transcends the temporal than through a temporal succession.

[301] *Ep.* 243 (IV.153–4). Further texts in Congar, p. 391.

prehension of theological necessities, shifts to the defence of Christian freedom—in the individual and the Church—from whose unfathomable glory all necessities are derived. Necessity is reduced more and more to a contradictory proposition, according to which the law of freedom is necessary, in so far as it is and cannot not be. To the same degree the perspectives are veiled in the eternal truth: what we see is only a reflection: 'as we are aware of the sun through its rays before we see it unveiled, so we are aware of God from the reflection (*speculatio*) of our reason: if we discover anything true in the light of truth, then we are aware at the same time of him by recognition and love in faith and hope. In the future we shall see him face to face. . . .'[302] So at the last there remains a yearning longing for glory, for the unveiled radiance of the Lord:

'He whose aim in serving is directed towards the recovery of the kingdom of eternal life strives to stick to God through thick and thin, and with unshakeable perserverance to place his whole trust im him. . . . Strong in patience, he rejoices in all things and says with the Psalmist: *Magna est gloria Domini*. This glory, even in this earthly pilgrimage, he has a taste of; he savours it; and as he savours he desires it; and with great desire he salutes it while yet far off. Thus he is supported by the hope of attaining it, and consoled by it in the midst of all earthly dangers, and he sings with great joy: *Magna est gloria Domini*.'[303]

The final thing here below is not vision, but being seen: *Johannes, certe vides, vides me. Ergo vide me, domine, vides me noscendo, vide me miserando. Vides et scis, vide ut sciam.*[304]

---

[302] *Simil.* 165 (692A).

[303] Address in Canterbury: Eadmer, *Vita* II.32 (*PL* 158.93).

[304] *Or.* 12 (III.48.106–7). [John, you behold certainly, you behold me. Therefore behold me, Lord, you behold me by knowing me, behold me by having mercy on me. You behold and you know, behold that I may know.]

BONAVENTURE

1. THE SERAPH AND THE STIGMATA

Of all the great scholastics, Bonaventure[1] is the one who offers the widest scope to the beautiful in his theology: not merely because he speaks of it most frequently, but because he clearly

[1] The works are quoted from the great Quaracchi edition: *Opera omnia*, 10 vols. (Quaracchi 1882–1902); Report A of the Collations on the Hexameron from F. Delorme's edition in *BFSMA* Vol. 8 (Quaracchi 1934); the *Quaestiones disputatae De caritate* and *De novissimis* from the edition of P. Glorieux (*La France franciscaine*, Docum. II, Paris, 1950); the *Quaestiones disputatae De theologia* from the edition by G. H. Tavard in *RThAM*. 17 (1950), 178–256. Particularly worthy of mention among the literature: on the doctrine of God, Albert Stohr, *Die Trinitätslehre des hl. Bonaventura*, pt. I: *Die wissenschaftliche Trinitätslehre*, Münster, 1923. On the teaching about the doctrine ideas, J.-M. Bissen, *L'exemplarisme divin selon S. Bonaventure* (1929). On christocentrism, Alexander Gerken, *Theologie des Wortes. Das Verhältnis von Schöpfung und Inkarnation bei Bonaventura* (in course of publication, with bibliography). On the doctrine of illumination, Gilson, *La philosophie de S. Bonaventure*, 3rd ed. 1953. On the doctrine of the spiritual senses, Karl Rahner, 'La doctrine des "sens spirituels" au Moyen-âge, en particulier chez S. Bonaventure', *RAM* 14 (1933), 263–299. On mysticism, E. Longpré, *La théologie mystique de S. Bonaventure* (AFH 14 [1921]). On the theology of history, J. Ratzinger, *Die Geschichtstheologie des hl. Bonaventura* (1959). On aesthetics, *cf.* especially Edgar de Bruyne, *Etudes d'esthétique médiévale*, 3 vols. (Bruges 1946), on Bonaventure Vol. 3, ch. 6 (III 189–226). Sr. E. J. M. Spargo, *The Category of the Aesthetic in the Philosophy of St. Bonaventure* (FIP.P N.11, 1953). Karl Peter, *Die Lehre von der Schönheit nach Bonaventura* (dissertation, Basel, 1961).
The treatise *De transcendentalibus entis conditionibus* may be a youthful work of Bonaventure (Cod. Assisi bibl. Com. 186): this is the first work to describe clearly the beautiful as the transcendent (edition by Dieter Halcour in *FS* 41 [1959], 41–106). On the development of the high scholastic aesthetic, *cf.* Dom Henri Pouillon, OSB, 'La beauté, propriété transcendentale chez les scholastiques (1220–1279)', *AHDL* 21 (1946), 263–329; Dieter Halcour, *Die Lehre vom Schönen im Rahmen der Transzendentalienlehre der Metaphysik der frühen Franziskanerschule von Paris* (dissertation, Freiburg i. Breisgau, 1957).
The commentary on the *Sentences* is quoted as follows: 3 d34 I, 1 q 3 = In 3. Sent., *distinctio 34, pars 1, articulus 1, quaestio 3.* Further, 3 d35 q4 = In 3. Sent., *distinctio 35, articulus unicus* (not identified), *quaestio 4. Fund = fundamentum*; c = *conclusio, dub = dubium*; S = *sermo*; a and b indicate the columns (of the Quaracchi edition).

thereby gives expression to his innermost experience and does this in new concepts that are his own. At a superficial level he could indeed appear simply to occupy a privileged place of convergence and confluence of all the ideological tendencies that from many sources water the mid-thirteenth century and make it fruitful: he could appear as the heart, wide as the world, that offers a place of shelter to each influence, that synthesises them all. The principal influence would still be from Augustine: a philosophy of love, of the image of the Trinity in the created spirit, of the degrees of being and correspondingly of beauty, of an illuminative shining and indwelling of the eternal truth as of the personal *magister interior* in the intellectual act of the creature. But Denys' influence would appear as strong, both directly and as mediated through the School of Chartres and Richard of St Victor: divine transcendence and mystical ecstasy that reaches towards it, creation as the effusion of God, now in combination with the Augustinian teaching on the Trinity, whereby a new pattern is produced—the reservation which characterises Augustine as much as Denys when they speak of the revelation and communication of the Trinity to the world disappears, and the Trinity is not (as for Denys) the absolutely separated and unknowable, nor (as for Augustine) is everything in the world that speaks of the divine Persons mere appropriation. Rather, the Trinity is truly revealed in its overflow into the world (in creation and the Incarnation of Christ), and shows itself thereby to be the a priori ground of everything that exists in the world. Thirdly we would have to mention Anselm, in that which is most peculiarly his, the 'ontological proof', which Bonaventure takes over. For him too this is only the highest example of an aesthetic and theological insight, just as in decisive passages it is precisely the hymn-like texts and the prayers of Anselm which are introduced. He it is who is allowed the last word when Bonaventure speaks of the overpowering of the creature made happy by God, the creature that does not grasp its happiness but rather is grasped by its happiness.[2]

[2] Anselm has the last word, at length, in *Breviloquium* VII 7 (*Opp.*V 290–291), but likewise in *De Sc. Chr.* q6 (V 35b), S 2 *Dom. 5 p. Pascha* (IX 313b); S 1 *Dom. 2 p. Pent.* (IX 359a). *Cf.* 1 dl, 3 q *ad* 2 (I 41a).

As a fourth and even more significant influence, we must
mention the spiritual theology of Bernard and his followers,
which had taken over Anselm's tone and developed it (especially in Bernard's sermons on the Song of Songs) more
decisively than anyone previously in the direction of a nuptial
theology. The foundations were indeed laid in Augustine's
theology of the *totus Christus*, head and body, Bridegroom and
Bride, but this was essentially restricted to the Church as a
whole; in Denys this is almost wholly absent (there are only
hints of it in the concept of eros). But in Bernard and his school,
this becomes a dominant theme: fundamentally, the Bride is the
Church, but in its membership of the Church so too is each
believing and loving soul; and mediating between the two, as
'personified Church' and soul identified with the Church (*anima
ecclesiastica*), is Mary, the mother of the Lord. In Bonaventure,
the nuptial theology and spirituality is omnipresent, permeating
everything as a matter of course; it comes to expression more
strongly the nearer he approaches the mystical peaks. In close
connection with this, and likewise particularly characteristic of
Bernard, is the idea of theology as *sapientia*, that is, precisely, as
sapida scientia,[3] which as such stands above theoretical and
practical science, 'for the recognition that Christ died for us, and
similar knowledge, moves to love, if a man is not a hardened
sinner—this is quite different from a proposition of geometry'.[4]
Finally, we must reckon Joachim of Fiore's theology of
salvation history as an important influence. In one respect he
gives new life to the historical aesthetic of Irenaeus (and of
Tertullian), though of course in an exceptionally literal manner
which does not correspond to the early Fathers, but which is
taken over by Bonaventure and built into his system. If the Old
Covenant is the period of the Father and the New Covenant the
period of the Son, then out of the parallelism of these periods,
which are read into each other and each interpreted by the
other, springs the understanding of the Spirit, because in the
dispensation of salvation the Spirit also proceeds from both the
Father and the Son. In the history of the Church, this interpreta-

[3] *Sex. al.* S 7 2 (VIII 148a).
[4] 1 *Sent. prooem.* q3 (I 13b).

tive understanding of the Spirit is something that develops, and according to Joachim and Bonaventure we stand at the dawning of the eschatological age, for which this understanding is reserved in a special way.[5] What for Joachim appeared as prophecy, appears to Bonaventure as fulfilled: as man came forth on the sixth day of creation, as God became man in the sixth age of the world, so when the sixth apocalyptic seal is opened the 'angel goes up from the rising of the sun, bearing the seal of the living God' (Rev 7.2):[6] who else but the stigmatised man of the Spirit, Francis?

When we speak of this event, we have at last mentioned the living, organising centre of Bonaventure's intellectual world, the thing that lifts it above the level of a mere interweaving of the threads of tradition. His world is Franciscan, and so is his theology, however many stones he may use to erect his spiritual cathedral over the mystery of humility and poverty, like another Baroque Portiuncula over the unpretentious original chapel. And yet, when we have established that the Franciscan mystery is the centre that crystallises all, we have not yet uncovered the ethos that is peculiar to Bonaventure. For Bonaventure does not only take Francis as his centre: he is his own sun and his mission. If we were to use here the categories which Gundolf developed for Goethe, we could distinguish between a wholly personal, fundamental experience and an experience of education which confronts one in the realm of history and brings the still shapeless fundamental experience to crystallisation.

At the origin lies an experience of *overpowering* by the fullness of reality, like a sea that emanates gloriously from the depths of God, eternally flowing and not to be restrained. As he encounters revelation and the endlessness of its meanings and possibilities of interpretation, there occur to Bonaventure words from the Old Testament about rivers and seas: 'All rivers flow into the sea, and the sea does not overflow, and the rivers

[5] On this, cf. J. Ratzinger, loc. cit.
[6] Legenda S. Franc. prol. (VIII 504b); for further applications of Rev 7.2 to Francis, cf. the scriptural index, Vol. X 263.

turn back to the place of their origin and flow on further.' The
mirabiles elationes maris are the Word of God, and those 'who
travel the sea in ships and do much work in the deep waters' are
the interpreters of the Word, but 'such endless depths—who can
plumb them?' Only the uncreated Wisdom makes this her
boast: 'I have my dwelling in the highest heights': at the
creation, 'my throne is in the pillar of the cloud'; in the
Incarnation, 'I trod through mighty waters'; in the Passion, 'I
plumbed the floor of the abyss'; in the investigation of the
Scriptures, for 'Jesus opened their meaning to them' after the
Resurrection. 'Endless variety' characterises this flowing
revelation: 'Manifold indeed is the flowing forth, from the
water in the clouds, from the rivers, from the springs, and all
comes from the sea.' But 'the earth receives' everything that
streams down from heaven, '. . . and brings forth a swarm of
wonderful growth (*facit pulcherrimas pullulationes*)'.

Nevertheless, 'like a drop that one takes from the sea, so are all
the *theoriae* that are produced when compared with those that
could be produced'.[7] And so nothing is more typical of the
author than the prologue to the whole commentary on the
Sentences. He writes that his subject is the four rivers of paradise:
the first is the triune, eternal flowing of God himself; the second
is the creation, which is wide and deep as the sea in whose depths
the dragon dwells; the third is the Incarnation of God, who in
Christ flows out of himself and flows back to himself: 'as in a
circle the last joins itself on to the first, so in the Incarnation the
highest joins itself on to the lowest, God unites himself with the
clay'; 'it belongs to the nature of water to mount up again to the
same extent as it sank down.' The fourth river is the sacraments,
that stream of 'the water of life, clear as crystal, that went forth
from the throne of God and of the Lamb', for 'from the side of
Christ as he slept flowed out the sacraments, as water and blood
streamed out'. But Bonaventure needs the image of the river
only because of the liveliness of the image of flowing; otherwise,
he replaces it with the image of the depths of the sea: 'The depth
of the eternal emanations (of the divine Persons) is the sublimity
of the divine nature . . . the depth of the creation is its futility: "I

[7] *Hex.* 13, 1–6 (V 388ab).

stick in deep mud and find no firm place to stand". . . . The
depth of the Incarnation is what Christ's manhood achieved. . . .
"You have thrown me into the depth of the heart of the sea, and
its waves closed together over me." This can be said about
Christ, who was brought so low that he can be described as one
thrown aside and rejected. . . . For Jesus' gentle heart beat in so
tender love for us that it did not seem to him too hard to endure
for us the extreme, harshest death. The depth of the dispensation
of salvation in the sacraments, however, is the efficacy of the
perfected means of salvation: "You led them on your way
through the depths of the sea, and they walked through the sea
as freed men." ' This is the content of the book that
Bonaventure intends to comment upon, dealing with the
revelatio quatuor absconditorum: 'The first hidden thing is the
greatness of the divine being . . . the second hidden thing is the
dispensation of the divine Wisdom (as Job says, "Where is
Wisdom to be found? Where is the place where she is known?
She is hidden from the eyes of all the living") . . . the third
hidden thing is the strength of the divine power . . .: Christ
hanging on the cross, where the strength of his power hid itself
under the mantle of powerlessness. . . . The fourth hidden thing
is the sweetness of the divine mercy, for the sweetness of his
mercy is truly hidden, and laid up for those who fear him' (Ps
102.17).[8]

The place of the rivers of paradise is taken in the *Soliloquium*
by the four dimensions in the Letter to the Ephesians: 'That you
may be able to understand, together with all the saints, the
length and breadth, height and depth, and that you may know
the love of Christ which surpasses all knowledge, so that you
may be filled with all the fulness of God' (Eph 3.18–19). These
four dimensions are 'the blessed cross on which you, consecrated
soul, must forever hang in contemplation with your gentlest

[8] *Sent. Prooem.* (I 1–5); *cf. Comm. in Eccl.* I (VI 13b); S 2 *Dom.* 2 *p. Pascha* (IX
299b); *Don. Sp. Sti.* 4, 14 (V 476b): revelation is compared to the waters of the
sea because of the depth of the mysteries. The sea is deep, man cannot walk
through it; and so powerful is the depth of the mysteries of sacred Scripture
that man, however enlightened he may be and however much he may strive, is
not able to penetrate to the bottom of the mysteries.

Bridegroom Jesus Christ'.⁹ The introduction to the *Breviloquium* chooses the same text to explain the nature of revelation and theology, and to elevate them above the more restricted area of philosophy: theology does not take its starting-point in human research, but in divine revelation that flows from the Father of lights; as theology progresses, it is 'not narrowed down by the rules of human logic, definitions, and distinctions', but 'embraces the whole as in one single epitome'; and the goal of theology is the 'fullness of eternal beatitude', so that 'our fulfilment may bring us into the entire fullness of God'.¹⁰

Because of this superabundance, revelation appears to the outsider like something 'uncertain, with no order, and like a kind of virgin forest (*silva opax*)'.¹¹ Even for the one who penetrates into it, the experience is the same: 'Who is capable of knowing the endlessness of the grains of seed, when in one single seed woods upon woods are hidden—and so once more endless seeds?'¹² But it is precisely this swarm, too vast for the eye, that is the beauty (*speciositas*) of revelation's starry sky: 'The swarm of meditations which spring forth from the faith outshines the shining of the stars.'¹³ It is 'an exceedingly rich turmoil' (*pullulationes uberrimae*);¹⁴ it is assuredly not without divine order, for indeed 'it is that which is most ordered of all, but its order is like the order of nature in the growth of the plants'.¹⁵ The ethos of the theology in Bonaventure is thereby quite different from the ethos in Thomas Aquinas, whose philosophical point of view tries to reflect the order of the world as rigorously and clearly as possible. In Bonaventure, there is something defeated from the very start; theology is an imposing upon that which is not to be imposed upon, a tireless proposing of new ordering, counting, classifying, gathering the 'blossoming wilderness' into bouquets. But in the face of this, the last word remains the experience of being out-trumped, of wonder, and of being transported out of oneself (*excessus*). The dizzying pyramids of concepts frequently lack a final necessity: that is to say, they do not satisfy the need for fullness, and it is often the case that a

⁹ *Solil. prol.* (VIII 28–29).
¹¹ *Ibid. prol.* 6 (V 208b).
¹³ *Hex.* 10, 1 (V 377a).
¹⁵ *Ibid.* 14, 5 (V 393b).
¹⁰ *Brevil. prol.* (V 201–202).
¹² *Hex.* 13, 2 (V 388a).
¹⁴ *Hex.* 14, 3 (V 393a).

lower degree leads itself to the last stage in a way which is not really surpassed in the subsequent higher degrees.[16] But the impossibility of mastering revelation does not give rise to doubt or an experience of anxious failure in Bonaventure: it is complete beatitude in the face of the inexhaustibility of God. The 'inconceivable Wisdom with her inscrutable ways'[17] is still *sapientia amorosa*;[18] it is a great beatitude to see how everything in the world bows down before the divine, like the stars in Joseph's dream—*ibi est magna delectatio*.[19] The nearer one draws to God, the higher becomes the experience of beauty: 'For there is great beauty in the construction of the world, and far greater beauty in the Church, which is adorned with the beauty of the gifts of grace of holiness, but the greatest beauty lies in the Jerusalem above, and the beauty greater than the greatest (*supermaxima*) is in the highest and most blessed Trinity.'[20]

With divine things, the business of grasping them in thought always involves a stage of being taken over and grasped, and it is the nature of the created spirit to be orientated precisely to this: 'For nothing satisfies the soul except what exceeds its power to grasp.'[21] The soul might be brought in six ways to what exceeds its capacity: through believing, thinking, wondering, contemplating, being transported out of itself, and comprehending. Faith by itself is imperfect and only a beginning, while it is only God who may comprehend God: so we are left with the pair: thinking and wondering (*arguendo—admirando*) for the earthly life, and for the heavenly life the pair: contemplating and being transported out of oneself (*contuendo—excedendo*). This is true even for the soul of Christ, which contemplates God indeed, yet does not grasp him. 'And this is why the astonished wondering

---

[16] So, for example, in the collations on the Hexameron, whose seven planned stages (Coll. 3, 24; V 347) break off incomplete at the fourth stage, but in this the essential has been said. In the same way, one must not press the three stages of the De triplici via (VIII 3–18) too hard: the first already leads to the nuptial love and to the elevation above all that is of the senses, all that may be imagined and understood.

[17] *Hex.* 8, 6 (V 370a).

[18] [the loving wisdom], *Hex.* 19, 2 (V 420a).

[19] *Hex.* 11, 21 (V 383b).

[20] *Brevil. prol.* 3 (V 205a).

[21] *De sc. Chr.* q7 c (V 35a).

has its place not only in this life, but also in the next life . . . for
what is seen (*apprehenditur*) is not thereby understood (*compre-
henditur*). When God is called inconceivable, however, it is not
because some part of him is kept concealed, but because of the
immeasurability of his simplicity.' Even the soul of Christ is
'taken up in plenitude and ecstasy' (*capitur per superexcedentiam et
excessum*) by the superabundance of God's Wisdom and goodness.[22] This ecstasy awaits the faithful in heaven also, and is
indeed more perfectly realised there than on earth.[23] For in
heaven, the whole incomprehensible fullness of the Godhead
offers itself to the one who contemplates, 'in the same kind of
way as the whole Seine offers itself to someone who brings a jug,
but is not grasped in its entirety, but only as much as the capacity
of the jug'.[24]

So no one should think that for the study of theology it
suffices to have 'reading without unction, speculation without
devotion, research without wondering, prudence without exultation, hard work without piety, cleverness without humility'.[25]
Rather, the purified soul 'is prepared by devotion, wondering
and exultation for the spiritual experiences of being transported
out of itself' which allow it to experience God 'as the highest
beauty'.[26] For 'we attain to ecstasy (*mentis alienatio*) for three
reasons: occasionally from an abundance of devotion, at other
times from an exceedingly great wondering, and at other times
again from extreme joy'.[27] For Bonaventure, this ecstasy
(usually described as *excessus*) is 'the highest and chief manner of
knowledge', but 'scarcely anyone understands it if he has not
experienced it, and one will experience it only if he "is rooted
and grounded in love, in order to understand with all the saints
the length and breadth and height and depth", which is what

---

[22] *Ibid.* V 35–36b.
[23] *Ibid.* q7 c (V 40a).
[24] *Ibid.* V 41a.
[25] *Itin.* (*Itinerarium*) prol. 4 (V 296a).
[26] *Itin.* 4, 3 (V 306b).
[27] *Perf. vit. ad sor.* (*De Perfectione vitae ad sorores*) 5, 6 (VIII 119a). These three
reasons are taken from Richard of St. Victor, who is quoted in the following
passage. *cf.* also S. 3 *Dom.* 3 *in Quadr.* (IX 229b).

truth that is experiential and genuine consists in.'[28] He makes a distinction between this normal spiritual experience and the *raptus*[29] which by a unique privilege mounts above the *status viatorum* and permits the direct sight of the being of God.[30] The ecstasy which belongs to a genuine knowledge of God (which cannot be only 'theoretical') is called, after Denys but using a psychologically richer language, *anagogicus excessus*,[31] 'elevation into the darkness', *docta ignorantia*,[32] contemplation in the strong sense of the word, with as its presupposition and its consequence a suspended lifting-up to God (*suspensio*).[33] We have here the Augustinian transcendence of man towards God, strengthened by the influence of Denys: *oportet . . . nos transcendere ad aeternum*,[34] *nullus potest esse beatus, nisi supra seipsum ascendat*[35] in an *ecstaticus excessus*.[36] This taking leave of the faculty of knowledge takes place *in vertice* as *unitio amoris*,[37] in accordance with the text of the Song of Songs, 'I sleep, and my heart is awake'; Bonaventure, advancing beyond Denys' *apophasis*, always understands the *ablatio* of this experience of ecstasy in a nuptial sense. The soul, with Moses, climbs 'up the mountain,

---

[28] *De sc. Chr.* q7 (V 43ab).

[29] *Hex.* 3, 30 (V 348a); *cf.* K. Rahner, 'Sens spirituels', *loc. cit.* 279, n. 89; 282, n. 98.

[30] 2 d23, 2 q3 c (II 544b).

[31] [anagogical ecstasy], 2 d23, 2 q3 *ad* 6 (II 546a).

[32] [learned ignorance], *ibid.*; *Brevil.* 5, 6 (V 260a).

[33] *Hoc autem videre non est nisi hominis suspensi ultra se in alta visione* [but to see this is granted only to a man suspended out of himself in a deep vision], *Hex.* 13, 11 (V 386a). *Contemplatio suspensa* [a suspended contemplation], *Hex.* 20, 1 (V 425a). The *Itinerarium* uses the six wings of the seraph as divisions of the work: the wings are understood as *sex illuminationum suspensiones* [six illuminative suspensions], through which the soul makes the transition *ad pacem per ecstaticos excessus sapientiae christianae* [to peace through the ecstatic raptures of Christian wisdom], *Prol.* 3 (V 295b).

[34] [it is necessary . . . that we pass over to what is eternal], *Itin.* 1, 2 (V 297a).

[35] [no one can be blessed, unless he ascends above himself], *ibid.* 1, 1 (V 296b). According to the teaching about the *apex mentis* [summit of the mind], this transition can also be termed *intrare in suum intimum et per consequens in summum suum ascendere* [to enter its inmost depth and consequently to ascend to its greatest height], *Hex.* 2, 31 (V 341b).

[36] [ecstatic rapture], *Hex.* 23, 27 (V 449a).

[37] [uniting of love], *Hex.* 2, 29 (V 341a).

enters the darkness, sees the "wholly desirable" Bridegroom; in this unitive love, the person is carried out of himself and united to the Bridegroom, enters God and is lost in him, sees (as far as that is possible) the face of the most beautiful Wisdom, and experiences unheard-of ecstasies of the spirit'.[38] It is certainly possible to apply the word 'mystical' to this experience of man's being overpowered by God in the act of the wondering ecstasy, and one can and must see in it a 'special' grace of God's gift; but, granted God's loving self-disclosure, this experience is nothing other than the human realisation of the objective revelation. In the same way, the message of a work of art will be truly grasped only by one who is delighted and carried out of himself by it. This is Bonaventure's 'fundamental experience'.

This 'fundamental experience' finds its crystallisation in the central image of the *stigmatisation of St. Francis* on Mount Alverna, and this from multiple points of view. Let us begin with the object of such experience: the whole tradition from Augustine, Denys, Bernard and the Victorines understood the divine glory as the beauty of his Wisdom: *forma sapientiae est mirabilis, et nullus eam aspicit sine admiratione et ecstasi.*[39] 'Many love beauty, but beauty is not in external things, which are only her image; the true beauty is in the beauty of Wisdom.'[40] This beauty of Wisdom appears to Francis in the form of the crucified seraph—it is almost as if the crucified one, who appears to the late Gothic (as late as Grünewald) in the form of pure distortion, must here make use of this clothing of Wisdom. But it is still the crucified who is the centre of the apparition: if the six wings of the seraph signify the six flights to Wisdom, yet 'there is no other path to Wisdom than through the most burning love for the crucified',[41] and the mystical *suspensio* is itself a reply to the crucified who is suspended 'between heaven and earth, as if he were unworthy to live or to die upon the earth'.[42] Ecstasy,

[38] *Hex. princip.* 2, 33, ed. Delorme 32.
[39] [the form of wisdom is wonderful, and no one looks on her without wonderment and ecstasy], *Hex.* 2, 7 (V 337b).
[40] *Hex.* 20, 24 (V 429b).
[41] *Itin. prol.* 2 (V 295b).
[42] *Perf. vit. ad sor.* 6, 3 (VIII 121a).

then, means a suspended transition: 'Let us then go with the crucified Christ out of this world to the Father.'[43] In this, the man's experience has a decisive role: the *via negativa et excessus* of Denys, leading to the Neo-Platonic simplicity, is now explained as a Franciscan stripping away of all things, that is to say, as poverty, and this is already understood in a nuptial sense— 'Contemplation can occur only in the highest simplicity (*simplicitas*), and the highest simplicity can occur only in the highest poverty, and thus it is appropriate for this Order. The intention of blessed Francis was to attain the highest form of poverty.'[44] Here above all the relationship between object and subject is made clear, and here we find the basic concepts that characterise the whole of Bonaventure's aesthetics, distinguishing him from the tradition: *expressio* and *impressio*.'

The crucified seraph is not only the object of contemplative loving meditation: he is also active and expresses himself by impressing himself, which is to say his wounds, in Francis. Such wounds are the only true *christiana sapientia . . . vere divinitus expressa*;[45] but again as the '*signaculum* of the crucified' they are equally '*in corpore ipsius (Francisci) impressum*, not through the power of nature, nor through the originality of art, but through the wonderful power of the living Spirit of God'.[46] The two words continually answer each other: 'That apparition of the seraph before Francis was *expressiva et impressiva*',[47] and, with a change of meaning, 'So the servant of the Lord bore on his breast *expresse impressam similitudinem Crucifixi*.'[48] It is significant that although the power of the expression goes out from the crucified, the bodily sign is imprinted only because Francis, through grace and his own inflamed love, had already himself become in spirit an expression of the love of the crucified. The

---

[43] *Itin.* 7, 6 (V 313b).

[44] *Hex.* 20, 30 (V 430b).

[45] [Christian wisdom . . . expressed in truly divine fashion], *Legenda S. Franc.* 13, 10 (VIII 545b).

[46] *Ibid. Prol.* 2 (VIII 505a). *Cf.* S *de S. Patre n. Franc.* 5: *contra naturam . . . supra artem* [contrary to nature . . . above art] (IX 593b).

[47] [expressive and imprinted], *Hex.* 22, 23 (V 441a).

[48] [expressly imprinted the likeness of the crucified], *Legenda minor* (VIII 576a).

stigmata are not in any way produced by his love, but come from God's power alone; but at the same time, the stigmata are the expression of his loving spirit, for God expressed himself thus only in the soft wax of a man so inflamed. When he saw the seraph, Francis understood that 'as he was consumed by spiritual fire he would be changed into an expressive image (*expressam similitudinem*) of the crucified. As the apparition disappeared, after a secret and interior conversation, it left his spirit inwardly kindled from a seraphic glow, and outwardly his flesh was branded with a reproduction of the image of the crucified, as if an imprint like a seal had followed the liquefying power of the fire.'[49] Notably the sermons about Francis set great store by this manner of production of the Franciscan *signum expressivum*:[50] even if Francis in no way looked forward to or prepared for anything like stigmatisation, nevertheless the stigmatisation is like a sign of his inward resemblance to the crucified, a sign that demands a bodily visibility; and the inner resemblance, no less than the bodily resemblance, was the work of the crucified God whose love sought to express itself.[51] The man's love makes the

[49] *Ibid.*

[50] [expressive sign], *Hex.* 23, 14 (V 447a); S 2 *de S. Patre Franc.* (IX 574b).

[51] *Legenda S. Franc.* 13, 5 (V 543b). *Cf.* S 2 *de S. Patre Franc.: Signaculum . . . transformatum per incendium dilectionis . . . expressum per exemplum perfectae virtutis, . . . expressivum per zelum supernae virtutis* [a seal . . . transformed by the fire of love . . . made eloquent by the zeal of heavenly virtue] (IX 547b). *Ponam te quasi signaculum, sc. in signis et stigmatibus impressis tibi Verbo Omnipotentis . . . quia servus meus es et humilis* [I shall set you as a seal, that is to say, in the signs and stigmata imprinted on you by the Word of the Almighty . . . because you are my servant, and lowly] (*ibid.* 576a). *Maximam habuit devotionem ad Christi incarnationem et Christi crucem; propter amorem . . . transformatus est in Christum crucifixum et habuit clavos* [he had a very great devotion to the Incarnation of Christ and the cross of Christ; because of his love . . . he was transformed into Christ crucified, and received the nails] (*ibid.* 580a). S 3: *Ipse enim voluit sequi Christum et portare crucem Christi. Unde ipsi . . . apparuit Seraphim unus et tunc apparuerunt in corpore ejus . . . stigmata passionis* [for he wished to follow Christ and to carry the cross of Christ. Therefore . . . one of the Seraphim appeared to him, and then there appeared on his body . . . the stigmata of the Passion] (*ibid.* 584b). S 4: *Sicut est de ferro, quod cum bene calet, ita quod liquescit, tunc potest imprimi in illud quaelibet forma vel figura: sic in corde bene fervente per amorem ad Christum crucifixum imprimitur ipse Crucifixus vel crux Crucifixi, et amans transfertur vel transformatur in Crucifixum, sicut fecit B. Franciscus. . . . Signum crucis impressum corpori ejus significabat affectum quem ipse habebat ad Christum*

wax of the heart soft, and God's love imprints the seal; and so every Christian may be urged, 'Like a seal in soft wax, so print Jesus the Bridegroom on your soul.'[52] Likewise: 'Long more forcefully for resemblance to God, through an explicit (*expressam*) following of the crucified Jesus.'[53]

It is decisive for Bonaventure's aesthetic theology that the stigmata were branded on the body precisely while the soul was in an ecstatic rapture: it is when the form of the divine beauty is seen that this divine beauty receives its form in the world. For Bonaventure, it is vital that ecstasy, even in its Dionysian aspects, is not a flight out of the world that leaves it behind, but rather the opening of the world for God, or more precisely the revelation of the fact that the world has already been grasped by God. Light is shed on this by Bonaventure's teaching about the number six, in which the patristic motif of the ages of history coalesces with the mystical motif of the six wings of the Isaianic-Franciscan seraph. For the traditional motif of the ages of history, the axiom *septima aetas currit cum sexta*, which Bonaventure adopts,[54] is characteristic: alongside the sixth age of the world, in which Christ is born and goes to heaven, the seventh age already runs its course. The sabbath of the world has already begun with the Ascension, and will last until the general resurrection; then is the dawn of the eighth day. Because through Christ heaven is now in principle open, mystical-eschatological contemplation and existence are already possible. The six wings correspond to the six-fold course of history as six ways of the knowledge of God, or 'six variations of illuminations', by which the spirit, transported to paradise on the

---

crucifixum [In the same way as iron, when it is very hot, liquefies and then any form or shape at all may be impressed on it, so it is with a heart that truly burns with love for Christ crucified: the crucified himself or the cross of the crucified is impressed on the heart, and the lover is carried over or transformed into the crucified, just as blessed Francis experienced it.... The sign of the cross imprinted on his body signified the devotion which he himself had for Christ crucified] (*ibid.* 589ab).

[52] *Perf. vit. ad sor.* 6 (VIII 123b).

[53] *De regim. animae* 7 (VIII 130a).

[54] [The seventh age runs alongside the sixth], *Brevil, Prol.* 2 (V 203b); *Hex.* 15, 18 (V 400b), 15, 12 (400a), 16, 2 (403b). On the tradition of the axiom, *cf.* Ratzinger, *loc. cit.* 17, n.3.

seventh day, 'resting in contemplation and sleeping, is led to the *arcanum* of the spiritual marriage'.[55] In the same way, the *Reductio artium* knows *sex illuminationes*,[56] and the *Itinerarium* knows *sex illuminationum suspensiones*,[57] in which the sixth step already grants what is in substance perfect (*iam venit ad quandam rem perfectam*), so that to look engenders that ecstatic wondering which as such is the transition to the seventh step: *nec aliquid iam amplius restet nisi dies requiei, in qua per mentis excessum requiescat humanae mentis perspicacitas.*[58] 'If by the sixth day someone has already reached the point where he can . . . meditate in the first and highest mediator between God and men . . . so it remains only, as one contemplates this (*haec speculando*), to make the transition.'[59] In the same way the work on the Hexameron arranges the visions in a sixfold scale, while the seventh vision is reserved for God.[60] Bonaventure's preference for the number six comes from its doubling of the number of the Trinity, which (in the creative sphere) is then distributed around two poles, right and left or upper and lower, which reflect each other: this parallel reflection is the ground scheme of Joachim's historical thinking, in which in each case a period of the Old Covenant and a similar period of the New Covenant reflect each other, and in this mirroring allow the Spirit to spring forth as the third age. In a similar way, the soul can realise her six capacities: below herself (as soul) the senses and the imagination, in herself

---

[55] *De plant. Par.* 15 (V 578b). Applied to a universal teaching on science: *In omni scientia sine Christo evanescit sciens; Christus enim, replens animam splendoribus, sex facit in ea illustrationes praemissas, in septima quiescens* [In any science that is without Christ, the scientist fades away; for Christ, filling the soul with splendours, sends six illuminations in it, and takes his rest in the seventh] (*Hex. Princip.* 1, Delorme 19). See below, ch. 2.

[56] [six illuminations], *De red. art.* (*De reductione artium ad theologiam*) 6 (V 321b).

[57] [six illuminative suspensions], *Itin. Prol.* 3 (V 295b).

[58] [nor does anything remain except the day of rest, in which the cleverness of the human mind comes to rest through an ecstasy of the mind], *Itin.* 6, 7 (V 312a).

[59] *Ibid.* 7, 1 (V 312ab). The book *De sex alis Seraphim*, treating the qualities of the rulers of the Order, locates these in the imitation of the founder: they must 'have spiritual wings' like the seraph which brought the marks of the wounds to Francis (VIII 133b).

[60] *Hex.* 3, 24f. (V 347ab).

(as reason) the abstract essences and the concrete ones (the angels), above herself (as related to God) speculation and the mystical union with God. If the soul realises these activities which belong to her, 'then she will become a wonderful mirror, rubbed smooth, in which she sees everything that has sparkle and beauty, just as the image is seen in the mirror'.[61]

All these varied applications should not lead us to forget that the central image is the crucified Christ hanging before Francis, and that here all the divine illuminations unite in this image of the cross, like rays in a lens. The twice three wings are the descent and ascent of the Son of Man,[62] the mystery of his nuptial love which contains both drunkenness and shame: 'Christ was drunk from love for his bride, and was exposed naked on the cross, and the evil Ham mocked him.'[63] The cross is the true manual of instruction, the only one which Francis continually read, and no one reaches understanding of revelation except through the cross, which we 'should take on ourselves as the book of wisdom, to contemplate it'.[64] The Christian should always 'see before him with the eyes of his heart Christ dying on the cross',[65] and should not only see him, 'but should enter fully through the door of the wound in his side, as far as his heart', while he 'ponders the utterly shameful death of the Bridegroom'.[66] All this takes place inescapably for me: 'God is mocked, so that you may be honoured; flogged, so that you may be consoled; crucified, so that you may be set free; the spotless Lamb is slaughtered, so that you may be fed; the lance brings forth water and blood from his side, so that you

[61] *Hex.* 5, 25 (V 358a). If the thought embraces the two seraphim by the ark of the covenant, who are turned one to the other and look to the middle of the sanctuary, then we have a new doubling: here, it is the twice six wings which together give the Biblical number twelve (found in the Old Testament, the New Testament, and apocalyptic), whereby the twelve articles of faith correspond to the twelve apostles. So Bonaventure can speak of a 'double seraphication' of the soul. *Hex.* 8, 8.12–17 (V 370–371).

[62] *Hex.* 8, 15 (V 371).

[63] *Ibid.* 14, 19 (V 396a).

[64] S 2 *in Parasc.* (IX 265b).

[65] *Perf. vit. ad sor.* 6 (VIII 120a). The same recommendation is made to the novices: *Regula Nov.* 4 (VIII 480b) and *passim*.

[66] *Ibid.* 120b.

may drink. . . . O Lord Jesus Christ, who for my sake did not spare yourself: wound my heart through your wounds, inebriate my spirit with your blood, so that wherever I may go, I may continually have you before my eyes as the crucified . . . and may be able to find nothing else but you.'[67] The marriage between God and creature takes place on the cross: 'Christ on the cross bows his head, waiting for you, that he may kiss you; he stretches out his arms, that he may embrace you; his hands are open, that he may enrich you; his body is spread out, that he may give himself totally; his feet are nailed, that he may stay there; his side is open for you, that he may let you enter there.'[68] This is 'the day of the marriage',[69] 'and he could not have a spotless bride before he had formed her out of his side . . . this wedding had to be celebrated in his Passion.'[70] Each Christian must 'long to become fully like the crucified',[71] just as 'the genuine love for Christ transformed the loving' Francis 'into the same image',[72] when the sword of compassionate pain pierced his soul;[73] just as Mary 'stood by that Martyr as a fellow-martyr, wounded together with him who was wounded, crucified together with him who was crucified, transfixed with him who was transfixed'.[74] This is how one abyss expresses itself in the other abyss, echoing the psalm: 'The abyss of the suffering of Christ calls to the other abyss of Christian compassion', for true Christians, 'by the weight of their grief and painful compassion for the suffering of the Lord, are made like him and transformed into the image of the crucified'.[75]

This calling of the abysses to one another is so much the centre and goal of all Wisdom that Bonaventure thinks all other knowledge insipid. '*Non sufficit ad habendam sapientiam scholastica*

---

[67] *Solil.* 1, 33–34 (VIII 39b–40a).
[68] *Ibid.* 1, 39 (VIII 41b).
[69] *Vitis myst.* 4, 3 (VIII 167a).
[70] S 1 *in Coena Dni.* (IX 247b).
[71] *Lignum Vitae, Prol.* (VIII 68a).
[72] *Legenda S. Franc.* 13 (VIII 543b).
[73] *Legenda minor* (VIII 575b).
[74] S 1 *Dom. infr. oct. Epiph.* (IX 172b).
[75] S 1 *Dom. 3 p. Pascha* (IX 307b).

sine monastica, for it is not through hearing alone but through following that a man becomes wise';[76] 'holiness is the direct aptitude for wisdom.'[77] 'There is no secure passage from learning to wisdom—one must go through an intermediary, namely, holiness. And the passage takes place through experimental practice: one turns from the study of learning and practises the study of holiness, and then again one makes the transition from the study of holiness to the study of wisdom.'[78] The seventh General of the Franciscan Order observed the scholastic rationalism of his time with increasing unease: like Thomas Aquinas, he draws more precisely than before the boundaries between belief and knowledge, but not (like Thomas) in order to safeguard reason's proper rights but, quite the contrary, in order to cause reason to retreat within its own proper limits.[79] This places him in an exceptionally exposed and lonely position between the ages: on the one hand, he sees the end of the sapiential theology drawing near and prophesies the coming of an eschatological epoch, when the defence of the faith through reason will be out-moded and the only valid preaching will be the way of life of the precursor of the end-time, St. Francis;[80] on the other hand, his distrust of the achievements of the autonomous reason means that he can only look with anxiety at the modern period as it dawns: the *mundus hodie*[81] with its secularisation and arrogance really admits only an apocalyptic interpretation, and so Bonaventure points back to the thorough study of Holy Scripture, and, with caution, to the *originalia sanctorum*.[82] 'There should not be so much water of philosophy mixed into the wine of Scripture that wine is turned into water: that would be a truly miserable miracle! . . . Besides, in the early Church they burned the philosophy books.'[83] He allows Thomas his Aristotelian, scientific future, and Augustine his

---

[76] *Hex.* 2, 3 (V 337a).
[77] *Ibid.* 2, 6 (V 337a).
[78] *Hex.* 19, 3 (V 420b).
[79] *Brevil.* 1, 1 (V 210b).
[80] *Hex.* 17, 28 (V 414b); Ratzinger, *loc. cit.* 155–159.
[81] [world today], *Hex.* 5, 9 (V 355b), and frequently.
[82] *Hex.* 19, 7–10 (V 421a–422a).
[83] *Ibid.* 14 (V 422b).

Platonic, sapiential past, and keeps for himself only the stigmatised Francis, whose existence of the end-time in poverty is not yet (or only very imperfectly) attained by his Order.

Because philosophy does not possess Christ, it cannot provide the final *resolutio* which would bring us to the true origins,[84] or at most it can do so *semiplene*.[85] Only one who knows the trinitarian mystery is a 'true metaphysician',[86] only one who knows Christ has the true *ethica generalis*;[87] 'the philosophers have no learning that forgives sins, not even in the *Summas* of the Masters.'[88] On the other hand, whoever loves the Christian revelation loves philosophy also, through which he confirms the faith; but philosophy in itself is the tree of the knowledge of good and evil[89]—it remains ambivalent until it is polarised through true (that is to say, existential) theology. If men cling to their researches, they love the darkness more than the light.[90] It is only the man who knows the nuptial mystery of Wisdom who knows also what virtue is: even the cardinal virtues derive from a conduct that imitates the divine;[91] no philosophical ethic has been able to achieve a system.[92] It is only when the teaching of Aristotle on virtue is taken up into a higher Christian sense that it assumes its true form.[93] It is not that reason is incapable of knowing anything: rather, it is precisely the beauty of Wisdom that seduces it to pride in knowing much, to satisfaction with the things of this world, and finally to a Faustian drive to experience: *vult (homo) cognoscere et cognita experiri et per consequens eis uniri*,[94] and therefore the nuptial mystery is perverted

[84] *De red. art.* 17f. (V 323b–324a).
[85] [half-fully], *Hex.* 11, 10 (V 381b).
[86] *Hex.* 1, 13 (V 331b).
[87] S 2 *in Nativ. Dni.* (IX 107b).
[88] *Hex.* 19, 7 (V 421a).
[89] S 2 *Dom.* 3 *Advent.* (IX 63a); cf. *Hex.* 17, 27 (V 413b). Ratzinger, *loc. cit.* 151f.
[90] S 1 *in Asc.* (IX 317b).
[91] *Hex.* 6, 10 (V 362 f.). Bonaventure develops here the noble image of the cardinal virtues as guardians of the four compass points of the soul, an image that Claudel took up in his Fifth Ode. Cf. *Coll.* 7, 15f. (V 367b).
[92] *Hex.* 5, 14 (V 356b).
[93] *Hex.* 5, 2 (V 354a–355b).
[94] [(man) wishes to know, and to experience what he knows, and consequently to be united to what he knows], *Hex.* 19, 2 (V 420b).

into an intellectual harlotry: *Abominatio maxima est, quod filia regis pulcherrima (scil. sapientia) offertur nobis in sponsam et potius volumus copulari ancillae turpissimae et meretricari.*[95] 'The danger of the sciences is that they may so extend themselves in their considerations that they cannot subsequently find their way back to the house of Scripture, but land in the house of Daedalus (the Labyrinth) and never find their way out of it. And it is better to hold the truth than the parable.'[96]

Certainly, the reason is the light that is the basis of all else and makes all else possible: 'Without this light implanted in man, he has nothing, neither faith nor grace nor the light of Wisdom.'[97] But reason is only the precondition of the communicability of God in his Word, both objectified as *Verbum incarnatum*, and interiorly as *Verbum inspiratum*, both having their source in the Word as *Verbum increatum*, which brings the inner being of God, and thereby the whole world also, to expression. The stigmatisation and the process which it makes perceptible to the senses belong to the *Verbum inspiratum*, for they are a coming of Christ into the human spirit: 'It is not possible to reach a clear revelation of the faith except by the coming of Christ into the rational spirit.'[98] *Verbum . . . inspiratum, secundum quod (Verbum) est in mente.*[99] This Word was 'in the prophets, but we perceive it because the Holy Spirit testifies that Christ is the truth'. The Holy Spirit has 'shone forth into the hearts of the preachers; it is he likewise who brought the Scriptures to birth in the spirits of the elect, and it is he who gives certainty to the Christian faith'.[100] And so the *Verbum inspiratum* can with precision be

[95] [It is a very great abomination, that the most beautiful daughter of the king (*i.e.*, wisdom) is offered to us as a bride, and we prefer to fornicate with a base servant-maid and resort to a prostitute], *Hex.* 2, 7 (V 337b); *cf.* 5, 21: *luxuriata est metaphysica* [metaphysics is given over to wantonness].

[96] *Hex.* 17, 25 (V 413ab); cf. 18, 3 (V 415a).

[97] *Hex.* 3, 25 (V 347a).

[98] S *theol.* 4, 3 (V 568b).

[99] [the inspired Word . . . in accordance with which (the Word) is in the mind], S 1 *in coena Dni.* (IX 249a); *cf.* S 1 *Dom. 2 p. Pascha* (IX 249b), S 3 *Dom. 2 p. Pascha* (IX 301b). 'It is impossible to arrive at a true revelation of the faith, *nisi per adventum Christi in mentem* [except through the coming of Christ into the mind]', S *theol.* 4, 3 (V 568b).

[100] *Hex.* 9, 6–8 (V 373b).

termed the Holy Spirit, in the whole breadth of his function of revelation and testimony.[101] In a quite central fashion, theology (understood as the comprehension of the objective revelation in the Church and its appropriation in the individual) is his domain: *theologia, tamquam scientia super fidem fundata et per Spiritum Sanctum revelata.*[102] *Verbum inspiratum* is that act of speaking by God *per quod omnia revelantur.*[103] This is why the Christian revelation (or, as Bonaventure usually has it in his later period, Holy Scripture) is 'highest certainty, because borne by the supernatural light of faith or of divine inspiration, which cannot err'.[104]

So *faith* is an inspired, irradiated, imprinted word of God, a ray of the eternal Spirit's light in us: 'Because the truth of the first principle (God) is infinitely greater than all created truth and infinitely more radiant than any light of our reason ... therefore even what surpasses the reason and contradicts sense-experience is true; if anyone denies this, he refuses to honour the highest truth as he should, because he prefers a judgment based on his own efforts to the command of the eternal light (*dictamini lucis aeternae*).'[105] Faith lies therefore between seeing and not seeing,[106] but it is certain, because it is based on a manifold seeing: 'The first depends on the spirits of the angels, the second on the spirits of the prophets, the third on the spirits of the apostles, and the interplay of these acts of seeing is the certainty of Holy Scripture.' According to Paul, the Law was transmitted to Moses through the angels: 'The angels issued it, they wrote it—they, who looked on the pure truth in the eternal light. And Moses was lifted up above all the prophets to see this ... to the

[101] *De Don. Sp. Sti.* 1, 7 (V 458b).
[102] [theology, in so far as it is a science founded upon faith and revealed by the Holy Spirit], *Brevil. Prol.* 3 (V 205a); *cf.* 5 (207a).
[103] [through which all things are revealed], *Hex.* 3, 2 (V 343a); 3, 22 (V 347a).
[104] *Qu. de Theol.* 1 resp. (Ed. Tavard *loc. cit.* 212, 12–13); *cf.* q3 *resp.*: *haec scientia est per divinam inspirationem* [this science is through divine inspiration], *ibid.* 226, 35.
[105] *Brevil.* 7 (V 260b).
[106] *Hex.* 8, 3 (V 369b).

intellectual act of seeing.'[107] The seeing of the prophets was in images (*imaginariae*), but that of the apostles combines the intellectual seeing with the bodily: so John can say that he has 'seen, heard and touched' the Word of life, 'and the blessed Virgin Mary, the teacher (*doctrix*) of the apostles and evangelists, touched this Word in her womb and at her breast. These three acts of seeing, or certainties, give to revelation the certainty of faith.'[108] In addition, there is the moral witness of the blamelessness of the preachers, the witness of the miracles and that of the martyrs, the full agreement of all the testimonies of Scripture, of the councils and of the writings of the saints, and so on. But these apologetic arguments are only a supplement: in the centre are the twelve mysteries of faith, which like the twelve constellations shine upon the world of faith and rule it. Not all of them are also *per rationem intelligibilia* (e.g., that Abraham begot Isaac), but others are both to be believed and to be understood, if there are strong arguments of reason for them. Here Bonaventure adopts the language of Anselm: *decentissimum fuit*,[110] *quae omnia necessario consequuntur et exiguntur. . . .*[111] In order for the spirit of man to attain to the knowledge of faith, it is necessary that a due proportionality with respect to God be established in the spirit, and this is produced through the light of faith, which is 'a presence of God in the soul' and 'transmits a kind of knowledge which is like a resemblance: not abstracted, but imprinted (*non abstracta, sed impressa*)'.[112] In the eternal seeing, this same act whereby God imprints himself in the created spirit will take place in a perfect manner:[113] hence Bonaventure loves to cite the aesthetic text of 2 Corinthians in his later writings: *Nos vero omnes, revelata facie gloriam Domini speculantes, in eandem imaginem transformamur a claritate in clari-*

[107] *Hex.* 9, 10–11 (V 374a); the final addition is only in Report A (Delorme 121).

[108] *Ibid.* 9, 12–14 (V 374b).

[109] *Hex.* 10, 1–4 (V 377–378; Delorme 126–127).

[110] [it was most fitting], *Brevil.* 4, 1 (V 241a).

[111] [all these follow necessarily, and are demanded logically], *Brevil.* 4, 10 (V 251a).

[112] 1 d3 1 q1 *ad* 5 (I 69–70).

[113] *Intellectus informatur (in patria) ad videndum Deum similitudine divinae essentiae impressa in ipso intellectu, non abstracta ab ipsa essentia divina* [the intellect

tatem, tamquam a Domini spiritu (2 Cor 3.18). The glory is the appearing of the Lord, and through the Spirit of the Lord, the *Verbum inspiratum*, the open seeing of faith and, more essentially, the configuration to the image in a process that stamps an impression are made possible in the unity between expression and impression that was found between the seraph and Francis.[114] This apparent *theologia gloriae*, for all the precision of the resemblance between expression and impression, remains nevertheless for Bonaventure—precisely in its blinding brilliance—a theology of *excessus* as the believer is confronted by the ever greater fullness of God: the superabundance of what may be revealed is the hiddenness that is the true characteristic of the Christian God; the superabundance of light that remains incomprehensible demands faith, the superabundance of love in the crucified demands pure humility and surrender of oneself, and finally the superabundance of the divine prodigality imperiously demands total poverty, which, as the human gesture of giving away everything, is the most exact answer possible for man to God's act of total abandonment even to the cross.

2. TRINITY, IDEA, *REDUCTIO*

Bonaventure's intellectual world is in its entirety an interpretation of the revelation of Scripture. Here the world and the spirit of man are each a function within the totality of God's act

---

is bent towards the vision of God (in the heavenly homeland) by the likeness of the divine essence which is imprinted in the intellect itself, a likeness that is not abstracted from the divine essence itself], *Qu. de Novissimis* 6 (ed. Glorieux, *loc. cit.* 59).

[114] The text is cited at: *Hex.* 2, 19 (V 339b), 10, 3 (V 377b), 11, 1 (V 379ab), 11, 2 (V 380a), 11, 22 (V 383b), 12, 1 (V 384a), 15, 11 (V 400a); *De Don. Sp. Sti.* 4, 2 (V 474a); *De Plant. Par.* 5 (V 576); *In Eccl.* 1 (VI 13b); *In Sap.* 4 (VI 134b); *Comm. in Joh.* 2 (VI 270b); 4 (VI 295b); 17 (VI 476b); 21 (VI 521a); *Coll. in Joh. Coll.* 62 (VI 611b); *In Lk.* 3 (VII 88b); 9 (VII 234b); *Legenda S. Franc.* 13 (VIII 543b: applied to Francis); *Legenda minor* (VIII 576b; likewise); S *feria* 2 *p. Dom.* 2 *in Quadr.* (IX 221b: the face of the contemplating soul should reflect the glory of Christ transfigured on Tabor); S 3 *Dom.* 3 *in Quadr.* (IX 229b); S 10 *Pent.* (IX 345b); S 3 *Dom.* 2 *p. Pent.* (IX 363b); S 5 *Dom.* 22 *p. Pent.* (IX 446a); S 6 *Dom* 22 *p. Pent.* (IX 449a).

of making himself known; there is complete interpenetration and interconnection between his understanding of the world and of God, such that for Bonaventure the world and man are intelligible in their being, and in their being what they are, only on the basis of the being, and the being what he is, of God in himself—and indeed, on the basis of the being, and the being what it is, of the divine revelation in Jesus Christ. If we give the key categories of Bonaventure's thought their place in this pattern, then we may say that the created world expresses God because at the origin God expresses himself and because, when he reveals himself outwardly, he wishes to make for himself a perfect self-expression in the God-man Jesus Christ: thus every worldly expression is a foreshadowing, an image, material directed to this end.

The cause that makes all things possible is therefore God's Trinity, in which the relationship of expression is located in the absolute being of God: this relationship is conceived purely in terms of Christian theology and has as little to do with Platonism as it has to do with Aristotelianism; Platonic ideas exist only with regard to the real world, since for any philosophy a relationship of expression based in the absolute is totally inaccessible. And God the Father does not beget the Son with a view to creation, and therefore we may not posit in the Son the beginning of a process of multiplication of the One of a mediating kind (as the Platonising fathers were inclined to suppose). Rather, the many thoughts of creation of God are possible only because the Son is unique, the only-begotten of the Father, and it is with a view to this oneness, and coming from this oneness, that all outward forms of expression and imitative images may be conceived. Bonaventure's picture of the world is accordingly in the highest degree christocentric— because all the copies that are imperfect expressions must be brought into relation with the one perfect Image of the Father, which expresses him with the highest precision, and so be made transparent in order to be comprehensible. But precisely in this his picture of the world is not Platonic.[115]

[115] In the theological sermon *Christus unus omnium magister*, Bonaventure weighs the achievements of the two Greeks against one another: Aristotle has

The present chapter, which forms a unity with that which follows, examines the relationship of expression in the first instance from three points of view: first, in so far as it is established in perfection in the being of God; second, in so far as this foundation in the Trinity is the root for every outward self-expression of God; third, in so far as every outward self-expression of God that occurs remains embraced and carried by his divine self-expression and must be interpreted, explained, traced back, and analysed with reference to this, so that it may be understood in terms of the conditions that make it possible, and so that it may be granted the conditions for its perfecting. The real structure of the cosmos does not yet come into sight in this three-fold examination: this will be developed in the following chapter, first, as the world in general; second, as man; third, as the God-man who perfects all things and establishes them. We reserve until the conclusion of the last chapter the problem of the freedom of the Incarnation—which must be free, even when the whole construction of the world is to be understood as effectively established in Christ. In the meantime, in the fourth chapter, the category of 'expression' is given its place in the ensemble of the theological teaching of Bonaventure about beauty, and in the fifth chapter we shall once again look back at the particular Christian situation of this aesthetic.

1. Only revelation teaches the Christian[116] that God is triune; but revelation indicates to the believer that he must think the highest of God. In the light of this principle,[117] the thinking

the gift of science, Plato the gift of wisdom; Aristotle is right to understand human knowledge 'as arising on the road of the senses, the memory and experience', and therefore he rightly rebukes Plato, 'who derives all certain knowledge from the intelligible or ideal world'; but Plato correctly posits the existence of these ideas or eternal grounds of being. The successful marriage of the ideal and the real was only finally achieved in the Old Covenant (Moses) and in the New Covenant (Paul), above all in Christ himself, inasmuch as he was *simul perfectus viator et comprehensor* [at the same time the perfect traveller and the perfect man of understanding] (V 572ab), and thereby possessed full knowledge, both a posteriori and a priori.

[116] I d3 I q4 (I 75–76).
[117] Already expressed implicitly in I d2 q2 (I 53), *ibid.* q4 (I 57), and

believer realises that it belongs to the perfection of being to bring forth what is of the same kind as itself; that the highest form of blessedness (which presupposes absolute goodness and selflessness), requires the highest form of self-communication within a perfect communitarian love; yet he also realises that, since God can be only the highest simplicity, a multiplication of his being cannot come into question, and that therefore the otherness of the Person must be compatible with the unity of the actual nature of God; finally, he realises that the plurality of the Persons can come only from a highest originality (*primitas*) of absolute fecundity (*fecunditas*).[118] The old Platonic axiom *bonum diffusivum sui* now in the light of Christian revelation no longer refers simply to God's relationship with the world but to his absolute being itself: and this opens the way for an explanation of the structure that belongs to the natural kinds in the world, makes it possible to trace them back to their origin without absorbing them monistically into the rays of the light that is their source. But in his thought the believer does not only follow the principle that the highest possible must be thought of God; he is also guided by the multiple reference of the relationships of expression among creatures, which all point to an absolute relationship of expression: '*Omnis creatura clamat generationem aeternam*, every creature proclaims the eternal process of generation, and this is expressed and represented by the twelve *generationes* that we find in the creatures.' Four means of radiation: illumination from light, warmth from fire, flowing from a spring, rain and dew from a cloud. But the ray of light is weaker than the source of light, the warmth is not an inmost part of the fire, the river departs in time from the spring, and only a part of its contents drips from the cloud. Four means of expression: the image of a figure is an expression of the object, the picture of the matrix, the word of the speaker, the concept an expression of the thinking spirit. But the image which appears is not the thing itself, the picture is extended in space, the

explicitly in the late period: *fides . . . dictat, de Deo esse sentiendum altissime et piissime* [faith . . . dictates that one should think about God in the highest and most devout manner], *Brevil.* 1, 2 (V 211a), developed in *Hex.* 9, 23f. (V 375b–376b); 11, 5f. (V 381b).
[118] 1 d2 q2 *fund.* 1–4 (I 53).

word is fragmented, the concept is contingent and does not give expression to the whole of the reason. Four means of reproduction: the seed of a plant produces the shoot, the root produces the tree, the mother's womb produces the child, the father's seed produces his descendant. The first, however, lacks a clear form, the second lacks equality of the form, the third is mainly passive, and the fourth lacks simultaneity. But all twelve express something (each in its own deficient way) that must include the fullness of the relationship of expression, in an inaccessible point of origin beyond this world.[119]

However, these twelve forms of expression may be reduced in number. The first four deal with the elements, at a stage before organic life. Among the second four, the concept and the picture have a pre-eminence: the concept, as an inner word which is amplified in the outward word, and the picture, to which the type of knowledge that comes from the object may be related back. In the last four, which deal with organic reproduction, everything can be reduced to the perfect natural begetting, fatherhood. So we have left, as decisive hints: word, image and Son. 'Now the word is nothing other than an explicit likeness which finds expression (*similitudo expressa et expressiva*), brought forth (or conceived through fertilisation = *concepta*) in the power of the rational spirit, when it contemplates and reflects on itself or something else. So it is clear that the content of the word "word", in addition to the contents of the words "being known", "generation" and "image", presupposes a "being known" in the intuition of the rational spirit, "generation" in the inner conception, and "image" in the resemblance which is in agreement on all sides: but the content "word" adds to all of this the content of the word "expression" (*superaddit intellectum expressionis*).' 'Being known' (*notitia*) is not applicable to the relationship of expression in the Trinity, because that is an absolute characteristic of God; so we are left with 'Son' for the generation, 'image' for the express correspondence with the one who proceeds forth, and finally 'Word', which contains all this in itself and, in addition, brings in the concepts of expression and revelation.[120]

---

[119] *Hex.* 11, 13–20 (V 382a–383a).   [120] I d27 II q4 (I 487–488).

It will be helpful here, before we go further, to look at the terminology used. *Expressivus* is frequently placed in contrast to *expressus*: *expressus* corresponds roughly to the German word '*ausdrücklich*' in the sense of 'precise', exact in reproduction, while *expressivus* corresponds to the German '*ausdrückend*', in which all the weight is placed upon the relationship of expression itself.[121] *Expressio* (expression) can be understood both in an active sense, as 'process of expressing' or as an 'original' (*exemplar*) that expresses itself, and in a passive sense, as the copy image which results from this.[122] But it is typical of Bonaventure that the exactness termed *expressus* is always understood and explained (so to speak) in the shadow of the expressive relationship, never *vice versa*: in other words, Bonaventure's concept of beauty (even when considered as 'exactness', as *aequalitas numerosa*) is always deployed in the framework of an ontology of expression (considered as the fecundity, self-abandon, love of being itself). So the copy or image is bound inwardly to the original: 'Where there is an image, there is imitation' (deriving *imago* from *imitago*).[123]

However, because only one substance can exist in God, the image which expresses him must be an 'absolute expression' (*expressio in summo*): this necessarily implies the uniqueness of this total expression.[124] In the world of creatures, the concept of (inner) 'word' comes closest to this, because in it the concept of image is most distinct, and at the same time mention is made of what proceeds naturally from the spirit in the act of knowing: 'Among all creatures, there is expression most of all in the "image", and likewise the pictorial relationship of expression is the most expressive of all; but the relationship of expression which resembles the eternal Word can only be the proceeding of the word from the spirit, and this then is the most expressive (*expressissima*), and it is applied in the appropriate way to God.'[125] If the Son from this point of view is *imitatio et similitudo*

[121] *Hex.* 12, 3 (V 385a).
[122] 1 d31 II, 1 q21 (I 540aᵃ). *Imago* thereby essentially is a copy, and it is an abuse of language to use it of the original (*ibid.* ab).
[123] *Ibid. fund. 4.*
[124] 1 d31 II, 1 q2 c (I 542a).
[125] 1 d27 II q4 *fund.* 1 (489a).

pura non permixta alicui dissimilitudini,[126] in which the being of the truth originally consists, it is likewise true, on the other hand, that this self-expression of God may not depend on his own free whim but must be rooted in his very nature as Spirit: 'The fecundity which belongs to the nature of the Father is necessarily the ground of his sharing his nature with the Other . . . but this necessity does not contradict his free will.'[127] In the generation of the Son God's freedom concurs with his nature, while in the spiration of the Holy Spirit the nature of God concurs with his freedom; if in the case of the Son the freedom did not concur with the divine nature, then the spiritual analogies from the world would have no value, but only the natural analogies (and even the natural procreations are works of eros!); and the basis of the principle *bonum diffusivum sui*, or the requirement to think the highest of the self-emanation of God, would remain unfulfilled. The generation of the Son takes place *per modum naturae, nihilominus ut dilectus*;[128] this is decisive for every aspect of theological ontology, and we must hold fast to it. The likeness of the *Verbum* needs here to be expanded by the likeness of the *Filius*, if it is not to be explained in a purely intellectual and logical way.

Originating being (*primitas*) and the fullness from which a spring flows (*fontalis plenitudo*) is the property not simply of the being of God, but rather of the Father as Father.[129] This fundamental spring of the Godhead is so powerful and free in its essence that it is able to reproduce itself out of its whole essence,

---

[126] [a pure imitation and likeness, not mixed with any unlikeness], 1 d8 I, 1 q1 c (I 151b).

[127] 1 d6 q1 *ad* 4 *et* c (I 126b,a).

[128] [the good is diffusive of itself] . . . [through nature's means, nevertheless as the beloved Son], *ibid.* q2 (I 128a).

[129] 1 d2 q2 c (I 54a); 1 d7 q1: *non tantum est essentiale appropriatum per additionem, immo etiam dicit proprium personae* [that which is of the essence is not merely appropriated through an *addition*, rather it is the name of something that *belongs* to the person] (I 136a); *cf. ibid.* q2 (I 139b); 1 d19 I q2 *sol.* 3: *emanatio personae non attenditur secundum rationem bonitatis essentiae, sed magis fecunditatis personae* [when the emanation of the Person is spoken of, this is not to be understood as caused by the essential *goodness*, but more as caused by the *fecundity* of the Person] (I 345b). On the *fontalis plenitudo Patris*: I d27 I q2 (esp. I 470b–471a).

'and only one whose essence can be one and entire in many can do this. Were this not possible for him, it would mean that if the begetter gave his entire essence to the one whom he begat, his whole essence would pass over to the one begotten, and he would necessarily lose his entire essence through the act of generation—but this is impossible. Therefore such a being must be able to be one and entire in many. Further, such a being must be simple in the highest degree, as only the divine being can be; in this essence of the highest simplicity, the one who is subject of the essence is no addition to it, and thereby neither limits nor restricts it, nor multiplies the form.'[130] As far as the Son is concerned, two things characterise this total gift of the divine nature: first, that in him the whole God is expressed, or (put in other words) that he is *God as he is in being expressed*, and thereby is the unsurpassable 'resemblance', 'assimilation', 'correspondence' and so 'truth';[131] second, that the one who proceeds is the one with the manner of the proceeding: 'There are two manners of proceeding, in accordance with the will and generosity (*liberalitas*): the first is the coming forth in the manner of generosity of that which itself is not generosity, but is born or given by generosity—it is in this way that the creatures proceed from God; then second the essential generosity (*ratio liberalitatis*) itself proceeds in this way from love—and it is in this way that the Holy Spirit goes forth as love, he who is the gift in which all other gifts are given. In the same way, there is a double procession in the manner of exemplification (*exemplaritas*): first, that in which what is properly speaking a copy is produced—it is in this way that the creature proceeds from God, as the copied image from the original (and thus the original is the formal cause of the copy); second, that in which that which proceeds in the manner of exemplification goes forth as essential archetypal originality (*ratio exemplandi*)—it is in this way that the Son, who

[130] 1 d9 q1 (I 181ab).
[131] *assimilatio ... secundum rationem exprimendi* [an assimilation ... in accordance with the proper manner of expression], 1 d39, 1 q1 *ad* 4 (1 686b); *expressio luminis non permixta obscuritati* [the manifestation of light, not mixed with any darkness], 1 d8 I, 1 q1 (I 151b); *aequalitas* (as *quantitas virtutis*) [equality as the quantity of virtue], 1 d19 I q1 (I 343a). *Haec similitudo sive Verbum est veritas* [this likeness or Word is the truth], *Hex*. 3, 8 (V 344b).

is named the Word of the Father, appears to go forth.'[132] If this is
said with a view to the creation, nevertheless it is true first of all
in the inner life of God, and this is confirmed by the statement
that the Son, by being the expression of the Father, is at the same
time *the* expression universally, *i.e.*, the expression of everything: 'The Word expresses the Father as the primal cause which
essentially underlies things, and in this way explains and
represents the generation of the Holy Spirit and its own
generation and the generation of the foundations of the earth.'[133]
And if witness is given in heaven from the three, Father, Son and
Spirit, 'this witness is expressed only by the Word, for the Word
gives expression to the Father and to itself and to the Holy
Spirit, and to everything else'.[134] The Son is therefore not only
the archetype, of which images are made in the world: he is God
as expression, that is, as truth, and therefore he is the principle of
the fact that the things in creation have been expressed and of the
fact that they express themselves as created essences: *'ratio
exprimendi est ipsius exemplaris*: the fact of being an expression
(which belongs to the creature) comes from the original. . . . All
things are true and have the capacity to express themselves by
virtue of the power of expression of that highest light', *i.e.*, of
the Word.[135]

As expression in God, the Son is a unifying centre between
Father and Spirit:[136] he gives expression both to his having been
begotten by the Father and to the Father's and his own spiration
of the Spirit. He is thereby the expression of an endless and
absolute event of love, and to that extent (precisely *as* expression) the Son himself journeys out of himself into the love
itself. Of this love, one can only say dialectically that it is both
expressed in the Son and taken up into the expression—but, at
the same time, it surpasses the sphere of expression of the Logos,
because the divine process finds its perfected end, not in the Son,
but in the Spirit. This dialectic runs through Bonaventure's
whole system, for while on the one hand he describes the Word

[132] 1 d6 q3 (I 129b).
[133] *Hex.* 3, 7 (V 344ab).
[134] *Hex.* 9, 2 (V 372b–373a).
[135] 1 d8 I, 1 q1 *ad* 4, 7 (I 151b).
[136] *Hex.* I, 12 (V 331ab).

from many points of view as the centre of all things, at the same
time he describes him as the centre which leads back to the
Father (and that means in the spiration of the Spirit), and which
surpasses itself, as this happens in love in the form of *affectus*,
excessus and *unio* in the silence of the understanding and indeed
in the turning-aside of the spiritual gaze (*amovendi sunt oculi
spirituales*).[137]

It is quite essential that we keep this in mind when
Bonaventure describes the position of the Son within the
Godhead not only as the place of truth but as the place of beauty.
But in order to make the whole meaning of this statement clear,
we must first discuss the position of the Son as archetype of the
world.

2. When he speaks of the relationship between the Trinity
and the creation of the world, Bonaventure clearly distances
himself from Augustine, in favour of the view of the Greek
fathers.[138] God behaves externally as he is, *i.e.*, as a trinitarian
being: therefore, though all his actions in the dispensation of
salvation are common to the Trinity, each expresses the individual position of the Persons; the positions of the Son as
expression of God and of the Spirit as the self-giving of God are
preserved externally just as much as in the inner life of the
Trinity. To speak of appropriation means therefore to indicate
the *propria* of the Persons, when we speak of these basic
articulations of God's communication of himself.[139] This means
nothing less than the grounding of the act of creation in the act
of generation within the Godhead—and at this point, we can
understand the whole influence of Bonaventure on German
mysticism.[140] To base the creation in the Trinity in this way
avoids both the danger of subordinationism which is found in
the early Greek Fathers, because every appearance of locating
the purpose of the generation of the Son in creation is avoided,
and likewise the danger of an absorption of the natural order in

[137] [the eyes of the spirit are to be turned away], *Hex.* 2, 32 (V 342a).
[138] A. Stohr, *Trinitätslehre, loc. cit.* 34 and frequently; A. Gerken, *loc. cit.*,
passim.
[139] *Cf., e.g.*, 1 d31 II, 2 q3 (esp. *ad* 7) (I 348–349).
[140] Kurt Ruh, *Bonaventura deutsch* (Berne, 1956).

the supernatural, because the natural order and the reason are unreservedly granted their relative independence.

However, in the generation of the Son, God (the Father) expresses himself uniquely and definitively—he expresses himself, and thereby his whole power and his whole capacity: *dixit similitudinem suam, et per consequens expressit omnia quae potuit;*[141] 'he gave utterance to his whole capacity: to what he was able to do and especially to what he wished to do. And all this he expressed in his Son, in the medium which is at the same time his art-form (*ars*).'[142] Art [*Kunst*] comes from capacity [*Können*], and therefore *ars* here speaks also of the artistic intelligence. But the Son would not be God, if he were not the realisation of the *entire* capacity of the Father and therefore a realisation that surpasses everything that is realised in the world of creatures. At this point Bonaventure applies the Anselmian formula, *Necesse est ut haec diffusio secundum totum posse sit in aliquo, quo majus cogitari non potest.*[143] If, therefore, the Father bestows the Son upon the world, 'then he gives it along with him (the Son) everything that he was, everything that he possessed, everything that he could'.[144] To the Father's capacity belongs everything real, everything possible; but the possible is utterly infinite, and in the power of God it is in fact infinite *actu*, and so it surpasses every created understanding, even that of Christ, *propter immensitatem et improportionalitatem.*[145] If the Father has really given expression in the Son to his whole being and capacity, then in the Son everything that is possible through God has taken on reality: if anything else outside God is realised through God, it can have possibility and reality only through the Son and in the Son. 'The divine truth expresses itself and

[141] [he has uttered his own likeness, and consequently he has given expression to all that he could], *Hex.* 1, 16 (V 332a).

[142] *Ibid.* 1, 13 (V 331b).

[143] [It is necessary that this total diffusion should be able to occur in something than which nothing greater can be thought of], *Hex.* 11, 11 (V 382a).

[144] S 1 *Vig. Nativ.* (IX 89a).

[145] [on account of the immensity (of God) and the greatness utterly out of proportion (to the smallness of man)], *De Sc. Chr.* 7, 10 (V 41b); 7, 14 (42a); 1c (5a); 1 d35 q5 *ad* 2 (I 612b).

everything else through the one unique highest expression.'[146]
The Son is *ars suprema*,[147] *ars Patris*:[148] thus he is the expression of
the entire divine capacity—*posse generare et posse creare est posse
unicum*.[149]

We come back, therefore, to what has already been said: the
Son is archetype, idea, exemplar of all things outside God, not
because he is first of all absolute content but because he is
absolute expression; Bonaventure never wearies of saying
this.[150] This is his sole reason for taking over the Platonic axiom
that the creatures 'are true, when they are as they are *in arte
aeterna*, or as they find expression there; but because they are not
perfectly matched to the idea which expresses or represents
them, every creature is a "lie", according to Augustine';[151] that 'I
shall see myself better in God than in myself',[152] that things are
more alive in God then in themselves.[153] The precise argument
runs as follows: *similitudo quae est ipsa veritas expressiva . . . melius
exprimit rem quam ipsa res seipsam, quia res ipsa accipit rationem
expressionis ab illa*.[154] Bonaventure subordinates his whole teaching on the *analogy of being* (which is very different from that of
Thomas) to this central proposition.

A *similitudo participationis* between God and creature 'is
entirely absent, because there is nothing in common. The
similitudo imitationis is quite slight (*modica*), for the finite can
imitate the infinite only in an insignificant way, so that the
dissimilarity always remains greater than the similarity: *semper
major est dissimilitudo quam similitudo*'.[155] What Bonaventure has

---

[146] 1 d39, 1 q1 *ad* 4 (I 686b).
[147] [the highest art], *De Sc. Chr.* 4 c (V 23b). On the theme of *ars* in general,
cf. 1 d1, 1 q1 *ad* 4 (1 31b); 2 d7 II, 2 q2 (II 202a); *Hex.* 5, 13 (V 356a).
[148] [the art of the Father], *De red. art.* 20 (V 324b).
[149] [to be able to beget and to be able to create is one and the same ability], 1
d7 q3 c (I 141b).
[150] *Cf.* text in the *Scholion*, I 603b–604a.
[151] *Hex.* 3, 8 (V 344b).
[152] *Hex.* 12, 9 (V 386a), Delorme 143.
[153] 1 d36, 2 q1 c (I 623–624).
[154] [the likeness which is the truth itself in its expressive power . . . better
expresses a thing than the thing expresses itself, for the thing itself receives the
power of expression from it (*i.e.*, from the likeness)], 1 d35 q1 *ad* 3 (I 602a).
[155] [the unlikeness is always greater than the likeness], *ibid. ad* 2 (I 601b).

to say about *proportionalitas* belongs here: unlike *proportio*, which is an analogous relationship between things of the same type (a:b = c:d), *proportionalitas* is a similar relationship between things which do not belong in the same common category and have nothing in common (*non communicantium*): *proportionalitas* 'posits no common character, for it compares only the relationship of two to two, and so it can exist, and does in fact exist, between things that are utterly different (*summe distantia*)'.[156] Over against this, we have the statement: *Similitudo vero expressionis est summa, quia causatur ab intentione veritatis . . . , quae est ipsa expressio.*[157] In contrast to the scarcely considered upwards-tending *analogia entis*, there is a very strong downwards-tending analogy: the eternal Word of expression knows better and says better what each thing wants to say than the thing itself knows.[158] And the creature receives its power to speak, to set it on its path, namely the *species*, which it emits from itself so that it may be grasped and understood in the sense-perception or intellect of another: but whereas the creature, through the resemblances which it causes itself, can give expression to nothing but itself, and even that only partially, 'the divine truth is able to give utterance to itself and to everything in one unique highest expression',[159] so that the self-utterance of a creature succeeds only when it is embraced by the self-utterance of the eternal light.[160] This is the archetype only

---

[156] 1 d48, 1 q1 (I 852b).

[157] [But the likeness of the expression is the highest, because it is caused by the intention of truth . . . which is itself expression], 1 d35 q1 *ad* 2 (I 601b). The concern of Karl Barth is here taken seriously and answered satisfactorily. The relation of the expression to what is expressed is fixed by the original. Bonaventure goes further in the direction of granting Barth's request when he distinguishes the creature's being-as-image *ex propria repraesentatione* [from its own character as a representation] from three other types of image, which are all given in the Biblical revelation: the prefigurations in prophecy, the taking on of an image by angels (*e.g.*, in the Angel of Yahweh), and the symbolic character granted in the act of institution, as in the sacraments, where in addition to the natural power of signifying a new relationship to what is signified is given from above: *Itin.* 2, 12 (V 303a). Revelation can raise all things to images (*facit figuras de omnibus*), *Hex.* 17, 20 (V 412b).

[158] *Cf.* n. 154.

[159] 1 d39, 1 q1 *ad* 4 (I 686b).

[160] 1 d8 I, 1 q1 *ad* 4. 7 (I 151b).

because of its being as light, only as *exprimens*, and as such it contains the *splendores exemplares*.[162] The *ratio radiandi* is the basis of the archetypical character, and the *species clarae*, the clear forms or concepts of light, lie in the power of expression, which in God is a spiritual power.[163] It will be clear at this point that Bonaventure's thought takes a middle path between Plato and Luther: his teaching on creatures contains a trinitarian doctrine of ideas which, if applied to christology (as he himself was later to do), supplies the ontological basis for the Lutheran doctrine of justification, including the idea of *justus et peccator*.

What is decisive here is that it is the one unique Word (*increatum–incarnatum*) who in himself is the sum of all the ideas of the world. He alone, as the total expression of God, gives expression in himself to all that can be created in its infinite multiplicity—and not only in general, but in the smallest particular details (*singulare*), in a *distinctissima expressio*,[164] 'just as the one unique light, for example, gives expression to many different colours'.[165] So 'he represents many things',[166] he is the Sophia of God, who bears in her womb the eternal thoughts of God;[167] 'from God's point of view only one thing corresponds to them—yet it has more power to represent many things than has any created plurality; nevertheless, although the truth is simple, it is infinite'.[168] It is as simple in relation to the many as God's creative power is simple in relation to the realisation of the many.[169] In himself, God possesses all things *sub omnimoda indifferentia reali*, but this does not prevent them from existing

---

[161] [giving expression], 1 d36, 2 q1 (I 624a).

[162] [exemplary splendours], *Hex.* 12, 14 (v 386b).

[163] *Ibid.* 12, 8 (V 385b).

[164] [most distinct expression], 1 d35 q2 *ad* 3 (I 606b); q4 c (I 610a); *De Sc. Chr.* 2 (V 9): *lucidissime, expressissime, distinctissime, integerrime* [most clearly, most explicitly, most distinctly, most wholly].

[165] 1 d35 q2 *ad* 2 (I 606b).

[166] *Hex.* 3, 4 (V 343b).

[167] *Ibid.* 20, 5 (V 426a); *Brevil.* 8 (V 216–217).

[168] *De sc. Chr.* 3, 17 (V, 16a).

[169] *Ibid.* 3 c (V 13b). It is therefore superfluous to ask whether the things are represented in the idea according to their differences, or only according to what they have in common; an answer is to be found in the superiority of the divine power of expression to every *genus* (*ibid. obj.* 13 and the reply).

outside God *sub differentia multiplici*.[170] For just as the three Persons in God are not in any genuine sense numerable (since the unity does not multiply itself but in each case is related to a hypostasis), so there is no number among the ideas, for the idea is only single, even if it is multiple through its relationship to the various things that may be expressed.[171] This teaching grounds finite being in God's will to expression, in a double way: first, in as much as the archetype in God is itself an expression, and second in so far as the individual being is the goal of a particular intention of expression on God's part, *expressissime* and *distinctissime* chosen to be as it is, and addressed by God with this intention. Thereby it is the destination of a particular act of God's condescension, of a particular form of speech of the eternal Word.

Everything created is therefore based in the generation of the Logos: 'God would never have been able to bring forth a creature on account of his will, if he had not brought forth the Son on account of his nature.'[172] 'Every procession is either a begetting or a consequence of this begetting.'[173] 'In the procession of the Word everything is said, in the procession of the Gift (the Holy Spirit) every other gift is given.'[174] 'If there is such a thing as the begetting of something dissimilar, it presupposes conceptually the begetting of what is similar. This may be proved as follows: the like is related to the unlike as the same is related to the different, the one to the many; but the same necessarily precedes the different, and the one necessarily precedes the many.... Accordingly, what is different does not proceed from the eternal substance until that which is the same is begotten.'[175]

Now we may anticipate somewhat and speak about the particular *association of beauty with the Son*, which Bonaventure treats as something wholly taken for granted; and we are aware that 'appropriation' means more in his writings than it does in Augustine and normally in modern theology. Peter Lombard,

---

[170] [in a general, real lack of diversity] . . . [in a multiple diversity], *ibid.* q3 *ad* 10 (V 15b).

[171] *Ibid. ad* 8 (V 15a).   [172] 1 d7 *dub.* 2 (I 144b).

[173] 1 d28 q4 c (I 503a).   [174] *Itin.* 6, 2 (V 311a).

[175] *Hex.* 11, 9 (V 381b).

who serves Bonaventure as a basis for his theology, had already
made the equation: 'The most perfect beauty (*pulchritudo*) is the
Son, that is, the truth of the Father, which never in any way
departs from him ... and which is the model (*forma*) of all
things.'[176] Later, Lombard takes over from Hilary[177] the
appropriation of *aeternitas* to the Father, of *species* to the image
(*i.e.*, the Son), and *usus* to the Spirit, and here the Master of the
Sentences interprets the word *species*, which is predicated of the
Son, in the sense of beauty, because between Son and Father
'there reigns the highest mutual concord and chiefest similarity
and chiefest resemblance, deviating in no point, dissimilar in no
point, unlike in no point, but responding in identity to him
whose image he is'.[178] Thus Bonaventure can rewrite the text
from Hilary forthwith as *aeternitas–formositas–jucunditas*;[179] the
statement of the Book of Wisdom leads him quite simply to
this, when it is said of the Wisdom of God that she is *candor lucis
aeternae et speculum sine macula*, she is *speciosior sole* (7:25ff.). He
comments: 'Where there is a mirror and an image and
brightness, there is necessarily also a representation
(*repraesentatio*) and beauty (*pulchritudo*)', and to this he adds at
once one of the Augustinian definitions of beauty: ' *"pulchritudo
nihil aliud est quam aequalitas numerosa"*; *ibi autem sunt rationes
numerosae ad unum reductae.*'[180] Ascending from the world, where
beauty consists (in Augustinian terms) in harmony and pro-

---

[176] Peter Lombard, 1 *Sent*. d 3 *pars* 1 *cap*. 1 (=I 63a). Lombard's model here
is Augustine's *De vera religione* c. 55 n. 113, where, however, only *forma*, not
pulchritudo, is used when speaking of the Son.

[177] *De Trin*. II n. 1, conclusion.

[178] Lombard, 1 d31 *pars* II *cap*. 2 (=I 530a).

[179] [eternity–beauty–joyfulness], *Hex*. 21, 11 (V 433a).

[180] ['beauty is nothing other than equality in number'; and there the
numerous causes are reduced to one], *Hex*. 6, 7 (V 361b–362a); *cf. De tripl. via*
7: *altitudo, pulchritudo, dulcedo. . . . Pulchritudo (attribuitur) Filio propter veritatem
et sapientiam. Nam sapientia multitudinem idearum, veritas autem aequalitatem
includit, 'pulchritudo autem nihil aliud est quam aequalitas numerosa'* [majesty,
beauty, sweetness. . . . Beauty (is attributed) to the Son because of truth and
wisdom. For wisdom includes the multitude of the ideas, while truth includes
equality (of number), and 'beauty is nothing other than equality in number']
(VIII 17b). Other passages on wisdom which make the same attribution: S *de
Trin*. (IX 352b); *cf. S theol*. 2, 14 (V 542b).

portion, one arrives by a process of reduction at unity—but not an empty unity, rather an absolute *aequalitas* in the Godhead between archetype and image, which, together with the absolute truth as correspondence (*respondens*), is the basis of absolute beauty.

Bonaventure sets this forth in a classical passage,[181] in which he shifts the weight from the concept of harmony to the initially less unambiguous concept of *species*. This has indeed a threefold meaning—the senses of the word seem at first sight to be united more by the word itself than by any conceptual unity: first, expressive image (in the sense of *eidos*, reproduced in Latin by *similitudo*), second, an image which imparts knowledge (as the object emits knowledge and imprints it on the subject's capacity to know: *species ex-* and *impressa*), finally, simply beauty, as indicated by the adjective *speciosus*. Clearly, the basis of this last meaning must lie in the two other meanings,[182] the first of which speaks of the (passive) character of the expression of an archetype, the second of which adds the idea of the (active) act of expressive mediation of this archetype as it expresses itself to the knowing subject. This, precisely, is the position of the Word in God: he gives expression to the Father who is the archetype, and himself becomes an expressive archetype in relation to the world, precisely in so far as he gives perfect expression to the paternal archetype. The Son is the perfect image of the Father, because he proceeds *per modum naturae*, 'for the divine nature begets what resembles it and is like it. Since, however, he possesses the content of the expressive likeness, he possesses likewise the content of knowledge, for the likeness which is expressed is the basis of knowledge. And since he is in himself the idea and source-idea (*ratio et exemplar*) of all things, in that he is in fullness the idea of similarity and knowledge, he realises in himself also the content of perfect beauty. For since he is the perfect and expressive form of resemblance, he is beautiful in comparison with him whom he expresses. And since he

---

[181] I d31 II, 2 q3 (I 543–545).

[182] Neither takes account of a further meaning of *species*, that of *forma totius* (*species* is then the opposite concept to *genus* and to *individuum*): precisely from this point of view, the term *species cannot* be applied to the God-man as such: 3 d2, 2 q3 (III 48b).

possesses the content of knowledge, and that not of some one single thing but of the entirety of all that is, 'he bears the beautiful world spiritually in himself, as the beautiful one' (Boethius), and he possesses beauty in relation to all beauty that is his image. These two relationships, taken together, result in the most perfect beauty: that particular kind of *speciositas* which springs from both.

We must add that the beauty of the image is twofold: 'An image is called beautiful if it is well painted, but it is also called beautiful when it perfectly represents the beauty of that which it copies.' In the first sense, 'an image of the devil is beautiful if it perfectly represents his ugliness', *i.e.*, if it exactly copies the original; in the second sense, we have also the luminosity, *i.e.*, the original makes itself clear and expresses itself in the copy itself. *Pulchritudo ita refertur ad prototypum, quod nihilominus est in imagine pulchritudo*: this becomes clear when, beyond the mere *aequalitas numerosa*, the purely formal correspondence between the two, the relationship of expression is added as the fundamental principle: as the principle which makes itself clear (from the Father to the Son) and which makes itself an expression (from the Son to the Father).[183] For here we have passed beyond the relationship of nature and spirit that is found in the world: here we are speaking of the nature of God's Spirit, where the personal relationships each imply both (with different emphases in the cases of the Son and of the Holy Spirit). Only so can it be understood why the Son, precisely as copied image, stands over against the world as archetype, that is, *species* that mediates knowledge: because as Son he wishes to be nothing else than the image of the Father, he transmits this image (as copy and as archetype) and thereby lays the foundation for every creaturely attitude before God. Such attitudes can be true and beautiful only in so far as they copy the attitude of the Son to the Father.[184]

3. On this view the Word of God, as total expression of God, is the 'archetypical world' in three respects: first, because,

---

[183] I d31 II, 2 q3 (I 544ab).

[184] On the reference back to the Father through the Son as a medium of knowledge, which is sent out (expressed) from the object, *cf. De red. art.* 8 (V 322a).

considered in relationship to the origin, he expresses this perfectly; second, because he serves the origin as a medium of expression (as the inward concept serves the thinker); and third, because in the Incarnation he is expressed in outward form by the origin, without losing his immanence in the Spirit, as the idea of that which was intended in the creation.[185] This means that every creature, in the distance of its otherness, can be only a 'deficient' and therefore necessarily a multiple copy of the original identical form of the image in God himself. 'In the archetypical world, there is the highest beauty, on the grounds of the absolute unity; but if there were unity in the world perceived by the senses, there would be no beauty, because neither order nor perfection would reign. If this world is to imitate the other in perfection and beauty, it must be multiple, so that the multiplicity may achieve what the unity cannot do.'[186] This is true in the case of the angels, who can imitate the highest hierarchy of the Trinity only through a 'gradation of the dissimilar': 'In the highest hierarchy, the most perfect beauty can reign through sheer equality of form and sheer equality of relationship, because the universal and highest truth holds sway in each of the equally ranked Persons. But since in the hierarchy of the angels each of the spirits who are ranged in their orders does not possess as an individual the highest perfection, a certain harmony of order and beauty must be attained through an appropriate differentiation in a relative gradation: as far as creatures are concerned, this is the highest perfection possible. It is the same in the sphere of holiness within the Church: there is an order of the apostles, another of the martyrs, another of the confessors, and so on, and there exists no absolute equality among them, because it can be said of every single saint, "No one was his like in keeping the commandment of the Most High" (Sir 44:20). . . . Because of the limitation of the created being, order and beauty in the creaturely hierarchy must be joined to difference and indeed to oppositeness, so that what could not be obtained from unity may be derived at least from the multiplicity of many.'[187]

[185] 1 d27 II, q4 c (I 490a).
[186] 2 d1 II, 1 q1 *ad* 3 (II 40b).
[187] 2 d9 q8 c *et ad* 4 (II 255b–256b).

According to Augustine, this drawing near through distance has three stages: trace (*vestigium*), image (*imago*), and resemblance (*similitudo*). In the 'trace' the trinitarian mystery of origin expresses itself only in an objective manner; in the 'image' this happens expressly in the structure of the subject, which through the form of its being as a spirit enters the relationship to the trinitarian spirit of its origin; in the 'resemblance' the archetype dwells in the copied image through sanctifying grace.[188] 'Just as the creature cannot have God as its origin without being configured to him in accordance with unity, truth and goodness, so it cannot have God as the object of its knowledge without grasping him through memory, understanding and will; and in the same way, it cannot have God in itself as a gift poured into it without becoming like him through faith, hope and love.'[189] The distinction of the various stages derives, then, from the degree of intimacy of the 'representation' of God.[190] But it is only in the light of the 'resemblance' effected by faith, to which the trinitarian mystery will disclose itself, that the 'image' in the human spirit can understand itself as trinitarian; and it is only when this is realised that the real significance of the 'trace' in all things can be grasped. Besides this, the insight of faith permits each of the three stages to be interpreted in a double sense (corresponding to the double relationship of the image to the beautiful, discussed above): as a 'reference' to the archetype, and as a 'representation' (and to this extent a vessel) of the archetype. Thus, the *Itinerarium mentis in Deum* is divided into six stages: trace, image and resemblance each as a pointer and as representation (*per speculum—in speculo*). The pointer is in each case prior: the world is 'as a whole a mirror, through which we come to God . . . wandering over as true Hebrews from Egypt into the promised land',[191] and in this way one achieves a proper understanding of the pointer as a representation, and an understanding of the self-fulfilment of creaturely being as an immanent sign of the indwelling of its origin in it.[192] The sequence is determinative of this theological aesthetic: the immanent beauty of the things of the world is visible in itself

[188] *De sc. Chr.* 4 (V 24a).   [189] *Brevil.* 2, 12 (V 230ab).
[190] 1 d3 I q2 (I 73ab).   [191] *Itin.* 1, 9 (V 298ab).
[192] *Itin.* 2, 1f. (V 299b f.).

only when the transient pointer to the archetypical beauty is understood and ratified. But in this, the pointer itself must of necessity be named beauty, because the creature can refer to its archetype only through itself. 'Anyone who is not illuminated by so much glory in created things is blind; anyone who does not awake amid such loud cries is deaf; anyone who does not praise God for such numerous works is dumb; anyone who does not sense the first origin from so many hints is stupid.'[193]

In contrast to the 'trace', the *imago* in man is an *assimilatio expressa* and *de proximo* to God:[194] in it, the objective self-expression of God returns subjectively to him—for in as much as the created spirit wakes up to itself, it must of necessity turn to its origin. When it becomes inwardly an illuminated being, its source and its goal must become clear to it. It is *capax Dei*,[195] and therefore *informabilis* by God;[196] it 'has the most excellent of all capabilities of conceiving the capacity to be united (*unibilitas*) with God'.[197] 'And for this reason it bears in itself from its origin the light of the divine countenance', and this precisely 'in what concerns the origin, order and distinction of its inner abilities, in which it resembles that distinction and interrelation which, in the divine Persons, belongs inwardly to God's nature'.[198] It is obvious that here lies the central point of Bonaventure's spirituality and of his aesthetic alike: the spirit of man can find self-fulfilment only in faith, for it is only in faith that he understands himself as the expression of the triune life, and it is only in the explicit turning (per *speculum*) to the trinitarian image that is above him that the image of the eternal God in him (in *speculo*) is truly illuminated. In as much as man is oriented towards the proper image that is in God, he is tending towards the image (*ad imaginem*), 'whereas the Son, in his whole being, *is* the image of the Father, and therefore *solum est Imago, non ad*

---

[193] *Itin.* 1, 15 (V 299b).

[194] [explicit assimilation from close at hand], 2 d16,1 q1 (II 394b–395a).

[195] [having a capacity for God], 1 d3 I q1 (I 69a); *Brevil.* 7, 1 (V 281a); 7, 7 (V 289b); *Itin.* 3, 3 (V 304a). *Tantae capacitatis es, ut nulla creatura infra Deum sufficit satiare tuum desiderium* [so great is your capacity that no creature lower than God suffices to satisfy your longing], *Solil.* 1, 6 (VIII 31b); *S theol.* 4 (V 571b).

[196] [able to be informed], *De Don. Sp. Sti.* 1, 5 (V 458a).

[197] *S* 2 *de Nativ.* (IX 110a).

[198] *Cf.* n. 194 and, on this point, the *Scholion* (II 396).

imaginem.[199] The orientation of man's being as image, for which
God is the *objectum motivum*,[200] the *ratio movens*,[201] means that
God is not only the transcendental object which is the goal of the
created spirit, but is also the object at the source, *objectum
fontanum*,[202] as Bonaventure puts it (using a magnificent formula
instead of the pale *objectum formale*), the *fontale principium illumi-
nationis cognitivae*.[203] The more the spirit actuates itself, therefore, the more immanent will it be in God, and God in it. With
Augustine, a distinction may be made between an *imago* which
shines more in transcendence (*memoria–intellectus–voluntas*) and
an *imago* which shines more in the spirit's act of grasping itself
(*mens–notitia–amor*):[204] but in so far as the second is actually
realised, it is once again only the relationship to God that
becomes a reality: 'Because the soul is the image of God, and
because whatever turns to the image and is configured to it turns
likewise to what is portrayed, the soul which reflects on itself
does not separate itself from the likeness of form.'[205] 'And so the
reality of the image is from one point of view to be found more
in the turning of the soul to God, and from another point of
view more in the turning of the soul to itself. It lies more in the
turning to God, because therein lies more beauty (*venustas*) and
resemblance; but in the turning to itself lies more similarity of
being and likeness'[206]—in so far as the single divine substance of
the three Persons is more visible in the self-realisation of the
human spirit in its three capacities. It is clear that here reflection
on itself is not meant purely theoretically, or even egotistically,
but rather as the self-understanding of the being that is man,

---

[199] [he is only the Image, he is not tending to the image], 2 d16 *dub.* 3 (II 407b).
[200] [motivating object], *S theol.* 4, 16 (V 571b).
[201] [moving cause], *De sc. Chr.* 4 (V 24a); *ratio motiva* (*ibid.* 23b).
[202] *Hex.* 5, 33 (V 359b).
[203] [principle from which springs forth the illumination that gives knowl-
edge], *S theol.* 4, 1 (V 567a).
[204] 1 d3 II, 2 q1 c: *praecedens fuit per conversionem animae ad Deum, haec est per
conversionem animae supra se* [that which has happened came through the
conversion of the soul to God, *i.e.* through the conversion of the soul above
itself] (I 89b).
[205] 1 d3 II, 1 q2 c (I 83b).
[206] *Ibid. ad* 5 (I 84b).

who does not exist in any way other than in this positing of self. Accordingly, although the image in man is 'substantially' prescribed in advance, and to this extent cannot be lost, nevertheless it can be lost in as much as it must be actualised intellectually,[207] for this actualisation can fail to occur.

Out of this dialectic in the created spirit between the progressive entering into itself and the progressive orientation towards God emerges the conclusion that the existential realisation of the self goes along with the existential polarity between copy and archetype. For this archetype, as the reality of the three Persons, is the highest reality that can present itself to the intellect—it is not in the least a mere 'idea' or 'conceptual realm'. The relation between archetype (the divine Word, as expression of the life of God in his wholeness) and copy is no formal relationship, but a profoundly personal relationship, and in Bonaventure this is even more unequivocal than in Augustine. The realisation by the created spirit of this relationship of persons (which is always real on God's part) in faith, prayer and contemplation is called by Bonaventure *regressus, reductio*, and *resolutio*; this is for him the fundamental act of a thinking and being that is worthy of man.

'If a ray of light strikes a polished object, it must be reflected back along the same path.'[208] 'The ray of understanding must be sent back (*reflectendus*) through meditation, so that it may return to the source of all good.'[209] Things are not simply set forth from God at creation: rather, they exist in a continuous emanation from him, and therefore it is required that they flow back,[210] in a 'pious act of pouring themselves back into their origin'.[211] It is, however, only with the help of the grace of the absolute Spirit that the *plena resolutio* succeeds,[212] while that of philosophy can

[207] 1 d3 II *dub.* 1 (I 93a).
[208] *De Don. Sp. Sti.* 1, 9 (V 459a).
[209] *De tripl. via* 2, 14 (VIII 6b).
[210] *Hex.* 21, 18: *continuatio–reductio* [continuation–reduction] (V 434a); *De Don. Sp. Sti* 1, 10: *reversio–conjunctio* [reversion–conjunction] (V 459a).
[211] *Creatura rationalis . . . non est pia, nisi refundat se super originem suam* [a rational creature . . . is not loving (to its creator) unless it pours itself back upon its origin], *De Don. Sp. Sti.* 3, 5 (V 469a).
[212] *Itin.* 3, 3 (V 304a).

succeed only *semiplene*.[213] For it is only in so far as the archetype freely discloses itself in the copy, and is recognised and acknowledged there as the 'inner teacher', that the impulse towards absoluteness in all intellectual knowing and striving will be correctly understood, and taken as the goal. The spirit necessarily comes into contact with this impulse, for the spirit is configured to the *rationes aeternae*.[214] And it is only when these become clear to it that it receives any definitive illumination. 'Christ is the inner teacher, and it is only through him that the truth is known: not through outward speech as with us, but through inner illumination. He is in the innermost part of every soul, and shines with his wholly bright concepts (*species*) over the dim concepts of our understanding.'[215] The sermon 'Christ is the one teacher of all' develops these thoughts in all their aspects.[216] All human theology is only the servant of the teaching of the unique Theologian, and, in accordance with this teacher, all the teachers of Christendom must strive after love, and so must agree in their opinions.[217]

The idea of the presence of the one teacher in all hearts, the idea of the one *Verbum increatum-incarnatum* that dwells in all spirits, known or unknown—this is ancient Alexandrian tradition. God is present to the soul in a much more intimate manner than the soul supposes, and therefore she has a necessary knowledge of him which does not rest simply on abstraction: 'Through the truth, God is present to the soul and to every understanding, and therefore it is not necessary to fashion an abstract concept of him in order that he may be known. Nevertheless, the reason that knows him receives the form of an image of knowledge (*notitia*), which is a kind of likeness—but this is not an abstraction, but something imprinted (*impressa*).'[218]

---

[213] *Hex.* 11, 10 (V 381b).

[214] [eternal causes]. *Inquantum est imago Dei . . . aeternas rationes attingit* [in as much as it is the image of God . . . it attains to the eternal causes], *De sc. Chr.* 4 (V 24a). *Portio illa, in qua est imago Dei, quae et aeternis regulis inhaerescit* [that portion in which is the image of God, which clings to the eternal rules] (*ibid.*).

[215] *Hex.* 12, 5 (V 385a).

[216] *S theol.* 4 (V 567–574).

[217] *Ibid.* 4, 24–26 (V 573b).

[218] 1 d3 I q1 *ad* 5 (I 70a).

For God is 'ever present in the spirit of man',[219] 'even if there are few who are willing to believe this, since it seems scarcely credible to the spirit that has not yet risen up to the contemplation of the things of eternity that it has God so present and so near'.[220] God is presence and reality in an absolute sense: *praesentissimum, actualissimum*.[221] Accordingly, 'the blindness of the understanding is a source of the greatest wonder. It does not notice what it sees first of all, it does not notice that without which it can know nothing. But just as the eye which attends to the difference of the colours does not see the light which permits it to see everything else, or does not notice it if it does see it, so it is with the eye of our spirit . . . it looks at the light of the highest being, but imagines that it sees nothing, and does not understand that it is precisely the darkness that is the highest illumination of our spirit.'[222] In reality, this light is inaccessible to the grasp: *lux est inaccessibilis, et tamen proxima animae, etiam plus quam ipsa sibi. Est etiam inalligabilis, et tamen summe intima.* But only the man who soars up in the highest vision can comprehend this.[223] Bonaventure is not in any sense an ontologist: here below God is not seen face to face, he is not seen openly, he is not seen without images presented to the senses.[224] On the other hand, God is active in every act of intellectual knowing, not merely as *principium et causa*, but as *objectum et ratio motiva*,[225] and we cannot interpret this (with Gilson) in the sense of a purely unknown medium of knowledge which is not objective. It has been said above that the light is not observed by the eye that is absorbed in the things; is it then not seen anywhere? 'The cause is luminous (*relucet*) in the effect, and the wisdom of the artist is revealed (*manifestatur*) in the work: so God, who is the artist and the cause of the creature, is known through the creature.'[226] The one who interprets the image is

[219] *De sc. Chr.* 4, 13 (V 25b).
[220] *Ibid.* 4, 19 (V 26a).
[221] [most present, most active], *Itin.* 5, 7 (V 309b).
[222] *Ibid.* 5, 4 (V 309a); 1 d1, 3 q2 (I 41a); *De sc. Chr.* 4, 31 (V 20b).
[223] *Hex.* 12, 11 (V 386a), Delorme 143.
[224] *S theol.* 4, 18 (V 572a).
[225] [principle and reason . . . object and moving cause], *ibid.* 4, 17 (V 571b).
[226] 1 d3 I q2 (I 72a).

drawn to what is portrayed by the image as it points beyond itself,[227] especially in the special case where what is objectively intended coincides with what first arouses the process of knowing, and both aspects together (beyond the distinction of object and subject) flow from the *Objectum fontanum*.[228] Accordingly, we must speak (with Gerken) of an 'implicit awareness' of God as the 'transcendental' subject-object,[229] which does not exist only formlessly as the primal light, but also as 'having form', in as much as the eternal (and then incarnate) Word is the exemplar of all forms in the world, both as light and as form, as we have seen.[230] Naturally, 'he stands in your midst as one whom you do not know' (Jn 1:26),[231] but true knowledge can take no other path than that of the progressive clarification of the source-object, the path of the progressive rendering more transparent of the archetypical idea through all the copies. This process is the *reductio*, the theological transcendental reduction, the theological demonstration of the conditions of the possibility of all knowledge and striving. Whereas the researcher who confines his attention to earthly things attains the *rationes aeternae* only *ut moventes*, as presupposed functions, the wise man, whose soul has been purified for this purpose, attains them *ut quietantes*, in their act of shining which has its own finality in itself.[232] This,

[227] 1 d3 II, 1 q2 (I 83b).
[228] [object that is the source], *Hex.* 5, 33 (V 359b). To understand this concept aright, *cf.* 1 d1, 3 q2 *concl.* 2: *objectum intelligibile excellens* (in God) *juvat et confortat, quia influentia talis cognoscibilis procedit ab intimis et intrat ipsam potentiam* ... ; *cum sit intimum ipso intellectui, in ejus perceptione virtus non dispergitur sed colligitur, et quanto virtus est magis unita, tanto fortior* [the object that is intelligible and most noble (in God) gives joy and consolation, because the influence of such a knowable object proceeds from the inmost depths (of God) and enters the power (of knowing) itself ... because it belongs intimately to the intellect itself, in the act of perceiving the power (of the intellect) is not diffused but rather is gathered into a unity: and the greater the unity of the power, the greater is its strength], (I 39b).
[229] A. Gerken, *loc. cit.*, Part I, ch. 2 II, 2.
[230] *Cf.* n. 163.
[231] *Hex.* 1, 20 (V 332b).
[232] *De sc. Chr.* 4 *sol.* 2 (V 24b). The eternal light shines for the researcher and the philosopher indirectly even in the general principles of natural knowledge, in a certain universal validity which as such belongs to the structure of knowledge: *non sequitur quod ipsa sit nobis nota secundum se, sed prout relucet in suis*

however, does not change the fact that even the former can know what is contingent (and thereby defective) only on the basis of full being.[233] 'Thus, no one would know that one thing is better than another, unless he knew that it has a greater resemblance to what is best.'[234] 'Therefore God cannot be thought of as not existing, as Anselm proves.'[235]

If the *reductio* is our way to God, it is also God's way to us, for God himself does not wish to see us in any way other than that in which we are conceived in his perfect image, the Son, and through the Son's redemption and our acceptance as God's children we have found our way back to this. Our good works by themselves could not have procured this for us: God had first to come down to us, to give us sanctifying grace. 'First of all he must accept his image and his will, for this is the achievement which comes from man . . . for no one can make himself better than he is, or perform a work that pleases God, unless he himself beforehand is pleasing to God, and God looks with favour first on him, and only then on his works.'[236] Just as for us all things possess the beauty and goodness that is their own when they are illuminated and made transparent with reference to the idea, that is to the divine Word, so the world, for the Father who created it, possesses its full goodness and beauty only in the Son, and in so far as the Son embraces it in himself at its origin as *exemplar*, and as Bridegroom draws it back to himself in nuptial love: 'God is inwardly hidden in everything that is perceived by the senses or intellectually known. And the fruit of all learning is that through all the sciences the faith is edified, God is honoured, and right living is furthered—and that from this, those consolations may be drawn forth which lie in the uniting of Bridegroom and Bride, as this is accomplished through *Caritas*. This is the goal of all revelation.'[237]

principiis et in sua generalitate [it does not follow that it is known to us as it is in itself, but rather it shines forth in its principles and in its generality], *ibid. sol.* 16 (V 25b).

[233] *Itin.* 3, 3 (V 304a), 3, 4 (V 305a).

[234] *Ibid.* 3, 4 (V 304b).

[235] *Hex.* 5, 31 (V 359b); *Itin.* 5, 3 (V 308b); 5, 6 (V 309b).

[236] *Brevil.* 5, 2 (V 254a).

[237] *De red. art.* 26 (V 325b).

3. FIRST AND SECOND ADAM

Up to this point, the phenomenon of 'expression' has been considered from a theological, a priori standpoint: we have considered how the expression within the Godhead determines every self-expression of God in the world, sustains this and refers it back to him. Now we must show the same phenomenon from the standpoint of the world, a posteriori, and then demonstrate the synthesis of descending and ascending expression in the God-man. For Bonaventure, man is the crowning of the process of the world's coming to be, and Christ is the crowning of the historical process: the sixth age of the world, in which God becomes man, corresponds to the sixth day of creation, when man is formed and appointed king of the world.[238] The following passage proves that the word 'process' may indeed properly be used here: 'The impulse (*appetitus*) which is in matter is ordered and directed to spiritual things, so that the process of coming to be (*generatio*) does not reach its term until such time as the spiritual soul is united with organic matter. By analogy to this, we can affirm that the highest and noblest perfection in the universe is not attained until such time as the nature that contains the germs that make for the spirit (*rationes seminales*) and the nature that contains the concepts of reason (*rationes intellectuales*) and the nature that contains the archetypical designs of the world (*rationes ideales*) are united to form one single person: and this happened at the Incarnation of the Son of God.'[239] The seeds that lie in the womb of nature cannot be brought to birth without the light of heaven which graciously imparts its radiance, and, in exactly the same way, man cannot develop to his full stature without the spiritual grace from heaven.[240] We must content ourselves with developing a few aspects of Bonaventure's teaching about the world, man and Christ which are significant for his aesthetics.

1. Here, for the last time within Christian theology, the doctrine of the *world* is considered in very close relationship to

---

[238] *Brevil. prol.* 2 (V 204a). [239] *De red. art.* 20 (V 324b).
[240] *Ibid.* 21 (V 324b).

the doctrine of the scriptural revelation. For Adam the 'book of the creatures' sufficed, that he might learn thereby 'to contemplate the light of the divine Wisdom': and this because he looked at things both as they were in themselves and as they were in the divine art, 'for things have a threefold manner of existence: in matter or in their own nature, in the created reason, and in the divine art'.[241] Their existence in the reason is in this way the midpoint and boundary between their existence as such and their existence in God, just as the human spirit at its peak attains to what is above, and has its roots in what is below, and is in this way a mediator between the creatures and God. For this reason, truth possesses in the soul a relationship to that double truth . . . from below, it receives a certainty *secundum quid*, but from above an absolute certainty.[242] Man himself is accordingly the proper ladder that leads to God—from the material existence which he penetrates, via his own intellectual midpoint, to the height of God's Spirit above him: and Christ unites all three stages in his own Person.[243] He appeared because the book of nature had become illegible to fallen man.[244] 'In the state of innocence, man possessed a knowledge of created things, and when they were present he was carried to God through them, so that he might praise and glorify and love God. That is why the creatures exist, and it is in this way that they are brought back to God. But when man had fallen and lost his knowledge, there was no longer anyone who could bring the creatures back to God. So that book—the world—was as if dead and obliterated; and thus another book was needed through which man might be enlightened to understand things again as parables: the book of Scripture, which employs the properties of things to make parables. The revelation of Scripture illuminates all things, and sets the whole cosmos free for God, who is to be praised, glorified and loved.'[245] If the world is interpreted in the light of Scripture, it once more gives its proofs of God, as it did at its origin.[246] For 'the creature is nothing else than a mirror-image of the divine Wisdom, its tangible image', 'a reflection of the

[241] *Brevil.* 2, 12 (V 230b).　　[242] *De sc. Chr.* 4 sol. 23–26 (V 26b).
[243] *Itin.* 1, 2–3 (V 297a).　　[244] *Hex.* 2, 20 (V 430a).
[245] *Hex.* 13, 12 (V 390a), using Delorme 150.
[246] *Ibid.*10, 10–18 (V 378–379).

divine Wisdom, though of course mingled with darkness', for 'the ray of sunshine which penetrates through the window-panes breaks up into many colours'. It is 'only the highest contemplatives' who can read this book aright, 'and not the philosophers who limit themselves to this world's nature, for these know only the nature of things, not the trace of God in them'.[247] Nature is a book with writing on its outside, but the scriptural revelation is a book with writing on its inside, and Christ the God-man is the apocalyptic book with writing on the outside and on the inside.[248]

As a whole, the world in its existence is ordered towards man; in Bonaventure's theology, matter has an *appetitus* towards form, and this *appetitus* gives it the capacity and disposes it for the taking-on of form.[249] To this extent, matter is not *privatio pura*, but in its very nature has already something of beauty and light in itself.[250] This is important in all organic life, and especially in that of man: 'The soul moves the body by means of the power and by means of the disposition of the body, which gives it the tendency to accept the influence of the soul.' This law is then transposed likewise to nature and grace: '... and in precisely the same way, God's light and love move the soul herself and give her life by means of the grace and wisdom poured into her.'[251] 'The bodies of men are therefore ordered towards the noblest form, the spiritual soul, and every *appetitus* of the sensual and bodily nature is oriented towards this and comes to rest in this.'[252] This means that there is a 'proportion' from the outset between body and soul; and because a spiritual soul must demand the highest from its instrument the body, the human body possesses 'the greatest variety of organs endowed with the greatest beauty and skill and manageableness'.[253] This proportion, this state in which the different parts are constructed in mutual orientation, unites in man 'natures which are the furthest distant from each other';[254] moreover, without 'pro-

---

[247] *Ibid.* 12, 14–16 (V 386b).

[248] *Ibid.* 14–17 (V 386b–387a); *Brevil.* 2, 11 (V 229a).

[249] *Hex.* 2, 2 (V 336b).　　　　　　[250] 2 d1 I, 1 q1 *ad* 2 (II 17b).

[251] *De sc. Chr.* 5 *ad* 11 (V 31a).　　[252] *Brevil.* 2, 4 (V 221b).

[253] *Ibid.* 2, 10 (V 228ab).　　　　　[254] *Ibid.* (V 228a).

cess'[255] and a gradual assimilation of matter to the spirit this would be quite impossible. 'Therefore it is absurd to hold that the final form could have been planted in the *materia prima* without a disposition or power [in the *materia prima*] oriented towards the final form, or without some mediating form.'[256]

Since animals and plants are but a mediating link between matter and man, their *generatio* can cease in the eschatological age: their cosmic aim has been attained.[257] But until then, the nature of the world shares a common fate with man and is affected in its inner existence by his condition: innocent with him, fallen with him, shaken, judged and purified with him.[258] For Bonaventure, the *light* is the great power that mediates between matter and life, life and spirit: it is illuminated and interiorised matter, it comes from 'heaven' and penetrates the shapeless 'earth'. This illuminating power of light, which appears of itself and requires no other illumination, but illuminates everything else, suddenly unites light and beauty as closely as possible—indeed, identifies them with each other. *Sicut enim rosa pulcher est inter flores, sic claritas lucis inter colores.*[259] Of its nature, light is the mediator, bridging the oppositions between bodies, between matter and life,[260] and thereby we may once again discern the connection between beauty and expression: the unitary light 'expresses itself' in the material medium which breaks it (in accordance with the variety of the elements)[261] in various ways as 'colour' and, precisely in this, diversifies itself into 'forms'; hence the summary opinion that every form is

---

[255] *Hex.* 4, 9 (V 350b).

[256] *Ibid.* 4, 10 (V 351a). *Nec alicui corpori unitur rationalis potentia absque vegetali et sensibili* [and the rational faculty is not united to any body without the physical and sensual faculties]: 2 d17, 2 q1 *fund.* 3 (II 419a).

[257] *Brevil.* 7, 4 (V 285b–286a).

[258] *Ibid.* 7, 4 (V 284b–285a).

[259] *S. fer.* 2 p. *Pascha* (IX 283a).

[260] [As the rose is beautiful among the flowers, so is the clearness of light among the colours], *Itin.* 2, 2 (V 300a); 2 d17, 2 q2 *ad* 1: *Lux ex aequalitate complexionis generata consurgens, et haec est illa lux quae facit corpus esse susceptibile vitae* [Light arises, born from the equality of the composition of the parts, and this is that light which makes the body capable of receiving life] (II 423ab).

[261] 4 d49 II *sect.* 2, 2 q1 *fund.* 3 (IV 1025a).

beautiful *qua* form[262] may be judged right, for the form possesses that illuminated inwardness which can express itself by presenting itself in a material. Form is the light from above which reconciles the opposition within matter,[263] as it draws on the unity of being.

To this we must add a second dimension of the world, *time and history*, to which Bonaventure (picking up and greatly developing themes from Augustine) accords the highest aesthetic significance. To the rhythm of reconciliation between matter and spirit corresponds in time the rhythm of the generations and of the historical periods, a rhythm that imparts a meaning to time. The first rhythm is the development in space of the species from their principles, the second 'consists in the bringing-forth of that which perdures through the periods, succeeding itself as it gives way to itself: from the order of this process there comes into being a particular beauty and perfection of unity.'[264] Looked at from the point of view of nature, the death of organic beings is taken account of in this rhythmical ordering: 'From the first in the conditions of paradise . . . the animals contributed to the beautifying of the whole by their dying on account of the succession of their generations. . . . Also, as they pursue each other and one nourishes itself from the flesh of the other . . . they contribute to making the whole a wonderful poem in which one syllable follows the other.'[265] This last image is from Augustine;[266] the image of the *pulcherrimum carmen* caused by the succession of periods is used again and again, especially in regard to that history which is the history of salvation. 'Just as a man who does not look at the wholeness of the strophe cannot realise the beauty of the poem, so one who does not contemplate the ordering and government of the world in their wholeness cannot realise their beauty'; but since no man lives long enough to experience the whole of

---

[262] *Omne autem, quod habet aliquam formam, habet pulchritudinem* [everything that has some form, has beauty], 2 d34, 2 q3 *fund*. 6 (II 814a).

[263] *Brevil.* 2, 3 (V 220b–221a).

[264] 2 d15, 2 q3 (II 387a); at *Hex.* 3, 6 *ordo naturae* and *ordo temporis* [the order of nature, the order of time] are derived together from eternity (V 344a).

[265] 2 d15, 2 q1 *ad* 4.5 (II 383b).

[266] *Civ. Dei* 11, 18; *Ver. rel. c.* 22 *n.* 42; *c.* 41 *n.* 77.

history, the Holy Spirit gives us the outlines of it in Scripture.[267] So true is this that Bonaventure holds that he can derive a kind of survey of world history from Scripture, and so (from the same position as Joachim of Fiore) he draws the most varied insights about salvation-history from the proportions of the Old and New Covenants, of which Christ is the temporal midpoint; for this, one must have the knowledge of the periods in a manner that is both contemplative and prophetic, *tempora scire*. 'For no one can know what is to come, unless he knows what is past. If I do not know of what tree this is the seed, I cannot know what tree will be produced from it. . . . Thus Moses, when he prophesied the future, through revelation related what was past.'[268] The agreement of the Church's teaching through all interpretations and periods is a proof of the truth of the Church.[269] The arrangement in stages and the ordering in the world's progress (*in profectu mundi*) also requires that the Incarnation of Christ ensues at a determined point of time.[270] Even the temporary disorder in the world that is caused by sin cannot really disturb the beauty of the ordering: 'for the whole has its beauty from the ordering, and this beauty is so constituted that it is a fitting proof of the highest wisdom. Therefore it cannot in any way be frustrated, and likewise there cannot exist even for a moment anything disordered in it—this is why sin is not separable from punishment.'[271]

This teaching about history subscribes in general to an optimism that understands the cosmos as an evolution towards the God-man: 'The development (*processus*) must ensue from the imperfect to the perfect, not the other way round. Therefore the Incarnation had to ensue at the end of time, so that just as man, the crown of all the material world, was created at the end

---

[267] *Brevil. prol.* 2 (V 204b).

[268] *Hex.* 15, 11 (V 400a). 'If anyone wishes to see how much evidence God gives concerning himself in his works, he must pay attention not merely to what he sees in the present but likewise to that which is past and that which is future, just as the beauty of a metre will not be perceived from one single syllable.' 2 d32, 3 q2 (II 774b).

[269] *Hex.* 11, 19f. (V 375ab).

[270] 3 d1, 2 q2 *fund.* 2 (III 31–32). The reasons are developed in the conclusion.

[271] 2 d36, 2 q1 (II 848b); I d44, 1 q3 c (I 786–787).

to bring perfection to the whole . . . so also the second man, the fulfilment of the whole in its redemption, in which the first cause was joined to the last, God to clay, came at the end of the ages . . . though not at the very end; for it was fitting that some of his members should precede the Mediator, and some should follow him.'[272] So Christ is the ideal end, as the high point of world and history (this is predominantly the perspective of Augustine's view of history); but precisely for this reason, he moves into the temporal midpoint, so that from the elevated position of the centre he may be able to synthesise the time before him and after him (this is the perspective of Joachim's view of history).[273] In this, he is the higher reflection of the first Adam, likewise appearing at the end of the ages of creation of the cosmos—but he appears in order to establish in himself the harmonious balance of the cosmos towards which the cosmos itself was oriented.

2. For Bonaventure, *man* is essentially the midpoint and summary of the world; this point must be made against anyone who would interpret his doctrine as one-sidedly spiritual, in flight from the world, ecstatic. The *impressio* of the stigmata is God's imprint on the material world. And (as we have already shown) the *excessus* comes about as an act of marvelling in the presence of God's nearness and immanence in the world. Man is the longing of all of nature, and the uniting of spirit and matter which takes place in him is the opposite of a falling-away of spirit from itself: 'The action whereby the soul unites itself with the human body and gives it life is neither accidental nor shameful. It is not accidental, because the soul is the substantial form in the body; it is not shameful, because in the body the soul becomes the noblest of all forms, and all the longing struggle of nature finds its goal in this soul. For the human body possesses the noblest constitution and organisation that exist in nature, and therefore it finds its complementary fulfilment only in the noblest form or nature. The character of the soul through which she is able to be united (*unibilis*) to a body is something that

---

[272] *Brevil.* 4, 4 (V 244b–245a).
[273] On this, *cf.* J. Ratzinger, *op. cit.*

touches what is most essential to her and is the most excellent character in the soul.'[274] Of all material systems of organisation, the human body possesses the highest 'illuminated quality (*luminositas*) and subtlety', its 'harmony is greater than that of any other substance', just as 'its dignity is great because of the high harmony of the proportion of its parts'; when once it is transfigured, it will be so elevated and perfected that it will most fittingly be given a place in the empyrean above the heavenly natures.[275] And the harmony of the body, through which it is ordered to the soul, 'is no sameness in every point, but has breadth (*latitudinem*) and stages, in accordance with the different conditions of man'.[276]

In virtue of his position at the centre, man is a summary of the world: 'Beyond a doubt, we are the goal of everything that exists.'[277] For man is the only being in the world who is free, and his freedom encompasses (*comprehendit*) all his sensual and intellectual faculties in itself, in order to surpass them.[278] His reason is disposed in such a way as to be able 'to reflect in outline the whole world in itself'.[279] The sensual faculties already are directed to this: 'See how much the senses can do: for the eye would take in the entire world in the point of the pupil, in the opinion of some, if there was nothing in the way. But the power of the imagination is able to grasp many such worlds.'[280] 'The spiritual soul is, in a certain measure, everything', according to Aristotle;[281] and so a body is placed at her service, the multiplicity of which corresponds to the multiple nature of the objects.[282] In this midpoint of the world, which unites both spirit and matter in itself, 'the divine archetype of the world is better represented': that is the first reason why God assumes a body here and not in the world of the angels. The second reason for

[274] 2 d1 II, 3 q2 c (II 50b).
[275] 2 d17, 2 q2 c *et ad* 6 (II 423ab); *cf.* 2 d2 II, 1 q2.
[276] 2 d17, 2 q3 c (II 425b).
[277] *Brevil.* 2, 4 (V 222a).
[278] *Ibid.* 2, 9 (V 227b).
[279] *Hex.* 4, 6 (V 349b).
[280] *S. theol.* 2, 9 (V 541b).
[281] 2 d17, 2 q1 *fund.* 1 (II 419a).
[282] *Ibid.* c (II 419b).

this is that the state of being united to matter 'makes it easier to accept the kindness of the divine mercy', or, to express this more deeply, because God's 'humble condescension is more clearly expressed in the assumption of mortal man than in the assumption of an immortal spirit'.[283] This is important, because it points both back and forwards to the link in Bonaventure's ethics between glory and humbling: this paradox is built by him into the foundations of anthropology.

Man, as midpoint of the world and its microcosm (*minor mundus*)[284] is the eye of the world that is open to God. As we have already seen, he is *capax Dei*, and he can be given rest only by God.[285] But (and this follows from what we have just said) he is this not as an isolated spirit-soul but as a being characterised as body-soul; therefore he must be eternal as a whole, with body and soul: 'The form of the composite is more perfect than any one part, because the parts are ordered towards the form of the composite. So the form of existence as man is more full and perfect than the form which the soul is by itself; since therefore the perfecting of grace and glory presupposes the perfection of nature, the whole man, not only the soul, must be transfigured',[286] though it is at the same time clear that the condition which permits this to man is his immortal soul, which as such is capable of blessedness (*beatificabilis*).[287] But man in his essence must bring his body into this blessedness, and through his body the whole physical world below which is ordered towards transfiguration through man.[288]

Hence we can understand the teaching about man's double nature, the Janus-like figure, in which Bonaventure admittedly takes over Patristic ideas (found especially in Origen), and yet transforms them in a way that corresponds to his own gifts. The whole man who was placed in paradise had received 'a double range of senses (*duplex sensus*), an inner and an outer, one in the reason and one in the flesh'. Correspondingly, he received 'a

---

[283] 3 d2, 1 q2 c *ad* 1 *fund.* 2 (III 40b–41a, 40a).
[284] *Ibid.* 40b.
[285] *Cf.* nn. 195f.
[286] 4 d43, 1 q1 *fund.* 5 (IV 883a).
[287] *Brevil.* 2, 9 (V 227a).
[288] 2 d17, 2 q1 (II 420a).

double movement: one reigning in the will, one executing the
will's decisions in the body. And he received a double
possession: one visible, the other invisible.' In addition, he
received God's help to interpret God's invisible wisdom in the
physical book of nature: the animal sees only the physical, the
angel the spiritual, but, 'for the sake of the perfecting of the
whole', man had to 'come to be, endowed with a double range
of senses, so that he could read the book written on the inside
and on the outside: the book of Wisdom and her works'.[289] Thus
sin became possible: 'Because his material nature did not press
forward to the immutable possession, his striving began to
address itself to the mutable possession.'[290] But the path to the
material nature is in itself by no means bad or dangerous, so long
as man remains in equilibrium. For Bonaventure, man's
function of being and of knowing lies so much in this
equilibrium that even in the act of knowing God the
equilibrium does not separate *sensus* and *ratio*, and he speaks of
an *inner* as well as an outer *material nature*. For him, knowledge
of God—even when this is 'negative'—is tied to the form of the
world, which can be interpreted by man only with intellect and
senses. And the *ratio* has such deep roots in the material nature,
indeed releases the senses from itself as its instruments in the
world, that it thinks only together with the senses, and only
together with the senses perceives the archetypical world
through the language of things, and is led by the functions of the
senses just as much as by inductive thinking. After the analysis of
the outward knowledge of the senses, in which (through the
material *species*) a transcendental *reductio* is accomplished to the
trinitarian *species* of the Son who reveals the Father,
Bonaventure says: 'Understand therefore that from the highest
reason, which can be known to the inner senses of our
intellectual reason (*mens*), there has flowed forth eternally a
likeness, an image, a Son.'[291] And immediately afterwards, since
he has mentioned the delight (*oblectamentum*) in the functioning
of the senses: 'In the same way, the sense of our heart (*sensus*

---

[289] *Brevil.* 2, 11 (V 229a). *Cf. duplex sensus* in the sense of childish–sensual and
adult–spiritual, *S. 2 Dom.* 1 *in Quadr.* (IX 208a).

[290] *Brevil.* 3, 3 (V 232b).

[291] *De red. art.* 8 (V 322a).

cordis) must longingly seek what is beautiful, or what sounds well, or what smells sweet, or what tastes sweet, or what is soft to touch—must find it with joy, and untiringly strive after it anew. In this way, the divine Wisdom is contained in a hidden manner in sense-knowledge, and the contemplation of the five spiritual senses is wonderful in its correspondence to the bodily senses.'[292]

One can form an idea of what is meant here if one looks at the state of fulfilment of man in heaven, where the body with its senses will have a full share in the overflowing of the joys of the Spirit in God: 'There all the faculties of sense will be exercised (*in actibus suis*): the eye will see the most marvellous beauty, the sense of taste will savour the sweetest taste, the sense of smell will smell the most lovely fragrance, the sense of touch will lay hold of the most precious object, the hearing will be refreshed by the most joyful sounds.'[293] The departed soul longs for this overflowing of the spiritual joy into the joy of the senses, 'and it is quite certain that the soul would never strive for the body to be assumed again, if the body, however transfigured it might be, were to disturb the contemplation of God in the least degree once it was assumed again. But as it is . . . the blessed do long for this, because without the body their blessedness cannot reach perfection, their exultation cannot be satisfied; indeed, so great is their longing, that it actually hinders and blocks their contemplation in some measure (*aliqualiter*).'[294]

After reading this statement, one cannot suppose that the outer and inner senses are two faculties separate from one another, perhaps indeed opposed to one another: rather, they must have their common root in the single intellectual-material nature of man, in which the general character of seeing, hearing, tasting, and so forth is based. Nor is this contradicted by the fact that (with Augustine) Bonaventure sees the specific characters of the senses as having taken on their diversity in response to the relationships of the elements of the material world: earth calls forth touch, water taste, air hearing, fire (smoke) smell,

---

[292] *Ibid.* 10 (V 322b).
[293] *Solil.* 4, 20 (VIII 63a).
[294] *Ibid.* 21 (VIII 63b–64a).

quintessence (light) sight.[295] We must add to this that just as the
elements themselves (again following Augustine) take on their
diverse characters through various mixtures of light with
matter, so the five senses are gradations of one single basic
faculty, that of sight.[296] Sight is the most intellectual sense, touch
the most material.[297] The three senses between the root and the
top of the tree of the senses admit the intermediate mixtures.
But all the senses, together with their specific qualities, mediate
what is held in common, as we find there number, size, shape,
rest, movement. 'The entire material world' penetrates
'through the senses as through five doors into man as micro-
cosmos',[298] and in this way man 'can understand all bodily
forms', because he possesses five organs which correspond to the
five elements.[299]

How can the transition be made from this teaching about the
senses, which is expressed wholly in this-worldly terms, to the
spiritual senses which are exercised upon God? The latter are
'the range of senses' for God, bestowed fundamentally with
grace and its ramifications (*ramificationes*) in the gifts of the
indwelling Holy Spirit: these ramifications are the infused
patterns of behaviour (*habitus*), the 'seven virtues', the 'seven
gifts' (which facilitate the practice of the virtues), the 'seven
beatitudes', which are manifested as acts as the 'twelve fruits of
the Holy Spirit' and the 'five spiritual senses'. It is firstly characteristic that the chief texts identify the eternal Word as the object
of this experience of God through the senses, the Word in his
nuptial relationship to redeemed and sanctified man.

The *Breviloquium.* Through the twelve fruits as 'the overflow
of the spiritual gifts, the holy soul is made glad, and thus man is
suited for contemplation and for the mutual beholding and
embracing of Bridegroom and Bride, as this takes place in
accordance with the spiritual senses. Then the sublime beauty of
Christ the Bridegroom is seen, in so far as he is splendour; the
highest harmony is heard, in so far as he is word; the greatest

[295] *Brevil.* 2, 9 (V 227a) and n. 5 there.
[296] *De red. art.* 3 (V 320a); 2 d13, 2 q2 *contra* 2, and n. 8 there (II 319b).
[297] 4 d49 I *sec.* 1, 3 q1 *arg.* 5 (IV 1018a).
[298] *Itin.* 2, 3–4 (V 300ab).
[299] *De red. art.* 3 (V 320ab).

sweetness is tasted, in so far as he is the wisdom that contains
both, word and splendour; the sublimest fragrance is smelled, in
so far as he is the word inspired in the heart; the greatest delight
is embraced, in so far as he is the incarnate Word, which dwells
bodily among us and gives itself to us to be touched, to be kissed,
to be embraced, through a most fiery love that leads our love
over from this world through *ecstasis* and *raptus* to the Father.'[300]
Here, the tree of the spiritual senses is related to the full height of
the form of God in his revelation: not indeed to the transcendent
God in himself (as the negative theology of the Areopagite
contemplates him), but precisely to the three dimensions of the
Word of revelation. The Word as the eternal expression of the
Father—ray of light, word, wisdom—is spiritually seen and
heard and tasted; as inspired prophetic word—fragrance—he is
breathed into the hearts (a subtle use of metaphor!); in his
incarnate state he is at last touched fully, and out of this contact
on the level of the earth grows the whole tree, up to the height:
in the same manner as Francis was caught up into the nuptial
ecstasy precisely in the palpability of the contact with the
wounds.

The *Itinerarium*. Here the spiritual senses appear at the second
of the three stages (contemplation of the world, contemplation
of self, contemplation of God, or: below oneself, in oneself,
above oneself), and in their second aspect, which contemplates
God *in* the image in the soul, not merely *through* the image in the
soul. The immanence in the image in the soul comes about
through grace, through faith, hope and love. And once again
the object of the soul which has received these gifts is Jesus
Christ as *Verbum increatum, inspiratum, incarnatum*: 'while she
accepts Christ, in her faith in him, as the uncreated Word, word
and splendour of the Father, she recovers the spiritual hearing
and sight—hearing that she may hear the address of Christ, sight
that she may look on the rays of his light. When, further, she
sighs in hope of receiving the inspired Word, she recovers the
spiritual sense of smell through longing and inclination. When
she embraces the incarnate Word in love, receiving pleasure
from him and passing over to him through ecstatic love, she

recovers taste and touch. Through the recovery of these senses
she now sees and hears her Bridegroom, she smells and tastes and
embraces him, and can exult like the Bride in the Song of Songs
... At this stage, the inner senses are restored, in order to
perceive what is most beautiful, to hear what sounds most
lovely, to smell what is most fragrant, to taste what is most
sweet, to touch what is most delightful: and through this the
soul is laid open to the intellectual ecstasies (*mentales excessus*),
i.e., through devotion, wonder, and exultation'.[301] In
comparison with the earlier text, it matters little that here the
five senses are arranged more harmoniously (two for the
Verbum increatum, one for the *Verbum inspiratum*, two for the
Verbum incarnatum); whereas before *sapere* was related to the
eternal *Sapientia* (not least, because of the verbal similarities),
here it is more correctly related to the experience of tasting the
incarnate Wisdom; but taken as a whole, the object of the senses
is the same: the entire vertical extension of the revelation in the
Word. What is decisive is the conclusion. If before it was from
the *tactus* on the level of the earth that the whole tree of the
senses grew up ecstatically, here it is the five-fold sense-
experience that brings the soul into the final readiness for the
ecstasy: disponitur *anima ad mentales excessus*, and this takes place
in the *devotio*, *admiratio* and *exultatio* which are attained in the
five-fold experience. This chief text in no way therefore speaks
of the spiritual senses as encompassing the experience of God in
ecstatic rapture (for example, as an immediate touching of the
divine essence), as we find this later in John of the Cross, in the
concept of *toques*: the senses remain ordered to the form of the
appearance of God in the Word, which of course reaches from
his form as man into his very form as divine expression, and can
be perceived only in the unity of this *one* inseparable form of
revelation, in faith, hope and love.[302]

Thus the spiritual senses are explicitly termed *perceptiones
mentales circa veritatem contemplandam*, a *contemplatio* which in the
prophets was directed to the actual historical revelation in its

[301] *Itin.* 4, 3 (V 306b).
[302] I disagree here with the interpretation of the spiritual senses in
Bonaventure given by Karl Rahner, *La doctrine . . ., loc. cit.*

three (Augustinian) stages of *visio corporalis, imaginaria* and *intellectualis,* while 'in the other righteous men it occurs in the manner of the *speculatio,* which begins with the senses and from there reaches the imagination, from the imagination goes to the reflective understanding, from the reflective understanding to the contemplating reason, from the contemplating reason to the intuition, and from the intuition to wisdom or even to the ecstatic perception.'[303] Both in the prophets and in those who contemplate, the spiritual senses accompany this entire ascent through the six faculties of knowledge, as these are arranged following Pseudo-Augustine (Alcher of Clairvaux). At the foot of this ascent, the spiritual senses touch the bodily senses, but they endure through all the stages of the intellect's perception until the ecstasy, which springs forth from the highest manner of the employment of the spiritual senses like fire from sticks that are rubbed together.

Bonaventure sometimes distinguishes two kinds of higher knowledge of God, one deriving from the workings of God's grace in the soul (*ex suo effectu*), the other residing in a certain immediacy (*in se,*[304] *per intimam unionem*);[305] but even if the second kind looks to the mystical theology of the Areopagite and to Moses' vision in the cloud, this distinction does not directly affect the spiritual senses. They are without any doubt actuated in the first mode of knowledge, in which a presence of God in the soul (through grace) is experienced; and this experience has the effect of a deepening which permits the contemplative perception of God through the world: 'If I experience God as present to me ... from his most personal working (*i.e.,* grace), then that is *contemplatio,* which is so much the higher the more a man feels the working of divine grace in himself, or the better he understands, in accordance with this, how to contemplate God in the external creatures.'[306] This grace-knowledge is for Bonaventure the knowledge of a wholly personal presence: 'it is as a holy soul feels when the Bridegroom addresses her, and she melts away because of

---

[303] *Brevil.* 5, 6 (V 260a).
[304] [in itself], *In Joh. coll.* 1, 43 (VI 255–256).
[305] [through intimate union], 3 d24 *dub.* 4 (III 531).
[306] 2 d23, 2 q3 (II 545a).

this.'[307] Beyond such grace-knowledge, there can be the flight
up into the 'darkness', if in ecstasy 'the sight of the eye (*oculi
aspectus*) can fix itself on God, so that it looks at (*aspiciat*) nothing
else, and yet does not perceive (*perspiciet*) him, nor is allowed to
see the splendour of his light, but on the contrary is raised up
into darkness and attains to the knowledge that Denys . . . calls
docta ignorantia.'[308] Bonaventure describes this ecstasy as that in
which love surpasses all knowledge;[309] in an extravagant way
(since other words are lacking) sensory experiences can be
adduced to shed light on the ineffable. But in any case, it is not a
'seeing' but rather a hearing of secret words,[310] and above all a
touching of one being by another.[311]

[307] *Ibid. ad* 5 (II 546a).

[308] [learned ignorance], *ibid. ad* 6 (II 546a).

[309] *Hex.* 2, 29: *in vertice est unitio amoris* [at the summit is the uniting of love].
2, 30: *sola affectiva vigilat et silentium omnibus aliis potentiis imponit, et tunc homo
alienatus est a sensibus et in ecstasi positus et audit arcana verba quae non licet homini
loqui, quia tantum sunt in affectu* [only the affective faculty remains awake, and
imposes silence on all the other faculties, and then man is estranged from the
senses and set in ecstasy, and hears secret words which a man may not utter,
because they exist only in the affective sense]. 2, 32: *mens oculis intellectualibus
aspicere non potest, et ideo amovendi sunt* [the mind cannot see with the eyes of the
intellect, and therefore they must be removed] (V 341ab–342a).

[310] *Cf.* preceding note.

[311] 3 d28, 2 q1 *ad* 6: *respectu objecti increati nobilior est modus apprehendendi per
modum tactus et amplexus quam per modum visus et intuitus* [in respect of an
uncreated object, the mode of perception by means of touch and embrace is
nobler than that by means of sight and beholding] (III 604b). The basic reason
for this is that (following Bernard) the spiritual senses of seeing and hearing are
to be related more to the soul's faculty of knowing, while the three others are
to be related more to the affective faculty, so that the sense of smell perceives
the object from afar, the taste in its drawing-near, and touch in the highest
uniting, *et sic tactus . . . est perfectior inter omnes sensus et spiritualior propter hoc
quod maxime unit ei qui est summus spiritus* [and so touch . . . is the most perfect
among all the senses, and the most spiritual, because it gives the greatest
uniting to him who is the highest spirit]: 3 d13 *dub.* 1 (III 292a). So in the
presence of God, the worldly tree of the senses seems to be inverted, and the
lowest sense becomes the highest: for Bonaventure this is justified, because for
him the earth is the most unpretentious, the humblest element and precisely
for this reason was chosen to be the midpoint of the world and of the proofs of
God's grace: 2 d17, 2 q2 (II 420a), 2 d15 *dub.* 2 (II 389a), *Hex.* 1, 22 (V 333a). It
must also be borne in mind that in actual fact the senses developed not from the
eye (as Augustine would have it), but from the sense of touch.

Thus on any view which sees the proper location of the spiritual senses as residing in the ecstasy, one would have to credit Bonaventure with all kinds of incoherence and internal disagreements.[312] Their dwelling-place, in which they develop in an organic unity, is not the lowest stage, the world of mere faith, nor the highest, the ecstasy, but the wide middle area of sapiential contemplation, which has as its object the total form of revelation that is the threefold Logos. It is here that the 'eyes of faith' and all the other spiritual senses that belong to them are brought into action. But it is here that they also have their *asceticism*, for their finality is not within themselves and they are not to be cultivated for the sake of their own pleasures but are measured against their object, which essentially is the crucified, who is put to death in all his senses. In the *Soliloquium*, the five senses are individually summoned back from their state of fallenness in the world: they ought really to have Jesus as their object, but they have turned adulterously to outward things.[313] In the rule for novices the *quinque sensuum revocatio* is also found, 'for if the invisible soul is configured to the invisible God, then she must forget all that is visible when she prays to God'.[314] We shall draw attention below to the seductive power of what is perceived by the senses, and to the *custodia sensuum*. At its basis, the mystery of faith is accessible to no bodily or spiritual sense-perception, especially in the wonder of the eucharist, where 'all the senses are disappointed, apart from hearing alone':[315] here all the faculties of knowing are put to shame, the *apprehensio sensitiva*, *imaginaria* and *intellectiva*.[316] The renunciation of an autonomous, acquisitive experiencing is the only preparation possible for the experiences which the Word of inspiration wishes to mediate itself: 'For no revelation takes place except

---

[312] As Karl Rahner is obliged to do: *op. cit.*, p. 276 ('un peu forcé'), p. 290 ('un peu arbitraire'), etc. The problem of the spiritual senses in Bonaventure cannot be solved (*cf.* J. Bonnefoy, *Le S. Esprit et ses dons selon S. Bonaventure*, Paris 1929, p. 212) until one adopts the viewpoint which I have developed in the first volume of this work.

[313] *Solil.* 1, 10–18 (VIII 33–35).

[314] *Reg. Nov.* 2, 2 (VIII 477a).

[315] *S.* 1 *in Coena Dni.* (IX 248b).

[316] *S.* 2 *in Coena Dni.* (IX 252a).

through the *Verbum inspiratum*. "Daniel understood the speech, for understanding is necessary to vision." If God's word does not sound in the ear of the heart, if the eternal splendour does not shine into the intellectual eye, if the fragrance of the almighty God cannot be felt by the sense of smell, if the sweetness cannot be felt by the taste, if eternity does not penetrate into the soul, then you are not ready to understand the visions. . . . For this, Daniel possessed a very pure soul, on which the divine inspirations breathed, that he might be raised up to the visions of the Almighty, to which nothing that is stained gains entry.'[317] For 'all the spiritual senses, all the spiritual impulses and charisms, stream down from Christ the Head'.[318]

3. *Christ* as *Verbum incarnatum* is the midpoint of all things; there is nothing that Bonaventure declared with greater fondness and detail. But he emphasises with equal force that Christ is the midpoint as mediator, that is, a midpoint that mediates. It is in this sense that the great outline is intended, showing Christ as the sevenfold *medium omnium scientiarum*.[319] Everything is created in him, and therefore everything has its place.[320] From him flows originally the context of meaning of the whole revelation,[321] 'in him lies the treasure of all being, all wisdom, all grace, all glory'.[322] He is 'the recapitulation of the first and the last, of the Word of God which is the beginning of all things, and of the human nature which was the last of all creatures'.[323] In the dynamic form of his revelation from uncreated Word to revealing (inspiring) Word to Word in the form of man, he is 'the key of all contemplation' and solves in himself the riddle of

---

[317] *Hex.* 3, 22 (V 347) and Delorme 43–44.

[318] *Ibid.* 1, 20 (V 332b).

[319] [midpoint of all the sciences], *ibid.* 1, 11 (V 331a); *cf.* as a preliminary stage to this *Coll. in Joh.* 1, Coll. 4 (VI 640–642). There is a short summary in *S.* 1 *Dom.* 22 *p. Pent.*: 'Christ is the source-principle and the origin of every human science. As the one sun sends out many rays, so the numerous and varied sciences proceed from the one spiritual sun, the one teacher' (IX 332a).

[320] *Brevil. prol.* 4 (V 205b).

[321] *Ibid. prol. init.* (V 201ab); *Hex.* 14, 16ff. (V 396f.).

[322] *S. theol.* 3, 30 (V 563a).

[323] *Brevil.* 4, 1 (V 241a).

philosophy, how the many can come to be from the one.[324] As the 'source-principle' of all knowledge, he contains all things, from the 'light of the uncreated Wisdom, which is Christ',[325] and in which alone the changeable truth of the changeable creatures has its final stability (*plenam immutabilitatem*),[326] via the truth of the revelation in history, since without the illumination of his light no one can penetrate into the secrets of the prophetic visions and of the faith,[327] to the nature of man, to which he condescends in his work of redemption and enlightenment so that he may be its inward measure as its 'hierarch'.[328]

The motive of the condescension is emphasised in many ways: the Incarnation is the loving *condescendere* of God, who takes flesh and makes himself visible for sinners, because they cannot any longer grasp his divinity.[329] It is also, quite apart from any intentions of redemption, a drawing-near on the part of love: 'For this reason I became a visible man: so that I might be seen and loved by you; for in my divinity I was unseen and in a certain sense (*quodammodo*) unloved.'[330] 'Men were animal, physical, and thus it was impossible to direct them upwards to the ineffable Word and to fix their eyes on the inaccessible light and the everlasting beauty; therefore the Word must come into the midst of men, or else they must persist in their folly.' Besides this, the Word 'had already created man after his own image, and made himself imitable. Our procreation, constitution, creation was in accordance with the image of the Word . . . and yet man's nature could not imitate the Word in its beauty and wisdom. The first angel wanted to imitate it in its beauty, and so he fell; Adam wanted to imitate it in its wisdom, and so was broken. So the Word deigned to come down in person to mankind, so that we might imitate him and form ourselves anew in following him.'[331] 'He was indeed our strength, but

[324] *Hex.* 3, 2–4 (V 343ab).
[325] *S. theol.* 4, 9 (V 569b).
[326] *Ibid.* 4, 7 (V 569a).
[327] *Ibid.* 4, 3 (V 568a).
[328] *Brevil. Prol.* 3 (V 205a); *Hex.* 3, 12 (V 345a).
[329] *Brevil.* 4, 1 (V 241b).
[330] *Vitis myst.* 24, 3 (VIII 189ab).
[331] *S.* 2 *Dom.* 3 *Advent.* (IX 60ab).

quite out of proportion to us (*improportionabilis*), and so it was fitting that strength should be weakened, and the mighty God become a little child. . . . He was the light, but inaccessible, and so he had to be overshadowed by the flesh, so that men could see and follow.'[332] 'As the word of the mind, when still unspoken, is not yet sensible, but once clothed in the voice can be received by us, so the incarnate Word before his birth was incomprehensible, but after his birth was like a word expressed by the voice, clothed in flesh and perceptible to the senses. . . . Indeed, the Word became visible, not only audible. For in itself it belongs more to the word to be heard than to be seen; but the Word of the Father could be neither seen nor heard, until through his birth he became visible and audible.'[333] This means also that the eternal Word, the expression of the Godhead, when become audible and visible can be understood only as the expression of the Godhead: in Jesus Christ, the whole Trinity gives witness to itself. The Father gives witness to himself in the fact (of the Incarnation), for he is the power; the Son in the utterance, for he is the Word; the Holy Spirit in the intention, for he is the love and the bond.[334] Without God's Trinity, the Incarnation of God cannot be understood, and the phenomenon of Jesus Christ cannot be interpreted: *Incarnatio non cognoscitur, nisi cognoscatur distinctio personarum*.[335]

When God experiences what it is to be man (*ut experiri posset*),[336] he descends and sets himself in that midpoint of the world where the descent to material nature and the ascent to God ensue. The skill of being able to do both, the descent into the act and the ascent into the contemplation,[337] is perfected for the first time in him, and so he becomes our 'exit and entrance', our ascent to God and descent to neighbour, our looking outwards into the book of nature and our looking inwards into

---

[332] *S.* 1 *Vig. Nativ.* (IX 90ab).

[333] *S.* 1 *Nativ.* (IX 103a).

[334] *S. theol.* 1, 8 (V 536b).

[335] [the Incarnation is not recognised unless the distinction of the persons is recognised], *Hex.* 8, 11 (V 371a).

[336] *Ibid.* 3, 15 (V 345b).

[337] *Ibid.* 20, 18 (V 428b).

the spiritual truth.[338] For he is the book written on the inside and on the outside.[339] And precisely in this he is 'lovely and refreshing to look upon in accordance with man's double power of sight: the inward sight which sees the divinity, the outward sight which sees the manhood'.[340] In that this midpoint of the world is the expression of God's descent, the descent within this world must be emphasised in it: it becomes the midpoint of humility, of poverty, of the cross. And in that God's descent reveals his immeasurable loftiness, the humility of Christ becomes the fundamental divine mystery: 'The depth of God-made-man, his humility, is so great that reason founders on it.'[341]

It is part of this essential humility of the Son, precisely because he is and desires nothing else than to be the expression of the Father, that he possesses no other midpoint than one that mediates: and therefore he continually makes himself nothing by pointing back in the Holy Spirit to the Father.[342] It is this perspective which governs the main lines of Bonaventure's entire christological science. In his metaphysics, Christ is the mediation of being along with himself, because he mediates being (as Father) as that which is like himself (*secundum se* = the Son) to the being which exists for himself (*propter se* = the Spirit), and precisely in this explains how there can exist a plurality of things in the world outside God; the christologist is *verus metaphysicus*.[343] The cosmologist who researches in the macrocosm and the doctor who researches in the world's microcosm are shown the incarnate Christ as the true sun and man's true heart (or head). If the earth's midpoint is the mathematical point of intersection of all lines, then Christ is

---

[338] *S. theol.* 4, 14 (V 571ab); *Franciscus ... aut ascendebat ad Deum aut descendebat ad proximum* [Francis ... either ascended to God or descended to his neighbour], *Legenda* 13, 1 (VIII 542a).

[339] *Vitis myst.* 24, 2 (VIII 188a).

[340] *S.* 1 *Dom. infr. Oct. Epiph.* (IX 171b).

[341] *Hex.* 8, 5 (V 370a).

[342] *De don. Sp. Sti.* 1, 10: *Istam reversionem servat humilitas ... Humilis continuatur cum sua origine ... Christus reduxit se in suum originale principium per humilitatem* [Humility preserves that turning-back. ... The humble man is in continuity with his origin. ... Christ through humility reduced himself to his fundamental principle of origin] (V 459ab).

[343] *Hex.* 1, 12–13 (V 331ab).

shown to the mathematician as the crucified, the one who has descended into hell, the saving and redeeming midpoint of the earth. For the logician, he is the exemplary syllogism in his Resurrection, for from the major term of his divinity and from the minor term of his death on the cross he draws the conclusion which only he could draw, the conclusion to which all the power of logic is reduced. For the moral philosopher, Christ as he ascends to heaven becomes the midpoint, for only the one who continually strives for a goal over and above what has already been achieved is in accord with moral principles, just as the Neo-Platonists had constructed a ladder to heaven from the virtues. For the jurist, he is the midpoint as judge of the world, for there alone is the source and the content of all justice and jurisdiction. For the theologian, finally, who studies the return (*reductio*) of all things to God and the universal reconciliation (*universalis conciliatio*) of the world in God, Christ is the eternally mediating midpoint through his eternal blessedness, for it is through 'the Lamb in the midst of the throne' that 'all blessedness is mediated'.[334] This last idea, of an eternal mediation even in heaven through the incarnate God, is familiar to Bonaventure.[345]

He can give expression to the mediating position of Christ in the midpoint in various ways, for example, by modifying the position of the concept of midpoint within the syllogism-form according to the logical tropes: either by placing it under the first concept and above the second, so that Christ mediates between man and God; or above both concepts, so that Christ mediates between man and angel; or placed below both concepts, so that he (as the last of men) mediates between man and man.[346] Again and again he takes as his starting-point the verse in John, *medius vestrum stetit quem vos nescitis*, and the unknownness of this mediating midpoint is underlined with pathos: 'Thus the eternal Lord stands in the midst of mortal men, the innocent

---

[334] *Ibid.* 1, 11–38 (V 331a–335b).

[345] *Cf.* 12 d2 II, 1 q1 *sol.* 1 (II 72a). *Ipse est principium influentiarum, per quas vivemus in futuro saeculo* [he is the principle of existence of the influences through which we shall live in the age to come], Hex. 3, 19 (V 346b). On this theme, *cf.* A. Gerken, *op. cit.* Part 2, appendix 1 to ch. 4.

[346] *Coll. in Joh. c.* 1 coll. 4, 5 (VI 540b–541a and note there).

lamb stands in the midst of the threatening sinners, the glorious redeemer stands in the midst of those who are perishing in their wretchedness, the all-wise stands in the midst of fools, the all-holy in the midst of despicable men, the all-blessed in the midst of the damned.'[347]

But when he stands thus in the midst, it is as the one who brings reconciliation, enlightenment, the one who leads back, who measures all things, who makes straight. In this mission lies his beauty: not only because he is the *rectitudo* of all that has deviated, but because he is able to make what has deviated come to resemble himself through the power of the radiance of his omnipotent heart. It is indeed true that as the measurement which appears and judges all things he is already the highest beauty, *perpulchrum*: 'It is this that gives all things their beauty: that he restores fair form to what has lost its shape, that he makes the beautiful more beautiful, and what is more beautiful he makes most beautiful.'[348] At this point, Bonaventure (with less hesitation than any other theologian) builds into his theology the questionable argument of Augustine that ultimately justifies the evil in the world and even everlasting hell on aesthetic grounds.[349] But this 'beauty' of mere righteousness remains in Bonaventure's system as a whole just as provisional as the Augustinian definition of beauty as *aequalitas numerosa*. The full concept requires an *expressio* from God—and fundamentally

---

[347] *S. 2 Dom. 3 Advent.* (IX 64b).

[348] *Hex.* 1, 34 (V 335a).

[349] The 'antitheses' belong to the beauty and perfection of the cosmos, the dark hue (evil) belongs to the beauty of the picture: 1 *de* 46 q6 (I 832a, 833b); 4 d44 II, 1 q1 (IV 921b); *S. theol.* 2, 45 (V 552b). Punishment suffices to guarantee the beauty of the order of the world at every moment: 2 d32, 3 q1 (II 770a); 2 d36, 2 q1 (II 848b). Part of this is the idea that more men are damned than redeemed (*Brevil.* 1, 9; V 218b), that at the *descensus* only the *electi* are saved (3 d22 q5; III 461b), and that intercessory prayer has therefore its boundaries in the fact of predestination: *incassum orarent* [they would pray in vain] (*Ep. de Imit. Chr.* 5; VIII 500b; and 4 d45, 3 q1ff.; IV 947ff.), that Christ will be angered at the last judgment (*Lignum vitae* 42; VIII 83b), that the redeemed rejoice in the presence of the damnation of the others because they are not damned along with them (*Solil.* 4, 2; VIII 58ab). This and similar passages indicate a limitation in this otherwise joyful and loving thinker that alienates, a barrier that comes from Augustine but that cannot be felt in Anselm.

this is a movement of love in God himself and from God to the world—and from the world comes the answering movement of *resolutio*, which succeeds only as the humble, obedient answer to the radiant light. Thus, in an eschatological contemplation of beauty, the designation of *aequalitas numerosa* is built into the all-embracing process of the shining forth of love and the assimilation of all to this radiating midpoint.

The heavenly Jerusalem needs neither sun nor moon, because the glory of God shines upon it and the Lamb is its light. 'The light of the Lamb gives it beauty and splendour, his divinity shines in the place of the sun, his manhood in the place of the moon.... Thus the Son, the Lamb, whose splendour and substance is eternal light and a mirror without spot, beautifies it. ... If, as Augustine says in the sixth book *De musica*, beauty is *aequalitas numerosa*, because a face is the more beautiful the more its parts are set in relationship and adjusted to one another because of their harmony with one another, how great must be the beauty of that city where the Son, who is the eternal art in all things, in whom from eternity all the principles and ideas of the things created in time are found, offers himself to the blessed spirits and gives them his presence as a most clear mirror, and is grasped by each one according to his power of comprehension and is known in a manifest manner.'[350]

He is primal beauty as the world of ideas, which contains God's pure thought of every deficient being. But he is this because he himself as the world of ideas is the pure expression of the primal divinity, and in himself has brought creation back into the archetypical glory: rising to eternal life, 'he displays in himself the exemplary beauty of the human bodies which are one day to be raised up'.[351] He is the 'blossoming again'[352] of the fallen earthly flesh upwards to God. As such, he is the glory of the tree of life in the supratemporal paradise, as Bonaventure loves to term him; the tree which, if not misused through curiosity, is at the same time the tree of knowledge.[353] Round

[350] S. 2 Omn. Sanct. (IX 601b).
[351] Lignum vitae 35 (VIII 81b).
[352] S. fer. 3 p. Pascha (IX 281f.; 286f.).
[353] Lignum vitae: VIII 68–86; tree of knowledge: ibid. 69b; De plant. Par. 9 and 12 (V 577ab).

about it in paradise other trees are planted, 'so that man through
the alternation of the fruits, through the varieties of the beauties
and tastes, might avoid the boredom which tends to ensue from
attention to one single thing, and that he might have the delight
that the perceptions of the spiritual senses derive from variety
and renewal.'[354] But all other fruits are only the unfolding of
faith in the one God revealed in Christ. This tree in the midst is
always at the same time the *Vitis mystica*,[355] which must be
staked and pruned and fenced in, that it may bear fruit. It is also
the book of life, 'in which God the Father has deposited all the
treasures of wisdom and knowledge: as God's firstborn and the
uncreated Word, he is the book of wisdom and the shining in
the spirit of the highest craftsman full of living and eternal first
principles; as inspired Word, he is in the spirits of the angels and
the blessed; as incarnate Word he is in the reasonable souls that
are united to a body: that thus the many-coloured Wisdom of
God might radiate forth from him and in him throughout the
whole realm, as from a marvellous mirror that contains all
forms and lights, and as from a book in which all stands
recorded in accordance with the unfathomable mysteries of
God.'[356]

4. THE STRUCTURE OF BEAUTY

In what has been so far said, one sees the statements about beauty
occupying so important a place in Bonaventure's theology that
one begins to be afraid that there is no unity to give shape to
their multiplicity. Externally there is no such point of reference,
because Bonaventure nowhere offers a developed treatise on the
beautiful. The reason for this may be that his trinitarian-triadic
thinking continually uses the three primary *transcendentalia*
(*unum, verum, bonum*) as a scheme of appropriation and as it were
systematically cannot manage an enlargement to four by the
inclusion of *pulchrum*. Nevertheless, as the sensitive study of Karl

---

[354] *De plant. Par.* 9 (V 577a).
[355] *Vitis myst.*: VIII 159–189. Doubts have been raised about the authenticity
of this work, especially because all sixteen manuscripts come from Germany.
[356] *Lignum vitae* 46 (VIII 84b–85a).

Peter has demonstrated, the beautiful can effectively be shown to be a transcendental property of all being, both inductively through its presence in all categories of being and deductively from some occasional remarks (such as, *cum igitur omnia sint pulchra et quodam modo delectabilia*)[357]—and this property is necessarily present in a *circumincessio* in the one, the true and the good. While it is true that these three mutually establish each other within the order of being 'so that the true presupposes the one, and the good presupposes the one as well as the true', and thus directly suggest the appropriation to the divine Persons who mutually establish each other,[358] Bonaventure (unlike the treatise on the *transcendentalia* in the Assisi Codex)[359] does not base the beautiful immediately and especially in the good; he rather follows the treatise in the Assisi Codex in the statement that *pulchrum circuit omnem causam et est commune ad ista (i.e., ad unum, verum, bonum).*[360] The beautiful completes the inner development of being as being in itself; it is the expression of its rounding-off in itself; and thus the paths to an understanding of the beautiful lead directly from the one as well as from the true and from the beautiful. But we must ask what the *ratio pulchri* is, over against the other fundamental properties of being.

An important text (*Breviloquium* 1, 6)[361] derives the *transcendentalia* each from a relationship of being to itself (*indivisio*): the one 'is the basis of its numerability, because it is not separated from itself', the true 'is the basis of its ability to be known, because it is not separated from its image (*species*)', the good 'is the basis of its communicability, because it is not separated from what it itself does'. Everything is what it is through the essence (*essentia*), and thereby an *unum* which is different from all others,

[357] [since therefore all are beautiful and in some manner delightful], *Itin.* 2, 10 (V 302b); *ibid.* 2, 9: *formosa omnia* [all are beautiful] (V 302a), *cf.* also the statement that all form is beautiful: 2 d34, 2 q3 *fund.* 6 (II 814a).

[358] *Brevil.* 1, 6 (V 215a).

[359] *Nam pulchrum praeintelligit bonum, et bonum verum, et verum unum, unum autem ipsum ens* [For the beautiful presupposes the good, and the good the one, and the one presupposes being itself], a 1 q1 (ed. Halcour, *loc. cit.* p. 65, lines 14–15).

[360] [The beautiful includes every cause and is common to those things (*i.e.*, the one, the true, the good)], *ibid.* lines 19–20.

[361] V 215a.

gathering in its parts (matter and form) and holding them together in itself. It is precisely on this that its knowability depends, in so far as the form in which it is known corresponds to the form of its being; and in its acts it communicates itself in accordance with the form of its essence and can thereby complement and complete another existing thing that lacks it. If one wished to deduce a corresponding formula for the beautiful from what Bonaventure elsewhere says about it, then (following Peter) this would have to run somewhat as follows: the beautiful is the basis of its physical appearing, because what is is not separated from being. Naturally, such a formula could be achieved 'at a price which Bonaventure was not willing to pay ... that of the elevation of sense-perception into the rank of irreducible being', something that the Platonic-Augustinian depreciation of sense-perception did not allow, even though perhaps no one in the Middle Ages evaluated sense-perception so positively as Bonaventure. If one were to take 'sense-perception' as 'a direct act of permitting to appear' at all levels (at the level of the five bodily senses, which in this are the opposite of an abstract knowledge; at the level of the intellect, when it simply permits itself to be met as *simplex apprehensio*, before it forms any judgment; and finally at the level of mysticism, where the spiritual senses permit a direct meeting with the divine essence),[362] then one might step beyond the general scholastic manner of thinking and speaking and speak of a 'transcendental sense-perception': from this collective term, one might try to solve the puzzles of Bonaventure's teaching about beauty. If one confined one's attention to the field of philosophy, this would round things off very satisfactorily.

Our question, however, is theological, and so it seems better to group Bonaventure's statements round the key theological and spiritual concept of *expressio* if we are to discover their unity. This has the advantage of remaining closer to the text and the period and, at the same time, of drawing out all the content of the category which Bonaventure himself furnished. As with

---

[362] For this analogy of the sense-perceptions (as an analogous *sentire*), we may cite 2 d8 I, 3 q2 *ad* 4 (II 222b), where there is a gradation of knowledge of the immediate presence of a thing, knowledge of its *hic et nunc*, and knowledge through the sense-organs of the body.

the philosophical enquiry just mentioned, we shall deal with the
'appearing' of what is, but the point of departure (as with the
one, the true and the good) remains primarily what is itself in
the movement of its act of presenting itself, and only secondarily the one who meets it (in the immediacy of its becoming
visible). Thus the trinitarian midpoint can be preserved here
also.

A few preparatory observations will indicate to us the
ramifications of the problem—ramifications that ought indeed
to be expected, if a discussion of the beautiful is a discussion of a
genuine *transcendentale*. The appropriation of beauty to the Son,
which we have already come across several times, hints at a
position in the midpoint which can be maintained only by
simultaneously surpassing both sides. The triads of appropriation taken over from the tradition are principally two,
modus–species–ordo and *mensura–numerus–pondus*; these can be
placed in relationship to one another, so that the mode of being
(substance) becomes the measure of being ordained by God and
corresponds to unity and to the *causa efficiens* (or *formalis*); the
form of being and of knowledge gives this essence its truth and
likewise its position in the entirety of things (thus it takes on
especially the aspect of beauty[363] and corresponds to the *causa
exemplaris*); the order gives it its gravitational pull towards God
and, mediating to it the way to God, its pull towards the other
creatures (this corresponds to the good and to the *causa finalis*).[364]

---

[363] *Ut autem comparatur ad res alias, sic attenditur in ea (re) species, sicut attenditur
pulchritudo partium secundum situm, quem habent in toto* [when it is compared
with other things, 'species' in the thing is understood to mean the same thing as
the beauty which the parts have according to the position they occupy in the
whole], 2 d35, 2 q1 (II 829b).

[364] Apart from the text cited here, *cf.* 1 d3 I *dub.* 3 (78b–79a), *Itin.* 1, 11 (V
298a): *pondus quoad situm ubi inclinantur, numerum quo distinguuntur, et mensuram
qua limitantur* [weight, in relation to the location where they lean down,
number, by which they are distinguished, measure, by which they are
bounded]. *Cf. Hex.* 2, 23 (V 340a) and *S. de Trin.* with the appropriation:
*mensura respicit Patrem, ut a quo creatura deficit propter Creatoris immensitatem, . . .
numerus vero respicit Filium propter ejus sapientiam omnia distinguentem et
cognoscentem, . . . pondus vero respicit Spiritum Sanctum propter sui bonitatem omnia
terminantem . . . Et istis tribus respondent alia tria . . . : modus, species et ordo, ita quod
modus mensurae, species numero, sed ordo ponderi attribuuntur . . .* [measurement
looks to the Father, as it is that by which the creature falls short because of the

But apart from the innate ambiguity of the word *species*, which has to cover both 'truth' and 'beauty' at the same time, its position with regard to *modus-mensura* is also unclear, because while the measurement of being is the basis of the unity of the essence, this unity seems to belong again to *species*, as the principle of numerability. At any rate, number as such belongs to *aequalitas*, which must be appropriated to the Son, and this uncovers the problems connected with the concept of unity.[365] Precisely in this, the *species* (as a unity which does not suffice for itself) transcends itself to *ordo-pondus*; one may attempt to introduce a double concept of order, one related to wisdom and the other to goodness,[366] but both must merge into each other, as happens in the Aquinas' concept of *ordo*. In these schemes, therefore, beauty appears formally as a midpoint in suspension, which embraces but surpasses them on both sides.

A second area indicated by the analogy of beauty is the domain formed by the gradation from the physical world to the inner world of the souls and the angels, to Christ, to the triune God: here one may 'see the beauty of the things of the senses, of the rational spirits, of the manhood of Christ, of the divinity of the one and triune God'.[367] Whereas Bonaventure discusses the

Creator's immeasurability . . . number looks to the Son because of his wisdom which distinguishes and knows all things . . . weight looks to the Holy Spirit who sets an end to all things because of his goodness. . . . And to these three correspond another three . . . : manner, *species* and order, such that manner is attributed to measurement, *species* to number, but order to weight . . .] (IX 353a). In this last text, the problems connected with the *transcendentalia* become especially obvious through the combination of 'distinguishing' and 'knowing' (in the case of the Son), because *species* has to stand for the true and for the good.

[365] Bonaventure is wholly aware of this: there is a unity towards what is below as communicability, and this is negative; and there is a unity towards what is above (grounded in the incommunicability of the form), and this is positive: 1 d24, 1 q1 (I 421b); *cf.* 1 d8 II, q1 and q2 (I 165–169).

[366] 1 d3 1 *dub.* 4 (I 80ab). *Cf.* likewise the distinction between *ordo partium in toto* [the ordering of the parts as a whole] and *ordo partium in finem* [the ordering of the parts towards a goal], and a corresponding double beauty: an unchanged beauty of the substances, and a beauty that is historical and makes for a goal: 1 d44, 1 q4 (I 786a).

[367] *S. theol.* 2, 14 (V 542b).

beauty of the physical in detail, the beauty of the soul, which consists in the inner ordering of the soul and in the realisation of her faculties for virtue, is only mentioned, not shown in its aesthetic essence. This inner beauty is the product of a purification from the stain of sin and the setting-up of a clear mirror, in which it is not first of all the beauty of the world that is reflected but rather (along with its quality as mirror) the created spirit's quality as image that appears, in the reflection of the self which is now possible. Once the purification has taken place, 'the soul, reflecting itself, can become a marvellous clear mirror, in which she looks on everything that radiates splendour and beauty': for this, she must take on the characteristics of a mirror—she must be able to catch the light (through steel or lead under the glass), she must be polished, and finally she must be exposed to the light—and this takes place through the lower, middle and highest virtues.[368] It is important here that the beauty of the soul is explained on the basis of her renewed transparency to her being as an image of God. This does not mean that it is not the activation of the order within the soul (what Bonaventure calls the 'hierarchisation' of the soul) which produces the beauty of this image.[369] The soul thereby finally becomes the heavenly Jerusalem itself, 'where God dwells and is seen',[370] and she is accordingly frequently compared to the apocalyptic woman clothed with sun, moon and stars.[371] So she becomes in this sense a kind of embodiment of the Church, in so far as she rests in this holy gazing on God, 'for the contemplative Church and the soul differ from one another only in this, that the soul possesses all things in herself, while the Church possesses them [distributed] among many'.[372] Thus the universalising of the soul, her power to grasp the whole kingdom of God within herself, belongs to the hierarchisation of the soul—and if this is true, it follows that the reflection of the macrocosm belongs also to her full beauty as a mirror, and so she becomes a fully developed monad. It should

[368] Hex. 5, 25 (V 358a).
[369] Hex. 20, 22 (V 429a); Hex. 22, 24 (V 441a); 22, 36f. (V 442b–443).
[370] Hex. 23, 2 (V 445a).
[371] De plant. Par. 4f. (V 575b–576a).
[372] Hex. 23, 4 (V 445b).

be noted, however, that it is precisely to the *anima contemplativa* alone that this beauty is attributed:

'Consider that in the contemplative soul the entire universe together with all the heavenly spirits writes its name, and each of these spirits carries the universe inscribed in himself, and finally that the ray above all being [the Word of God] writes his name in her—he who contains both the universe and all the spirits in himself. Thus wonderful lights and a wonderful beauty reign in the contemplative soul. In the same manner, the universe, which is beautiful from its summit to its depths, from beginning to end, forms a mirror as it inscribes itself in the soul, and every spirit is a mirror, and thus there comes to be in the soul a marvellous multiplicity, a most sublime order, a sublime proportion. The world of the spirits is [likewise] beautiful. And as often as the ordering of the universe, and that of the blessed spirits, and that of the ray above all being shine out in the soul in this manner, a marvellous illumination takes place in her. . . .'[373] The impulse of beauty here lies undoubtedly not in the quantitative; but in the possibility for the totality of being in the world to reflect itself and express itself in the soul which has been purified and trained so that it may recover the original image of God; we have here a monadology, but without a 'pre-established harmony'—a monadology within the framework of a cosmos of wholly mutual expression. For Bonaventure, this beauty of the spirits is the real beauty because it is the nearest to the original world of divine expression: 'There are many who love beauty, but beauty does not dwell in what is external—that is merely its copy; the true beauty dwells in the beauty of wisdom.'[374] But in so far as the incarnate Word is also the beloved Bridegroom, the original objective beauty is joined indissolubly in him to the subjective beauty of eros: he is *sponsus speciosissimus et desiderabilis totus*,[375] he is *pulchritudo pulchrificativa universorum*.[376] But he is this, in the final analysis, because he is *Splendor* and *Verbum*, the expression of the Father.[377]

[373] *Hex.* 20, 8 (V 426b).
[374] *Hex.* 20, 24 (V 429b).
[375] *Brevil.* 5, 6 (V 260a).
[376] *S. 2 Nativ. Virg.* (IX 709a).
[377] *Brevil.* 5, 7 (V 261a).

A third analogy of beauty must be mentioned before we go further. Bonaventure's principal aesthetic text (*Itinerarium* ch. 2), which deals with the perception by the five senses of what is beautiful in the world, and therefore of the mutual workings of object and subject in this perception, makes a number of subtle and original distinctions in its identification of the aesthetic perceptions. The point of departure here, as generally in this great text, is the idea of the entry of the macrocosm into man's microcosm, in this case through the door of the senses. The macrocosmos itself consists of generative forces, the basic elements and especially the light, 'which reconciles the oppositions among the elements' and prompts them to construct minerals, plants, animals and human bodies, which are the things generated. The five senses (following Augustine) correspond to the various mixtures of light with the four elements, as we have set out above: thus the senses, in their specific characteristics, stand a priori in a particular proportionality to the world, and it is this that explains the pleasure which such encounter gives: *omnis delectatio est ratione proportionalitatis.* As things themselves are generated from the elements and light, so they generate themselves once again in the faculty of sense-perception, with their mysterious power of expression through which they generate an image (*species*) from themselves in the medium of air: this image enters the organ, and through this enters the *potentia apprehensiva.* But this encounter (through proportion a priori and generation a posteriori), which in any case creates sensuous joy (*oblectatio*), can now be further distinguished according to whether it is the objective form (*species*) which generates this joy: in the eye, which sees the *speciositas*, beauty in the narrower sense, and identifies it; or the power (*virtus*) of the object which penetrates and dominates the middle ground (between object and subject): in the ear and the nose, which perceive what is soft and sweet (*suavitas*), 'in so far as the active power is not out of proportion to the faculties of the senses it encounters'; or finally, the operation (*operatio, efficacia, impressio*) which is wholly impressed upon the subjective faculty and is proportionate when the active object satisfies a passive need through its impress (*imprimendo*)—as with taste and touch, which chiefly identify what is proper, healthy (*salubre*). In this delicate gradation, while the basic proportion remains the same, the perception of beauty passes over more and more from the object into the subject: the eye sees and identifies the beauty of things, the ear and the nose are in equilibrium between outside and inside, the taste and touch, at their strongest in the service of the vegetative-sensitive life, are primarily concerned with subjective pleasurable sensations. Yet, if the world is open to the eye in the pure act of beholding what is illuminated, the eye sees chiefly an *image* of the world, while step by step up to the faculty of touch it is the substantial *reality* in its resistant character which penetrates the subject, in order to satisfy its needs.[378] The threefold joy of the encounter is immediate; in the intellectual man, the act of judgement (*dijudicatio*) follows this joy, asking *inter alia* why a thing gives pleasure; abstracting from the gradation between *pulchrum, suave* and *salubre*, it identifies the *proportio aequalitatis* as the unifying precondition—but with this Augustinian and mathematical definition of beauty we have reached only an abstract relationship between object and subject, and have done justice neither to the objective catching sight of the beauty of form by the eye, nor to the impulse of the satisfaction of need, which unambiguously points to the realm of the *bonum*. Nevertheless, it is Bonaventure's chief concern to make this whole texture of the aesthetic sense-perceptions transparent to the theological and trinitarian. For if (to begin with) the perceived appearance of the thing is its generally uniform generation in the medium of the air and then in the sense organ, in order to bring the one who perceives into communication with the thing itself, this circumstance clearly points (*manifeste insinuat*) to a generation in the eternal light itself which makes this possible; it points to the eternally omnipresent consubstantial ray of the Father, which is united to the created spirit (as to an organ) through the Holy Spirit and should bring home this created spirit to the principle and object at its source, the Father. In the same way, the threefold joy (at what is beautiful, what is pleasant and what is healthy) points back to a corresponding primal relationship in God, for in the Godhead the basis of everything is laid in an absolute, archetypical

---

[378] *Cf.* n. 311.

proportionalitas between Father and Son in the Spirit, which then becomes objective for the eye of the believer,[379] is inwardly assimilated by the believer without *phantasma* through the power (*virtus*) of the word of revelation (as the medium), and as an imprint (*impresso*) into its being banishes and heals all distress and satisfies every need. The joy of the senses, with its three levels, has therefore its theological equivalent in the beholding of the truth, in the experience of intimacy, and in the receiving of the satisfying fullness (*veritas, intimitas, plenitudo*). But all this takes place no longer on the basis of a relationship *between* man and God, but through man's participation by grace in a proportion and joy within the Godhead; for man experiences thereby 'that the true *delectatio* which is the source of joy is in God alone, and that all other pleasures are for us a signpost, so that we may seek that joy'. The spiritual judgement, finally, points beyond the experience of the senses to man's participation in the absolute and ideal light of the Logos, without whose illumination no absolutely certain thought about what is perceived by the senses would be possible.[380]

This is the rich text which develops the structure of beauty more fully than any other in Bonaventure, by distinguishing the levels first in the object itself, then in the subject, and finally in the relationships of both, to find its ultimate goal in the mystery of expression within the Godhead. Indeed, the only reason for undertaking the whole analysis was to ground the experience of beauty through the senses in a relation of expression of the object to the subject, which in turn is a relation grounded in the eternal expression in God himself.

We have now obtained three ways of approaching the theologically beautiful. The first runs from the concept of being

---

[379] This link, because it is implicitly included in the train of thought, must be introduced here, so that the parallel between the material copy and the theological archetype becomes fully obvious (*Itin.* 2, 8; V 301b, lines 19–20).

[380] *Itin.* 2, 1–9 (V 299b–302a). The differentiation of *pulchrum–suave–salubre* has an approximate parallel in the triad of appropriation of *altitudo* (Father), *pulchritudo* (Son), *dulcedo* (Holy Spirit), where the first should be rendered by 'excellence' (dignity, sublimity, glory), the second by 'beauty' more in the sense of attractiveness, and the third by the subjective emotion of 'pleasure', 'delight' (*De tripl. via* 3§7 n. 12; VIII 17b).

and its transcendental dimensions, which point to the trinitarian mystery; the second from the levels of being and thereby of beauty; the third from the texture of the experience of beauty through the senses, which points to an absolute structure of the beautiful. In the first metaphysical connection, however, the content of beauty was very difficult to grasp, for although it overlapped the traditional location of truth it remained something that circled all the *transcendentalia* (*pulchrum circuit omnem causam*), and could not be identified unambiguously. The relationship between the stages leads to an important conclusion, which has so far not been drawn: that in each case the lower form of beauty must be abandoned for the sake of the higher, and that since the more spiritual forms of beauty are continually more hidden for earthly man, the ascent to God can appear as a renunciation of all familiar beauty. In the context of the objective–subjective experience of beauty, one may wonder how far the structure accessible to the senses really does expose the trinitarian mystery so 'obviously', and what of this mystery is ultimately comprehensible as archetypical beauty. In the metaphysical context, the beautiful appears primarily in the general setting of the problems concerning unity, and the metaphysical definitions of beauty which Bonaventure likes to quote from Augustine all revolve around the question of number, of resemblance, of proportion, of rhythm, and thus of the changes of oneness. In the context of the levels it is the question of truth that presses, because the possibility of unity between beautiful appearance and substantial reality of being becomes stronger from level to level. In the context of the interwoven relationship of object and subject, we have looked to *oblectatio*, i.e., to the good, to explain this, both in regard to the self-giving of the object and in regard to the need and the satisfaction of the subject. All three points of view find their grounding, and thereby likewise their complete mutual penetration, in the teaching about expression.

1. Definitions of beauty offered on the basis of its relation to oneness assume that the impression of beauty comes from the sight or experience of an objective conformity of things, whether this is merely a numerical distinction of things that are

the same (*aequalitas numerosa*,[381] *pluralitas et aequalitas*[382]) or the agreement and proportion of things that are different (*convenientia disparium*,[383] *proportionalitas*,[384] *congruentia partium*[385]). All these definitions envisage not number as such but rather its evidential reference to unity, the appearing of unity in numbers, their being held together by the unity which contains them. The numerable is beautiful only by virtue of its *reductio* to the unity of the divine wisdom and idea, where the *rationes numerosae ad unum reductae* exist.[386] It is only in this sense that, following Boethius, the Pythagorean/late-Platonic maxim may be stated, *numerus est praecipuum (maximum) in animo Conditoris exemplar*.[387] This is, as it stands, a hint that mere relationships of number, by themselves, would never call forth the delight in the beautiful (they would be more likely to induce the utmost boredom) unless other impulses were also present. Thus even Augustine was careful to add to the 'relationships of the parts' the *suavitas coloris*,[388] *i.e.*, an impulse of that which enchants and casts a spell. The pleasure of the game of numbers does not lie alone or chiefly in the quantitative; in the idea itself there are no actual numbers, just as there is none in the Trinity, which exists *per replicationem ejusdem unitatis circa diversas hypostases*.[389] And

---

[381] [equality of number], 1 d31 II, 1 q3 *ad* 5 (I 544b); *Itin.* 2, 5 and 2, 10 (V 300b, 302b); *Hex.* 6, 7 (V 362a); *S. theol.* 2, 14 (V 542b), etc.

[382] [plurality and equality], 2 d9 *praenot.* (II 238a); Brevil. prol. 2, 4 (V 204b: *varietas, multiplicitas et aequitas, ordo, rectitudo et pulchritudo* [variety, multiplicity and equity, order, rightness and beauty]).

[383] [the agreement of things dissimilar], 2 d9 q8c and *ad* 2 (II 256ab).

[384] [proportionality], *Itin.* 2, 5 and 6 (V 300b–301a).

[385] [the agreement of the parts], 4 d49 II *sect.* 1 a 2 q1 *ad* 4, 5 (IV 1016b).

[386] *Hex.* 6, 7 (V 362a).

[387] [number is the chief (greatest) exemplar in the mind of the creator], *De sc. Chr.* 3, 8 (V 11a): *Itin.* 2, 10 (V 302b). From *lib.* I *Arithmet.* ch. 2. The Pythagorean element appears at *Brevil.* 2, 3, where the structure of the universe and the intervals of the spheres are described: *universum, quod secundum numerales proportiones ordinatum dicitur* [the universe, which is said to be ordered following arithmetical proportions] (V 221a). *Cf.* also the *Scholia* of the Quaracchi Edition, Vol. I 58–59; Vol. II 253, n. 4.

[388] [sweetness of colour], *Civ. Dei* 22, 19; 4 d49 II *sect.* 2 a2 q1 *fund.* 1 (IV 1025a); *Itin.* 2, 5 (V 300b–301a).

[389] [by the replication of the same unity in regard to the different hypostases], *De sc. Chr.* 3, 8 (V 15a).

the numerical proportions in the world are beautiful to the extent to which they represent their origin which is above number;[390] the periods of time are beautiful only in so far as they are adapted (*aptata*) to the Word of life.[391] What is measured is beautiful if it is measured rightly against the idea, against Christ, against God: in this way everything that is numerable in the world has its measure in the created spirit, which must maintain its proportion to Christ: 'Man fights against his own salvation if he does not understand how to measure himself. For what advantage is it to him to be able to measure the other things, but not to know how to measure himself?'[392] This measure does not lie in number: rather, what is created must become an adequate expression of the idea above number through its ordering (*hierarchizatio*), and thus it transcends itself by virtue of its inner structure. Now this tendency in what is created to reveal the divine points back to the power of God the Word to express himself—and so it points back to a pleasure of the creator; and the Word itself points back to the relationship of expression within the Godhead, to the Father's joy in begetting. The perfect act of generation in God is the ground of the beauty of the absolute equality and unity between Father and Son in the Holy Spirit.

2. In this way light is also shed on the relationship of expression in the sign of truth. For truth is not demonstrated by merely formal agreement (correctness); truth demands the relationship of a generative and creative self-illumination. Truth is found as enlightenment, revelation, expression of the depth of substance: *veritas est declarativum esse*,[393] and the *intentio veritatis* is *ipsa expressio*.[394] This is based in the absolute self-utterance of God, and so in the absolute relationship of expression: *omnia vera sunt et nata sunt se exprimere per expressionem illius summi*

---

[390] *Brevil.* 2, 3 (V 221a).

[391] *Itin.* 1, 12 (V 298b).

[392] *Hex.* 1, 24 (V 333a).

[393] [truth = to possess the character of making affirmation], 1 d3 I *dub.* 4 (I 79b), following Hilary but in a free formulation.

[394] [the intention of truth is the expression itself], 1 d35 q1 (I 601b).

luminis.[395] All Being, since it is grounded in the Word of God, is revelation, *manifestatio,*[396] *similitudo exprimens.*[397] Bonaventure never ceases to wonder at the mystery that the things of the world possess the power to emit an expressive image of themselves into the entire medium which surrounds them, and that thereby of themselves they shine and reveal themselves to a potential knowing subject.[398] The emanation of things, as they mutually offer their *species,* is somehow innumerable, is an immeasurable reduplication of themselves, an ability to be outside themselves, a power to 'appear', in which they of course preserve their boundaries and proportions and let themselves appear as such. In dealing with the illumination of the things themselves, Bonaventure (in contrast to Thomas, who above all marvels at the power of abstraction possessed by the *intellectus agens* in the subject, and makes this the object of his research) is occupied entirely with the mystery of the objective self-disclosure of things. It is in their being light and in their act of self-expression that the substances' resemblance to God lies; in this they express God, though it is rather he who expresses himself in them. This mystery of light as the creative power of revelation is broken up into the colours in their various illuminations, and into the forms, which ultimately are only various stamps of expression.[399]

All this speaks of the success of the divine power of utterance and reveals an infinite power both in the invention of qualitative words of essence and plans of being and in the certainty with which everything is set forth by God into what is not God, and given the power to manifest itself once more, powerfully and

[395] [all things are true and are born to express themselves through the expression of his supreme light], 1 d8 I, 1 q1 (I 151b).

[396] [manifestation], 1 d3 I, q1 (I 69a).

[397] [a likeness that makes expression], 1 d35 q2 *ad* 3 (I 606b).

[398] *Objectum in toto medio suo generat similitudinem* [the object generates a likeness in the whole of its medium], *Itin.* 2, 7 (V 301b). '*Et hoc est mirabile, quomodo talis species generatur* [and the manner by which such a *species* is generated is marvellous]. . . . It occurs out of a *naturalis fecunditas* [natural fertility] given by God to accompany it on its path' (*Hex.* 11, 23; V 383b).

[399] *Pulchritudinem autem rerum, secundum varietatem luminum, figurarum et colorum* [the beauty of the things, in accord with the variety of lights, forms and colours], *Itin.* 1, 14 (V 299a).

inventively, by appearing in what is outside itself and by bearing witness. It is precisely this ability of things to be outside themselves in the creative revelation of their *species* that is equally the danger of beauty—a double danger: that one may find satisfaction in the colourful reflection and neglect the *reductio* to the substance, and second, that one may come to a stop at the finite substance which is expressing itself instead of seeing in it the expression of absolute truth and beauty. This double danger, to which Adam succumbed, was definitively banished only by Christ, who, as the perfect expression of eternal Wisdom, gives expression also to what all things wish to utter in the intention of the divine Wisdom. In his utterance about God he brings all things with him to utterance, he makes them become a word in him, he brings them to be in tune with their idea, which he himself is. As the incarnate art of God (*ars divina*), he is the appearing of absolute beauty, and this appearing is free from all empty outward show, for it is in itself the substantial truth. Everything that appears in it is guaranteed through that which is.

To look on the nature of the world in the *Verbum incarnatum* means to understand this nature for the first time genuinely as an expression, and so to see it in its own proper beauty. So it is said of Francis: 'He looked at him who is most beautiful of all in the things that are beautiful, and pursued the beloved in the traces he had imprinted everywhere. . . . In the urgency of an unheard-of devotion he tasted that fountain of goodness in the individual creatures as in water-channels; and, as though he perceived a heavenly concert in the harmony of the powers and actions which God had bestowed on them, he exhorted them gently to praise God.'[400] This ability to interpret nature, the flowers and birds, the powers of the elements, the whole of being as it makes its appearance, has its root in God: the eternal Son is radiating light (*splendor pulcherrimus*)[401] as God illuminated and expressed, and Francis gives expression in his *Canticle of the Sun* both to the Father's joy at having completely expressed all that he is and can do and to the love of the Holy Spirit, in which the illumination

---

[400] *Leg. major* 9, 1 (VIII 530a).
[401] [most beautiful splendour], *Hex.* 21, 1 (V 431a).

of the Son substantially transcends itself in becoming gift and blessedness. Here thinking in images breaks down; for the Son is not the copy of an archetype, which he would therefore have to reproduce as faithfully as possible but the expression of the archetype itself and thereby absolute expression: this makes him the archetype of every further expression of God in what is not divine. One therefore cannot say that the Son is beautiful because he reproduces the beauty of the Father, whereas everything in the world is beautiful because it reproduces the beauty of God expressed in the Son; rather, the Father himself shows himself (as fountain of the Godhead) in the Son, for apart from this act he is not Father. Therefore the action of expressing is integrated into the outcome of the expression; into the 'Word' or 'form' goes what lies at the source, what is original, what is inventive, what is absolutely unique in the generation. If the trace and image of this were not in all genuine beauty in the world, such beauty could not point to the absolute beauty.

3. Neither harmony nor the revelation of the depth of being would suffice to explain beauty as *expressio*: a third aspect is also necessary, the aspect of disinterested self-giving, the *diffusio sui* which is thereby *impressio* in the other—the aspect of the Holy Spirit. This is far more than a mere relationship of the satisfying of need, more than a mere *salubritas* which by itself would remain in the sphere of what is useful and thus of what is not selfless. God is not, in respect of his creative self-effusion, under obligation to any passive potency which he needs to satisfy; nor is the primary concern of the things of the world in their mutual self-revelation the satisfaction of need. In every offer of the beautiful there is an element of gratuitousness, of freedom and disinterestedness, which makes itself known in the experience of the receiving of beauty by those in need. The things are able to testify to this gratuitousness only because they are a trace and copy of the trinitarian beauty, which is under obligation to no one in its self-giving. The one who encounters beauty cannot therefore respond to this offer primarily with self-interest but only with reverent marvelling: [*per*] *stuporem admirationis*.[402] The

---

[402] [through the astonishment of wondering], *Itin.* 6, 3 (V 311a). *Cf. Perf. vit. ad sor.* 5, 8: *summae pulchritudinis admiratione suspensa tam vehementi stupore*

power of ravishment (*excessus*) of the beauty which reveals itself lies in its objective revelation (*expressio*), in so far as this is seen by the subject (*impressio*). The resulting ecstasy does not exist as a phenomenon of the soul for its own sake, but, as Bonaventure continually insists, in order to bring it back to the essence and to the idea. The Son leads to the Father. The image which gives knowledge (*species*) leads in its beauty (*speciositas*) to the thing itself. This does not mean that disinterested beauty finally becomes subordinated to a goal at this point, for if beauty is interpreted as it presents itself, then the ecstasy which it produces *is* the act of transition which it wishes to effect. Therefore the true question is: 'Who is able to interpret beauty aright in its appearing?' For Bonaventure, only the pure heart can do this, the heart that understands the love which reveals itself through beauty as love and is already prepared to respond with love: the potential sacrifice in the heart of the one who is addressed, touched, and inflamed answers to the gratuitousness of the beauty which offers itself as a gift. There is in ecstasy an element of adoration, directed not to the appearance but to the reality which appears there: *reverentia, adoratio, excessus . . . ad modum inclinationis, genuflexionis, prostrationis.*[403] But adoration implies a letting-go precisely in the ecstatic encounter; it implies a readiness to give back to him who is glorious the glory which offers itself, to leave the Bridegroom who reveals himself full power of disposal over his handmaid.[404] At this point, negative theology (in its Christian intention) is of one voice with aesthetic theology, as we see in the following text.

'Man must lift himself above all that is of the senses, all that may be imagined and conceived. First of all, he must . . . reflect, and say that he whom he loves is not physical, for he cannot be seen nor heard nor smelled nor tasted nor touched, and therefore he is not physical, but as a whole he can only be longed

---

concutitur [caught up in wonder at the highest beauty, it is stunned by so mighty an astonishment] (VIII 119b).

[403] [reverence, adoration, ecstasy . . . directed to bowing, genuflection, prostration], *De tripl. via* 2§3, 6 (VIII 9a).

[404] *Perf. vit. ad sor.* 5, 4 (VIII 118b): *valde indecens est . . . ut dimidius cor dirigatur in coelum et dimidius retineatur in terra* [it is highly unfitting . . . that half of the heart should be directed towards heaven, and half kept back on earth].

for. Next he must say that he is not imaginable, for he cannot be held in boundaries, forms, numbers, outlines, nor figures of speech, and therefore he is not imaginable, but as a whole he can only be longed for. Finally, he must say that he is not conceivable, for he may not be proved nor defined, nor can he be the object of choice, nor may a value be set upon him, nor may he be investigated, and therefore he is not conceivable, but as a whole he can only be longed for.'[405] The longing which is caught up above every form that may be grasped is the exact response to the form of beauty in which God reveals himself.

The lower a form of beauty is in the gradation of the substances, the more it must be made transparent; and the more one must renounce it for the sake of a higher beauty. 'Gradually, everything that is outside and is encountered outside begins to be oppressive and tedious, because one perceives that it displeases him who is observed and senses within.'[406] Bodily beauty can be a *causa inducens* to a good marriage, 'because beauty naturally draws the soul to love'; 'thus there may be many *causae inducentes* which draw on without sin, provided that one does not stop there, such as charm, beauty, riches, reward, wisdom, virtue. . . .'[407] If the wise man says, 'Beauty is vain', this applies initially to bodily beauty, which must be given up freely for the sake of the inner, spiritual beauty.[408] And if Paul says that the *figura* of this world is passing away, he means 'the outward countenance or beauty of things, and this will pass away'; in as much as the word *figura* is derived from *fingere*, and is linked to *fragilitas*, it will pass away, while its substance will remain.[409] A call of love from God can give the summons to leave all the beauty of the world and to enter into the immediate nuptial love: 'Give glory, O soul, to God the Father alone in all his gifts and blessings, for it is he who *per occultam inspirationem* called you out of the world with the words, Return, return, O Sunamite!'[410]

---

[405] *De tripl. via* 1§3, 17 (VIII 7ab).
[406] *De 5 Festiv.* 1, 1 (VIII 89a); *Epist.* 25 *memorab. prol.* 1 (VIII 491ab).
[407] 4 d30 *dub.* 6 (IV 713b).
[408] 4 d24 I, 1 q1 *ad* 3 (IV 609a).
[409] 4 d48, 2 q3 *ad* 1 (IV 993b).
[410] *De 5 Festiv.* 5, 3 (VIII 94b).

Because the beauty of things is the expression of God, it is objectively something that has a further reference. This is true of the spiritual virtues also: 'They have beauty because they achieve a resemblance to God, and through this beauty they delight us and attract us; yet one must not rest and pause at them, for so they lose their beauty. For "virtues which relate to themselves are proud and puffed-up" ' (quoting Augustine).[411] Beauty, as the radiant appearance of the essence, can shine so strongly that the testimony to God in the beauty is overlooked, and thus it 'becomes a mouse-trap, for the beauty of the creature allures men';[412] so beauty directly satisfies the lust which strives 'to know what is concealed, to look at what is beautiful, to possess what is lovely and valuable'.[413] Lucifer 'did not consider that he had been created out of nothing, but rather looked at his charm, his beauty', and through this he fell from his own beauty into the utmost ugliness.[414] He took his own beauty and dignity as his highest good and glorified himself in this and took delight in himself:[415] but this was possible only because God had created the angels in the same way as men, so that they must decide for God in freedom, and rise above themselves to him.[416] God himself had not yet revealed his beauty directly to Lucifer, and so the crucial question was whether he would understand how to interpret his own beauty as a pointer to the absolute beauty, and to receive it as such. Because beauty always affirms something final and conclusive (*circuit omnem causam*), it is harder with it than with the other *transcendentalia* to remain in the *analogia entis*. Thus the wise man spoke mildly of those pagans who elevated the glorious constellations in the sky to gods (Wis 13:6f.). For this reason, the Christian must 'keep his senses thoroughly under control' on his path to God,[417] and 'keep his

---

[411] I d1, 3 q2 *ad* 4 (I 42a).

[412] *Hex.* 17, 17 (V 412a).

[413] *De tripl. via* I§1, 5 (VIII 4b); *cf. S.* 1 *Dom.* 1 *Quadr.* (IX 207a).

[414] *Perf. vit. ad sor.* 2, 2 (VIII 110b). Concerning the way in which Lucifer's ugliness appears, *cf.* 2 d5, 2 q2 *ad* 1 (II 153b).

[415] 2 d5, 1 q1 (II 145f.); *Brevil.* 2, 7 (V 225a).

[416] *Brevil.* 2, 7 (V 226b); *cf.* Henri de Lubac, *Surnaturel* (Paris: Aubier, 1946), and Karl Peter, *op. cit.*, 'Schönheit und Sünde'.

[417] *Ep. de 25 Memorab.* 10 (VIII 494a).

heart free, not imprinting on it any images of visible things, so that it may be alienated from all creatures and rest without hindrance in the creator alone'.[418] If the beauty of the creatures disappears and the light of God remains for a time intolerably bright, a night may fall in which the created spirit seems to pass over into what is dark and empty: 'Why is it that the radiance of God blinds (*excaecat*), where it ought rather to give illumination? But this blinding is the highest illumination, because it takes place at the peak of the spiritual soul, on the far side of anything that man's reason can discover.'[419] For Bonaventure, the final point is not a beauty that is measure but a beauty of that which is immeasurable and expresses itself in measure, coming from the sovereign fullness of God, and received in man in the aesthetical-mystical ecstasy of wonderment and inflamed adoration. God is for Bonaventure, as for Gregory of Nyssa, *anelpiston kallos*, 'beauty past all hope'.[420]

5. THE HEART, THE CROSS AND THE GLORY

It is now time to identify what is decisively Franciscan in the structure of beauty. This is not something superficially imposed but springs from the heart of what has been said. Although Augustine and Dionysius made important contributions to the means of its expression, the intuition itself, around which everything crystallises, does not derive from them.

The Father has given expression to himself in the Son, because he has the incomprehensible power to be one and the same God in another than himself; Bonaventure says that it is only this power that prevents him from ceasing to exist when he makes the total gift of his being as God.[421] Thus it is again the same power which enables God to give expression to himself outside himself, in what is no longer the divine, because the Father has given expression in the Son to everything, and so to every possible world. Because the absolute expression is in God,

[418] *Ibid.* 17 (VIII 495a).
[419] *Hex.* 20, 11 (V 427a).
[420] *Hom.* 12 *in Cant.* (PG 44, 1037C).
[421] *Cf.* n. 130 above.

he may dare to make expression in what is nothing. The act of descending into what is nothing in order to express himself is God's humility, his condescension (*synkatabasis, condescensio*), his going outside his own riches to become poor.

Bonaventure speaks continually of this *condescensio* of God:[422] creation, revelation, grace, and Incarnation are all God's humble act of adapting himself to the increasingly diminishing dimensions of the creature. 'The eternal God bends down in humility (*humiliter se inclinans*) when he raises up the clay of our nature into the unity of his Person.'[423] This *humilitas Dei*[424] is the most profound thing that God reveals of himself in his Incarnation and especially in his cross. The cross is absolutely the key to everything; *omnia in cruce manifestantur*,[425] not only sin, not only man, but God himself. Thus it is in the humbling of self (*se ipsum vilificare pro Christo*) that the height of the imitation of God lies.[426] In this imitation, self-humbling is not in the least hypocrisy but truth, and indeed the experiential knowledge of one's own reality.[427] None of this imitation surpasses God's humbling in Christ, 'who willed to serve the servants, and washed the feet of peasants and fishermen',[428] 'bent down even to their feet',[429] 'humbles himself in order to raise others up, even to the shameful death of thieves and murderers',[430] and indeed 'was humbled lower than all men'.[431] 'He was not content to possess his glory alone, and so he went forth (*exivit*), took on the form of a slave, to bring home many sons with him into his glory through his work and instruction.'[432] But the path of descent and humbling of self is the bitter path of abandon-

---

[422] *De perf. evang.* 1 (V 121b); *Brevil.* 4, 1 (V 241b), 5, 1 (V 252b); *Hex.* 7, 7 (V 366b); 9, 4 (V 373a). Many texts are cited by Alexander Gerken, *op. cit.*

[423] *S.* 2 *Nat. Dni.* (IX 106b).

[424] [humility of God], *S.* 1 *Dom. Oct. Epiph.* (IX 172a).

[425] [all things are revealed in the cross], *De tripl. via* 3§3 (VIII 14a); *cf. S.* 2 *Parasc.* (IX 265ab).

[426] *De perf. evang.* 1 (V 117–124).

[427] *Ibid.* 123.

[428] *S.* 1 *Dom.* 22 *p. Pent.* (IX 442b).

[429] *Ep. de imit. Chr.* 4 (VIII 500a).

[430] *S.* 5 *Dom. p. Pascha* (IX 305b).

[431] *Vitis myst.* 2, 2 (VIII 161a).

[432] *Sex al. seraph.* 3, 5 (VIII 133b).

ment and betrayal: Bonaventure draws up the list, for the first time, of the *traditores Jesu*: 'How many there are who betray you! The heavenly Father has handed you over ... and you yourself have handed yourself over.... O truly marvellous exchange! ... You have handed yourself over into the hand of the betrayer, the traitorous apostle, and this betrayer handed you over to the Jews. These wicked betrayers handed you over to the Gentiles, to be mocked and spat upon and scourged and crucified.'[433]

This 'stepping out' into what is nothing makes his appearing something hidden, causes his proper beauty to be distorted and deformed. Augustine was the first to speak of the *Christus deformis*, and this is greatly developed by Bonaventure. *Admirare igitur immensam potestatem annihilari, speciositatem decolorari, felicitatem tormentari.*[434] *Formosus deformis apparuit in conspectu paternae gloriae.*[435] Just as 'no tree is more plain and stunted than the vine, which seems completely useless and contemptible, as though it could never be useful in any way to anyone', so was Christ in his Passion, when, in accordance with what Isaiah said, he had neither beauty nor comeliness. 'Who would look for beauty of form now in such a roughly-handled body? The most beloved Lord is stripped naked, so that you may be able to see the formlessness of the most pure body.' 'But along with the outward formlessness, inwardly beauty was preserved. ... Men saw the most beautiful of the sons of men on the cross, and since they look only at what is external they saw him as one who possessed neither beauty nor form, for his face was despised and his posture out of joint; yet it was from this formlessness of our Saviour that the price paid for our beauty streamed forth. ... But who may find words for his inner beauty, since the entire fullness of the divinity dwells in him? So may we outwardly in our body become formless together with the formless Jesus, so

---

[433] *Vitis myst.* 5, 5 (VIII 170ab).

[434] [Marvel therefore at the immeasurable power as it is destroyed, at the beauty that is robbed of its colour, at the felicity that is tortured], *De tripl. via* 3§3 (VIII 13a).

[435] [The beautiful one appeared ugly in the presence of the Father's glory], *Lignum vitae* 29 (VIII 79b).

that inwardly we may be formed anew together with the most beautiful Jesus.'[436]

We can only touch on the question whether this distinction in Bonaventure between inward and outward goes deep enough; in other words, whether he has taken sufficient account in his christology of the inward suffering of the Son abandoned by God on the cross.[437] But the resolution of all such problems is found in the love of Jesus' heart, which in its solidarity both with God and with men was capable of the uttermost suffering on the cross.[438] For the heart, for Bonaventure, is the true midpoint of man.[439] And as the eternal Word 'was conceived in the heart of the Father . . . so he redeems no one who does not receive him with faith in the heart'.[440] Holy Scripture reveals the 'heart of God',[441] the 'high heart' (cor altum) which has become cor humiliatum et contritum on the cross, the cor humillimum altissimi Jesu.[442] This heart which has been opened and made accessible through the wound in the side contains in itself an insoluble mystery: for whence comes this wound? 'For this reason was your heart wounded, that through the visible wound the invisible wound of love might be made visible to us. . . . There-

---

[436] Vitīs myst. 5 (VIII 168–171).

[437] This appears at least questionable in the light of statements such as Vit. myst. 10 (VIII 175–176). The depth of his suffering is all too easily explained by means of his complexio tenerrima [most tender disposition] (S. 2 Parasc., IX 264a; cf. V 250b). The description of the Passion in Lignum Vitae confines itself to the external, and for this reason may easily appear sentimental (VIII 75ff.); reference to the abandonment by God is lacking at decisive passages (Perf. vit. ad sor. 6; VIII 120f.); suffering in the superior part of the soul seems at first impossible (Brevil. 4, 7; V 248a), but is then allowed by means of a curious distinction—the Spirit of Christ is at one and the same time 'as ratio' and because of its unity with God in the highest delight in God, and 'as nature' and because of its unity with what is lower 'in the deepest suffering' (ibid. 4, 9; V 250b).

[438] Ibid. 250b.

[439] Hex. 1, 19 (V 332b).

[440] Brevil 6, 8 (V 272b).

[441] Hex. 12, 17 (V 387a); cf. Hex. 21, 33, the statement that the love of the seraphim is usque ad cor Dei penetrativus [penetrates even to the heart of God] (V 436b).

[442] [the most lowly heart of the most high Jesus], Vitis myst. 24 (VIII 187–189).

fore the wound in the flesh reveals a wound in the spirit.' As it says in the Song of Songs, 'You have wounded my heart, my sister, my bride, you have wounded my heart.' Who then is the one who wounds, ultimately—is it the enemies? Or do these merely accomplish externally the work which the sister–bride has already accomplished internally? 'The sister-bride has caused both wounds; it is as though the bridegroom wished to say, "Because you have wounded me with the zeal of your love, I was also hurt by the soldier's lance." '[443] More deeply still, if God's heart were not already in itself vulnerable, how could the love of the bride have wounded it? Thus it is God's going forth into the danger and the nothingness of the creation that reveals his heart to be at its origin vulnerable; in the humility of this vulnerability lies God's condescenscion (*condescensio*) and thus his fundamental readiness to go to the very end of love on the cross.

This entire immeasurable concealment becomes precisely the highest expression of God: it possesses a power of expression which sheds its rays over all other images, draws them to itself, and includes them in itself. The revelation of God's heart in the heart of Jesus discloses the mystery at God's source *a fonte, scilicet cordis arcano profusum*,[444] as had already been expressed thematically in the prologue to the *Commentary on the Sentences*.[445] The stigmatisation of the father of the Franciscan Order forbids even the least doubt of the power of expression of what God said through the cross: for in it the final word about God and man has been uttered. The appearing of beauty in what is nothing is here transfigured in the double mystery of Christ's humility and poverty, and of the humility and poverty of the saint's heart which has been estranged from himself and turned to Christ. The poverty caused by love is a making room, so that the descending ray of God's love as beauty, its *species expressa*, may find no hindrance precisely in the *organon* in which it wishes to imprint itself. Francis himself had understood poverty as nup-

[443] *Ibid.* 3 (VIII 163–164).
[444] [from the fountain, *i.e.*, from the secret place of the heart, flowing forth], *Lignum vitae* 30 (VIII 79b).
[445] 1 *Sent. prol.* (I 4a).

tial; Bonaventure sees poverty as perfected on the cross,[446] but the cross as 'your wedding-day'.[447] Poverty remains the *consilium principale, fundamentale*,[448] because the total removal of what is multiple in the world creates the presupposition for the encounter with God as the absolutely simple and single: 'Contemplation can take place only in the highest simplicity, and the highest simplicity is unattainable except in the highest poverty, and thus this Order strives for it. The intention of the blessed Francis was directed to the highest poverty.'[449] 'Blessed are the poor in spirit, for theirs is the kingdom of heaven ... because that kingdom is the simplest thing of all, but the covetous man is the most complicated thing of all; for he depends on so many things in the world, and thus he is composed of many parts. ... Further, that kingdom is the thing that of all things is most held in common, whereas the covetous man is the most greedy thing of all, for he wants to make everything his own.'[450] Bonaventure is therefore not dependent on any external beauty of the Church and her liturgy: 'All the ornament of the ceremonies presents nothing other than the sufferings of Christ; while the Mass is going on, there is nothing more important than to think of the death of Christ.'[451] Although he has much to say about the hierarchy of God and of the angels, and about the inner hierarchisation of the soul, he speaks very little, and quite without emphasis, about the hierarchy of the Church, and considers this above all in its usefulness for souls.[452] His sole concern is with the movement of love in the nuptial kiss of the cross between the God who has become poor and the man who has become poor. The embrace of this kiss has its origin in the

[446] *Pauper in nativitate, pauperior in vita, pauperrimus in cruce* [poor in his birth, poorer in his life, poorest in the cross], *Vit. myst.* 2, 3 (VIII 161b).

[447] *Vitis myst.* 5, 4 (VIII 170a).

[448] [the basic, fundamental counsel], *De perf. evang.* 2, 1 c (V 129a).

[449] *Hex.* 20, 30 (V 430b).

[450] *S. theol.* 2, 25 (V 545b–546a).

[451] *Praep. ad miss.* 10 (VIII 103a).

[452] 2 d9 q9 c (II 257ab): 'The multitude in the Church is so constituted that it can err, and therefore it needs a head and a government; and since one man cannot do everything, the ecclesiastical offices and authorities must be distributed according to what is greater and what is less': 4 d24 I, 2 q1 c (IV 614b–615a).

incarnate Word, 'in whom is accomplished the union of the sublimest love and of the mutual embracing of the two natures, whereby God kisses us and we kiss God'.[453] The entire descent of God is nuptial: *descendit ut sponsus suavissimus*,[454] and the Bride is the one true Church,[455] and only in her and with her the individual soul;[456] 'but the marriage bed was the womb of the Virgin'.[457] The appearing of the glory of this marriage is eschatological,[458] and for Bonaventure (here influenced by Joachim) this implies something of the end of the *ages*: the religious Order of the end of the ages, as the perfect expression of the history of the world and of salvation-history, will be the true appearing of the cross of Christ in his mystical body[459]— which is the appearing of his glory[460]—by virtue of its contemplative poverty (putting into practice what the Poverello himself wanted). There will be accomplished the mystery of the nuptial uniting of God with the world: in '*susceptio, revelatio, unio*, beyond which the spirit can penetrate no further. Therein lies also the embodiment of the Song of Songs: that is, in chaste, more chaste, and most chaste conceptions, in chaste, more chaste, and most chaste beholdings, in chaste, more chaste, and most chaste unitings.'[461]

The cross's nuptial poverty which reveals the heart of God— this thought flows over in many ways into the mysticism of the

---

[453] *Comm. in Luc.* 15, 34 (VII 395b).

[454] [he descended as a most sweet bridegroom], *S.* 22 *Dom.* 1 *Adv.* (IX 44a).

[455] *Ecclesiam unicam Christi sponsam* [the Church, the sole bride of Christ], *Brevil.* 6, 5 (V 270a). Christ is the only one who can make the Church fertile: *S.* 2 *Dom.* 3 *Adv.* (IX 65a).

[456] *Sponsam, scil. totam Ecclesiam et quamlibet animam sanctam* [the Bride, *i.e.*, the whole Church and in a sense the holy soul], *Itin.* 4, 5 (V 307b).

[457] *S. theol.* 2, 38 (V 549b).

[458] *Lignum vitae* 44 (VIII 81ab).

[459] *Hex.* 22, 23 (V 441a): *Et dicebat (Bonaventura) quod illa apparitio Seraph beato Francisco, quae fuit expressiva et impressa, ostendebat, quod ille ordo illi respondere debeat, sed tamen pervenire ad hoc per tribulationes* [and he (Bonaventure) used to say that that appearing of the Seraph to blessed Francis, both giving an expression and imprinted on him, show what that Order ought to do as response to him (*i.e.*, Francis); but the Order would attain this through tribulations].

[460] *Cf.* n. 458.

[461] *Hex.* 22, 27 (V 441b).

Rhineland, which was fascinated by it and refused to know any other beauty than this, giving expression to it in pictorial art also. Pseudo-Tauler's *Book of Spiritual Poverty* draws the themes together: the imitation of Christ in total poverty is the imitation of God who is poor because he is above simplicity, and the imitation of his love that surrenders everything.[462] This Franciscan doctrine is in Bonaventure the crowning conclusion (and not the breaking-off) of his whole teaching about beauty, in as much as the ecstatic love which is enkindled by the forms of expression of the self-sacrificing love of God penetrates through to the ultimate source from which all beauty in its appearing flows. The name of this source and centre is, without qualification, love, in its incomprehensible passing over from itself into what is other than itself: love as the eternal generation of the Son from the Father, as God's act of creation directed into the nothingness—a passing over that reveals at one and the same time the absolute power and fruitfulness of God and his disposition of poverty, which wishes to have and hold on to nothing for itself. This disposition becomes visible in the creation, and fully in redemption, as a descent into nothingness and fruitlessness.[463]

But it is precisely in this act of pouring itself into what is nothing that God's heart glorifies itself, and thereby fulfils all the 'glory' of being, as this is based in the transcendental power of self-expression: *Hoc ipso quod despectus fuit, hoc ipso fuit gloriosus.*[464] This is the measure of all Christian and ecclesiastical glory: 'So all those who are set above others must look to themselves: the higher they stand, so much the more must they bend low in mercy; the more glorious they are, so much the lower must they stand in their own eyes. Princes must carry others, not be carried by them—especially the princes of the Church.'[465] The power of expression possessed by God's humility requires its concealment, and accordingly requires faith

[462] Edited by Heinrich Denifle, 1877.

[463] *Cf.* the sublime exposition of the vanity of Christian action in *De sex alis Seraphim* ch. 3 and 4 (VIII 136–140).

[464] [He was glorious in what caused him to be despised], *S.* 1 *Epiph.* (IX 148a).

[465] *Ibid.* (148b).

also, for the expressive image which is prepared in his revelation will be understood in its full beauty only in the eschaton; in the meantime, the Church and the souls stand in the sign of the mystery of the moon, whose closest approach to the sun can occur only at the new moon, and thus in the darkness.[466] The fulfilment of the mystery of the eros of Plato's *Symposium* takes place here also; this eros desires to generate in what is beautiful, but as such is not beautiful. 'As the Bride desires the Bridegroom, as matter desires form and the ugly desires the beautiful, so the soul in the rapture of contemplation desires to be united; then it happens that the outer man loses his form, and man loses speech. And so the saying in the Song of Songs is right, "Do not look on me, for I am black, the sun has distorted my colour"; for precisely then is man most united through inner rays of light. . . . This is what happened to Jacob or Israel, the strong man, who was strengthened in wrestling with the angel, although the sinew of his hip became loose, and he began to limp. For contemplation makes the soul of man seem ugly (*vilem*) when it is united to the highest sun.'[467] But the soul has seen enough in faith to enable it to renounce for a while all glory that appears outwardly. This she does for the sake of the glory of the marriage on the cross which appears only in the eschaton, and thus she completes all the stages of the path of beauty, preferring the highest beauty to the lower; she does not renounce for the sake of renunciation, but so that absolute love may glorify itself in her.

In as much as everything in Bonaventure's theology starts from the central image of the cross and returns there, it is this which forms the proper standard of what is theologically necessary. Therefore, as A. Gerken has shown, the question of another order of world and history than the actual order (and by the same token the question whether the eternal Word would have become man if Adam had not sinned) cannot seriously be entertained by him. He inquires only about the *ratio praecipua* of the Incarnation which has actually taken place,[468] and he affirms

---

[466] *Hex.* 20, 16f. (V 428ab). Hugo Rahner, 'Mysterium Lunae', *ZKT* (1939), pp. 311–349, 428–442; (1940), 61–80, 121–131.

[467] *Hex.* 20, 19 (V 428b–429a).

[468] 3 d1, 2 q3 (III 28f.).

nothing other than the highest fittingness everywhere in revelation,[469] but this follows the principle that 'in the actions of Christ
it is always what is most appropriate that happens'.[470] This
necessity is so far from encroaching upon the free decisions of
the creator that it positively exposes the sovereign logic of these
decisions to view. The existence of an *ordo naturae purae* is not
denied, but this cannot appear even on the horizon of
theological thought as a serious thesis: only what is actual is
interesting and worthy of contemplation. Only in Christ, as he
actually is, do we experience what God's true plan for the world
was. Only in his *missio* is the *emantio* within the Godhead
revealed,[471] only in him do we know who we ourselves are[472]
and so are able to be what we ought to be. For the Son is the
image, and therefore our archetype: we are merely directed
towards the image (*ad imaginem*).[473] Only in him do we experience the meaning of the lowliness of the earth; precisely because
it is so needy, it is a more fitting womb for the descent of God
than the more glorious nature of the angels.[474] And finally, to
the vexation of every philosophical anthropology, man, who
consists of body and soul, bears in himself a 'requirement'
directed to the creator, that of the resurrection of the body:
*requirit natura, . . . partes sunt ordinatae ad resurrectionem secundum
ordinem necessitatis.* But it was God who imprinted this requirement on nature (*impressit naturae*), a requirement which it
cannot satisfy through its own resources, for it can raise none of
the dead; 'but since the divine providence could create nothing
in vain, it is indispensable that the body should be restored
through God's own power . . . *salva tota veritatae naturae*'.[475]

---

[469] *Ibid.*, closely following Anselm; *cf.* 3 d2, 1 q1 *fund.* 1 (III 37a), *ibid.* q2 (III
40f.).

[470] *Hex. princip. coll.* 1; Delorme 14.

[471] 1 d15, 1 q4 (I 265b); *cf.* also I 484f., I 239f.; I 245; I 279.

[472] *Cf.* 1 d6 q3 *ad* 4 (I 130b).

[473] 2 d16 *dub.* 3 (II 407ab).

[474] 3 d2, 1 q2 *ad* 1 (III 41a). *Quia terra inter cetera elementa minus est decora, ideo
magis indiguit decorari* [since the earth is the least beautiful among the elements,
it had the greatest need to be made beautiful], 2 d15 *dub.* 2 (II 389a).

[475] [preserving the whole truth of the nature], *Brevil.* 7, 5 (V 287a). This is
Bonaventure's continuous teaching. *Cf. Brevil.* 7, 7: 'The soul cannot be fully
blessed without the body, because she has *inclinationem naturaliter insertam* [an

Only Christ in his Resurrection can draw the conclusion from these premises of nature, for his whole power comes from the *assumptio minoris*, from the introduction of the minor proposition that is the cross. *Haec est logica nostra*.[476]

inclination which is integrated in her by nature] oriented to being reunited with the body' (V 289b). *Hex.* 7, 5: 'Full peace is found only in the reuniting of body and soul—this is certain. For if the soul has an essential inclination towards the body, then she can never come fully to peace unless the body is restored to her' (V 366a). 4 d43, 1 q1: 'The form of manhood is more complete and more perfect than the form of the soul alone. Therefore, since the perfecting of grace and glory presupposes the perfecting of nature, it is necessary that the whole man—not only the soul—be glorified' (IV 883a). *Cf.* IV 1013a; *Solil.* 4, 21 (VIII 63b–64a).

[476] [This is our logic], *Hex.* 1, 30 (V 334b).

INDEX OF PROPER NAMES